Fodor's Inside

Mexico City

CONTENTS

ABOUT THIS GUIDE

Inside Mexico City shows you the city like you've never seen it. Written entirely by locals, it includes features on the city's street art and galleries and plenty of insider tips. The result is a curated compilation infused with authentic Mexico City flavor, accompanied by easy-to-use maps and transit information.

Whether you're visiting Mexico City for the first time or a seasoned traveler looking to explore a new neighborhood, this is the guide for you. We've handpicked the top things to do and rated the sights, shopping, dining, and nightlife in the city's most dynamic neighborhoods. Truly exceptional experiences in all categories are marked with a ★ .

Restaurants, bars, and coffee shops are a huge part of Mexico City's appeal, of course, and you'll find plenty to savor in its diverse neighborhoods. We cover cuisines at all price points, with everything from enduring institutions and groundbreaking chefs to the perfect late-night street snack; use the $ to $$$$ price charts below to estimate meal costs. We cover hotels in the Experience section at the front of this guide. We list adult prices for

#FODORSONTHEGO

We've highlighted fun neighborhood facts throughout this guide. As you explore Mexico City, we invite you to use **#FodorsOnTheGo** to share your favorite discoveries with us.

sights; ask about discounts when purchasing tickets.

Mexico City is constantly changing. All prices, opening times, and other details in this guide were accurate at this writing. Always confirm information when it matters, especially when making a detour to a specific place. Visit Fodors.com for expanded restaurant and hotel reviews, additional recommendations, news, and features.

What It Costs: Restaurants			
$	$$	$$$	$$$$
under MX$150	MX$150–MX$300	MX$300–MX$450	over MX$450

Prices are the average cost of a main course at dinner or, if dinner is not served, at lunch.

1

Experience
Mexico City

POLANCO

SANTA MARÍA
LA RIBERA

SAN
RAFAEL

ALAMEDA CENTRAL

CENTRO
HISTÓRICO

BOSQUE DE
CHAPULTEPEC

JUÁREZ AND
ANZURES

ROMA

CONDESA

BENITO
JUÁREZ

SAN ÁNGEL

COYOACÁN

WELCOME TO MEXICO CITY

First-time visitors who catch a glimpse of Mexico City's breathtaking vastness as their plane descends are often surprised by the manageable pace and pleasing scale that defines many of its neighborhoods, from ritzy Polanco and San Ángel to quaintly historic Coyoacán and Condesa. Although slightly more populous than New York City, it's far less densely populated and less expensive. As a wonderfully vibrant, culturally blessed metropolis that can keep museum-hoppers, discerning gourmands, history buffs, and design-minded shoppers entertained for days, Mexico City also feels remarkably easy to navigate. It's little wonder that its cachet as a sophisticated, world-class travel destination continues to soar.

MEXICO CITY TODAY

Mexico's sprawling, energetic, and sometimes deeply complicated capital city offers a study in contradictions. Its venerable heritage traces back centuries before the Spaniards arrived in 1519, and yet as the largest metropolis in North America, it is a remarkably contemporary destination with a fashion-forward design scene, cutting-edge art galleries, and sceney restaurants and bars. As a whole, Mexico is a deeply Catholic nation in which men and women of all ages generally dress conservatively (locals rarely wear shorts), but same-sex marriage was legalized in 2009 and abortion in 2007, and it's common to spot younger locals smoking weed and snuggling and making out on park benches in public. And despite its enormity and the often crushing traffic and packed public transportation that comes with it, drivers and pedestrians move at a relatively relaxed pace. Chilangos, as residents here are known, generally speak slower than other Latin Americans and are quite patient with visitors who aren't fluent in Spanish. Indeed, the sometimes seemingly contradictory social and stylistic forces at work in CDMX appear to be a significant part of Mexico City's appeal.

THE PRE-HISPANIC ERA TO THE COLONIAL PERIOD

Nestled beneath the jagged peaks of the Sierra Nevada range, few places in the Western Hemisphere have hosted human settlements longer than Mexico City, the present-day site of which has been continuously inhabited since at least the early 1300s. Archaeological evidence, however, confirms that nomadic tribes first settled Valle de México and the surrounding region as far back as 17,000 years ago. The region's two most prominent archaeological sites, Cuicuilco in the south of the city and the formidable pyramids of Teotihuacán about 60 km (37 miles) northeast, supported thriving civilizations centuries before the Aztecs established the city of Tenochtitlan—now Mexico City—in 1325.

At the height of Tenochtitlan's prominence as the center of indigenous Mexican civilization, Spanish explorer Hernán Cortés arrived in 1519 with perhaps 1,000 troops and a considerably larger auxiliary force of anti-Aztec natives. By 1521, the once mighty Aztec Empire had been completely decimated through war and disease. Cortés razed Tenochtitlan and in its place built Mexico City, which would serve as the capital of colonial New Spain for the next 300 years.

MEXICO: INDEPENDENCE, REVOLUTION, AND THE PRESENT

The country's first 100 years as a sovereign nation, starting with the long and bloody 11-year War of Independence, which resulted in nationhood and a complete separation from the Spanish crown in 1821, was marked by a series of military engagements. These included two separate campaigns with France, the second of which (from 1861 to 1867) saw the French occupy Mexico City for four years. There was also the loss of Texas in 1836 and then, following the country's defeat during the Mexican-American War of 1847–48, Mexico lost California and most of the current southwestern United States.

Although President Porfirio Díaz ruled the country through most of its largely stable and prosperous 36-year period following the second war with France, he maintained his power through ruthless means and governed as an elitist despot. In 1910, he was overthrown and exiled, and Mexico entered yet another tumultuous period of political and military upheaval. Over the next decade or so, a series of presidents and revolutionary leaders—including Pancho Villa, Emiliano Zapata, and Venustiano Carranza—were elected or installed by coup and then subsequently assassinated. The revolution ended in 1920, at which time Álvaro Obregón assumed the presidency and served out his term successfully (Obregón was reelected in 1928 but was killed by an assassin's bullet shortly before he officially assumed office for a second time).

Throughout the past century, Mexico and the capital have enjoyed relative stability and fairly consistent growth, with the exception of several economic downturns. The city's metro population has skyrocketed from around 500,000 in 1900 to more than 21.6 million today, and it has thrived as a center of art, literature, music, and culture since Obregón's tenure.

WHAT'S WHERE IN MEXICO CITY

Mexico City is organized into 16 official *delegaciones* (similar to boroughs), which can in turn be subdivided into hundreds of informal *colonias* (neighborhoods). This book focuses on about 15 of the colonias that contain the lion's share of notable points of interest, most of them extending west, contiguously, from the city's downtown core (Centro Histórico) out to the giant park, Bosque de Chapultepec and the Polanco neighborhood just north of it. Additionally, three chapters stretch south through the Benito Juárez delegacion to the charming historic centers of Coyoacán and San Ángel. And a final Greater Mexico City chapter covers points of interest set beyond the city's core, from relatively close colonias to a few entirely separate municipalities on the region's periphery. To help you organize your visit, here's a rundown of the areas we cover in this book. The numbers refer to chapter numbers.

2. CENTRO HISTÓRICO
The city's historic core and part of the Cuauhtémoc delegacion, Centro Histórico occupies nearly 700 blocks, and more than 1,500 of its 9,000 buildings are of historical importance. Here you'll find Latin America's largest Zócalo and a slew of essential museums and historic sites, plus a number of venerable restaurants, cantinas, hotels, and shops.

3. ALAMEDA CENTRAL
Named for the charming park—the oldest in the Western Hemisphere—that anchors it, Alameda Central comprises a few colonias immediately west of Centro Histórico, and though smaller, it's nevertheless rife with important cultural attractions. The southern half of the neighborhood, especially near its border with Juárez, is steadily gentrifying.

4. JUÁREZ AND ANZURES WITH LA ZONA ROSA
Bisected by Paseo de la Reforma, the grand Parisian-style boulevard that connects Centro Histórico with Bosque Chapultepec, this section of the city takes in the colonias of Juárez, Cuauhtémoc (a colonia

within the greater Cuauhtémoc delegacion), and Anzures. Juárez includes the LGBTQ and nightlife-driven Zona Rosa quarter as well as a mix of historic blocks with hip retail and dining that somewhat resemble neighboring Roma. Cuauhtémoc is home to a number of modern office and hotel towers, and Anzures is a mostly residential center of upper-middle-class professionals that borders Polanco to the west.

5. SAN RAFAEL AND SANTA MARÍA LA RIBERA

Two historic neighborhoods that lie north of Cuauhtémoc and Juárez, the colonias San Rafael and Santa María la Ribera were laid out in the late 19th century and contain a wealth of impressive Porfirio Díaz mansions. The neighborhoods fell on tougher times during the late 20th century, but lately have begun to supplant Roma and Condesa as the more affordable and free-spirited bastions of edgy art and entrepreneurialism in the city.

6. POLANCO AND BOSQUE DE CHAPULTEPEC

Mexico City's "green lung," 1,695-acre Bosque de Chapultepec (often referred to as Parque Chapultepec) lies at the west end of Paseo de la Reforma and contains an utterly enchanting array of museums, shaded paths, gardens, and both historic and newer attractions. Immediately north, the sprawling and wealthy Polanco neighborhood is sometimes called Mexico's Beverly Hills and abounds with high-end boutiques, hotels, and restaurants.

7. ROMA

One of the hippest neighborhoods in North America—its considerable stock of regal Porfirio Díaz mansions now occupied by see-and-be-seen bistros, third-wave coffeehouses, artisanal mezcalerías, avant-garde art galleries, and exquisitely curated lifestyle shops—Roma has few formal attractions but a seemingly endless supply of pleasing hangouts.

8. CONDESA

A grand neighborhood of winding streets and verdant pocket parks flanked by Porfirian mansions, art deco buildings, and striking contemporary structures, Condesa has transitioned from faded but elegant to artsy and edgy to hip and upwardly mobile in recent years. Now a little less trendy than adjacent Roma, it's nevertheless rife with cool bars, eateries, shops, and B&Bs.

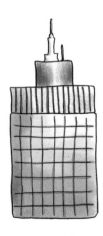

9. BENITO JUÁREZ

A sweeping delegacion made up of several unassuming, mostly middle-class colonias that lie between Condesa and Roma to the north and Coyoacán and San Ángel to the south, Benito Juárez contains a number of lesser-known gems—from leafy parks to old-school fondas.

10. COYOACÁN

Closely identified with the former home (now a museum) of its most famous resident, Frida Kahlo, the historic core of Coyoacán is one of the most appealing colonial neighborhoods in the Americas, a charming warren of tree-lined streets, gracious old homes, and bohemian cafés and bars.

11. SAN ÁNGEL

Like its neighbor to the east Coyoacán, this lively and historic colonia that Diego Rivera called home is richly historic. It's also just plain old rich, with a number of fashionable restaurants and a colorful central plaza that's famous for its antiques, art, and crafts shops.

12. GREATER MEXICO CITY

Some of the city's top attractions—the pyramids of Teotihuacán, the canals of Xochimilco, the cultural institutions of UNAM (Universidad Nacional Autónoma de México)—lie outside the city center. In addition, you'll find everything from alpine national parks to vaunted restaurants to charming historic districts in these regions surrounding Mexico City.

TOP EXPERIENCES

In a city that's reputed to have more museums than any other in the world, you could fill a trip here with nothing but museum visits and come away culturally starstruck. Yet there is so much more to see and do in the capital. Some of the best neighborhoods for touring, such as Roma and Condesa, have few formal attractions and instead tempt the senses with amazing dining, shopping, and nightlife options. In other parts of Mexico City, simply getting out and strolling the historic tree-lined streets or trekking through a verdant park will leave you enchanted. Here are some of the best ways to make the most of your time in CDMX.

FRIDA AND DIEGO

Among the most recognizable creative duos of the 20th century, artists Frida Kahlo and Diego Rivera resided in the south of the city—at various times together and separately—in two different compounds that are both now fascinating museums. Plan to visit each of them: the stark, modernist **Museo Casa Estudio Diego Rivera y Frida Kahlo** in San Ángel and the far more famous **Casa Azul,** in neighboring Coyoacán, that served as Frida Kahlo's family compound until her death in 1954. You'll find several other prominent sites related to the pair in this part of the city, including Rivera's **Museo Anahuacalli,** a striking volcanic-rock, temple-like structure that houses his vast trove of prehispanic art, and **Museo Dolores Olmedo,** which contains impressive collections of artwork by both Frida and Diego.

TRADITIONAL MERCADOS

In addition to being excellent sources of mouthwatering—and bargain-priced—tacos, posole, ceviche tostadas, quesadillas, and other classic Mexican street food, the city's bounty of bustling *mercados,* or markets, offers a compelling look at how many residents continue to shop for both everyday necessities and special treats and gifts. The best of these mercados, such as foodie-favored **San Juan** in Alameda Central and colorful **Medellín** in Roma Sur, continue to thrive, even in the face of growing competition from bland big-box stores and multinational chains. Beyond prepared foods, great things to buy in these old-school mercados include fresh-squeezed juices and *licuados* (similar to smoothies), flowers, candy, mole pastes and salsas, and pottery.

ARCHAEOLOGICAL RUINS AND ARTIFACTS

Remarkably, you can visit several incredible archaeological sites within CDMX city limits, including the 3,600-year-old remains of **Cuicuilco.** But just an hour's drive northeast, you can also visit one of the most significant intact Mesoamerican cities—complete with massive pyramids circa AD 200—in the world, **Teotihuacán.** And right in the heart of the city, you'll find a pair of beautifully designed museums filled with artifacts and commentary that shed light on Mexico's rich indigenous heritage: the expansive **Museo Nacional de Antropología** in Bosque de Chapultepec, and **Museo del Templo Mayor,** which lies in Centro Histórico atop the ruins of the most important Aztec temple of ancient Tenochtitlan.

WORLD-ACCLAIMED RESTAURANTS

If you're serious about dining at the city's most venerable temples of gastronomy (think names like **Pujol, Quintonil,** and to a slightly lesser extent **Sud 777, Maximo Bistrot,** and **KoMa**), consider making reservations the minute after you've booked your flights to CDMX. But also take heart that some of the city's must-eat experiences, while still best booked a day or two in advance, are relatively affordable and easygoing. You can experience longtime bastions of creative cooking, such as **Rosetta, Nicos,** and **Contramar,** and more recently anointed hot spots like **Carmela y Sal, Meroma,** and **Loretta Chic Bistro.**

SHOPPING IN SAN ÁNGEL

The affluent and historic colonia adjacent to Coyoacán in the south of the city is justly well-regarded by shoppers for its **Bazaar Sábado,** which indeed takes place only on Saturday and features two floors of mid- to high-end art, crafts, fashion, and home goods. Definitely give yourself a couple of hours to explore the bazaar, but if you're a serious shopper, allow at least another three to four hours to check out the less-expensive art dealers and craft vendors who set up stalls outside on historic Plaza San Jacinto and to visit the dozens of fine shops on the surrounding blocks.

BOSQUE DE CHAPULTEPEC

A vast swatch of thoughtfully planned greenery that comprises three distinct sections, **Bosque de Chapultepec** is where seemingly half the city congregates on weekends. Set aside at least a half day or even return a second day to allow time to see the park's top sights, all of which are in the first section nearest Polanco and Condesa. These include the incomparable **Museo Nacional de Antropología,** the Tamayo and modern art museums, kid-approved **Zoológico de Chapultepec,** and the towering, grandiose **Castillo de Chapultepec.** But leave some time as well to simply stroll the miles of colorful pathways.

THE CONTEMPORARY ART SCENE

There are two highly rewarding ways to see world-class, avant-garde visual arts in Mexico City. First, see what's on at the several museums that focus on the genre—your first choices should be **Museo Jumex** in Polanco, **Museo Tamayo Arte Contemporáneo** in Bosque de Chapultepec, **Museo Universitario Arte Contemporáneo (MUAC)** on the campus of UNAM, and **Museo de Arte Carrillo Gil** in San Ángel. The second path worth pursuing is visiting some of the city's superb galleries, many of which are in Roma, San Miguel Chapultepec, and Polanco. Impressive venues that are almost always sure to stand out include **Proyectos Monclova** and **Galería OMR** in Roma and **Kurimanzutto** in San Miguel Chapultepec.

HISTORIC WALKS

Despite Mexico City's sheer immensity and considerable auto traffic, it remains a wonderfully inviting destination for scenic urban walks through beguiling Spanish Colonial and late 19th- to early 20th-century neighborhoods shaded by purple-flowering jacaranda trees and brilliant bougainvilleas. Perhaps the most charming spot in the city for just such a ramble is **Avenida Francisco Sosa,** which connects the historic heart of Coyoacán with the edge of San Ángel and is lined with grand homes and charming cafés. Closer to the city center, the grand Porfirian-era neighborhoods of Roma, Condesa, Juárez, San Rafael, and Santa María la Ribera offer a different style—think European-inspired beaux arts and art nouveau buildings—but no less enchanting sidewalks for early morning and late afternoon walks. If you have time to wander along just one street in this part of the city, make it **Avenida Amsterdam,** a leafy ellipse in the center of Condesa's most alluring restaurant and retail district.

ARCHITECTURAL LANDMARKS

Mexico City abounds with noteworthy examples of architecture that date all the way back to Hernán Cortés in 1521. A walk through Centro Histórico reveals the imposing **Catedral Metropolitana,** which was constructed in sections over 250 years, as well as a number of grand colonial buildings on the blocks west all the way to iconic **Palacio de Bellas Artes,** a wedding cake of art nouveau and neoclassical splendor. Design buffs will also want to devote time to seeing the city's countless examples of boldly innovative modern design, from the mid-century campus of the **National Autonomous University of Mexico (UNAM)** to the home-studio of legendary architect **Luis Barragán** to the geometric, natural-light-drenched **Biblioteca Vasconcelos.**

MADE IN MEXICO CITY

As the centuries-old trading hub of a country with vibrant traditions of both indigenous and colonial handicrafts, CDMX is a superb place to pick up gifts and goods made locally or elsewhere in Mexico. In addition, the maker culture thrives among the city's rising crop of entrepreneurs, which includes fashion designers, artists, furniture makers, and artisanal food producers.

ARTS AND CRAFTS

Traditional mercados as well as a number of shops around Centro Histórico are an excellent source of both inexpensive and higher-end decorative items made by artisans. Favorites include Día de Muertos figurines, miniature ofrendas, and *alebrijes,* colorfully painted carved-wood animals from Oaxaca. If you want to be sure of authenticity and quality, stick with any of the vendors who sell their goods at Bazaar Sábado on Saturday in San Ángel,

the exceptional nonprofit gift shop at Museo de Arte Popular, or any of the city's several FONART stores. You can also pick up authentic Talavera pottery, which has been produced in nearby Puebla for generations, at Uriate, a prestigious maker with shops in San Ángel and Polanco.

APPAREL AND ACCESSORIES

Mexico City has a growing crop of talented fashion designers earning international acclaim, among them Sandra Weil, Carla Fernández, and Suzzan Atala of Tuza. You'll find the best selection of fashion boutiques in Roma, Condesa, Juárez, and Polanco. Additionally, in the more traditional shops and markets, keep an eye out for distinctive traditional Mexican textiles, like embroidered huipil blouses, intricately patterned rebozo scarves, handwoven Zapotec rugs from Oaxaca, and ornate Tenango embroidery from Hidalgo. And, of course, these areas also provide opportunities to stock up on cheap, gaudy, and fun lucha libre masks.

COFFEE AND LIQUOR

A number of excellent cafés—including Cafe Avellaneda, Quentin, Cafe Negro, and Camino a Comala—sell high-quality, artisan-roasted coffee beans from the country's three prime coffee-producing states: Oaxaca, Chiapas, and Veracruz. Although tequila will forever remain a great buy in Mexico, and you can pick up some truly buzzworthy small-batch brands at excellent prices in liquor stores, mezcal has become the favored spirit for gifts (or for just bringing a few bottles back for yourself). Condesa's tiny Sabrá Dios shop has one of the best selections of top-quality mezcals; if you're just looking for a mid-price but consistently excellent brand widely available in liquor stores, Alipús and 400 Conejos are excellent choices.

CANDY AND SALSAS

Mexican candies are worth seeking out, from the old-fashioned treats sold at Dulceria de Celaya to the exquisite artisan bonbons available from Que Bo! and Tout Chocolat. The city's traditional mercados are also excellent sources for local spices, salsas, and mole and smoked-chile pastes and powders. And if you're keen on making your own spice blend or guacamole at home, pick up a *molcajete*. Similar to a mortar and pestle, these bowls are typically made of volcanic basalt, and simple rough-hewn ones sell quite cheaply.

FOOD AND DRINK

Mexico City is remarkable for its variety of intriguing culinary experiences as well as for its relative value. It's beloved as a place to snack on flavorful yet humble dishes doled out by street vendors in exchange for a few coins and as a destination that's home to several of the world's top-ranked temples of haute cuisine. Buen provecho!

STREET FOOD

Even in the city's upscale neighborhoods, you'll find street corners or entire blocks lined with vendors serving up short-order Mexican delicacies—not just the familiar tacos, quesadillas, and tamales, but slow-roasted goat and lamb barbacoa, *tortas* (sandwiches) overflowing with grilled meats and fixings, *tlacoyos* (fried or grilled American football–shape corn-masa cakes filled with beans, cheeses, and meats), *sopes* (fried-masa discs with pinched edges topped with a slew of ingredients), and several others. Oh, and don't pass up the chance to snack on charred street corn slathered in chile powder, lime, cotija cheese, and either mayo or sour cream; these delicacies are known as *elote* when served on the cob or *esquites*, with the kernals served in a cup.

Many of these foods, as well as rich posole and birria stews, are also served by taquerias, which can be anything from tiny walk-up counters to cavernous dining rooms with table service. As far as dining on the street goes, especially if you're a bit prone toward an upset stomach, consider entering the swimming pool slowly: start with a snack a day or two after you've arrived and had a chance to acclimate, and don't hesitate to choose a vendor with a slight or even long line of customers ahead of you. It's a sign that you've found a good one, and also that the food doesn't sit for long before it's served.

OLD MEXICO, NEW MEXICO

When it comes to food, Mexico is a hugely diverse nation, and CDMX offers cuisines from every region. There's tender *cochinita pibil,* the slow-roasted pork dish of the Yucatán; moles, the intensely complex sauces of fruits, nuts, chiles, and spices most typically associated with Oaxaca and Puebla; and *aguachile,* the ceviche-like dish of raw shrimp or fish cured in a concoction of lime, cilantro, sliced onions, and chiles that's a staple of Sinaloa. Much of the food served in Mexican restaurants around the world—burritos and gorditas with sides of rice, refried beans, and gooey cheeses—

reflect the culinary styles of the country's northern states, and other dishes you may think of as Mexican, such as fajitas, chili, and chimichangas, are fusion inventions of Texas and the southwest United States.

At traditional restaurants in Mexico City, you're apt to find both mildly seasoned and spicy fare (if you like it hot, there are virtually always fiery salsas available on request), and it's a near certainty that you'll encounter dishes on the menu that feature less commonly used parts of animals, including tongue, feet, stomachs, and kidneys. Insects, from grasshoppers (*chapulines*) to ant larvae (*escamoles*), often make appearances as well. And although it's landlocked, Mexico City thrives when it comes to seafood; its relative proximity to the Pacific, Caribbean, and Gulf coasts ensures both freshness and variety.

Throughout the capital—and especially in trendier neighborhoods like Roma, Condesa, and Polanco—restaurants helmed by chefs committed to reinterpreting traditional dishes with new twists, seasonal ingredients, and global influences like Mediterranean and Japanese are commonplace and account in part for the city's increasingly impressive reputation as a legit culinary destination. Slowly but surely, first-rate international restaurants are also starting to make their mark. This is a fairly easy city to find excellent sushi and ramen, wood-fired pizzas and handmade pastas, and well-prepared steak

tartare and moules-frites. Truly memorable Thai, Korean, Indian, Chinese, Peruvian, and Eastern European cuisine is harder to come by, but the city's global-food map is expanding rapidly.

MEZCAL, PULQUE, WINE, AND BEER

Over the past 15 years, Mexico City has vastly upped its beverage game. More and more restaurants serve a significant selection of international wines as well as fine bottles produced domestically (Baja's Valle de Guadalupe is the leader in the Mexican wine industry). By the glass options still tend to be limited, but this is changing, too. And mixology-driven cocktail programs, with artisan mezcals from Oaxaca and beyond, now proliferate in both bars and restaurants.

Also produced from agave, using its fermented milky and slightly tart sap, pulque has been enjoyed in Mexico for centuries, declined somewhat in popularity throughout the 20th century, and is now experiencing a renaissance. Its initial fall coincided with the rise in beer consumption in Mexico, and also until quite recently, the country generally favored mass-produced, German-style lagers like Negra Modelo and Dos Esquis Amber. Thankfully for beer lovers, Mexico City's thirst for innovative craft brews—both domestic and imported—has skyrocketed since the mid-2010s, and you'll now find a good selection of *cerveza artesanal* on most menus.

WHAT TO WATCH AND READ

It's perhaps not surprising that many of the most memorable films and books about Mexico City explore themes of death, violence, and economic inequality, but often with a darkly or absurdly comedic bent. This massive, vibrant metropolis with a history that's at once inspiring and heartbreaking is an apt setting for tales that capture the full spectrum of the human condition. Here are some key works that shine a bold light on one of the world's most complex cities.

AMORES PERROS
This darkly funny, gritty anthology film from 2000 helped launch director Alejandro González Iñárritu into the current realm of Mexican cinematic royalty. Said to be influenced by Buñuel's *Los Olvidados*, the movie was shot in some of the capital's roughest neighborhoods.

DOWN AND DELIRIOUS IN MEXICO CITY BY DANIEL HERNANDEZ
Young California-born and -bred journalist Daniel Hernandez chronicles his efforts to get in touch with his Mexican roots by partaking in a series of adventures in CDMX. The result is a colorful portrait of the capital and its subcultures in the 21st century.

FRIDA
Salma Hayek's portrayal of Frida Kahlo in this vivid 2002 biopic helped turn the artist into one of Mexico's most recognized and canonized figures, and her former home, Casa Azul—which appears in the film—into one of the city's most hallowed attractions.

I'LL SELL YOU A DOG BY JUAN PABLO VILLALOBOS
The novelist Juan Pablo Villalobos set his comically absurd third novel in a Mexico City retirement-apartment complex filled with memorably odd and endearing characters.

THE INTERIOR CIRCUIT: A MEXICO CITY CHRONICLE BY FRACISCO GOLDMAN
Francisco Goldman followed up the raw, shattering memoir about his wife's death in a freak accident, *Say Her Name*, with this deeply personal account of learning to drive in his home city of CDMX, and subsequently exploring both its beauty and its social challenges.

THE LABYRINTH OF SOLITUDE BY OCTAVIO PAZ
The lionized Mexico City poet and Nobel Laureate Octavio Paz wrote

this richly lyrical series of essays in 1950. They explore the country's complex identity, from its revolutions to its embrace of mortality by way of its Día de Muertos celebration.

LA CASA DE LAS FLORES

One of several Netflix original shows filmed in Mexico, this over-the-top and morosely funny paean to Mexican telenovelas recounts the desperate travails of a dysfunctional, wealthy Mexico City family.

LOS OLVIDADOS

The iconic Spanish auteur film-maker and sometime Mexico City resident Luis Buñuel made this despairing, realist 1950 portrait of impoverished urchins trying to scrape by in a grim D.F. slum. It was shot largely in the Romita section of Roma.

MADE IN MEXICO

Check out this often rollicking, at other times lyrical, documentary that showcases—and interviews—many of Mexico's most revered contemporary musicians and bands, including Lila Downs, Natalia Lafourcade, Kinky, Carla Morrison, Gloria Trevi, Adan Jodorowsky, Julieta Venegas, Molotov, and the amazing Chavela Vargas, who passed away in 2012, the year the film was released. A number of other cultural notables are also interviewed, from actors Diego Luna and Daniel Giménez Cacho to wrestler Blue Demon.

MASSACRE IN MEXICO BY ELENA PONIATOWSKA

In one of her most critically acclaimed works, celebrated French-Mexican journalist Elena Poniatowska provides a harrowing, carefully researched, and witness-corroborated account of the 1968 student massacre at Tlatelolco, shortly before the Summer Olympics.

ROMA

Alfonso Cuarón's mesmerizing semi-autobiographical tour de force masterfully and affectionately re-creates the Mexico City of his early 1970s childhood. The 2018 film is filtered through the unvarnished yet nevertheless poignantly sentimental lens of his family's maid, nanny, and confidant. It also should be noted that although much of Cuarón's captivating 2001 road-trip classic *Y Tu Mamá También* takes place in and on the way to Oaxaca, the first half is set and filmed in the capital.

THIS IS NOT BERLIN

This briskly paced, often quite funny film is based on director Hari Sama's wild coming-of-age in mid-1980s Mexico City and its queer and iconoclastic punk, art, and club scene.

MEXICO CITY TIMELINE

Continuously inhabited since the 1300s (and sporadically inhabited for many centuries prior), Mexico City has seen its fortunes wax and wane over the millennia. Here are some of the key events that have shaped the city's, and the country's, development.

15,000–12,000 BC: Earliest nomadic tribes inhabit the lakes of Valle de México, the site of present-day Mexico City.

1400 BC–150 CE: Believed to be the oldest city in the Valle de México, Cuicuilco is inhabited, initially as a series of smaller communities and then becoming more concentrated from 800 to 600 BC, when the settlement's great pyramid was constructed.

600–200 BC: Small villages take root in the Teotihuacán Valley.

100 BC–700 CE: Teotihuacán thrives and then collapses over this 800-year period, with construction on the Pyramid of the Moon and Pyramid of the Sun having likely begun around AD 200. The ancient city's population is estimated to have reached its peak of about 200,000 around the 4th and 5th centuries.

245–315 CE: Xitle, an ash cone volcano, erupts, destroying what's left of Cuicuilco and creating the vast lava fields that still underlie a good bit of the southern half of the city.

900–1150 CE: The region is dominated by Toltec culture, which gives way to the Mexica (Aztecs) after the fall of the Toltec Empire in 1122.

1325–1521: The Aztecs establish the city-state of Tenochtitlan—the exact site of Mexico City's present day city center—on a series of islands in the middle of Lake Texcoco in 1325. The Aztec Empire and Tenochtitlan thrive over the next two centuries, with the city-state attaining a top population estimated to be anywhere between 300,000 and 700,000 inhabitants.

1519: The Spanish, led by Hernán Cortés, arrive in Tenochtitlan, having traveled from their landing point in Veracruz, and are initially received warmly by the city's Aztec ruler, Moctezuma II.

1521: Following more than a year of tensions, during which the Spanish fled the city for the community of Coyoacán, Cortés and his troops return and overrun Tenochtitlan, forcing the city's new king, Cuauhtémoc, to surrender. Although they keep much of Tenochtitlan's layout, the Spanish virtually destroy the Aztec city, building the city of Mexico—now the capital of New Spain—on top of it.

1521–1821: Over the next three centuries, as the kingdom of New Spain grows to include additional territories throughout Latin America, Mexico City grows rapidly in population and both economic and cultural clout, a period during which the valley's lakes are drained as settlement expands outwardly.

1810–1821: During a decade of insurgency and war, Mexico secures its complete independence from Spain on September 27, 1821, with Mexico City continuing its role as capital of the new nation.

1847–1848: U.S. troops occupy Mexico City during the Mexican-American War, an engagement that followed the U.S. annexation of Texas in 1845 and the ambitious expansionist designs of American President James K. Polk. The war ends with Mexico's defeat and the signing of the Treaty of Guadalupe Hidalgo in 1848. As a result, Mexico cedes present-day California and most of the current southwestern states to the United States.

1861–1867: The second and larger of two 19th-century wars between Mexico and France results in French occupation of Mexico City from 1863 through 1867, when Mexico prevails and the republic is restored.

1877–1911: A heroic general of the French-Mexican War, Porfirio Díaz assumes the presidency of Mexico by coup in 1877 and remains in

this role, except for one term from 1880 to 1884, for seven more terms, until 1911. The full 36-year epoch is referred to as the *Porfiriato*.

1900: Greater Mexico City's population stands at about 500,000 (compared with 3.5 million in New York City and 5 million in London).

1910–1920: The onset of the Mexican Revolution brings an abrupt end to the Porfirio Díaz regime and dramatically transforms the nation's, and Mexico City's, culture and government. The revolution ends in 1920, with Álvaro Obregón—a former commander of revolutionary forces—elected president.

1921: Secretary of Education José Vasconcelos launches the Mexican Muralist movement as a way to promote the ideals of the Mexican Revolution. Its heyday lasts into the 1970s and brings worldwide acclaim to numerous painters, particularly Diego Rivera, José Clemente Orozco, and David Alfaro Siqueiros.

1930: Greater Mexico City's population reaches 1 million.

1952: Construction begins on the massive and architecturally significant 2,500-acre main campus of National Autonomous University of Mexico (UNAM), which is named a UNESCO World Heritage Site in 2007.

1956: Torre Latinoamericana becomes Mexico City's first skyscraper and remains the country's tallest building, at 545 feet tall, until the

1982 construction of Torre Ejecutiva Pemex.

1958: Four years after Frida Kahlo's death, her former husband Diego Rivera donated her iconic blue Coyoacán house, Casa Azul, and its contents for it to become a museum.

1960: Greater Mexico City's population stands at 5.5 million.

1968: In October, Mexico City hosts the Summer Olympics. Just 10 days before the Opening Ceremonies, government forces murder 300 to 400 protesters gathered in Plaza de las Tres Culturas in Tlatelolco.

1971: Around 120 protesters, most of them students, are killed by government-trained forces in June's *Halconazo,* or Corpus Christi Massacre.

1985: More than 5,000 people are killed and 3,500 buildings are severely damaged or destroyed in an 8.1 magnitude earthquake.

1990: The population of greater Mexico City reaches 15 million.

1992: Mexico signs the North American Free Trade Agreement (NAFTA) with the United States and Canada (it's renegotiated as USMCA in 2019).

1994: The home and studio that Mexico's most influential modern architect Luis Barragán designed and lived in until his death in 1988 is turned into a museum.

2000: Vicente Fox is elected president on the PAN (Partido Acción Nacional) ticket, becoming the first non-PRI (Partido Revolucionario Institucional) in 71 years.

2016: At 807 feet tall, Torre Reforma becomes the city's tallest building.

2017: Exactly 32 years to the day after the 1985 quake, a 7.1 magnitude earthquake causes widespread damage and 370 deaths.

2018: Alfonso Cuarón's Mexico City–centered *Roma* becomes the first Mexican film to win Best Foreign Film at the Academy Awards (it also wins Best Cinematography and Best Director).

2019: Pujol is named the best restaurant in North America and the 12th best in the world by the U.K.'s prestigious *Restaurant* magazine. Quintonil clocks in at 24, and Sud 777 as 58th.

2020: The population of greater Mexico City stands at about 21.6 million, although growth has slowed from a high of 63% during the 1950s to 7.5%.

BEST EVENTS AND FESTIVALS

Some of the best times of the year to visit Mexico City revolve around cultural celebrations, some that have been taking place for 500 years and others that are still relatively new. In addition to these high-spirited gatherings, keep in mind that Mexico City also observes a number of public holidays, during which normal business hours may be affected; a few to watch for, beyond Christmas and New Year's, include Dia de la Constitucion on Feburary 5, Benito Juárez's birthday on March 21, Easter week, Labor Day on May 1, and Dia de la Revolución on November 20.

FEBRUARY

Zona MACO

Held over five days and growing in size and prestige every year, this remarkable contemporary art festival draws both national and international talents to feature their work at dozens of noteworthy galleries and art museums around the city. Additionally, a massive art and design expo takes place at Centro Banamex event and convention center northwest of Polanco, featuring art, furniture, jewelry, antiques, photography, and more. *Early Feb.*

MARCH

Vive Latino

This two-day pan-Latin outdoor music festival takes place at Foro Sol, near the airport, and draws an impressive roster of internationally renowned talents in a variety of genres. In more recent years, non-Latin bands like Gun N' Roses, the Cardigans, and Portugal the Man have also been included in the lineup. *Mid-Mar.*

Spring Equinox at Teotihuacán

During this day on which indigenous tribes throughout the Americas once ushered in the new growing season and gave praise to the sun's energy, tens of thousands of visitors—many dressed in the traditional attire of all white with one red garment, such as a ribbon or scarf—descend on the 2,200-year-old complex of pyramids north of the city. *Mar. 20–21*

APRIL

Festival del Centro Histórico

Begun following the 1985 earthquake to help reinvigorate the city center, this 17-day cultural extravaganza features dozens of concerts, dance recitals, readings, kids' activities, art exhibits, and other performances. Some are free and take place in churches, palaces, and other public squares while others are held in the top arts venues of Centro Histórico and Alameda Central and require buying tickets. *Late Mar.–mid-Apr.*

JUNE
Marcha del Orgullo LGBT
Typically held the last weekend in June, the nation's largest and wildest Gay Pride celebration is centered around the cluster of queer bars in Zona Rosa and features a hugely attended parade that commences at El Ángel de la Independencia and proceeds along Avenida Paseo de la Reforma to the Zócalo. A growing number of bars, hotels, restaurants, and even cultural attractions now hold related parties and events throughout the preceding week. *Late June*

AUGUST
Festival Internacional de Artes Escénica
This 10-day cultural series features some 40 theater, music, and dance companies from throughout Mexico as well as about a dozen other

countries. Concerts are held at more than 20 scenic venues, from theaters to outdoor spaces. A number of free dance, theater, and circus workshops are also offered. *Mid-Aug.*

SEPTEMBER
Día de la Independencia
Here in Mexico, the beer-sodden Cinco de Mayo celebration that's so popularly hailed in the United States is barely even acknowledged (it's a celebration of Mexico's 1862 victory over the French during the Battle of Puebla). But Mexico's true Independence Day, which marks the start of Catholic priest Miguel Hidalgo's brave uprising in 1810, is hugely important. Throngs gather at the Zócalo outside Palacio Nacional on September 15 to loudly commemorate with fireworks and great fanfare Hidalgo's *"el grito de Dolores,"* or "cry of Dolores" (Dolores, now Dolores Hidalgo, being the small town in Guanajuato where he initiated the rebellion). A huge parade is held the following day. *Sept. 15 and 16*

NOVEMBER
Día de Muertos
The Day of the Dead has become increasingly popular throughout the city in recent years (and, just before it, Halloween for that matter). Mexicans joyfully honor their dead by creating lavish and both joyful and poignant *ofrendas*—altars with *papel picado*, photos, images of saints, favorite foods, *pan de muerto* (Day of the Dead bread), candles, incense, and *cempasúchiles* (marigolds). It's celebrated with particular color

and fervor in the historic plazas in Coyoacán, Xochimilco, Bosque de Chapultepec, and the small, off-the-beaten-path colonia of San Andrés Mixquic; there's a Day of the Dead Parade on Paseo de la Reforma too. Many attendees dress in skeleton costumes and wear skull makeup, and countless museums and other businesses set up impressive ofrenda exhibits during the weeks before or after. *Nov. 1 and 2*

Corona Capital
Held over a weekend at Autódromo Hermanos Rodríguez racetrack near the airport, this Coachella-inspired music festival features performances by around 60 top rock, alternative, and pop talents. Headliners in recent years have featured The Strokes, Franz Ferdinand, Billie Eilish, and Keane. *Mid-Nov.*

DECEMBER
Día de la Virgen de Guadalupe
On this day in 1531, an indigenous man claimed to have encountered the ghost of the Virgin Mary. Ever since, millions of Mexicans have made the pilgrimage to the site, which is now encased within the Basilica of Our Lady of Guadalupe on the city's north side. A good many of those pilgrims trek here—many on foot—on December 11 and 12, and throughout the city and country, midnight mass is held at churches and even local makeshift altars. *Dec. 11 and 12*

BEST BETS

Mexico City has enough world-class cultural attractions and culinary draws to keep you busy for weeks. Even on a short visit, however, if you focus on these recommendations of the very top places to visit in a wide range of categories, you can make the most of your time and see as many must-sees as possible. Search the neighborhood chapters for more recommendations.

ACTIVITIES AND SIGHTS

ARCHITECTURE

Biblioteca Vasconcelos, Santa María la Ribera

Casa Luis Barragán, San Miguel de Chapultepec

Monumento a la Independencia, Juárez

Monumento a la Revolución, Alameda Central

Museo Soumaya Plaza Carso, Polanco

HISTORIC SITES

Avenida Sosa, Coyoacán

Castillo de Chapultepec, Bosque de Chapultepec

Catedral Metropolitana, Centro Histórico

Museo del Templo Mayor, Centro Histórico

Palacio Nacional, Centro Histórico

Teotihuacán, Greater Mexico City

Tlalpan Centro, Greater Mexico City

MUSEUMS AND GALLERIES

Galería OMR, Roma

Kurimanzutto, San Miguel de Chapultepec

Museo de Arte Popular, Alameda Central

Museo de Frida Kahlo, Coyoacán

Museo del Carmen, San Ángel

Museo Dolores Olmedo Patiño, Greater Mexico City

Museo Nacional de Antropología, Bosque de Chapultepec

Museo Tamayo Arte Contemporáneo, Santa María la Ribera

Museo Universitario Arte Contemporáneo (MUAC), Greater Mexico City

Museo Universitario del Chopo, Santa María la Ribera

Palacio de Bellas Artes, Alameda Central

PARKS AND GREEN SPACES

Bosque de Chapultepec, Bosque de Chapultepec

Parque Bicentenario, Greater Mexico City

Parque Lincoln, Polanco

Parque México, Condesa

Parque Nacional Desierto de los Leones, Greater Mexico City

Viveros de Coyoacán, Coyoacán

DRINKS

CANTINAS

Bar El Sella, Roma

Bar Mancera, Centro Histórico

Covadonga, Roma

El Centenario, Condesa

La Faena, Centro Histórico

La Jalisciense, Greater Mexico City

COCKTAILS

Baltra, Condesa

Hanky Panky, Juárez

Hotel Casa Awolly, Roma

Jules Basement, Polanco

Licoreria Limantour, Roma

Maison Artemisia, Roma

Parker & Lenox, Juárez

COFFEE AND TEA

Cafe Avellaneda, Coyoacán

Camino a Comala, Santa María la Ribera

Casa Tassel, Roma

Quentin Cafe, Condesa

CRAFT BEER

El Depósito, San Ángel

El Trappist, Condesa

Jupiter Cerveceria, Roma

Krox International Beer, Greater Mexico City

Tasting Room, Roma

MEZCAL AND PULQUE

Bosforo, Alameda Central

Corazon de Maguey, Coyoacán

La Clandestina, Condesa

La Paloma Azul, Benito Juárez

Pulqueria Los Insurgentes, Roma

FOOD

ASIAN AND MIDDLE EASTERN FARE

Galanga Thai Kitchen, Roma

Jardín de Anatolia, Benito Juárez

Kura Izakaya, Roma

Masala y Maiz, Juárez

Merkavá, Condesa

Mog Bistro, Roma

Rokai, Cuauhtémoc

DESSERTS AND
BAKED GOODS
Cafe Nin, Juárez

Cafe Ruta de la Seda,
Coyoacán

Churreria El Moro,
Roma Norte

Diario Delicatessan,
Juárez

EUROPEAN
Huset, Roma

Lardo, Condesa

Loretta Chic Bistrot,
San Ángel

María Ciento 38, Santa
María la Ribera

Meroma, Roma

Rosetta, Roma

MODERN MEXICAN
Carlota, San Ángel

Carmela y Sal, Greater
Mexico City

Comedor Jacinta,
Polanco

Contramar, Roma

Piloncillo y Cascabel,
Benito Juárez

Restaurante Sin Nombre, Alameda Central

Tetetlán, Greater
Mexico City

TACOS AND
STREET FOOD
El Turix, Polanco

Los Cocuyos, Centro
Histórico

**Mercado de Antojitos
Mexicanos,** Coyoacán

Tacos Hola, Condesa

Tacos Los Güeros,
Greater Mexico City

Tortas Robles, Alameda Central

TRADITIONAL
MEXICAN
Azul Condesa,
Condesa

Café de Tacuba,
Centro Histórico

El Bajío, Polanco

El Tajín, Coyoacán

Fonda Mi Lupita,
Alameda Central

La Oveja Negra, Santa
María la Ribera

Los Tolucos, Greater
Mexico City

Nicos, Greater Mexico
City

Pasillo de Humo,
Condesa

Restaurante Bar Chon,
Centro Histórico

UPSCALE AND
FARM-TO-TABLE
KoMa, Greater Mexico
City

Limosneros, Centro
Histórico

Maximo Bistrot, Roma

Pujol, Polanco

Quintonil, Polanco

Restaurante Milia,
Cuauhtémoc

Sud 777, Greater
Mexico City

SHOPPING
BOOKSTORES
Cafebrería El Péndulo,
San Ángel

**Centro Cultural Elena
Garro,** Coyoacán

**Libreria del Fondo de
Cultura Economica,**
Condesa

Libreria Jorge Cuesta, Juárez

CLOTHING, JEWELRY, AND ACCESSORIES
Carla Fernández, Juárez

Carmen Rion, Condesa

HomoHabilis, Coyoacán

Sangre de mi Sangre, Roma

Tane, Polanco

Tuza, Roma

VOID, Condesa

FOOD AND DRINK
Dulcería de Celaya, Centro Histórico

Maizajo, Molino y Tortilleria, Greater Mexico City

Sabrá Dios, Condesa

Tout Chocolat, Condesa

HOME GOODS AND ACCESSORIES
Bazar Fusion, Juárez

El Bazaar Sabado, San Ángel

Local Mexico, San Ángel

Onora, Polanco

Roma Quince, Roma

Taller Experimental de Ceramica, Coyoacán

Uriarte Talavera, San Ángel

MARKETS
Mercado Artesanal de la Ciudadela, Alameda Central

Mercado Coyoacán, Coyoacán

Mercado Lagunilla, Centro Histórico

Mercado Medellín, Roma

Mercado San Juan, Alameda Central

Portales de Mercaderes, Centro Histórico

NIGHTLIFE AND PERFORMING ARTS
CONCERT AND PERFORMANCE VENUES
Centro Cultural Helenico, San Ángel

Centro Cultural Universitario de la UNAM, Greater Mexico City

Palacio Bellas Artes, Alameda Central

Teatro Bar El Vicio, Coyoacán

THEATER AND CINEMA
CENART (Centro Nacional de las Artes), Greater Mexico City

Centro Cultural Universitario de la UNAM, Greater Mexico City

Cine Tonalá, Roma

Cineteca Nacional, Benito Juárez

Foro Shakespeare, Condesa

Teatro La Capilla, Coyoacán

TOURS WORTH TAKING

In Mexico City, you'll find dozens of companies offering guided tours, in both English and Spanish, many of them fairly standard group excursions around the most prominent neighborhoods or out to Teotihuacán (which, because of its immensity as well as its distance from the city center, can be easiest to explore on an organized trip). Look beyond the usual fare, however, and you'll find several excellent outfitters that can provide an inside look at some of the city's most fascinating aspects, from mezcal and street food to LGBTQ history and street art.

Go Man Go!/Mexico at Max This company's enthusiastic, local guides offer regularly scheduled tours with a rich variety of themes, including Jewish history, LGBTQ heritage (available in three parts), food, shopping, the Zócalo, and Coyoacán. They also offer side-trip adventures that include an LGBTQ Cuernavaca adventure and trips to Teotihuacán. ⊠ *Mexico City* ☎ *55/1355–2122* ⊕ *www.mexicoatmax.com* ✉ *From MX$720.*

Mexico Bike Tour Run by a staff who have been ardent advocates of improving the city's bike infrastructure (which now includes several bike-share systems), this company also offers fun, guided daily rides through Chapultepec, Condesa, and Reforma as well as a Frida-theme pedal around historic Coyoacán. ⊠ *Mexico City* ☎ *55/5180–2287 Coyoacán, 55/2428–1488 Reforma* ⊕ *www.mexicobiketour.com.mx* ✉ *From MX$650.*

Mexico Urban Adventures This internationally acclaimed company offers more expected Teotihuacán and Hidden Mexico excursions, but it stands out for some more unusual tours, such as a night of experiencing mariachi, licha libre, and old-school cantinas; a quest for street food in some of the city's best mercados; and a *New York Times*–partnered behind-the-scenes visit with artists, designers, chefs, and other top local makers. ⊠ *Mexico City* ⊕ *www.urbanadventures.com* ✉ *From MX$920.*

Sabores México Food Tours Although several outfitters have a culinary excursion in their tour line-ups, Sabores specializes exclusively in the city's most intriguing culinary offerings. Options include eating your way through Centro Histórico and Roma's top eateries as well as a particularly stimulating beer, mezcal, and taqueria adventure. ⊠ *Mexico City* ☎ *55/5350–9565*

⊕ www.saboresmexicofoodtours.com
🎫 From MX$1400.

Street Art Chilango Married
couple and highly knowledgeable
art experts Abril and Chris give
wonderfully enlightening tours of
Roma's incredible trove of street
art every Saturday morning at
11:30 am. There's no need to book
ahead—just show up at the address
listed and bring US$25 per person.
If you can't make this date and time,
the couple does offer private art
tours by arrangement. ✉ Av. Álvaro
Obregón and Calle Orizaba, Roma
Norte ☎ 55/1364–0818 ⊕ www.stree-
tartchilango.com 🎫 From MX$500
Ⓜ Insurgentes.

COOL PLACES TO STAY

Look past the city's many chain properties and business hotels, and you'll find a bounty of distinctive lodgings that stand out for their chic design, historic charm, fashionable settings, or perhaps all three. Condesa and Roma contain many of the top smaller properties in town, but you'll find memorable lodgings throughout the city's core, from Centro Histórico to Polanco.

ALAMEDA CENTRAL

Chaya B&B Boutique Situated just across the city's oldest public park and from magnificent Palacio de Bellas Artes, this cute, bright, and reasonably priced inn sits on the top floor of a restored 1920s building. It has simple, chic furnishings, verdant plants, and an enchanting inner courtyard with hammocks and a view of San Hipolito Ex-Convent. Rates include a substantial breakfast, and there are two good restaurants on-site as well as a handful of hip boutiques elsewhere in the building. *Rooms from: MX$2,000* ⊠ *Calle Dr Mora 9* ☎ *55/5512–9074* ⊕ *www.chayabnb.com.*

CENTRO HISTÓRICO

Gran Hotel Ciudad de Mexico The rooms in this 1895 art nouveau beauty face either the iconic (but bustling) Zócalo or a less dramatic garden. The roomy accommodations are traditionally furnished, if a bit staid, but service is exceptional and the location in the historic heart of the city is exhilarating. An utterly spectacular four-story stained-glass atrium ceiling adds to the charm. *Rooms from: MX$2900* ⊠ *Calle 16 de Septiembre 82* ☎ *55/1083–7700* ⊕ *www.granhoteldelaciudaddemexico. com.mx.*

Hotel Downtown Mexico Enjoy close proximity to the Zócalo and Alameda Central from your boho-minimalist hideaway in this exquisitely restored 17th-century building. The lobby-level collection of scene-y restaurants and boutiques have made Downtown a favorite gathering point in the city. One of the building's best attributes is its gorgeous rooftop terrace, which includes a snazzy cocktail bar as well as a lap pool, sunken hot tub, and sun deck. *Rooms from: MX$3800* ⊠ *Calle Isabel la Catolica 30* ☎ *55/5130–6830* ⊕ *www.downtownmexico.com.*

CUAUHTÉMOC

Hotel Carlota Catering to a youthful, see-and-be-seen crowd of clubbers and fashionistas, this uber-cool design hotel also houses a hipster-approved lifestyle boutique and a buzzy mod-Mex restaurant. There's also an oft-Instagrammed glass-walled swimming pool. It's the kind of place where you'll want to laze by the pool and sip cocktails with friends, and although the rooms—with concrete floors and eye-catching low-slung furniture—are beautiful, they can also be noisy. *Rooms from: MX$2250 ⊠ Calle Rio Amazonas 73 ☎ 55/5511–6300 ⊕ www.hotelcarlota.mx.*

JUÁREZ

Four Seasons Mexico City. Among the most luxurious hotels in the capital, this eight-story oasis with a traditional inner courtyard was modeled after the 18th-century Iturbide Palace. It has airy, spacious rooms with French doors separating the sleeping and living spaces and opulent marble baths. The two outstanding restaurants (Italian and Pacific Coast Mexican), a gastropub, and a French bakeshop are all superb, and you can pamper yourself in the lavish spa with a roof deck and pool. *Rooms from: MX$11,600 ⊠ Paseo de la Reforma 500 ☎ 55/5230–1818 ⊕ www.fourseasons.com/mexico.*

Room Mate Valentina A favorite with LGBTQ travelers because of its handy (although somewhat noisy) location near Zona Rosa nightlife, this lone Mexico outpost of the hip Spain-based budget boutique chain is also an easy stroll from Roma, Condesa, and Parque de Chapultepec. Rooms have boldly colored, pop-art-inspired designs and are quite spacious for the price. Amenities include a reasonably priced

breakfast buffet and a small gym. *Rooms from: MX$1400 ⊠ Calle Amberes 27 ☎ 55/9596–8035 ⊕ roommatehotels.com/en/valentina.*

CONDESA

Condesa DF. It's all about the details at this hip hotel with a quiet, picturesque setting overlooking Parque España, from rooms outfitted with eye-catching custom-designed furniture and Malin & Goetz bath products to a library of coffee-table books about Mexican history and culture. The white corridors surround a central courtyard, where the hotel restaurant serves a delicious fusion of French and Mexican cuisine. The swanky rooftop terrace serves Japanese bar fare and well-crafted cocktails with sweeping views of the leafy neighborhood. *Rooms from: MX$5000 ⊠ Av. Veracruz 102 ☎ 55/5241–2600 ⊕ www.condesadf.com.*

Red Tree House Set in a charmingly restored, art-filled 1930s compound just off delightful Avenida Amsterdam and steps from a slew of great bars and restaurants, this tranquil inn offers a range of accommodations, from simple, wallet-friendly garden units to fanciful suites and two-bedroom apartments with full kitchens and terraces. Rates include a hearty breakfast, which you can enjoy in the skylight-ceilinged dining room or on the terrace. *Rooms from: MX$2500 ⊠ Calle Culiacan 6 ☎ 55/5584–3829 ⊕ www.theredtreehouse.com.*

ROMA NORTE

Ignacia Guest House One of the most alluring of the several posh, intimate B&Bs that occupy stately Porfirian-era mansions in Roma, this 1913 house has been enlarged with a dramatic glass-and-metal contemporary addition that encircles a peaceful courtyard with a living wall, cactus garden, and fountain that functions as social focal point—and is also just a wonderfully relaxing place to read or relax. The softy lit, uncluttered rooms have sumptuous beds and bathrooms, and rates include an artfully presented breakfast as well as an evening cocktail hour. *Rooms from: MX$4400 ⊠ Calle Jalapa 208B ☎ 55/2121–0966 ⊕ www.ignacia.mx.*

La Valise The Terrace Suite at La Valise is one of the most dramatic guest rooms in the city, with a plush king-size bed on tracks that allows it to slide right out onto the rooftop balcony, where you have the option of spending the night beneath a canopy of stars. But the other two rooms in this magical little B&B also exude character—and luxury. Located above the hip Almanegra Café, this is where you go when you're looking to celebrate a special occasion, but book early, as it fills up fast. *Rooms from: MX$6700 ⊠ Calle Tonalá 53 ☎ 55/5965–2585 ⊕ www.lavalise.com.*

POLANCO

Las Alcobas A favorite roost of celebrities and dignitaries, this boutique member of Marriott's Luxury Collection is on Polanco's most exclusive shopping street, a block from charming Parque Lincoln Polanco. Set in a mid-century building that's been breathtakingly reimagined by famed design firm Yabu Pushelberg, the hotel features posh rooms done with custom rosewood furniture, state-of-the-art Bose entertainment systems, and roomy baths—some with separate rain showers. *Rooms from: MX$7400 ⊠ Av. Pdte. Masaryk 390 ☎ 55/3300–3900 ⊕ www.lasalcobas.com.*

Wild Oscar This handsome, contemporary apartment-style hotel abounds with handy perks, from in-room 42-inch smart TVs and iPhone docks to laundry facilities, free parking, a great gym, and a cute little restaurant and bar. Dozens of fine eateries and shops as well as Museo Nacional de Antropología and the rest of Bosque de Chapultepec are an easy, scenic walk. *Rooms from: MX$5200 ⊠ Lamartine 516 ☎ 55/6844–0300 ⊕ www.thewildoscar.mx.*

SAN ÁNGEL

Krystal Grand Suites Hotels are rare in the city's southern neighborhoods, but this stylish all-suites property steps from San Ángel's main shopping and sights is also a great base for visiting Coyoacán, Tlalpan, and UNAM. The spacious, upscale rooms have floor-to-ceiling windows, wooden floors, kitchenettes, and comfy sitting areas, and there's a good-size gym. *Rooms from: MX$2400 ⊠ Av. Insurgentes Sur 1991 ☎ 55/5322–1580 ⊕ www.krystal-grand-suites.com.*

QUICK SIDE TRIPS

From the capital's central location, nestled high in the Sierra Nevada, you can find magnificent scenery and well-preserved villages and cities in just about any direction. Because it can take an hour or more just to travel across the city, keep in mind that while all of the destinations mentioned in this section can be visited in one long day, you'll have a more relaxing time if you consider overnighting, or stopping in these places as part of a longer regional road trip.

PUEBLA AND CHOLULA

Just 130 km (81 miles) east of CDMX, on the other side of the humongous Iztaccihuatl and very active Popocatépetl volcanoes, Mexico's fourth-largest city is a handsome if rather traditional hub of ornate Spanish Colonial architecture and classic old-world cuisine. In a day, you can explore the city core, strolling around its grand Zócalo and visiting the absolutely spectacular Catedral de Puebla and the trove of art—ancient and contemporary—and artifacts at Museo Amparo. Plan on one meal at the venerable El Mural de los Poblanos, which is justly famous for the city's most famous dish, mole, then enjoy sunset from the chic rooftop terrace at the Azul Talavera Hotel or the Hotel La Purificadora. With an extra day, you could also venture a bit farther afield to Museo Internacional del Barraco, with its spectacular design by Japanese architect Toyo Ito as well as the small and walk-able adjacent city of Cholulu, with its sweeping views of Popocatépetl and Iztaccíhuatl, its outstanding Museo de la Ciudad de Cholula, and Tlachihualtepetl—the great pyramid of Cholula, which dates to the 3rd century BC.

Timing: Buses make the two-hour trip from Mexico City to Puebla all day long, and from Puebla, it's a 20-minute taxi ride or hour-long train ride to Cholula. Going by Uber from CDMX to Puebla costs about MX$2,000 each way, and it's an additional MX$100 for an Uber ride from Puebla to Cholula.

TEPOZTLÁN AND CUERNAVACA

Reached via a dramatically twisting and turning mountain highway, the state of Morelos is home to a number of worthwhile destinations, including the historic capital city of Cuernavaca, with its proliferation of fancy haciendas that many Chilangos own as weekend retreats (a few are now swanky hotels). The bustling Zócalo de Cuernavaca is surrounded by inviting restaurants and bars as well as a few notable sights, among them the excellent MMAPO Museo Morelense de Arte Popular, the quirky Museo Casa Robert Brady art museum, and the lush greenery of Jardín Borda.

Set in a sweeping, emerald valley fringed by jagged mountains, the popular village of Tepoztlán is reached via a side road off the highway between Mexico City and Cuernavaca. Beyond the gorgeous scenery, which you can best appreciate by hiking up a steep mountainside to the Aztec Pirámide Tepozteco, you'll find a number of funky and chic boutique hotels, eateries, and New Age spa resorts. An excellent crafts market takes place in the village center on weekends, and you should make every effort to tour the fascinating Templo y Ex-Convento de la Natividad, a 16th-century church and Dominican monastery filled with ancient frescoes. If you're driving, you can also continue east to Puebla (about a 2½-hour drive) or make the 90-minute drive south to one of the country's most delightful alpine villages, the colonial silver-mining town of Taxco.

Timing: There's cheap and frequent bus service from CDMX's Taxqueña bus station to both Cuernavaca and Tepoztlán. Ubering to either community costs about MX$1,000 each way.

TOLUCA AND MALINALCO

A city of about 500,000 that lies just west of the capital, Toluca has a scenic and historic colonial core and a handful of noteworthy attractions, including the superb Museo de Antropologia e Historia and the Jardín Botánico Cosmovitral with its ornate stained-glass mural. But the city is also the stepping off point for Nevado de Toluca, a 15,433-foot extinct volcano that anchors a wonderful scenic park with great hiking, cross-country skiing, and wildlife watching. From Toluca, it's also just an hour west to one of central Mexico's most delightful little retreats, Valle de Bravo, with its azure alpine lake and great variety of boutique hotels and inviting restaurants. A stunningly picturesque 75-minute drive or bus ride through the mountains south from Toluca, tiny Malinalco enjoys a spectacular setting in a lush valley framed by sheer cliffs, with hiking trails that lead to Aztec temples. Its tiny colonial center is anchored by a pair of lovely plazas and—while mellower than Tepoztlán—cultivates an increasingly hip, New Age-y vibe, with some notable dining, shopping, and lodging options.

Timing: There's frequent bus service to Toluca, and less frequent but very affordable buses from there or from Mexico City to Malinalco. From the capital, a one-way Uber runs about MX$1,000 to Toluca (one hour), and another MX$1,300 from Toluca to Malinalco (two hours).

Centro Histórico

GO FOR

History galore

Authentic street food

Art and architecture

POLANCO

SANTA MARÍA LA RIBERA

SAN RAFAEL

ALAMEDA CENTRAL

CENTRO HISTÓRICO

BOSQUE DE CHAPULTEPEC

JUÁREZ AND ANZURES

ROMA

CONDESA

BENITO JUÁREZ

SAN ÁNGEL

COYOACÁN

The Centro Histórico is not only the heart of Mexico City, but it is where the modern history of the Americas began. Since its time as the center of the great Aztec city of Tenochtitlan, founded in 1325 on an island in the shallows of Lake Texcoco, the modern-day historic center has been the axis around which Mexico revolves. This is where the Aztec kings performed their sacred rites (the pediments of their great stone pyramid are still visible just below street level at the Museum of the Templo Mayor), where the Spanish invaders established their colonial capital, and where modern Mexico has consummated its many revolutions. Centered on a grand ceremonial square, called the Zócalo, the neighborhood is both a living museum crowded with historic monuments, and also the most democratic space in a highly stratified city of more than 20 million people. On any given day, people from across the city and country flock here to shop for toys, school uniforms, or fabrics by the yard, to protest under the Zócalo's arcades, or simply to marvel at the nation's magnificent heritage as they wander down crowded pedestrian streets like Madero and Regina. Dotted with street stalls, cantinas, and precarious-looking churches—their foundations tilted from centuries of earthquakes—the Centro is still the chaotic, graceful soul of the Western Hemisphere's greatest metropolis.

—by Michael Snyder

Centro Histórico North

Sights

Antiguo Colegio de San Ildefonso
Located in a colonial building with lovely patios, this former college started out in the 18th century as a Jesuit school for the sons of wealthy Mexicans. Frida Kahlo also famously studied here as an adolescent. It's now a splendid museum that showcases outstanding regional exhibitions, but the best reason to visit is the interior murals by Diego Rivera, José Clemente Orozco, and Fernando Leal. ✉ *Calle Justo Sierra 16, Centro Histórico* ☎ *55/3602–0000* 🌐 *www.sanildefonso.org.mx* 🎫 *MX$50; free Sun.* ⏲ *Closed Mon.* Ⓜ *Zócalo.*

Arena Coliseo
The smaller and less polished of the city's two lucha libre arenas, the Coliseo is (as its name suggests) round and (belying its grandiose namesake) has seen better days. But the space allows proximity to the crowd, which means the fighters

ramp up spectators to compensate for the lack of bright lights and spectacle in their other home, Arena México. The best fights start on Saturday at 7:30 pm; tickets are available at the box office or through Ticketmaster. ⊠ *República de Perú 77, Centro Histórico* ☎ *55/5588–0266* ⊕ *www.cmll.com* Ⓜ *Garibaldi.*

Casa de los Azulejos *(House of Tiles)*
Originally built in the 16th century, the "House of Tiles" only acquired the celebrated facade that lends it its name a century later when the material was likely introduced from the workshop of the Dominican friars in the nearby city of Puebla. The dazzling designs, along with the facade's iron balconies and bronze handrails, the latter imported from China, make it one of the most singular baroque structures in the city. The interior is also worth seeing for its Moorish patio, monumental staircase, and mural by Orozco. The building is currently occupied by Sanborns, a chain store and restaurant; if you have plenty of time (service is slow), this is a good place to stop for a meal—especially breakfast, when older men gather to read their newspapers around the snaking bar. There's also a store with a pharmacy, bakery, candy counter, and an ATM. ⊠ *Calle Madero 4, at Callejón de la Condesa, Centro Histórico* ⊕ *www.sanborns.com.mx* Ⓜ *Bellas Artes, Allende.*

★ Catedral Metropolitana

The majestic cathedral that forms the northern side of the Zócalo is nothing less than the heart

GETTING HERE

As its name suggests, the Centro Histórico is, historically, the city's geographic heart. Situated to the east of Juarez, it marks the northeastern extreme of the neighborhoods most visitors are likely to visit. Well-served by public transit, the Centro is best reached by Metro lines 1 and 2 (tickets are just MX$5); most useful are the stops at Pino Suárez, a major transit point that houses a poorly restored Aztec temple, and Zócalo, in the heart of the central plaza. If coming or going early in the morning or late at night, Uber is also a good option, but the heavily congested streets can make entering in a private vehicle during the day more complicated.

of Mexico City, its most famous building, and the backdrop to many of the country's most important historical events. Construction on the largest and one of the oldest Latin American cathedrals began in the late 16th century and continued intermittently throughout the next 300 years. The result is a medley of baroque and neoclassical touches. There are 5 altars and 14 chapels, mostly in the ornate churrigueresque style, named for Spanish architect José Benito Churriguera (1665–1725). Like most Mexican churches, the cathedral is all but overwhelmed by innumerable paintings, altarpieces, and statues—in graphic color—of Christ and the saints. Over the centuries, this cathedral began to sink into the spongy subsoil, but a major engineering project to stabilize it was declared successful in 2000. The older-looking church attached to the cathedral is the 18th-century Sagrario chapel. Guided tours of the bell towers were discontinued following the 2017 earthquake, but crypt tours in Spanish are available daily from 11 am to 5 pm for MX$40 per person; inquire at the main entrance. ⊠ *Zócalo, Centro Histórico* ☎ *55/4165–4013* ⊕ *www.catedralmetropolitanacdmx.org* ✉ *Free* Ⓜ *Zócalo.*

Centro Cultural de España

The Cultural Center of Spain is an art space, restaurant, and bar in the heart of the neighborhood, just steps away from the Cathedral and the Templo Mayor and with beautiful views of both from its open-air rooftop. It was built in an area that Hernán Cortés himself assigned to his butler, Diego de Soto, though the land changed hands many times and the current building was constructed in the 18th century, well after the years of Cortés. Temporary exhibits housed in the seven exhibition rooms often highlight young artists and showcase current artistic trends. While the exhibitions are worth a look, there are also conferences and workshops held on a nearly daily basis for anyone interested in art and culture. The rooftop bar, which hosts frequent live music events, is one of the neighborhood's better-kept secrets, with a balcony opening directly onto the Cathedral's magnificent dome and buttresses: easily one of the area's best views. Check out the center's website for listings. ⊠ *Guatemala 18, Centro Histórico* ☎ *55/6592–9926* ⊕ *www.ccemx.org* ✉ *Free* ⊙ *Closed Mon.* Ⓜ *Zócalo.*

Ex-Teresa Arte Actual

One of the more disorienting buildings in the Centro, the Ex-Teresa was first established in 1616 as a Carmelite convent and now runs as a contemporary art space. The convent was shut down after 250 years, but the space reopened in its current iteration in 1993. The two primary chapels lean precariously against one another, unsettled by centuries of seismic activity and resulting in a gravity-warping physical experience when you step inside. The space transforms dramatically with each new installation, but its vertigo-inducing power is constant. ⊠ *Licenciado Verdad 8, off Calle Moneda, Centro Histórico* ☎ *55/4122–8020* ⊕ *www.exteresa. bellasartes.gob.mx* ⊙ *Closed Mon.* Ⓜ *Zócalo.*

Mercado Abelardo Rodriguez

Built in 1934 as a cultural complex and prototype for modern marketplaces around Mexico, the Mercado Abelardo Rodriguez is largely an ordinary neighborhood mercado today, with butchers, vegetable vendors, juice stalls, and some outstanding carnitas served at a stall called Don One. The market's real claim to fame is its murals, painted by disciples of the greats in the arched entrances. ⊠ *Callejón Girón, Centro Histórico* ⊕ *www.facebook. com/MercadoAbelardoLRodriguez* Ⓜ *Zócalo.*

Museo Archivo de la Fotografía
(Museum of the Photography Archive)
The building that now houses the Museum of the Photography Archive is one of the oldest on the Zócalo, first built in the late 16th century as part of the property of the Nava Chávez family, founded by the canon priest Pedro Nava Chávez and passed down through his niece, Catalina de Nava. Decorated in a neo-Moorish style popular in Mexico's colonial period, the house became famous in 2006 when archaeologists uncovered a monolithic statue of the goddess Tlaltecuhtli under its floors. That same year, the building opened its doors for regular photography exhibitions, often focused on the work of Mexico's finest photojournalists. ⊠ *República de Guatemala 34, Centro Histórico* ☎ *55/2616-7057* ⊕ *www.cultura.cdmx.gob.mx* ⊘ *Closed Mon.* Ⓜ *Zócalo.*

Museo del Estanquillo
First built as a jewelry store in 1892, the belle epoque–style Esmeralda Building has had various uses over the years, including as a government office, a bank, a disco called La Opulencia, and, since 2006, as the Museo de Estanquillo, housing the eclectic collection of the great 20th-century journalist, Carlos Monsiváis. The museum takes its name from the term used through the 19th and early 20th centuries for small neighborhood convenience shops, which stocked virtually everything a person could need. It's an appropriate name for a museum dedicated to rotating exhibitions drawn from a total collection of 20,000 individual pieces. Shows might range from cartoons, stamps, and etchings to photos, lithographs, drawings, and paintings from some of the greatest names in Mexican art; the collection is as diverse and democratic as Monsiváis was in his writing. The rooftop café and bookstore offer a stunning view over the domes of San Felipe Neri la Profesa and the hubbub of Madero below. ⊠ *Isabel la Católica 26, at Av. Madero, Centro Histórico* ☎ *55/5521-3052* ⊕ *www.museodelestanquillo.com* ▧ *Free* ⊘ *Closed Tues.* Ⓜ *Zócalo or Allende.*

Museo José Luis Cuevas
Found within the refurbished Santa Inés convent, this inviting museum displays international modern art as well as work by Mexico's *enfant terrible*, José Luis Cuevas, one of the country's best-known modern artists (1934–2017). The highlight is the sensational *La Giganta (The Giantess)*, Cuevas's eight-ton bronze sculpture in the central patio. It represents male-female duality and pays homage to Charles Baudelaire's poem of the same name. Up-and-coming Latin American artists appear in temporary exhibitions throughout the year. ⊠ *Academia 13, at Calle Moneda, Centro Histórico* ☎ *55/5522-0156* ⊕ *www.museojoseluiscuevas.com.mx* ▧ *MX$30; free Sun.* ⊘ *Closed Mon.* Ⓜ *Zócalo.*

Calle Galeana

Calle Degollado

Mosqueta

Lázaro Cárdenas

Avenida Paseo de la Reforma Norte

1

Guerrero

M GARIBALDI/ LAGUNILLA

2

Calle Comonfort

Calle Nunó

Calle Libertad

López Rayón

Avenida Peralvillo

LAGUNILLA **M**

Calle Jesús Carranza

C. República de Ecuador

C. República de Paraguay

Peatonal República de Honduras

3

Calle Ignacio Allende

Calle República de Perú

4

Centro Histórico North

Calle Belisario Domínguez

5

Lázaro Cárdenas

15

14 Calle República de Cuba

6

C. República de Argentina

7

Calle Donceles

13

12

BELLAS ARTES

16 **17**

18

19 C. Tacuba

ALLENDE **M**

Calle República de Chile

Calle Palma Norte

C. República de Brasil

11

Bellas Artes

M **47**

46 **45**

C. 5 de Mayo

40 **39**

48 **49**

Francisco I. Madero

34

20

21 **22**

23

24

50

51

44

43

41

35

31

29

ZOCALO

28

52

42 **38** **36**

32

30

M

37

33

16 de Septiembre

Calle Simón Bolívar

C. Venustiano Carranza

C. República de Uruguay

Lázaro Cárdenas

Centro Histórico South

C. Matamoros

Morelos

Calle Caridad

Calle Tenochtitlán

Calle Aztecas

Calle Florida

Tepito

Héroe de Granaditas

Calle González Ortega

C. República de Costa Rica

Plaza del Estudiante · Calle Peña y Peña

C. República de Bolivia

Calle del Carmen

C. República de Colombia

C. General **9** Miguel Alemáin

3

C. San Antonio Tomatlájn

C. Mixcalco

10

C. República de Guatemala

C. Correo Mayor

25

C. C. Jesús María

26

27

C. la Soledad

C. Corregidora

0 ——— 500 ft

0 ——— 100 m

Museo Mexicano del Diseño

This museum with a big gift shop (or shop with a small museum) and café features small expositions of contemporary Mexican design. The goals of the museum are to provide a space for design, to assist local designers, and to offer a location in which designers can make money from their craft. Exhibitions, open only through guided tours in Spanish every half hour from 10 am to 8 pm, are shown in a back room made of brick, where you can see the old archways from Cortés's patio, which was built, in part, on top of Moctezuma's pyramid. The shop is open to the public. ⊠ *Madero 74, Centro Histórico* ☎ *55/5510–8609* ⊕ *www.mumedi.mx* ✉ *MX$50* Ⓜ *Zócalo.*

Museo Nacional de Arte (MUNAL)
(National Art Museum)

The collections of the National Art Museum occupy one of the Centro's most impressive neoclassical buildings, designed by Italian architect Silvio Contri in the early 20th century. The works in the permanent collection, organized in galleries around a gracious open patio and grand central staircase, span nearly every school of Mexican art, with a concentration on work produced between 1810 and 1950. José María Velasco's *Vista del Valle de México desde el Cerro de Santa Isabel* (*View of the Valley of Mexico from the Hill of Santa Isabel*) is on display; the collection also includes artists such as Diego Rivera and Ramón Cano Manilla. Keep an eye out for temporary exhibitions of works by Mexican and international masters. Guided tours in English are available for free if you book ahead (email visitasguiadas@munal.inba. gob.mx to do so). ⊠ *Calle Tacuba 8, Centro Histórico* ☎ *55/8647–5430* ⊕ *www.munal.mx* ✉ *MX$70* ۩ *Closed Mon.* Ⓜ *Bellas Artes or Allende.*

Museo Palacio Cultural Banamex
(Palacio de Iturbide)

Built between 1779 and 1785, this baroque palace—note the imposing door and its carved-stone trimmings—was originally a residence for the Counts of Moncada and the Marquises of Jaral de Berrio, a title created only five years earlier. The palace takes its name from Agustín de Iturbide, who stayed here for a short time in 1822. One of the military heroes of the independence movement, the misguided Iturbide proclaimed himself emperor of Mexico once the country finally achieved freedom from Spain. He was staying in the palace when he became emperor, a position he held for less than a year before being driven into exile. In the two centuries since, the house has been a school, a café, and a hotel. In 1964, the Palacio Iturbide became the property of Banamex, which oversaw its restoration and eventually reopened the space in 2004 as a cultural center, showing major exhibitions in the grand central atrium. ⊠ *Calle Madero 17, Centro Histórico* ☎ *55/1226–0004* ⊕ *www. fomentoculturalbanamex.org* ✉ *Free* Ⓜ *Bellas Artes, Zocalo.*

★ Palacio Nacional

The center of government in Mexico City since the time of the Aztecs, the National Palace's long, volcanic stone facade is both a symbol of political power and a staging ground for acts of resistance. Construction of the national palace was initiated by Cortés on the site of Moctezuma II's royal residence and remodeled by the viceroys. Its current form dates from 1693, although its third floor was added in 1926. The entire building is worth a look, even just for the novel experience of wandering freely through an influential nation's primary seat of government, but most visitors come for Diego Rivera's sweeping murals on the second floor of the main courtyard. For more than 20 years, starting in 1929, Rivera and his assistants mounted scaffolds day and night, perfecting techniques adapted from Renaissance Italy's frescoes. The result is nearly 1,200 square feet of vividly painted wall space, titled *Epica del Pueblo Mexicano en su Lucha por la Libertad y la Independencia* (*Epic of the Mexican People in Their Struggle for Freedom and Independence*). The paintings represent two millennia of Mexican history, filtered through Rivera's imagination; only a few vignettes acknowledge the more violent elements of some pre-Hispanic societies. As you walk around, you'll pass images of the savagery of the conquest and the hypocrisy of the Spanish priests, the noble independence movement, and the bloody revolution. Marx appears amid scenes of class struggle, toiling workers, industrialization (which Rivera idealized), bourgeois decadence, and nuclear holocaust. These are among Rivera's finest works—as well as the most accessible and probably the most visited. The palace also houses a minor museum that focuses on 19th-century president Benito Juárez and the Mexican Congress. Other exhibition spaces house rotating, and sometimes quite extraordinary, exhibitions, typically advertised on a large billboard in the Zócalo.

The liberty bell rung by Padre Hidalgo to proclaim independence in 1810 hangs high on the central facade. It chimes every eve of September 16, while from the balcony the president repeats the historic shout of independence to throngs of citizens below. Though remarkably accessible, the Palacio Nacional can be closed with little notice for government functions.

In order to enter, you might have to leave an ID at the entrance; it's smart to bring yours just in case. ⊠ *East side of the Zócalo, Centro Histórico* ✛ *Entrance through side door on Moneda* ⊕ *www.hacienda.gob. mx/cultura/museo_virtual_pal_nac/ index.htm* 🖾 *Free* Ⓜ *Zócalo.*

Palacio Postal (Dirección General de Correos)

Mexico City's main post office building, designed by Italian architect Adamo Boari and Mexican engineer Gonzalo Garita, is a fine example of Renaissance Revival architecture. Constructed of cream-color sandstone from Teayo, Puebla, and Carrara, Italy, it epitomizes the grand Eurocentric architecture common in Mexico during the Porfiriato—the long dictatorship of Porfirio Díaz (1876–1911). For many, it's one of Mexico's most splendid buildings. Though the Palacio's on-site museum is currently closed for renovations, tours in Spanish are available at 6 pm on the last Wednesday of every month. Tours in English can be arranged over the phone with two days advance notice. ⊠ *Calle Tacuba 1, at Eje Central Lázaro Cárdenas, Centro Histórico* ☎ *55/5510-2999 museum, 55/4130-4000* ⊕ *www.gob.mx/correosdemexico* 🖾 *Free* Ⓜ *Bellas Artes.*

★ Plaza de Santo Domingo

Of all the plazas and public spaces in Mexico City, there is none more beautiful or harmonious than the Plaza Santo Domingo. The Aztec emperor Cuauhtémoc built a palace here, where heretics were later burned at the stake during

the Spanish Inquisition. The plaza was the intellectual hub of the city during the colonial era and it remains one of the only places in the city to have maintained nearly all of its original 18th-century buildings. Today Santo Domingo's most iconic feature is the Portal de los Evangelistas, a sagging arcade casting shade over scribes working at typewriters and stands printing business cards and other stationery on old-fashioned ink presses. On the northern side of the plaza, the baroque Santo Domingo Church is all that remains of the first Dominican convent in New Spain. The convent building was demolished in 1861 under the Reform laws that forced clerics to turn over all religious buildings not used for worship to the government. ⊠ *Bounded by República de Cuba, República de Brasil, República de Venezuela, and Palma, Centro Histórico* Ⓜ *Zócalo.*

★ Secretaria de Educación Pública (SEP) *(Ministry of Public Education)*

Diego Rivera painted his finest suite of murals in the arcaded patios of the Ministry of Public Education, which occupies the former convent of Santa María de la Incarnación del Divino Verbo. Led from 1921 to 1924 by the writer José Vasconcelos, the Secretariat of Public Education was arguably the single most influential institution of post-Revolution Mexico. From his post as Minister, Vasconcelos instituted substantial education reforms, particularly in rural Mexico, while also becoming a major sponsor of the muralist movement in the city. Together, those dual efforts played a fundamental role in redirecting the aesthetic and intellectual orientation of Mexico's cultural elites toward local and indigenous traditions (albiet sometimes in ways that bordered on the paternalistic and reductive). Rivera's murals at the SEP building include depictions of farmers and factory workers, sweeping landscapes from the desert north, festivities from Mexico's countryside and urban centers, and, on the upper floors, satirical send-ups of American capitalist greed. In February and March, towering jacaranda trees carpet the back patio in purple flowers. ⊠ *República de Argentina 28, Centro Histórico* ☎ *55/3601–7599* ⊕ *murales. sep.gob.mx* ⊗ *Closed weekends.*

Sinagoga Justo Sierra

This was the first center for the Ashkenazi Jewish community that arrived in Mexico after fleeing eastern Europe in the first decades of the 20th century; the synagogue fell out of regular use just two decades after its founding in 1941, when the community starting moving out to more prosperous districts of the city. Restored in 2010, it's now once again a community center, open daily to the general public and hosting frequent cultural activities, from seminars to musical performances to lending studio space to local artists. Guided tours of the synagogue are available on the first and third Sunday of each month at 11:30 am (MX$50) and tours of the surrounding neighborhood, where many Jewish migrants once lived, are offered the second Sunday of each month at 10 am (MX$150). For guided tours outside those dates contact the synagogue directly by phone or email (info@sinagogajustosierra.com). ⊠ *Justo Sierra 71, Centro Histórico* ☎ *55/5522–4828* ⊕ *www.sinagogajustosierra.com* Ⓜ *Zócalo.*

Templo de San Francisco

On the site of Mexico's first convent (1524), this church has served as a barracks, a hotel, a circus, a theater, and a Methodist temple. The main sanctuary's elaborate baroque facade is set past an iron gate and down a pretty flight of steps from street level. Inside, the Templo is one of the best places in the Centro to get a sense of the seismic shifts that continue to unsettle Mexico City. Stand at the back of the nave and note the chandeliers, which appear frozen mid-swing: an effect of gravity combined with the incline of the aisle, which has sunken unevenly over the centuries. The church next store, in a French neo-Gothic style, was added later. ⊠ *Madero 7, Centro Histórico* ☎ *55/5521–7331* Ⓜ *Bellas Artes or Allende.*

★ Templo Mayor

The ruins of the sacred axis of the Aztec empire, built here beginning in the 14th century, were unearthed accidentally in 1978 by telephone repairmen and the vast, 3-acre archaeological site has since become the old city's most compelling museum. At this temple, whose two twin shrines were dedicated to the sun god Huitzilopochtli and the rain god Tláloc, captives from the empire's near-constant wars of conquest were sacrificed in rituals commemorated in carvings of skulls visible deep in the temple compound. The adjacent Museo del Templo Mayor contains thousands of pieces unearthed from the site and others across central Mexico, including ceramic warriors, stone carvings and knives, skulls of sacrificial victims, models and scale reproductions, and a room on the Spaniards' destruction of Tenochtitlán. The centerpiece is an 8-ton disk unearthed at the Templo Mayor depicting the dismembered moon goddess Coyolxauhqui. ⊠ *Seminario 8, Centro Histórico*

☎ *55/4040–5600* ⊕ *www.templomayor. inah.gob.mx* 🎟 *MX$75* ⊙ *Closed Mon.* Ⓜ *Zócalo.*

★ Torre Latinoamericana

At the time of its completion in 1956, after eight long years of construction, the 44-story Torre Latina was Latin America's tallest building, a marvel of local engineering that proclaimed Mexico City as the most important metropolis in the

Spanish-speaking world. Some of the best views of the city can be seen from the museums, restaurants, and cafés on floors 37 to 41 while the observation deck is on floor 44. Stop off at floor 38 to visit a museum that focuses on the history of the tower and the city or on the 40th floor for a drink at Bar Nivel 40, which gives you basically the same view for just the cost of a drink. In addition, the Bicentennial Museum on the 36th floor has documents from the early independence era. ⊠ *Eje Central Lázaro Cárdenas 2 , at Calle Madero, Centro Histórico* ⊕ *www.torrelatinoamericana.com. mx* 🎫 *Observation deck MX$120, city museum MX$30, Bicentennial Museum MX$20* Ⓜ *Bellas Artes.*

★ Zócalo

One of the world's largest urban squares, Mexico City's Zócalo is the clearest expression of the city's immense importance as the capital of New Spain: a showpiece of colonial power and wealth and, after independence, a symbol for every element of Mexico's complex political identity.

Zócalo literally means "pedestal" or "base"; in the mid-19th century, an independence monument was planned for the square, but only the base was built. The term stuck, however, and now the word "zócalo" is applied to the main plazas in many Mexican cities. Mexico City's Zócalo (because it's the original, it's always capitalized) is used for government rallies, protests, sit-ins, and festive events. It's the focal point for Independence Day celebra-

tions on the eve of September 16 and is a maze of lights, tinsel, and traders during the Christmas season. Flag-raising and -lowering ceremonies take place here in the early morning and late afternoon.

Formally called the Plaza de la Constitución, the enormous paved square, the largest in the Western Hemisphere, occupies the site of the ceremonial center of Tenochtitlán, the capital of the Aztec empire, which once comprised 78 buildings. From the early 18th century until the mid-1900s, the plaza housed a market known as El Parián, specializing in luxury goods imported from Asia on the Manila Galleons, Spanish trading ships that crossed the Pacific from the Philippines to Acapulco. And while the Zócalo has seen the rise and fall of governments and movements for seven centuries, many of the rust-red facades that ring the plaza today—save for the first two floors of the emblematic Palacio Nacional and the Cathedral—were only added in the early 20th century, built in the neo-colonial style in fashion following the Revolution.

The Zócalo is the heart of the Centro Histórico, and many of the neighborhood's sights are on the plaza's borders or just a few short blocks away. Even as the Mexican economy has gradually begun to centralize in recent years, the Zócalo remains the indisputable center of the nation. ⊠ *Bounded 16 de Septiembre, Av. 5 de Mayo, Pino Suárez, and Monte de Piedad, Centro Histórico* Ⓜ *Zócalo.*

LA MERCED

Since the late 1980s, the largest market in Mexico City has been the Central de Abastos in the southeastern district of Iztapalapa—a market so large that it has its own postal code. But for 450 years before that, almost every product sold in the capital and every person arriving from the provinces made a first stop in La Merced at the eastern edge of the historic center. And while La Merced may no longer be the city's largest market, it remains its most iconic. Under high, modernist vaults built in the 1950s and charred in places from fires that have devastated but never destroyed it, the market sprawls in a maze of stalls selling fruits, vegetables, mounds of blood-red dried chilies, and fragrant bundles of medicinal herbs. Radiating out from the center are other stalls selling big bowls of chicken soup and *huaraches* (fried masa dough) of beans, cheese, and squash blossom while old women from the countryside sell farm fresh eggs, homemade tortillas, and beans in shades of cream, orange, and purple. There is still no better place to get a sense of Mexico's bounty.

Shopping

Dulcería de Celaya

A haven for anyone with a sweet tooth since 1874, Dulcería Celaya specializes in candied pineapple, guava, and other exotic fruits; almond paste; candied walnut rolls; and *cajeta,* a thick caramelized milk similar to Argentine dulce de leche. There's another branch in La Roma, but you have to come to the Centro for the atmosphere. ⊠ *5 de Mayo 39* ☎ *55/5521–1787.*

★ La Lagunilla

Enormous La Lagunilla has been the site of trade and bartering for more than five centuries. It's open every Sunday, when vendors set up along Confort Street and along the alley connecting to Paseo de la Reforma, selling everything from antique paintings and furniture to old magazines and plastic toys. Dress down, and watch out for pickpockets. ⊠ *On Calle Bocanegra from Comonfort to Reforma, and on Paseo de la Reforma from Allende to Matamoros, Centro Histórico* Ⓜ *Garibaldi, Lagunilla.*

Mercado Lagunilla

If you're en route to the Lagunilla antiques market, which constitutes a small corner of the larger Lagunilla Sunday market, don't forget to make a stop at the brick-and-mortar Mercado Lagunilla, which specializes in quinceañera and wedding dresses. Inside, the low ceilings and narrow aisles are crowded blossoming taffeta skirts, first communion gowns, and mariachi outfits. ⊠ *López Rayón 46, Centro Histórico* ✛ *Entrances on Allende, Ecuador, Comonfort, and López Rayón.*

Oaxaca en Mexico

Opened six decades ago, this family-run shop in the shadow of the Parroquia de la Sanísima Trinidad sells fresh products imported weekly from Oaxaca. Expect to find cheeses, herbs, chiles, and chocolate along with simple green-glazed pottery. ⊠ *Calle Santísima 16, Centro Histórico* ☎ *55/5522–0296* Ⓜ *Zócalo, Merced.*

★ Portales de Mercaderes

This arcade on the Zócalo has attracted merchants since 1524. It's lined with jewelry shops selling gold (often by the gram) and authentic Taxco silver at prices lower than those in Taxco, where the overhead is higher. The best shop is Sombreros Tardán, which specializes in fashionable hats of every shape and style; it's more or less in the middle of the arcade. ⊠ *Extending length of west side of Zócalo between Calles Madero and 16 de Septiembre, Centro Histórico* Ⓜ *Zócalo.*

Shops at the Downtown Hotel

Seven years ago, the 17th-century palace of the Miravalle family was turned into the Centro's coolest hotel, which brought with it a collection of worthwhile shops arranged around its interior patios. The best stores in the small, charming complex are branches of well-known designers and clothing brands like Carla Fernanez, Remigio (by Oaxacan designer Remigio Mestas Revilla), and Fábrica Social, all focused on contemporary clothing crafted from handmade Mexican textiles. ⊠ *Isabel la Católica 30, Centro Histórico* Ⓜ *Zócalo, Isabel la Católica, Allende.*

🍵 Coffee and Quick Bites

Café Rio

$ | Lebanese. A sliver of patina tables and walls painted with tropical foliage on a stretch of Donceles devoted mostly to camera stores, Café Rio has been the preferred coffee shop near the Zócalo since it opened in 1961. Run by the indomitable Gema Hauayek and her family, the café has hosted writers, journalists, and presidents who come for fresh pastries and strong, well-made espresso. **Known for:** famed date pie; old-world charm; Lebanese lunch on Wednesday afternoon. *Average main: 30 MP* ⊠ *Donceles 86, Centro Histórico* ☎ *55/5510–2250* ⊙ *No dinner Sun.* ▤ *No credit cards* Ⓜ *Allende.*

Huaraches Doña Mary

$ | Mexican. The southern edge of the Plaza Santo Domingo, where Calle República de Cuba crosses República de Brasil and becomes (for a span of one block) Luis González Obregón, is lined with stalls selling tacos, tortas, quesadillas, and huaraches. They're all pretty similar, but the best is Doña Mary, on the Cuba side, where you can grab a stool and enjoy your *huarache de quelites*—think of it as a big quesadilla stuffed with wilted wild greens—with a perfect view of the Centro's prettiest plaza. **Known for:** fast-paced street-stall atmosphere; filling antojitos; no-nonsense service. *Average main: 47 MP* ⊠ *República de Cuba 99, Centro Histórico* ✥ *On southwest corner with Brasil* ▤ *No credit cards.*

★ Pastelería Ideal

$ | Bakery. Since 1927, this venerable bakery has been supplying Chilangos with traditional European and Mexican pastries as well as savory rustic breads. Give yourself a little time to wander the aisles and make your way up to the second level to see the cake decorating area. **Known for:** dizzyingly enormous selection of desserts; Christmas cookies and roscas de reyes (king cakes); ornately decorated cakes. *Average main: 50 MP* ⊠ *República de Uruguay 74, Centro Histórico* ☎ *55/5512–2522* ⊕ *www. pasteleria ideal.com.mx.*

★ Tacos de Canasta Los Especiales

$ | Mexican. According to some food historians, *tacos de canasta* (literally "basket tacos") are the original taco and a street food par excellence as closely associated with the capital's unique culinary culture as tacos al pastor. Mostly made in the neighboring state of Tlaxcala and carried into the city in baskets (hence the name), tacos de canasta are cheap and tasty, slicked with fat and moisture from their journey, and stuffed with simple fillings like beans, potatoes, or chicken in adobo. **Known for:** quick and cheap dining; local classic; famed spot for tacos de canasta. *Average main: 50 MP* ⊠ *Madero 71, Centro Histórico* ✛ *West of the Zócalo* ▭ *No credit cards* Ⓜ *Zócalo.*

🍴 Dining

★ Café de Tacuba

$$$ | Mexican. An essential, if touristy, breakfast, lunch, dinner, or snack stop downtown, this Mexican classic opened in 1912 in a section of an old convent. At the entrance to the main dining room are huge 18th-century oil paintings depicting the invention of mole poblano, a complex sauce featuring a variety of chiles and chocolate that was created by the nuns in the Santa Rosa Convent in Puebla. **Known for:** live music by students dressed in medieval attire; classic tamales; old-school atmosphere. *Average main: 300 MP* ⊠ *Calle Tacuba 28, at Allende, Centro Histórico* ☎ *55/5521–2048* ⊕ *www.cafedetacuba.com.mx* Ⓜ *Allende.*

Café La Pagoda

$ | Mexican. Think of this as Mexico City's equivalent of your favorite all-day diner: open from 7 am to 3 am every day of the year, La Pagoda is the best of several (admittedly very similar) old school cafés lined up along the northern side of Avenida 5 de Mayo. The food is far from extraordinary, but the atmosphere is beyond charming, with its long bar and bright lights, service that borders on the maternal (expect to be called *mi amor* or *mi vida* at least once), solid breakfast dishes served all day, and a perfect café con leche to snap you out of a late-night or early-morning stupor. **Known for:** chilaquiles con cecina; all-day dining; late-night pozole, a traditional Mexican stew. *Average* *main: 80 MP* ✉ *Av. 5 de Mayo 10, Centro Histórico* ⊕ *www.cafelapagoda.com.mx* ⊟ *No credit cards* Ⓜ *Bellas Artes, Allende.*

Casa de España

$$ | Spanish. Housed on the mezzanine floor of the magnificent Casino Español, the restaurant Casa de España is as classic as it gets: white tablecloths, coffered ceilings, formal service, and food straight out of the Iberian Peninsula, with a particular focus on dishes from the northern regions of Galicia, Asturias, and País Basco. The Casino was founded in 1863 as a club for Spanish immigrants to independent Mexico and relocated to its current, opulent home in 1905. **Known for:** amazing architecture; great carajillos (Mexico's beloved after-lunch coffee cocktail); early closing at 6 pm. *Average main: 200 MP* ✉ *Isabel la Católica 29, Centro Histórico* ☎ *55/5521–8894* ⊕ *www.cassatt.mx* ☾ *No dinner* Ⓜ *Allende, Zócalo, Isabel la Católica.*

★ Casa Nela

$ | Mexican. For 60 years, the shop Aquí es Oaxaca has anchored this block of Calle Santísima that serves as the Centro's unofficial Little Oaxaca, selling tamales as well as the mole pastes and cured meats known in the region. When visitors started asking for full meals, Casa Nela was born, and so up a distressingly narrow flight of spiral stairs you'll find Oaxacan classics served in surprisingly peaceful surroundings. **Known for:** traditional mole negro; tlayudas, a typical Oaxcan dish; nice view over Calle Santísima.

Average main: 90 MP ✉ *Soledad 42, Centro Histórico* ✛ *Entrance on Santísima* ☎ *55/5461–5412* ☾ *Closed Tues.* ⊟ *No credit cards* Ⓜ *Zócalo.*

★ Don Vergas Mariscos

$$ | Mexican. What started as an eight-seat market stall became so popular that the chef, originally from the northern state of Sinaloa, had to move operations to this hangarlike cantina. Only open on weekends, Don Vergas serves some of the city's best seafood in an atmosphere imported straight from the fun, rambunctious north. **Known for:** raw whole scallops and grilled octopus; aguachile, a type of spicy ceviche; long waits unless you arrive early. *Average main: 200 MP* ✉ *Motolinia 32, Centro Histórico* ☾ *Closed weekdays* Ⓜ *Bellas Artes, Allende, San Juan de Letrán.*

El Cardenal

$$ | Mexican. An institution known for its classic Mexican cooking, today El Cardenal has locations all over the city, but the branch to try is on Calle Palma, in a three-story building in the florid style of the late 19th century. Inside, the atmosphere (think beige walls and white tablecloths) and food are old school; the best time to come is breakfast, when trays of pan dulces make for a pleasant prelude to eggs or chilaquiles. **Known for:** perfect Mexican breakfast; Oaxacan-style moles; family favorite for special-occasion dining. *Average main: 210 MP* ✉ *Calle Palma 23, Centro Histórico* ☎ *55/5521–8815* ⊕ *www.restauranteelcardenal.com* ☾ *No dinner* Ⓜ *Allende, Zócalo.*

Hostería de Santo Domingo

$$ | Mexican. Once part of the Santo Domingo convent, this genteel institution near the Plaza Santo Domingo has been serving colonial dishes in a delightful townhouse since 1860, making it one of the oldest restaurants in the city. Feast on shrimp-stuffed fish, house-made chorizo, or hearty *puchero* stew consisting of pork, chicken, chickpeas, and corn. **Known for:** chiles en nogada (stuffed poblano chile in walnut puree); lively atmosphere; good alcohol selection, including tequila and mezcal. *Average main: 200 MP* ⌧ *Belisario Domínguez 70–72, Centro Histórico* ☎ *55/5510–1434* ⊕ *www.hosteriadesantodomingo.mx.*

La Casa de las Sirenas

$$ | Mexican. The oldest portions of this 16th-century mansion were built using stones torn down from the Templo Mayor, which lies just feet away. At lunchtime, you may want to reserve a table on the atmospheric second-floor terrace overlooking the Zócalo, cathedral, and national palace, or simply stop at the ground floor patio for a drink in the shade of the towering cathedral across the street. **Known for:** nice craft beer and mezcal selection; mix of international and Mexican cuisine; outdoor seating. *Average main: 250 MP* ⌧ *República de Guatemala 32, Centro Histórico* ☎ *55/5704–3273* ⊕ *www.lacasadelas-sirenas.com.mx* ☾ *No dinner Sun.*

★ Limosneros

$$$ | Modern Mexican. With its dramatic volcanic-stone walls and sisal-rope ceiling, this upscale restaurant offers adventurously modern reinterpretations of pre-Hispanic Mexican cuisine. Start your meal with made-to-order tableside salsa (it's best with chapulines) and a sampling of several smaller dishes—like rabbit carnitas and beef tongue tamales—before graduating to a bigger plate of crawfish with a Yucatán relleno negro stew or octopus grilled with black onions, peas, and cherry tomatoes. **Known for:** interesting cocktails using Mexican spirits; emphasis on authentically indigenous Mexican ingredients; creative taco menu de dégustation. *Average main: 320 MP* ⌧ *Ignacio Allende 3, Centro Histórico* ☎ *55/5521–5576* ⊕ *www.limosneros. com.mx* ☾ *No dinner Sun.*

Los Girasoles

$$ | Mexican. When Los Girasoles ("the sunflowers") opened more than 30 years ago in the Centro, it became the first in a wave of modern Mexican restaurants to take on a neighborhood dominated by century-old classics. Now it remains a good place to sip a cold beer and enjoy pre-Hispanic delicacies like *escamoles* (ant eggs), *gusanos de maguey* (agave worms), and *chapulines* (fried grasshoppers). **Known for:** outdoor dining; great views of one of the city's most gorgeous plazas; sunny decor. *Average main: 200 MP* ⌧ *Plaza Manuel Tolsá, Xicotencatl 1, Centro Histórico* ☎ *55/5510–0630* Ⓜ *Allende, Bellas Artes.*

Restaurante San Francisco

$ | **Mexican.** Part of the Casa Tlaxcala, a space developed nearly 40 years ago to promote the culture of the nearby state of Tlaxcala, the Restaurante San Francisco serves simple but tasty comida corrida in a lovely, peaceful 18th-century courtyard behind the Zócalo. After lunch, stop into the shop selling Tlaxcalteca crafts at the entrance to the house. **Known for:** outdoor seating; chile traspatio filled with three cheeses; Tlaxcalan home-cooking. *Average main: 100 MP* ⊠ *San Ildefonso 40, Centro Histórico* ☎ *55/5702–9620 for Casa Tlaxcala offices* ☉ *Closed Sun.* ▭ *No credit cards* Ⓜ *Zócalo.*

Sanborns

$ | **Mexican.** In 1917, the Sanborn brothers took over the iconic Casa de los Azulejos building to expand their drugstore business and now the popular stores-cum-restaurants, owned by billionaire Carlos Slim, populate every major town in Mexico. The menu plays it safe with decent Mexican standards and international options like burgers, soups, and club sandwiches, but the long, winding counter is one of the best places around for a solo coffee and breakfast, while happy hour deals at the endearingly old-fashioned upstairs bar are hard to beat. **Known for:** quality enchiladas; spectacular colonial setting; old-school atmosphere. *Average main: 120 MP* ⊠ *Calle Madero 4, at Cinco de Mayo, Centro Histórico* ☎ *55/5512–9820* ⊕ *www.sanborns.com.mx.*

 Bars and Nightlife

Cabaret La Perla

The tiny, gritty Cabaret La Perla dates from 1946 and is now one of several popular gay bars lining the western end of Calle República de Cuba. Weekend drag shows are some of the city's best, with performances focusing on Mexican pop divas. Friday and Saturday shows are at 11:30 pm and 1:30 am, but come before 10 pm to get a table. ⊠ *República de Cuba 44, Centro Histórico* ☎ *55/1997–9001.*

La Botica

A small *mezcalería* located in the Hotel Downtown, La Botica is easily the best place in the Centro Histórico for a mezcal. Though mezcalerías have proliferated in the area in the hopes of luring in tourists, few serve such a respectable a selection in such a pleasant spot, with a list of 35 distillates from across the county and balcony views over the street below. ⊠ *Hotel Downtown, Isabel la Católica 30, 2nd fl., Mexico City* ☎ *55/5510–4015* Ⓜ *Zócalo.*

La Ópera

One of the city's classic watering holes has attracted top personalities since it opened in 1870. Don't forget to have your waiter point out the bullet hole in the ceiling allegedly left by Mexican revolutionary hero Pancho Villa. Come at night for live mariachi and good tequila. ⊠ *5 de Mayo 10, at Filomeno Mata, Centro Histórico* ☎ *55/5512–8959* ⊕ *www.barlaopera.com.*

Marrakech Salón
A decade after opening its doors on the gay-friendly end of Calle República de Cuba, El Marra (as this chaotic little slip of a place is affectionately known) remains as wild, crowded, and joyful as ever. Open to everyone, the crowd here skews young, queer, and ready to dance. ⊠ *República de Cuba 18, Centro Histórico* ☎ *22/2362–2627* Ⓜ *Bellas Artes, Allende.*

Pasagüero
In the early 2000s, this became one of the first bars to draw hip crowds from other parts of town to the Centro. Since then, things have calmed down, but the bar remains a pleasant spot for an afternoon beer and a lively spot for live music, which might range from salsa to hip-hop to trap, on weekend nights after 9 pm. For a complete listing of upcoming events, visit their Facebook page. ⊠ *Motolinía 33, Centro Histórico* ☎ *55/5521–6112* ⊕ *www.facebook.com/Pasaguero.*

Salón Corona
The famed *cervecería* opened this flagship cantina in 1928, three years after Corona beer was launched. Still a popular hangout for people who live or work in the neighborhood, it is one of the friendliest joints in town, and now boasts three other locations in the Centro (all inexplicably within a two-block radius) and another in the Zona Rosa. Try a torta of *pulpo* (octopus) or *pierna* (roast pork leg) with your giant mug of beer. Photos on the wall show the clientele reacting to the 1986 World Cup at the heartbreaking moment defeat was snatched from the jaws of victory by the national team. ⊠ *Calle Bolívar 24, Mexico City* ☎ *55/5512–9007* ⊕ *www.saloncorona.com.mx.*

Salón Tenampa
Juan Hernández opened Salón Tenampa in 1925, and was the first to introduce mariachi, originally a folk music of his home state of Jalisco, to Plaza Garibaldi. Now Plaza Garibaldi is *the* place to hear (and hire) not only mariachis, but also groups playing regional music styles from around Mexico. Spend the night under Salón Tenampa's historic brick arches sipping on tequila and hiring the mariachis by the song (prepare, if you can, to sing along). Plaza Garibaldi and the surrounding streets can be dodgy at night so it's wise to take a car here and back. ⊠ *Plaza Garibaldi 12, Centro Histórico* ☎ *55/5526–6176* ⊕ *www.salontenampa.com.*

Zinco Jazz Club
A moody subterranean jazz bar tucked into the basement of an art deco building straight out of Gotham, Zinco is as chic a place to pass a night as the Centro has to offer. Keep an eye on their website for up-to-date performances of some of the city's best musicians. ⊠ *Motolinía 20, Centro Histórico* ☎ *55/1131–7760 reservations* ⊕ *www.zincojazz.com* Ⓜ *Allende.*

Centro Histórico South

👁 Sights

⭐ Museo de la Ciudad de México

One of the Centro's most beautiful colonial palaces, built on land originally owned by Hernán Cortés's son Juan Gutiérrez de Altamirano, the Museo is both an excellent example of Mexico City's baronial 18th-century architecture and an interesting place for rotating exhibitions covering a wide range of subjects and interests. The original building was lost, with the current structure dating from 1778 when it was rebuilt as a palatial home for the counts of Santiago y Calimaya. By the early 20th century, the expansive structure had been broken into small, modest apartments, including one where the painter Joaquín Clausell (1866–1935) lived after arriving in Mexico City to study law. Claussel never finished his degree, instead going into exile due to his vocal opposition to the dictatorship of Porfirio Díaz. While in Europe, he learned to paint and ended up becoming one of the most important Impressionist painters in Mexican history. The museum displays historical objects from Mexico City, including antique maps. Clausell's studio is also open to the public, and its walls are covered with his work. Keep an eye out for the stone serpent's head, likely pilfered from the nearby Templo Mayor, embedded in the building's foundations on the corner of Pino Suárez and El Salvador. ✉ *Pino Suárez 30, Centro Histórico* ☎ *55/5542–0487* ⊕ *www.cultura.cdmx.gob.mx* 🎟 *MX$34; free Wed.* 🕐 *Closed Mon.* Ⓜ *Pino Suárez.*

Shopping

Antigua Madero Librería

Of all the secondhand bookstores in the Centro, none is lovelier than the Antigua Librería Madero. Previously located on the street that gave it its name, the bookstore moved to a leafy corner on San Jerónimo in 2011. The collection covers every Mexico-related subject imaginable, and is run by the most knowledgeable and resourceful booksellers in the city. ✉ *Isabel la Católica 97, Centro Histórico* ☎ *55/5510–2068* Ⓜ *Isabel la Católica.*

Cerería de Jesús

It's easy to miss this century-old candle shop in the thrum of pedestrian traffic along the eastern stretch of Venustiano Carranza Street, but step inside and you'll find marvelous creations in technicolor wax, from graceful taper candles in every shade of white, bone, and cream to elaborate towers of flowers dyed jade, ocher, and violet. ✉ *Venustiano Carranza 122–C, Centro Histórico* ☎ *55/5542–5473* ⊕ *www.cereriadejesus.com* Ⓜ *Zócalo.*

El Palacio de Hierro

Upscale department store El Palacio de Hierro is noted for items by well-known designers and its seductive advertising campaigns. There are freestanding branches throughout the city, as well as anchor stores in malls such as Centro Santa Fe,

Mexico's largest mall. If you're in need of any practical purchases, there's a good chance you'll find them here, but otherwise, it's not much different from any other department store. ⊠ *Av. 20 de Noviembre 3, Centro Histórico* ☎ *55/5728-9905* ⊕ *www.elpalaciode-hierro.com.*

☕ Coffee and Quick Bites

Antojitos Mexicanos Las Escaleras
$ | Mexican. So named for its location blocking access to a narrow staircase, this tiny stall is known for its deep-fried quesadillas, a notch above others in the neighborhood. **Known for:** almost literal hole-in-the-wall location; takes orders by phone; delicious quesadillas de requesón. *Average main: 26 MP* ⊠ *5 de Febrero 52, Centro Histórico* ⊹ *Look for a cluster of people gathered around an open doorway* ☎ *55/5709-1554* ▭ *No credit cards* Ⓜ *Pino Suarez, Isabel la Católica.*

Baltazar
$ | Mexican. Before Mexico City had *al pastor* tacos, Puebla had tacos *arabes*, a kind of schwarma brought here by Lebanese immigrants in the early 20th century and adapted to the flavors and ingredients of the New World. Baltazar serves arguably the best rendition of the dish in town along with some light, crisp falafel for vegetarians. **Known for:** retro diner-meets-taco stall aesthetic; good vegetarian options; delivery available. *Average main: 80 MP* ⊠ *Bolívar 100, Centro Histórico*

☎ *55/5709-7967* ▭ *No credit cards* Ⓜ *Isabel la Católica, Salto de Agua.*

Café Bagdad
$ | Mexican. Open since 1955, Café Bagdad occupies a long narrow room in an 18th-century house on the Plaza de la Aguilita, one of several plazas in the Centro's rundown and hectic but charming eastern side. Coffee beans are toasted and ground on-site and simple but hearty *comida corrida* (all-inclusive meals that include soup of the day, rice, beans, tortillas, and fruit juice) comes at an affordable MX$70. **Known for:** great breakfasts; outdoor seating; pretty setting in an often-ignored corner of town. *Average main: 70 MP* ⊠ *Plaza de la Aguilita, Plaza de San Juan José Baz 4, Centro Histórico* ☎ *55/5542-3802* ▭ *No credit cards* Ⓜ *Merced.*

Café Equis
$ | Mexican. Open since 1930, this coffee spot on one of the Centro's most hectic streets is easily the prettiest place in town to sip a *cortado* (espresso mixed with warm milk). Café Equis is by no means a third-wave coffee joint—the beans here, entirely from Mexico, are a touch over-roasted and you won't find any plant milks on offer—but with its painted walls and lively air, it's a bona fide institution. **Known for:** beautiful paintings; great break spot near La Merced; long history in the Mexico City coffee world. *Average main: 15 MP* ⊠ *Roldán 16, Centro Histórico* ☎ *55/5522-4263* ⊙ *Closed Sun.* ▭ *No credit cards* Ⓜ *Merced.*

Café Jekemir

$ | Lebanese. The main location of a small local chain founded in 1938 by a family of Lebanese immigrants, Jekemir recently moved to one of the Centro's prettiest plazas, at the end of the pedestrianized Calle Regina. One of precious few places in Centro to sit outside, Jekemir is still a family-owned operation. **Known for:** rare sidewalk seating; peaceful atmosphere; decent pastries. *Average main: 30 MP ⊠ Regina 7, Centro Histórico ☎ 55/5709–7086 ⊕ www.cafejekemir. com ⊗ Closed Sun. Ⓜ Isabel la Católica.*

El Moro

$ | Mexican. In the past few years, this classic *churrería* (churro shop) has exploded across the city, opening branches decked out in chic blue-and-white. But the original location, open since 1935 on the Eje Central (previously Avenida San Juan Letrán), is a cozy, two-story maze of wooden beams, ceramic tiles, and stained glass. **Known for:** some of the city's best churros; delicious hot chocolate; 24-hour dining. *Average main: 85 MP ⊠ Eje Central Lázaro Cárdenas 42, Centro Histórico ☎ 55/5512–0896 ⊕ www.elmoro.mx Ⓜ San Juan Letrán, Salto de Agua.*

★ Los Cocuyos

$ | Mexican. The Centro's most famous tacos are available all day from this hole-in-the-wall *puesto* (stall), but are best experienced in the early hours of the morning after several rounds of beer. The tacos here are all beef and are small, so plan on trying at least three. **Known for:** late-night dining; tacos de campechano (tacos with multiple layers of longaniza and suadero); unique beef tongue tacos. *Average main: 18 MP ⊠ Bolívar 57, Centro Histórico ☎ 55/5518–4231 ▤ No credit cards Ⓜ Salto de Agua, San Juan Letrán, Isabel la Católica.*

Rica Barbacoa Regina

$ | Mexican. On weekend mornings there's hardly a corner in Mexico City without a stall selling *barbacoa*, a traditional dish made by slow-cooking meat in an underground pit. This cozy spot on Calle Regina is a notch above the usual: warm, friendly, and family-run, with good tacos, *consomé* (soup made from the drippings of the meat), and a superior selection of salsas. **Known for:** friendly atmosphere; outdoor seating; good option for brunch. *Average main: 15 MP ⊠ Regina 45, Centro Histórico ⊗ Closed weekdays ▤ No credit cards Ⓜ Isabel la Católica.*

Taquería Los Paisas

$ | Mexican. You'll know this all-day taco spot (open 8 am to midnight, seven days a week) from the crowds that take over the corner outside.

The main draw here are tacos de bistec—thin cuts of beef cooked on a flat top—and a staggering array of toppings from mashed potatoes to boiled beans to pico de gallo that could make a solid meal on their own. **Known for:** tacos with impressive showmanship; tortillas straight off the press; cheerful, family-friendly atmosphere. *Average main: 20 MP ⊠ Jesus María 131–C, Centro Histórico ⊟ No credit cards Ⓜ Pino Suarez, Merced.*

⑬ Dining

Al Andalus
$$ | Middle Eastern. Housed in a magnificent 17th-century building, Al Andaluz makes some of the best Lebanese food in the capital and is a landmark for the Lebanese immigrant community that has been present here since the late 19th century. Its proximity to La Merced means that the numerous menu options—from classic spreads like hummus and baba ghanoush to delicate plates of raw kibbeh nayeh—are made with the freshest ingredients. **Known for:** outdoor dining; Arabic coffee; perfect baklava. *Average main: 150 MP ⊠ Mesones 171, at Las Cruces, Centro Histórico ☎ 55/5522–2528 ⊘ No dinner.*

Coox Hanal
$ | Mexican. Located up two flights of stairs, this neighborhood institution has turned out solid fare from the Yucatán since 1953 in a big, sunny spot filled with families and, on most afternoons, live music. If you turn up on a weekend lunch hour (usually from around 2 to 4 pm), expect to find a line winding down the staircase. **Known for:** cochinita pibíl, a popular slow-roasted pork dish from the Yucatán; family-friendly atmosphere and weekend crowds; sunny back patio. *Average main: 60 MP ⊠ Isabel la Católica 83, 3rd fl., Centro Histórico ☎ 55/5709–3613 ⊕ www.cooxhanal. com ⊟ No credit cards Ⓜ Isabel la Católica.*

Danubio
$$ | Spanish. Prior to opening as a Basque-style seafood restaurant in the mid-1930s, Danubio was, as its name suggests, a German bar. Today, the place veritably reeks of old-world charm, with its formal service, pressed table linens, and a bar of whole fish for diners to choose from. **Known for:** long history of traditional fine dining; seafood power lunches; business friendly clientele. *Average main: 240 MP ⊠ Uruguay 3, Centro Histórico ☎ 55/5512–0912 ⊕ www.danubio.com Ⓜ San Juan Letrán.*

Helu's
$ | Lebanese. After 70 years in a tiny alley of a shop deep in the Centro's fabric district on Calle El Salvador, Lebanese grocer and baker Helu's moved to bigger, shinier digs on Mesones, where they serve tasty shawarma on homemade *pan arabe* and empanadas *libanesas* stuffed with spinach, cheese, or meat. There are also Lebanese groceries like labneh and tahini for sale, popular with members of the community coming through

the neighborhood for work. **Known for:** traditional baklava; homemade ingredients; community atmosphere. *Average main: 80 MP* ✉ *Mesones 90, Centro Histórico* ☎ *55/5522-5130* ⊕ **www.productoshelus.com.mx** ☉ *Closed Sun. No dinner* Ⓜ *Pino Suarez.*

La Corte

$ | **Mexican.** Open since 1932, La Corte is a sunny, cheerful spot for breakfast or a particularly ambitious rendition of what's known in Mexico as *comida corrida*: three-course meals at a set cost designed to eat quickly during a work lunch break. **Known for:** classic and substantial comida corrida; tasty enchiladas; great horchata. *Average main: 100 MP* ✉ *República de Uruguay 115, Centro Histórico* ☎ *55/5542-7358* ☉ *Closed Sun.* Ⓜ *Pino Suárez.*

★ Restaurante Bar Chon

$$ | **Mexican.** This unpretentious family-style restaurant, deep in a working-class corner of the Centro not far from La Merced, is known for its menu of pre-Hispanic dishes. A knowledge of zoology, Spanish, and Nahuatl helps in making sense of a menu that includes ingredients from throughout the republic that have been used by indigenous people for centuries. *Escamoles de hormiga* (red-ant roe) is known as the "caviar of Mexico" for its texture and costliness; other exotic dishes may include armadillo, crocodile, and the frightening-looking gar fish—all sourced responsibly and sustainably. **Known for:** rare indigenous dishes, including red-ant roe (the caviar of Mexico); charming,

kitschy atmosphere; an oasis on a particularly hectic street. *Average main: 220 MP* ✉ *Regina 160, just off Plaza de la Aguilita, Centro Histórico* ☎ *55/5542-0873* ☉ *No dinner.*

★ Roldán 37

$$ | **Mexican.** Just a handful of blocks from the entrance to La Merced, Roldán 37 may well be the Centro's most surprising restaurant. Set over two floors in a 200-year-old house, the restaurant, run by chef Rómulo Mendoza, is an elegant oasis of high ceilings, French doors, and lovingly prepared family recipes, some drawn from Mendoza's grandmother's handwritten cookbook, which he keeps out of sight but on the premises. **Known for:** dishes made from long-standing family recipes; peace and quiet in an often busy neighborhood; lovely views over Calle Roldán. *Average main: 220 MP* ✉ *Roldán 37, Centro Histórico* ☎ *55/5542-1951* ☉ *No dinner* ☞ *Closes at 7 pm daily* Ⓜ *Merced.*

Zéfiro

$$ | **Mexican.** The restaurant attached to the culinary school at the Claustro Sor Juana is one of the Centro's best-kept secrets and one of its few options for fine dining. The cooking here leans toward the traditional with well-executed moles and classic antojitos like corundas and gorditas, but the space, tucked inside the school's quiet campus, is old-world elegant and the service is impeccable. **Known for:** regularly changing fixed-price menus; educating aspiring cooks; affordable fine dining. *Average main: 180 MP* ✉ *San Jerónimo 24, Centro Histórico*

☎ 55/5130–3385 ⊕ www.ucsj.edu.
mx/zefiro ⊘ Closed Sun. and Mon.
Ⓜ Isabel la Católica.

🍸 Bars and Nightlife

★ Bar Mancera
Dim and elegant with a long wooden
bar, stained glass, and high-backed
chairs, Bar Mancera is perhaps the
best preserved of all the Centro's
early 20th-century watering holes.
Founded in 1912, just two years
after the beginning of the Mexican
Revolution, this is the perfect place
to sit back with a tequila or a beer
and imagine yourself living in the
optimistic days after the fighting had
ended and a new political order had
emerged. ⊠ Venustiano Carranza
49, Centro Histórico ☎ 55/5521–9755
Ⓜ Isabel la Católica, Zócalo.

El Depósito
The Centro branch of one of the
city's best craft beer bars has a
handful of outdoor tables on a pretty
pedestrian street and serves up
to 150 beers, roughly 80% of them
made in Mexico. Look out for beer
brands like Colimita, Wendlandt,
and Insurgentes. ⊠ Isabel la Católica
96, Centro Histórico ☎ 55/5709–2404
⊕ www.eldeposito.com.mx Ⓜ Isabel
la Católica.

★ Hostería La Bota
Open since 2005 as part of a larger
project to revitalize the Centro
Histórico, La Bota has since become
a neighborhood institution. Set in
a long, convivial room, its walls
plastered with pictures and objects,
the space participates in cultural
and literary projects for the neighborhood while providing one of the
warmest, coziest places around for
a beer and Spanish-inflected snacks
like pan de tomateand cheese and
meat boards. ⊠ San Jerónimo 40,
Mexico City ✠ Corner of Isabel la
Católica ☎ 55/5709–9016 Ⓜ Isabel la
Católica.

La Faena
With its endearingly faded elegance
and beguiling collection of vintage
bullfighting artwork, costumes, and
memorabilia, this cavernous cantina
from the 1950s feels decidedly
from another era. Along with its
wonderful neighbor, Bar Mancera,
it occupies the 1535 Palacio del
Marqués de Selva Nevada. Although
international hipsters have gained
a foothold, La Faena still entices a
steady flow of old-timers and often
features mariachis, live Latin jazz,
and dancing. ⊠ Calle de Venustiano
Carranza 49, Centro Histórico
☎ 55/5510–4417.

★ La Mascota
One of the Centro's most atmospheric cantinas, La Mascota seems
perpetually packed, even when in
reality only a few tables are full.
Cheerful, bright, and frenetic,
it's also among the relatively few
remaining cantinas to offer free
botanas (snacks), listed on a short
rotating menu, with every drink.
⊠ Mesones 20, Centro Histórico
☎ 55/5709–3414 Ⓜ Isabel la Católica.

Alameda Central

SANTA MARÍA LA RIBERA

SAN RAFAEL

POLANCO

JUÁREZ AND ANZURES

BOSQUE DE CHAPULTEPEC

ALAMEDA CENTRAL

CENTRO HISTÓRICO

ROMA

CONDESA

BENITO JUÁREZ

SAN ÁNGEL

COYOACÁN

First built in the 16th century as a patch of public green space at the western edge of the capital, the Alameda has long been a place where the city and its residents could show off, whether it was wealthy residents in the late 18th century who came here to perform their elaborately choreographed courtships, the dictator Porfirio Díaz in the late 19th century who chose this as the site for his grand belle epoque monument to the arts, the Palacio Bellas Artes, or gay men in the 1960s who came for late-night rendezvous under cover of the decaying historic center's anonymous darkness.—*by Michael Snyder*

Long overshadowed by the Torre Latina and the Palacio Bellas Artes, two of Mexico City's most iconic landmarks, the Alameda was renovated in 2012 and has once again become a lively center of public life in the city, as well as a flash point for conflicts over gentrification in the city's historic *barrios populares*.

Immediately surrounding the plaza you'll find a discordant mix of restaurant chains and local institutions hanging on to their foothold in the neighborhood with impressive ferocity even as real estate developers attempt to push them out (be sure to patronize the latter and skip the former). South of the Alameda, the fancy facades along Avenida Juarez give way to fluorescent-light minimalls filled with lighting stores, some of the city's best food and craft markets, and a small Chinatown. To the north, the Colonia Guerrero remains somewhat dicey at night, but it's nevertheless one of the city's more interesting central neighborhoods with a few sights worth checking out.

◉ Sights

★ Alameda Central

The manicured gardens of the Alameda Central at the western edge of the Centro have been the heart of Mexico City life since the height of the city's pre-Hispanic glory, when informal markets were held here. Strolling around the park today remains a great way to break up sightseeing in the neighborhood. During the week it's quite lively, but you'll be able to find a shaded bench for a few moments of rest before heading off to more museums. There are food vendors throughout the park, selling all kinds of snacks, from ice cream to grilled corn on the cob. In the early days of the viceroyalty, the Inquisition burned its victims at the stake here. Later, national leaders, from 18th-century viceroys to Emperor Maximilian and the dictator Porfirio Díaz, envisioned the park as a symbol of civic pride and prosperity. *Life in Mexico*, one of the quintessential texts on daily life in the colonial period, written by the British countess Frances

Calderón de la Barca, describes how women donned their finest jewels to walk around the park even after independence. Over the centuries it has been fitted out with fountains and ash, willow, and poplar trees; through the middle of the 20th century, it became a popular gay cruising ground. Today, the Alameda is one of the best places in town to see people from all walks of life, mingling in the shadow of some of the city's most iconic buildings. ⊠ *Bordered by Av. Juárez, Eje Central Lázaro Cárdenas, and Av. Hidalgo, Alameda Central* Ⓜ *Bellas Artes, Hidalgo.*

Arena México

In operation for more than 80 years, this is Mexico's biggest venue for lucha libre. Pyrotechnic matches, complete with big screens and grand entrances, are held every week on Tuesday at 7:30 pm, Friday at 8:30 pm, and Sunday at 5 pm. Tickets range from MX$55 to MX$450 depending on quality of seats and the day of the week, with the more expensive matches typically held on Friday and Sunday. Tickets are available through Ticketmaster or at the venue. ⊠ *Dr. Lavista, between Dr. Carmona and Dr. Lucio, Alameda Central* ☎ *55/5588–0266* ⊕ *www.cmll.com.*

Biblioteca de México José Vasconcelos

The building that now houses one of several national libraries scattered around the city was first designed as a cigarette factory at the end of the 18th century. A grid of nine square

GETTING HERE

Separated from the Centro Histórico by the Eje Central in the east and the colonia Juárez by Avenida Bucareli in the west, Alameda Central is easy to reach by car and connected to virtually every corner of the city by public transit. Metro lines 1, 2, 3, and 8 all stop here at the major hubs Balderas, Salto de Agua, Bellas Artes, and Hidalgo. Four lines of the Metrobus stop in or near the neighborhood, with lines 3, 4, and 7 all making stops at Hidalgo (3 runs south to La Roma, 4 loops around the Centro, and 7 follows Reforma east and west). Metrobus line 1, which follows Insurgentes, the city's longest avenue, from north to south, stops just west of the Revolution Monument in neighboring Tabacalera.

modules, including open courtyards lined with neoclassical columns, construction on the building lasted from 1793 through 1807. Within a year, the building had taken on other uses, including as a prison. By the middle of the struggle for Mexican independence, which lasted from 1810 to 1821, the building had become an armory. After decades of multiple uses, a substantial part of the building was dedicated as part of the new national library system and eventually inaugurated as such in 1946. Today, the library houses the collections of several of Mexico's most celebrated writers. It's also a beautiful place to sit with a book of your own. Guided tours through the library's elegantly staid courtyards are available by request from Tuesday through Saturday. For more information, visit the library's website. ⊠ *Plaza de la Ciudadela 4, Alameda Central* ☎ *55/4155–0830* ⊕ *www.bibliotecademexico.gob.mx* Ⓜ *Balderas.*

Casa Rivas Mercado

Built by the renowned architect Antonio Rivas Mercado between 1893 and 1898, the recently restored Rivas Mercado House is among the finest freestanding homes in the city's central neighborhoods and one of the remaining reminders of the *colonia* Guerrero's heyday as one of the city's more fashionable districts. The house was also the childhood home of writer and intellectual Antonieta Rivas Mercado, a great cultural gatekeeper of early 20th-century Mexico. A contributor to the avant-garde Teatro Ulises and the now-legendary literary magazine *Los Contemporáneos*, Rivas Mercado died tragically in 1931 at age 30 by shooting herself on the altar at Notre Dame. The house, reopened in 2017, is now open for guided tours at 10 am and noon on weekends, reserved via email, at a cost of MX$200 per person. ⊠ *Heroes 45, Alameda Central* ☎ *55/2591–6666* ⊕ *www.casarivas-mercado.com* ⊘ *Closed weekdays* Ⓜ *Hidalgo.*

Centro Cultural Universitario Tlatelolco

If you fly into Mexico City at night, there's a good chance you'll spot the tower of this museum; located on the south side of the Plaza de las Tres Culturas, its stoic modernist facade is clad in Moorish star-bursts of red and purple neon. The museum hosts regularly rotating exhibitions of contemporary art, often experimental in nature, and a moving permanent memorial to the 1968 massacre that occurred on the plaza, installed in honor of that event's 50th anniversary. ⊠*Av. Ricardo Flores Magón 1, Alameda Central* ☎ *55/5583–4092* ⊕ *www. tlatelolco.unam.mx* ⊘ *Closed Mon.* Ⓜ *Garibaldi-Lagunilla.*

★ Centro de la Imagen

One of the city's most interesting museums, the Centro de la Imagen shares the old Ciudadela building with the Biblioteca de México. Remodeled just a few years back, the extensive gallery spaces work cleverly to transect and interact with the historic structure and are devoted to reflections on photographs as both historical documents and art. The library near the entrance has a significant collection of photobooks. Guided tours in English can be arranged for free via the website with several weeks' notice. ⊠ *Plaza de la Ciudadela 2, Alameda Central* ☎ *55/4155–0850* ⊕ *centrodelaimagen.cultura.gob.mx* ⊘ *Closed Mon.* Ⓜ *Balderas.*

Colonia Doctores

If you were speculating on which Mexico City neighborhoods are primed for an imminent renaissance, Doctores would likely be a good place to consider investing some pesos. Named for the fact that many of its main thoroughfares are named for noted medical doctors, the neighborhood was established in the late 1890s, right before Roma and Condesa. Home to the 42-acre campus of prestigious Hospital General de México, the famous lucha libre venue Arena México, and a number of prominent governmental buildings as well as some impressive old mansions, Doctores abounds with cantinas, bars, nightclubs, and pulquerías—some a bit dodgy, but others with increasing cachet among in-the-know locals. The northern and western areas, closest to Roma and Centro Histórico, are where a select number of entrepreneurs have recently begun taking advantage of lower costs to start new businesses. Doctores does have a reputation for crime, especially as you venture farther east and south; the issues are more commonly robbery and car theft than violent crime, but do exercise common sense when walking around this neighborhood, and go with friends or by Uber after dark. ✉ *Bound by Av. Cuauhtémoc, Eje 3 Sur/Dr. Ignacio Morones Prieto, Eje Central/Lázaro Cárdenas, and Av. Chapultepec/Av. Arcos de Belén, Doctores* Ⓜ *Balderas.*

Karen Huber Gallery

Open since 2014, this white-box gallery up a flight of stairs on Avenida Bucareli focuses primarily on contemporary painting. It is one among a crop of art- and design-focused spaces to have opened recently near the Alameda, and has launched the careers of several artists currently on the rise in the international art scene. ✉ *Av. Bucareli 120, 2nd fl., Alameda Central* ☎ *55/5086-6210* ⊕ *www.karen-huber. com* Ⓜ *Balderas.*

Laboratorio Arte Alameda

The facade of this refurbished building from the 1950s has a colonial air, but inside is one of the most contemporary art museums in town, with a mission to explore how art intersects with science and technology. There is a space for contemporary and often experi-mental art, a display area for video and photographs, and a room where artists whose works are not displayed in other museums and galleries can exhibit. These are not necessarily young artists, but those who have yet to become truly estab-lished. ✉ *Dr. Mora 7, Alameda Central* ☎ *55/8647-5660* ⊕ *www.artealameda. bellasartes.gob.mx* ✉ *MX$35; free Sun.* ☉ *Closed Mon.* Ⓜ *Hidalgo.*

Lodos Gallery

A small, experimental gallery space in the beautifully refurbished Humboldt Building, Lodos has spent the last seven years mounting group and solo shows from a diverse range of artists, both local and international. Named for the great Prussian naturalist Alexander von Humboldt, the Humboldt Building also houses the offices of art editorials, fashion designers, and other members of the city's vibrant creative community. ✉ *Edificio Humboldt, Artículo 123–116, Apt. 301, Alameda Central* ☎ *55/2121-0045* ⊕ *www.lodosgallery.info* ☉ *Closed Sat.–Tues.* Ⓜ *Juarez, Hidalgo.*

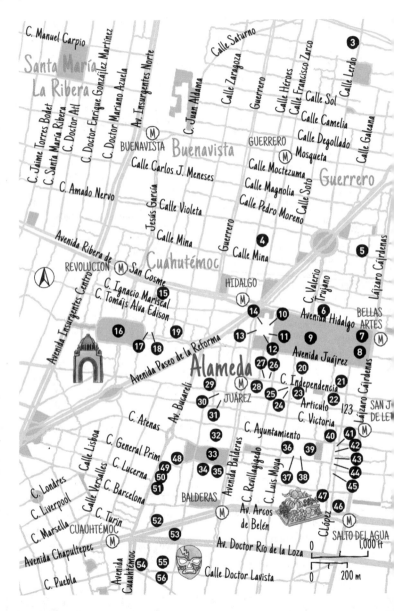

Morelos

① ②

Av. Ricardo Flores Magón

Lázaro Cárdenas

Av. Paseo de la Reforma Norte

Calle Nunó
Calle Libertad
(M) GARIBALDI
López Rayón
LAGUNILLA
(M)

C. República de Ecuador
C. República de Paraguay
Peatonal República de Honduras

Calle Ignacio Allende

C. República de Perú

C. República de Brasil

Calle Belisario Domínguez
Calle República de Cuba
Calle Donceles
C. Tacuba (M) ALLENDE

C. República de Argentina

C. República de Chile

C. 5 de Mayo

ZOCALO
Zócalo (M)

16 de Septiembre
AN
RÁN C. Venustiano Carranza
Centro
C. República de Uruguay
Histórico
C. República de El Salvador

Calle Ignacio Allende

Calle Mesones

Calle Regina
Calle San Jerónimo

Avenida José María Izazaga
ISABEL LA CATOLICA (M)
Calle Nezahualcoyotl
PINO SUÁREZ

③⑦

Av. Fray Servando Teresa de Mier

⭐ Monumento a la Revolución

The bronze art deco dome of the monument commemorating Mexico's bloody, decade-long revolution, which began in 1910, gleams like a beacon at the end of Avenida Juarez, one of the Alameda's busiest thoroughfares. Take an elevator to the observation deck up top, which offers 360-degree views of the city, or admire the Oliverio Martinez sculptures that adorn the four corners of the monument from below. There's also a small café and museum devoted to the history of the Revolution accessible at an additional cost. Lit up nightly at 10 pm, the monument is a moving sight. At the base of the pillars lie the remains of important figures from 20th-century Mexican history, including those of Pancho Villa. ⊠ *Plaza de la República, Alameda Central* ☎ *55/5592–2038* ⊕ *www.mrm. mx* 🎫 *From MX$60* Ⓜ *Revolución*.

⭐ Museo de Arte Popular

Set in an art deco former fire station (the building itself is reason enough for a visit), the Muso de Arte Popular maintains a gloriously diverse collection of folk art from all of Mexico's 32 states. Expect to find elaborately painted pottery from Guerrero, trees of life fashioned from clay in Mexico State, textiles woven in Oaxaca and Chiapas, and carved masks from Michoacán. Don't forget to stop at the on-site store on your way out for an exceptional collection of crafts sourced directly from communities around the country, by far the highest quality products you'll find in the city. ⊠ *Revillagigedo 11, Alameda Central* ✛ *Entrance on Independencia* ☎ *55/5510–2201* ⊕ *www.map.cdmx. gob.mx* 🎫 *MX$60; free Sun.* ☉ *Closed Mon.* Ⓜ *Juárez or Hidalgo*.

Museo Franz Mayer

Housed in the 16th-century Hospital de San Juan de Dios, this museum houses thousands of works collected by Franz Mayer, who emigrated from his native Germany to Mexico in 1905 and went on to become an important stockbroker. The permanent collection includes 16th- and 17th-century antiques, such as wooden chests inlaid with ivory, tortoiseshell, and ebony; tapestries, paintings, and lacquerware; rococo clocks, glassware, and architectural ornamentation; and an unusually large assortment of Talavera (blue-and-white) ceramics. The museum also has more than 700 editions of Cervantes's *Don Quixote.* The old hospital building is faithfully restored, with pieces of the original frescoes peeking through. You can also enjoy a great number of temporary exhibitions, often focused on modern applied arts. Tours in English are available with one week's notice by emailing museo@franzmayer.org.mx (MX$20 per person). ⊠ *Av. Hidalgo 45, at Plaza Santa Veracruz, Alameda Central* ☎ *55/5518–2266* ⊕ *www.franzmayer.org.mx* ✉ *MX$60* ⊘ *Closed Mon.* Ⓜ *Bellas Artes or Hidalgo.*

Museo Memoria y Tolerancia

Located inside a gleaming building by Ricardo Legorreta and situated across the street from Alameda Central, this impressive museum presents a poignant, thoughtful, and appropriately disturbing examination of the Holocaust and other atrocities around the world, including the genocides in Armenia, Cambodia, Guatemala, Rawanda, the former Yugoslavia, and Darfur. Compelling rotating exhibits have shined a light on Gandhi, LGBTQ rights, migrants and refugees, and other issues related to human rights. ⊠ *Av. Juárez 8, Alameda Central* ☎ *55/5130–5555* ⊕ *www.myt. org.mx/myt* ✉ *MX$95* ⊘ *Closed Mon.*

★ Museo Mural Diego Rivera

Each one of Diego Rivera's Mexico City murals is equal parts aesthetic revelation and history lesson, offering large overviews of Mexican history, allegorical vignettes from daily life, or, in the case of the single mural on display at the Museo Mural Diego Rivera, a visual rolodex of important figures in the nation's history. That mural, *Sueño de una Tarde Dominical en el Parque Alameda* (*Sunday Afternoon Dream in the Alameda Park*), was originally painted on a lobby wall of the Hotel Del Prado in 1947–48 with the controversial inscription "God does not exist," which was later replaced with the bland "Conference of San Juan de Letrán" to placate Mexico's conservative Catholic elites. The 1985 earthquake destroyed the hotel but not the mural, and this small, laser-focused museum was built across the street to house it. Like most of Rivera's murals, this one serves a didactic purpose as well, providing a veritable who's who of Mexico's most important historical figures; their identities are helpfully outlined in English and Spanish on panels facing the painting. ⊠ *Balderas 202, Alameda Central* ⊕ *Entrance on Calle Colón*

☎ *55/1555–1900* ⊕ *www.museomu-raldiegorivera.inba.gob.mx* ✉ *MX$35; free Sun.* ☾ *Closed Mon.* Ⓜ *Hidalgo.*

Museo Nacional de San Carlos

The San Carlos collection occupies a handsome, 18th-century palace built by Manuel de Tolsá in the final years of Mexico's colonial period. Centered on an unusual oval courtyard, the neoclassical mansion became a cigarette factory in the mid-19th century, lending the *colonia* its current name of Tabacalera. In 1968, the building became a museum, housing a collection of some 2,000 works of European art, primarily paintings and prints, with a few examples of sculpture and decorative arts ranging in styles. The Museo San Carlos is also the only museum in Mexico to offer tactile tours for the blind on weekends. ✉ *Puente de Alvarado 50, Alameda Central* ☎ *55/8647–5800* ⊕ *www.mnsan-carlos.inba.gob.mx* ✉ *MX$50; free Sun.* ☾ *Closed Mon.* Ⓜ *Revolución or Hidalgo.*

★ **Palacio de Bellas Artes**

Of all the monumental structures in Mexico City's city center, there is probably none more iconic than the Palacio Bellas Arts, with its orange dome, its elaborate belle epoque facade, and its magnificent interior murals. Construction on this colossal white-marble opera house began in 1904 under the direction of the Europhilic dictator Porfirio Díaz. The striking structure is the work of Italian architect Adamo

Boari, who also designed the city's post office; pre-Hispanic motifs trim the facade, which leans toward the opulence of the belle epoque while also curiously hinting at the pared-down art deco style that would take hold in the Mexican capital in just a few years. The beginning of the Revolution in 1910 brought construction to a halt and threw the country into economic turmoil for a decade. By the time construction commenced again, the political, economic, and aesthetic world of Mexico had changed dramatically, resulting in an interior clad in red, black, and pink marble quarried in Mexico (the white exterior is from Carrara, Italy) and clear, straight lines that complement the murals by the great Mexican triumvirate of Siqueiros, Orozco, and Rivera, which you can visit for a fee. There are interesting temporary art exhibitions as well, plus an elegant cafeteria and a bookshop with a great selection of art books and magazines. ✉ *Eje Central Lázaro Cárdenas and Av. Juárez, Alameda Central* ☎ *55/1000–4622* ⊕ *www.palacio.inba. gob.mx* ✉ *MX$70; free Sun.* ☾ *Closed Mon.* Ⓜ *Bellas Artes.*

Plaza de la Ciudadela

Located between the craft market of the same name and the 18th-century building that today houses one of the city's most important libraries and a photography museum, the Plaza Ciudadela is one of the liveliest squares in town, particularly on weekends when older couples come to dance. After lingering (or stepping in for a dance lesson of your own), browse the book and record stalls that line Balderas, the major avenue that borders the plaza toward the east. ⊠ *Between Av. Balderas, Emilio Donde to north, José María Morelos to south, and Enrico Martínez to west, Alameda Central* Ⓜ *Balderas.*

★ **Plaza de las Tres Culturas**
A short distance north of the Centro and Alameda, the neighborhood of Tlatelolco, with the Plaza de las Tres Culturas at its heart, is easily among the most historically signifi-cant corners of the city. Before the arrival of the Spanish, Tlatelolco was a breakaway city-state from the great Mexica city of Tenochtitlan. Memorialized in Rivera's murals at the Palacio Nacional, its market was the commercial heart of both cities. The ruins of Tlatelolco, no less impressive than those of the Templo Mayor but much less frequently visited, form the center of the Plaza de las Tres Culturas, surrounded by important build-ings from different stages of the city's history. To the east, the 16th-century Colegio de Santa Cruz de Tlatelolco, the first European institution of higher learning in the Americas, stands in slender profile against the monolithic block of the Tlatelolco housing projects, a masterpiece of Mexican modernism built between 1960 and 1965 by the legendary architect Mario Pani. In 1968, this became the backdrop for the infamous Tlatelolco massacre,

when the Mexican military opened fire, at the orders of the president, into a crowd of peaceful student protestors, arguably the city's most important political moment since the Revolution. Short of the Zócalo itself, there is no place in Mexico City more heavily imbued with history. ⊠ *Plaza de las Tres Culturas, Tlatelolco, Alameda Central* ✛ *North across Reforma from Lagunilla antiques market* ⊕ *www.tlatelolco. inah.gob.mx* Ⓜ *Garibaldi-Lagunilla, Tlatelolco.*

Shopping

Cihuah

French designer Vanessa Guckel moved to Mexico City in 2008 as an architect and five years later, she started her label Cihuah ("woman" in Nahuatl) to explore the intersections of architecture and clothing, the built environments closest to our bodies. At her studio and showroom in the Edificio Humboldt (buzz up from the street), Guckel displays clothing that uses experimental materials and geometric forms ranging from the indigenous Mexican *huipil* to elongated rectangles of cloth that zip into skirts and capes. ⊠ *Edificio Humboldt, Artículo 123 116, Suite 207–208, Alameda Central* ☎ *55/5518–5021* ⊕ *www.cihuah.com* Ⓜ *Juarez, Hidalgo.*

El 123

A shop, restaurant, and gallery at the far edge of the Centro, Artículo 123 first opened in this area otherwise dominated by electricians and hardware stores back in 2012. The food leans toward southeast Asian while the shop up front sells pretty keepsakes and gifts sourced from around Mexico, from carved stone mezcal glasses to cotton napkins and woven hats. ⊠ *Artículo 123 123, Alameda Central* ☎ *55/5511–1772* ⊕ *www.articulo123.com* Ⓜ *Hidalgo.*

★ Mercado de Artesanías la Ciudadela

This market, a 10- to 15-minute walk from the Alameda, is your best bet for a one-stop shop for all the gifts, souvenirs, and keepsakes you might need. Loaded with stalls selling everything from hammocks to beaded Huichol jewelry to woven palm hats, Ciudadela is a mixed bag to say the least, both in terms of quality and prices. But with a little patience (and a high tolerance for bright colors), you will almost certainly find something that meets your needs. ⊠ *Balderas and Plaza de la Ciudadela, Alameda Central* ⊹ *Entrances on plaza and Balderas* ☎ *55/5510–1828* ⊕ *www.laciudadela.com.mx* Ⓜ *Balderas.*

★ Mercado San Juan

Over the years, this traditional neighborhood market has refashioned itself as the city's gourmet food market. Its stalls are crowded with edible flowers, wild mushrooms, fresh seafood flown in from the coast, and spots that specialize in insect snacks like *chicatanas* (a species of flying ants) and *gusano de maguey* (agave grubs). Notably pricey, this is not a place where most people come for their daily shopping, but it's atmospheric nonetheless, with its cheeses, cured meats, and a great espresso bar in the form of Triana Café Gourmet

that serves good drinks with a smile over a bright orange counter. ⊠ *Ernesto Pugibet 21, Alameda Central* Ⓜ *Salto de Agua, San Juan Letrán*.

Tienda del MAP

The shop at the entrance to the Museo de Artes Populares is easily the best place in town to buy high-quality crafts from around the country. Even if you don't have time to visit the museum's galleries, the museum store itself is a sort of minimuseum with its shelves and racks stocked with textiles and pottery from many of the region's major craft regions, each piece marked with the name of the artisan who made it. Prices are higher here than in other places around town, but so is the quality and the overall financial benefit to the artist. ⊠ *Revillagigedo 11, Alameda Central* ✛ *Corner of Independencia* ☎ *55/5510–3133* ⊕ *www.tiendamap. com.mx*.

 Coffee and Quick Bites

Café El Cordobés

$ | **Café.** A corner coffee spot clad in dark wood with an impossibly narrow upstairs balcony, El Chavelete is a pleasant spot to stop for a pick-me-up in the vicinity of San Juan. **Known for:** faux-colonial aesthetic; repairs and sales of coffee equipment; fun vantage point over a bustling street. *Average main: 35 MP* ⊠ *Ayuntamiento 18, Alameda Central* ☎ *55/5512–5545* ⊕ *www. elchavalete.com* Ⓜ *San Juan Letrán*.

Café Moscú

$ | **Café.** Mexico City's city center finally has its very own third-wave coffee shop: a sunny, playful upstairs parlor decked out with terrazzo and color-blocked laminate tables, serving good coffee in one of the prettiest rooms the city has to offer. Despite the coffee-friendly menu, note that the café is closed weekday morning. **Known for:** calm oasis above street level; homemade breads; great decor. *Average main: 40 MP* ⊠ *Av. Independencia 46, 2nd fl., Alameda Central* ☎ *55/5266–5531* ⊙ *Closed Mon.* Ⓜ *Hidalgo*.

★ Café Trevi

$ | **Italian.** The coffee cups are mismatched, the vinyl banquettes are cracked, the pan dulce is too sweet, and the coffee is too bitter, yet there's no mistaking (or resisting) the inimitable charm of this Alameda institution, open since 1955 and still fighting tooth and nail against the gentrification of its neighborhood. Take a seat for a quick espresso with a beautiful view of the park before visiting the Museo Mural Diego Rivera just down the block. **Known for:** retro atmosphere; local favorite; neighborhood-friendly atmosphere. *Average main: 40 MP* ⊠ *Colón 1, Alameda Central* ☎ *55/5512–3020* ▭ *No credit cards* Ⓜ *Hidalgo, Juarez*.

El Huequito

$ | **Mexican.** General consensus says that this miniscule taco stand on the border between the Plaza San Juan and Chinatown serves the best al pastor in the Centro, and has been doing so since 1959. There are now three branches around the neighborhood, and several more scattered around town, but the original remains the best by far. **Known for:** crowded but quick meals; sidewalk dining; legendary tacos. *Average main: 19 MP ⊠ Ayuntamiento 21, Alameda Central ☎ 55/5518–3313 ⊕ www.elhuequito.com.mx Ⓜ San Juan Letrán.*

Panque de Nata Queretanas
$ | Bakery. You'll know this tiny storefront by the cluster of people waiting patiently on the sidewalk for a full loaf or single serving of *panque de nata*, pound cake made in a style traditional to the nearby state of Queretaro. Pillowy, buttery, and sweet, a piece makes for a perfect snack while winding your way through the nearby Ciudadela and San Juan markets. **Known for:** hole-in-the-wall atmosphere; delicious homemade pastries; quick service. *Average main: 15 MP ⊠ Luis Moya 82, Alameda Central ⊟ No credit cards Ⓜ Balderas, Juarez.*

Ricos Tacos Toluca
$ | Mexican. You'll recognize this bustling corner stall near the Mercado San Juan by the tangling garlands of chorizo hanging over its flat top. And while the taqueros here serve perfectly good tacos of many varieties, the reason you're here is the fragrant, herbal chorizo *verde* , or green chorizo, from the nearby city of Toluca, stained emerald with herbs and green chilies. **Known for:** fast and buzzy stall open one day a week; sidewalk dining; city's best chorizo verde. *Average main: 20*

MP ⊠ Lopez 87–C, Alameda Central ⊘ Closed Sat.–Mon. ⊟ No credit cards Ⓜ San Juan Letrán, Salto de Agua.

Taco de Oro XEW
$ | Mexican. Founded 65 years ago and moved to its current location three decades back, Taco de Oro specializes in *cochinita pibíl* , the beloved dish of slow-roasted pork from the Yucatán. **Known for:** bright and cheerful decor; quick service; family specializing in Yucatán stew. *Average main: 10 MP ⊠ Lopeze 107, Alameda Central ⊟ No credit cards Ⓜ Salto de Agua.*

★ Tortas Robles
$ | Mexican. Café Trevi's neighbor and partner in the fight to keep this classic block away from gentrifiers, Tortas Robles is a 12-seat sandwich shop that has been turning out simple tortas of *pierna* and *milanesa* for more than 70 years. It moved from around the corner to its current location in the early 1990s. **Known for:** family-owned and -run; chatty atmosphere; simple but delicious tortas. *Average main: 38 MP ⊠ Cristobal Colón 1–D, Alameda Central ☎ 55/5521–1624 ⊟ No credit cards Ⓜ Hidalgo, Juarez.*

Tostadas de Don Chucho
$ | Mexican. The Arcos de Belén Market, located just outside the Salto de Agua metro stop, has plenty of good food to recommend within it, but nothing tops Don Chucho's impeccable tostadas (thin, round corn crisps). Topped with one of three traditional toppings (*tinga* [pulled chicked], *salpicón* [shredded beef, tomato, onion, and cilantro],

and *pata* [pickled pig trotters]),
these are some of the city's best
quick bites. **Known for:** one of the
city's best market stalls; cheap eats;
lively atmosphere. *Average main: 14
MP ⊠ Av. Arcos de Belén, between Eje
Central and López, Alameda Central
⨁ 2nd aisle from Arcos de Belén
entrance ⊗ Closed Sun. ⊟ No credit
cards* Ⓜ *Salto de Agua.*

🍴 Dining

★ Arongo
$$$ | Modern Mexican. Exceptional
modern French-Mexican cuisine,
charming service, and—most of
all—spectacular floor-to-ceiling
views of Monumento de Revolución
and the Reforma skyline create
a memorable experience at this
stylish restaurant perched dramatically atop an art deco office building
in Tabacalera. Food highlights
include esquites with braised oxtail,
duck confit with fragrant and fruity
mole sauce, and a classic beef bour-
guignonne. **Known for:** dramatic
skyline views; creative versions of
French and Mexican dishes; well-
crafted cocktails. *Average main:
360 MP ⊠ Av. de la República 157,
Alameda Central ☎ 55/5705-5034
⊕ www.arangorestaurante.com.*

★ Bar Fritz
$$ | German. Close to the border of
the Juárez neighborhood sits this
locals' favorite German restaurant,
which has been in business in
neighboring Doctores since 1947.
Serving up authentic German food
and a very extensive list of German

beers, it has been paid a visit by
many famous players in Mexican
history, as proudly displayed on
the walls near the bar. **Known for:**
house-made pretzels and mustard;
pork sauerbraten in creamy
gingersnap sauce; hard-to-find
German beers. *Average main: 250
MP ⊠ Av. Dr. Río de la Loza 221,
Doctores ⊕ www.elfritz.rest* Ⓜ *Cuauhtémoc, Balderas.*

El Puerto de Alvarado
$ | Mexican. This seafood stand in
the Mercado San Juan sells some
of the market's freshest fish, which
are also served up as ceviches and
tostadas for diners who stop at the
tables across the aisle. This is the
place to try fresh *almejas chocolatas*
("chocolate" clams, named for
the color of their giant shells), so
fresh they'll move under a squirt of
lime juice. **Known for:** raw seafood
including excellent ceviche; incredibly fresh fish; traditional market
atmosphere. *Average main: 120 MP
⊠ Mercado San Juan, Ernesto Pugibet
21, Alameda Central ⨁ Enter market
and head down 1st aisle inside door
☎ 55/5512-6095 ⊟ No credit cards
Ⓜ San Juan Letrán, Salto de Agua.*

El Rancho Birrieria
$ | Mexican. When the last match
ends at Arena Mexico, slip outside
and down the block to this spot for
a big bowl of *birria*, a hearty beef
stew ideal for a chilly night. The
vibe is all neon, metal chairs, and
blaring banda music, a continuation
of the zero-subtlety atmosphere
at the arena, but the birria is tasty
and the doors open late. **Known for:**

live banda, salsa, or rock on Friday night; loud and raucous crowds; deals on beers. *Average main: 100 MP* ⊠ *Doctor Carmena y Valle 31, Alameda Central* ☎ *55/5588-2387* ⊕ *www.restaurantebarelrancho.com* Ⓜ *Cuauhtemoc.*

Farmacia Internacional
$ | Café. Located on Bucareli, a grand avenue lined with opulent turn-of-the-century apartment buildings, Farmacia Internacional is a perfect specimen of a café: all warm wood, pleasant light, good coffee, and the kind of light, simple cooking that can feel hard to come by in this neighborhood. Stop in for a freshly baked cookie in the morning, a glass of wine in the evening, or a midday salad. **Known for:** fantastic egg dishes; nice, concise wine list; cozy atmosphere. *Average main: 80 MP* ⊠ *Bucareli 128, Alameda Central* ☎ *55/5086-6220* ⊕ *www.facebook. com/internacional.farmacia* ☉ *No dinner Sun.* Ⓜ *Juarez, Balderas.*

★ Fonda Mi Lupita
$ | Mexican. Some of the best mole to be found in central Mexico City comes out of a giant clay pot that, at first glance, looks bigger than the entire dining room of this modest, family-run fonda. Opened in 1957, Fonda Mi Lupita specializes in mole from the eastern side of Mexico state, where the dish leans toward the rich, savory flavors of *mu lato* chilies. **Known for:** authentic home cooking; traditional atmosphere; enchiladas en mole. *Average main: 100 MP* ⊠ *Buen Tono 22, Local 4, Alameda Central* ⟐ *Entrance on Calle*

Delicias ☎ *55/5521-1962* ⊟ *No credit cards* Ⓜ *Salto de Agua.*

Gran Cocina Mi Fonda
$ | Mexican. If you're looking for the platonic ideal of a Mexico City fonda (the small, home-style restaurants that feed much of the city's population each day), you need look no farther than this sunny mainstay between the Mercados San Juan and Arcos de Belén. The food here is simple, classic, and always served with love, from the famous paella to the daily, three-course comida corrida. **Known for:** time-warp 1950s decor; home-style cooking; prix-fixe lunches. *Average main: 90 MP* ⊠ *López 101, Alameda Central* ☎ *55/5521-0002* ☉ *Closed Mon.* ⊟ *No credit cards* Ⓜ *Salto de Agua.*

★ Restaurante Sin Nombre
$$ | Mexican. This sleek little fonda alongside beloved mezcalería Bosforo adapts the integrity of flavor and care for ingredients and technique that defines the best of Mexico's countryside to the produce (and space constraints) of the country's capital. The result is one of the neighborhood's most pleasurable dining experiences: romantic, hip, honest, and, above all, delicious. **Known for:** good vegetarian options; stellar guacamole with chapulines; homemade totopos straight from the comal. *Average main: 200 MP* ⊠ *Luis Moya 31, Local 3, Alameda Central* ☎ *55/6708-9660* ☉ *Closed Sun. and Mon.* Ⓜ *Juarez, San Juan Letrán, Hidalgo.*

Tirasavia

$ | Mexican. A pretty café on the border of the Centro and Juarez, Tirasavia is a sweet, sunny spot for a coffee, breakfast, or a cold beer or glass of wine in the afternoon. Set in the street-level corner of a spare, glass-and-concrete modernist building occupied by architecture firms, photo studios, and a design company, this place is the happy cousin to its moodier, bolder neighbors and as pleasant a place as any for a quick refuel. **Known for:** gorgeous design with onyx counters and sage-green walls; pretty presentations of breakfast standards; outdoor tables. *Average main: 120 MP* ⊠ *Bucareli 108, Alameda Central* ⊙ *Closed Sun. No dinner* Ⓜ *Juarez, Balderas.*

⍟ Bars and Nightlife

★ Bosforo

There's only one thing in Mexico City about which there is neither controversy nor argument: Bosforo is the absolute best place in town for mezcal (as the weekend crowds can attest). The music is trippy, the vibe is sexy, and the selection of mezcals, many served from unmarked bottles by small producers, comes from across the country. No place in town—and few places in all of Mexico—offers such a rich variety of flavors and styles. Dark, steamy, and nearly always packed, this is a place to surrender and drink whatever comes your way.

⊠ *Luis Moya 31, Alameda Central* ☎ *55/5512–1991.*

Cantina Tío Pepe

One of a handful of cantinas competing for the title of oldest in Mexico (it was founded over a century ago), Tío Pepe is about as atmospheric as it gets. A Tiffany-style stained glass window, a heavy wooden bar running the length of the room, swinging wooden doors, and unflattering fluorescent lights add up to make this the paradigmatic Mexico City cantina. ⊠ *Av. Independencia 26, Alameda Central* ☎ *55/5521–9136* Ⓜ *Bellas Artes, San Juan Letrán.*

Enigma AntroBar

This nightclub is known for its drag contests, musical tributes, and overall exciting entertainment. Things get going on the later side and reservations are recommended. Thursday night is drag night, which is when it gets especially animated and busy. Drinks come tableside from attentive servers, with all seats in the house having a solid view of the stage. ⊠ *Calle General Prim 9, Juárez* ☎ *55/1321–2239* ⊕ *www.facebook.com/EnigmaAntroBar* Ⓜ *Balderas.*

5 Caudillos

A classic cantina in the colonia Tabacalera, 5 Caudillos serves up botanas that rotate through weekly specials, with options like *chamorro* (roasted pork shank) and *solomillo* (pork loin) drawing crowds on Thursday. Musicians play daily after 4 pm. ⊠ *Av. Plaza de la República*

127–B, Alameda Central ☏ 55/5705–3003 Ⓜ Hidalgo, Revolución.

Jardín Juarez

What was until recently an empty lot on one of the city's busiest avenues is now the closest thing Mexico City has to a beer garden: there's a small green lawn, picnic tables, potted plants hanging from a post-industrial steel grid, and big open windows in the concrete facade that open onto the traffic outside. The bar serves a wide range of craft beers, including several on tap that are made in-house. The food tends toward barbecue standards like burgers and hot dogs. ⊠ Av. Chapultepec 61, Alameda Central ⊕ www.facebook.com/JardinJuarezcdmx Ⓜ Balderas.

La Azotea

One of relatively few terrace bars in the city, La Azotea ("The Rooftop") occupies a small space in the restored art deco building known as Barrio Alameda. Technically a restaurant serving sandwiches and grilled meat, La Azotea is a beautiful place for an afternoon beer (they have a good list of craft brews) with gorgeous views over the trees of the Alameda and the spire of the Torre Latino. ⊠ Calle Dr. Mora 9, Alameda Central ☏ 55/5518–5023 ⊕ www.barrioalameda.com Ⓜ Hidalgo.

Las Duelistas

One of the best, and certainly the most famous, of the city's remaining pulquerías, La Duelistas is most first-timers' bar of choice for sampling fermented agave sap. Always busy, Las Duelistas is a psychedelic trip of a place. Try a sampler of the day's curados (pulques flavored with pureed fruits and vegetables). ⊠ Aranda 28, Alameda Central ☏ 55/1394–0958 Ⓜ Salto de Agua.

Pulquería La Hija de los Apaches

An emblematic pulquería of the colonia Doctores, Hija de los Apaches is a perfect place for a prefight drink before wandering a block over to Arena México. Serving up mugs of fermented agave, flavored in house with pureed fruits and vegetables, Hija de los Apaches turns into a salsa club most evenings of the week. There's no doubt its a lively, down-to-earth, singularly Mexico City kind of place. ⊠ Doctor Claudio Bernal 149, 2nd fl., Alameda Central Ⓜ Cuauhtemoc.

Punto Gozadera

A feminist art, music, and exhibition space, Punto Gozadera has become one of the best and most diverse queer spaces in the city over the past few years. Spread over two floors and opening onto the leafy Plaza de San Juan, Punto Gozadera operates as a restaurant, café, gallery, event space, and, on nights and weekends, a great bar that throws inclusive dance parties (sometimes with modest cover charges of MX$20 or so) that usually wind down around 3 am. Come into this space respectfully as a guest (it's by no means exclusively aimed at queer women), and you'll feel right at home in no time. ⊠ Plaza San Juan 15, Alameda Central ☏ 55/8235–3036 Ⓜ Salto de Agua.

★ Salón Los Angeles

The slogan of this classic dance halls says it all: "Whoever doesn't know Los Angeles doesn't know Mexico." When Salón Los Angeles turned 80 in 2017, a who's who of Mexico City turned out to celebrate, from actors and writers to politicians and ambassadors. A flashback to the hot pink splendor of Mexico's mid-century boom years (it opened in 1937), Salón Los Angeles is a fairly quiet place on most nights, where older couples from the surrounding neighborhood come to dance to live bands playing salsa, cumbia, and danzón. But when big acts come through town, the hall, large enough for 600 people, bursts to life. These are the nights to be here, so keep an eye on the line-up on their website. Note that La Guerrero can be dangerous at night, so it's best to come and go by Uber. ⊠ *Lerdo 206, Alameda Central* ☎ *55/5597-8847* ⊕ *www.salonlos-angeles.mx.*

Terraza Cha Cha Chá

This expansive rooftop bar at the edge of the Plaza de República combines elements of modernist chic, tiki bar greenery, and Mexican crafts in a way that, against all odds, works beautifully. Combine that with extraordinary views and this makes for a great place to spend an afternoon or evening over beers (or something stronger). ⊠ *Av. de la República 157, 6th fl., Alameda Central* ☎ *55/5705-2272* Ⓜ *Revolución.*

 **Performing Arts**

Ballet Folklórico de México

The world-renowned Ballet Folklórico de México is a visual feast of Mexican regional folk dances in whirling colors. Lavish and professional, it's one of the country's most popular shows. Though the offices and rehearsal space are in the colonia Guerrero, performances are held at the Palacio de Bellas Artes on Wednesday at 8:30 pm and Sunday at 9:30 am and 8:30 pm, with additional shows scheduled intermittently throughout the year (check the website for more information). Tickets range in price MX$300–MX$1,180 and can be purchased via Ticketmaster or directly at the Bellas Artes box office. Most hotels and travel agencies can also secure tickets. ⊠ *Violeta 31, Alameda Central* ☎ *55/5529-9320 box office, 55/5529-9320 theater* ⊕ *www.balletfolklorico-demexico.com.mx.*

Foro Normandie

One of the city's premier venues for electronic music, Normandie is hidden in plain sight, just south of the Alameda. A subterranean concrete cave, complete with rough, spiked walls, Normandie is equal parts brutalist-chic and gothic grotto. Check the website for upcoming events and ticket prices. ⊠ *López 15, Alameda Central* ☎ *55/7826-5314* ⊕ *www.foronor-mandie.com* Ⓜ *Bellas Artes.*

Orquesta Sinfónica Nacional

Mexico's National Symphony Orchestra plays regularly throughout the season at the Palacio Bellas Artes, along with visiting orchestras from around the globe. It's one of the best (and most affordable) excuses to enter the iconic building's spectacular main hall. Tickets range from MX$80 to MX$160. ⊠ *Hidalgo 1, Alameda Central* ☎ *55/8647–2500* ⊕ *www.osn. inba.gob.mx* Ⓜ *Bellas Artes.*

Teatro Metropólitan

Opened in the 1940s as a cinema, the Metropólitan closed down following the 1985 earthquake that devastated the city and did not reopen until more than a decade later when it reopened the doors to its neoclassical hall in the form of a top concert venue. Today, the Teatro Metropólitan plays host to major pop and rock acts from Mexico and around the world. ⊠ *Av. Independencia 90, Alameda Central* ☎ *55/5510–1035 box office* ⊕ *www. ocesa.com.mx* Ⓜ *Juarez.*

4

Juárez and Anzures with La Zona Rosa

POLANCO

SANTA MARÍA LA RIBERA

SAN RAFAEL

ALAMEDA CENTRAL

CENTRO HISTÓRICO

BOSQUE DE CHAPULTEPEC

JUÁREZ AND ANZURES

ROMA

CONDESA

BENITO JUÁREZ

SAN ÁNGEL

COYOACÁN

Sightseeing ★★★☆☆ | Shopping ★★★★☆ | Dining ★★★★☆ | Nightlife ★★★★☆

Adjacent to the Centro Historico, Colonia Juárez is essentially an extension of the city center and represents Mexico's eclectic, European-focused period of architecture that engulfed the city in the late 19th and early 20th century. As politicians, bankers, and other high society types began moving from the city's bustling center, La Juárez became a sort of suburb for the downtown area. Recently it's regained popularity with a multitude of new restaurants, bars, and shops. Just north of La Roma, it's positioned to receive the inevitable overflow of that booming neighborhood, while maintaining an off-the-beaten path feel and a friendliness to the city's artists.—*by Megan Frye*

La Zona Rosa is part of La Juárez and makes its home in the southwest corner of the colonia, nestled between Reforma Avenue and Insurgentes. "The Pink Zone" has been known for decades as the city's main LGBTQ neighborhood. With its streets lined with kitschy sex shops, beauty salons, nail parlors, gay bars, karaoke clubs, Asian restaurants, and the occasional embassy, this is one neighborhood that truly never sleeps.

Separated from Juárez by Paseo de la Reforma Avenue, one of Mexico City's broadest and most connected thoroughfares, Colonia Cuauhtémoc is at once big business and residential. With many international banks and other companies, it is one of the main business sections of the city. But take a step away from busy Reforma and you'll find the neighborhood is also home to office workers and people who lived in the area before any of its tall buildings appeared. Colonia Cuauhtémoc also has a number of small restaurants that cater to its inhabitants, who are increasingly diverse.

Just northwest of Juárez and bordering the northeast side of Bosque de Chapultepec (the city's main park), Anzures is a small colonia lined with leafy boulevards and two-story art deco homes, its skyline dotted only by a few tall apartment and office buildings. Quiet by nature, and even more so since the 2017 earthquake left some of its buildings uninhabitable, it functions as a suburb of neighboring Polanco and Cuauhtémoc while still effectively being right

in the middle of all the action. The charm of this neighborhood is simply how peaceful it is.

Sights

Diana la Cazadora

Constructed over the course of four years and completed in 1942 by Mexican sculptor Juan Fernando Olaguíbel Rosenzweig, this celebrated fountain of Diana the Huntress stands nine feet tall. The one-ton bronze homage to the Roman goddess was originally designed nude, then was covered for more than two decades due to public and political outcry until she was liberated into her natural form again in 1967. She had originally been unveiled at Bosque de Chapultepec and then moved to an obscure location, from which she was rescued and moved to the city's bustling Paseo de la Reforma in 1992. ⊠ *Paseo de la Reforma and Calle Sevilla, Mexico City* Ⓜ *Sevilla.*

El Museo del Chocolate

This museum tells the history of chocolate, referencing archaeological evidence of the magical substance from different locations across Mesoamerica. You will see what a fresh cacao pod looks like, and will be able to taste toasted seeds. Learn about the cultural significance that chocolate has played in Mexico over a millennia, as well as the role it plays in the world today. From a room dedicated to sculptures made of chocolate to utensils used to prepare chocolate to the insects that dominate its

GETTING HERE

Bordering the Centro Histórico, Roma Norte, Condesa, Polanco, and the Bosque de Chapultepec, these neighborhoods (including Colonia Cuauhtémoc) are extremely well situated for exploring the city. Uber fares from the airport and the Centro Histórico range from MX$70 to MX$170, depending on traffic. The area, with the exception of Anzures, is well-served by public transport, with two subway lines (1 and 3) and the Metrobus (line 1). There's a lot to see in these neighborhoods, so traveling by foot is recommended when possible. Zona Rosa is often busy, and where it's busy in Mexico City, there are usually pickpocketers, but in general, these neighborhoods are considered safe both night and day. Exercise extra caution on lonely streets at night on the eastern edge of La Juárez.

growing regions and cultivation, there is little you'll be lacking in chocolate knowledge once you spend an afternoon here. ⊠ *Calle Milán 45, Juárez* ☎ *55/5514–1737* ⊕ *www.mucho.org.mx* Ⓜ *Cuauhtémoc, Balderas.*

★ Monumento a la Independencia
(Ángel de la Independencia)

Known as El Angel, this Corinthian column topped by a gilt angel is the city's most uplifting monument, built to celebrate the 100 anniversary of Mexico's War of Independence. Beneath the pedestal lie the remains of the principal heroes of the independence movement; an eternal flame burns in their honor. As you pass by, you may see one or more couples dressed in their wedding apparel, posing for pictures on the steps of the monument. Many couples stop off here before or after they get married, as a tribute to their own personal independence from their parents. ✉ *Traffic circle bounded by Calle Río Tiber, Paseo de la Reforma, and Calle Florencia, Juárez* Ⓜ *Insurgentes.*

★ Zona Rosa LGBTQ District

Mexico City is home to one of the world's largest and—increasingly so since the early 2000s—most visible LGBTQ communities. Although you'll find gay or very mixed hangouts all over town, the epicenter of queer nightlife and rainbow flags is the Zona Rosa district of Juárez. Within this always bustling quadrant, you'll find nearly 20 LGBTQ bars and clubs, a handful of sex boutiques, and dozens of other more mainstream lounges, fast-food restaurants, music clubs, and the like. On a weekend evening, Zona Rosa pulses with revelers from all walks of life, the majority under 35 or so; pedestrianized Calle Génova almost feels like the CDMX equivalent of Bourbon Street in New Orleans. The more gay-frequented spots, including venerable hangouts like Kinky and Boy Bar, are predominantly along calles Amberes and Florencia south of Paseo de la Reforma, but there are a few notable exceptions—such as Baby and Rico—farther east on the Avenida Insurgentes side of the neighborhood. ✉ *Bound by Av. Insurgentes Sur, Paseo de la Reforma,*

For more than 40 years, Zona Rosa has hosted a yearly Pride march, bringing attention to inequalities faced by the LGBTQ community. The parade, always on a weekend in late June, brings hundreds of thousands of participants and spectators to the neighborhood. Crosswalks and business fronts are painted in rainbow colors from Paseo de la Reforma to Chapultepec. Take a walk around and try to find the crosswalk signal featuring a same-sex couple holding hands.

Av. Chapultepec, and Calle Florencia, Juárez Ⓜ *Sevilla, Cuautémoc.*

 Shopping

★ Bazar Fusion

One of the best places in the city to go souvenir or gift shopping, Bazar Fusion specializes in Mexican-made clothing, beauty products, shoes, and goodies like mezcal and salsa. On weekends, it expands with vendors taking over the hallways selling different items, mostly based on local and organic themes (think bath products, jewelry, accessories, and cooking goods), as well as art. Spanning various aesthetics, artisan products from all across Mexico are featured; as big and diverse as the country is, Bazar Fusion does a good job at representing much of it with textiles and other artistry from across the Republic. ✉ *Londres 37, Juárez* ☎ *55 /5511-6328* ⊕ *www. casafusion.com.mx* Ⓜ *Cuauhtémoc.*

Buut's Basement

Although its name stems from the Mayan word for "smoke," calling Buuts a smokeshop would be limiting, even though it does specialize in unique pipes, rolling papers, and floral blends for smoking. Basically, whatever a marijuana or tobacco connoisseur might be into can be found in this concept shop, but it's much more than that, too. The literally underground shop is curated well and prides itself on being a space for LGBTQ folks, selling erotic art and a notable gay-friendly version of the classic Mexican *lotería* game. ⊠ *Havre 68, Juárez* ☎ *55/5514-7853* ⊕ *www.facebook. com/BuutsBasement* Ⓜ *Cuauhtémoc.*

★ Carla Fernández

One of the country's most vaunted fashion labels, Carla Fernández displays and sells its gorgeously edgy women's garments—known for their geometric patterns and Mexican textiles—in this spacious boutique in Juárez. The original store is a few blocks away in Roma and there's a third outpost in Centro Histórico. ⊠ *Calle Marsella 72, Juárez* ☎ *55/5511-0001* ⊕ *www.carlafernandez.com* Ⓜ *Insurgentes.*

Casa Caballería

A store for the modern gentleman, Casa Caballería is designed to offer styles for men from different walks of life and varied interests. The space is well organized in what feels like a tailor's shop from more chivalrous times. From suits and colognes to jewelry and satchels, it has a boutique vibe with personalized service. The majority of goods here are from Mexican designers, though some Spanish and South American clothing can be found, too. ⊠ *Havre 64, Juárez* ☎ *55/5207-3216* ⊕ *www.casacaballeria.com* Ⓜ *Cuauhtémoc.*

Fonart

Located on the ground floor of the Secretariat of Welfare building on Paseo de la Reforma, the main retail outlet FONART (the National Fund for the Promotion of Handicrafts) is one of the country's best sources for authentic Mexican crafts: colorful embroidered textiles, ornate glassware, folk dolls, terra-cotta cookery, carved wood boxes, Day of the Dead figures, and more. You'll pay a bit more here than in many other markets and shops around the city, but FONART products are carefully selected directly from the best artisans in the country, who are in turn guaranteed a fair wage. There are a few other FONART locations around the city, including a very large branch in Benito Juárez on Avenida Patriotismo. ⊠ *Paseo de la Reforma 116, Juárez* ☎ *55/5546-7163* ⊕ *www. gob.mx/fonart* Ⓜ *Juarez.*

Joem

Among the numerous shops in Zona Rosa selling sex toys and erotica, Joem stands out as a place that sells under- and outerwear for daily use. Made in Colombia, the brand specializes in both men and women's wear: everything from (practical) thongs to hoodies and T-shirts, all made from sturdy nylon, elastic blends, and cotton. ⊠ *Calle Amberes 9, Juárez* ✢ *Zona Rosa*

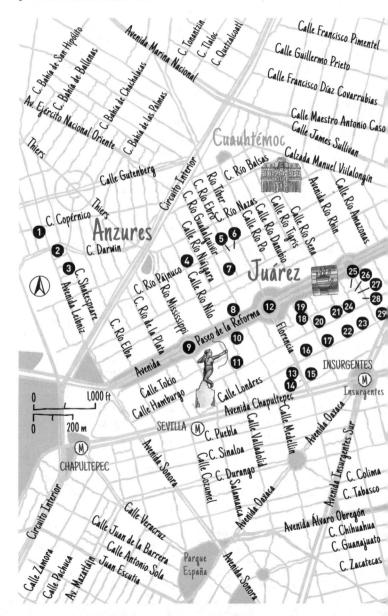

☎ 55/5122–7423 ⊕ www.facebook.
com/JoemHombre Ⓜ Sevilla.

⭐ **Jorge Cuesta Librería de Paso**

With volumes in multiple languages, Jorge Cuesta Librería de Paso is a great spot to find academic writing on any number of subjects in Mexico, as well as out-of-print copies of international and Mexican literature. The bookstore, named after a Mexican poet and scientist, is packed to the gills with antiques too (some of which are for sale), on which nary an inch is spared for all the books within its walls. ✉ Calle Liverpool 12, Juárez ☎ 55/5546–1742 Ⓜ Cuauhtémoc.

Loose Blues

Selling vintage clothing with a heavy emphasis on Japanese style, from shoes to denim to ceramics, the space is both well curated and slightly unexpected. Head upstairs for a privileged view of the hip Juárez neighborhood, where a restaurant serves Japanese fare including sushi, noodle dishes, and tea. ✉ Calle Dinamarca 44, Juárez ☎ 55/5546–4359 ⊕ www.facebook.
com/LOOSEBLUES44 Ⓜ Cuauhtémoc.

Mercado Insurgentes de Artesanías y Platería

Also referred to as either Mercado Zona Rosa or Mercado Londres, this is the neighborhood's largest crafts market, featuring artistry from across Mexico, including jewelry, ceramics, and clothing. Vendors here can be intense, calling you to their stalls with promises of low prices (which you may or may not find). The market is an entire block deep, with entrances on both Londres and Liverpool. Most of the stalls sell silver and pewter, or crafts like serapes and ponchos, baskets, pottery, fossils, jade, obsidian, amber, and onyx. Expect to pay slightly higher prices here than at the Mercado Artesanal de la Ciudadela. Opposite the market's Londres entrance is Plaza del Angel, a small, upscale shopping mall, the halls of which are crowded by antiques vendors on weekends. ✉ Londres 154, between Florencia and Amberes, Juárez ⊕ Tlatelolco, Garibaldi-Lagunilla.

Plaza del Angel

Shopping in the maze of antiques stores of Plaza del Angel is at its liveliest on Saturday. Combine a trip here with one to the Mercado Insurgentes, the crafts market across the way, for a full day of shopping. ✉ Between Londres and Hamburgo, opposite Mercado Insurgentes, Juárez Ⓜ Centro Médico.

Somos Voces

This inclusive store prides itself on being a bookshop, cultural space, and café geared toward LGBTQ customers. Colorful and stocked with magazines, games, gifts, and a variety of books on sexuality, it gives way to a quiet coffee shop with excellent pastries. The space is ideal for working or meeting in small groups. Open mike nights, book club meetings, and drag shows make up the regular event listings. ✉ Calle Niza 23, La Zona Rosa ☎ 55/5533–7116 ⊕ www.somosvoces.
com.mx Ⓜ Cuauhtémoc.

AIRBNB IN MEXICO CITY

Since the foreign tourism to Mexico City boom began around 2015, several key neighborhoods in the city have changed dramatically, with new restaurants and bars popping up that cater to more upscale tastes and budgets. La Juárez is one of these zones, and it's also one of the city's colonias with the highest number of Airbnbs, the now famous online platform for short-term apartment stays.

Some former tenants say they have been forcefully and illegally evicted from their homes as entire apartment buildings are renovated for Airbnbs with higher per-night rates; in some cases, the one-night price for an apartment equates to an entire week's salary for the average Mexican. Rents have doubled or tripled in La Juárez and other neighborhoods over the past several years and the September 19, 2017, earthquake didn't help, as many buildings crumbled or were left uninhabitable, making for even fewer housing options in an already overwhelmed city. That same year, Mexico City's government ruled to enforce a 3% accommodation tax for anyone who seeks to stay in the city, instead of just for guests of the city's hotels. No other legal measures have been taken to regulate Airbnb or other similar platforms yet, much to the distress of many city residents.

Tienda INAH

Next to the city's offices of the National Institute of Anthropology and History is a gift shop similar to what you'd find at the National Museum of Anthropology down the road. With ancestral Mexican handicrafts such as ceramics, weavings, and jewelry as well as books, magazines, and other media about Mexico's pre-Columbian past, it's a great spot to peruse if you don't have time to make it to the museum. ⊠ *Hamburgo 135, La Zona Rosa* ☎ *55/4166-0770* Ⓜ *Sevilla, Cuauhtémoc.*

 Coffee and Quick Bites

Café NIN

$$ | **International.** This exquisitely designed eatery feels like entering a mansion. A bit like a labyrinth, the service is quick and the menu extensive with breakfast through dinner options specializing in fresh ingredients. **Known for:** excellent coffee and fresh juice blends; beautifully designed space; international vibe. *Average main: 185 MP* ⊠ *Havre 73, Juárez* ☎ *55/9155-4805* ⊕ *www. cafenin.com.mx* Ⓜ *Cuauhtémoc.*

Cicatriz

$ | **Café.** Depending on when you drop by, this hip hangout can serve as a cheerful breakfast nook for chia pudding and egg sandwiches, an afternoon coffee or teahouse with light salads and a delicious smoked-eggplant-harissa dip, or an evening lounge with craft cocktails and well-curated (though pricey) wines. Whatever the time of day, there's almost always a crowd that tends toward the fashionable, arty side. **Known for:** creative, healthy salads, snacks, and baked goods; first-rate coffees and cocktails; trendy people-watching. *Average main: 140 MP* ✉ *Calle Dinamarca 44, Juárez* ⊕ *www.cicatrizcafe.com* Ⓜ *Cuauhtémoc.*

★ Diario Delicatessen & Gourmet Shop

$$ | **Deli.** This small, design-focused deli and café has preserved its original wood ceiling, which sits high over the few two-person tables. The menu is small but high quality, with meat and cheese plates, sandwiches, bagels, and salads along with an impressive tea and coffee selection. **Known for:** Mexican coffee varieties; mezcal, wine, honey, and other goods for sale; some of the best charcuterie boards in the city. *Average main: 200 MP* ✉ *Calle Lucerna 50b, Juárez* ☎ *55/5131–8009* ⊕ *www.diariodelicatessen.com* ⊘ *Closed Sun.* Ⓜ *Cuauhtémoc.*

Joe Gelato

$ | **Italian.** This gelato shop features flavors that are inventive, inspired by the Mexican palate. Friendly service from the owner himself gives it a homey vibe, where you can sit and enjoy your dessert or order coffee and tea. **Known for:** home-made quality gelato; unique flavors like beet and bergamot, avocado, and cacao and pistachio; quiet nook for relaxing. *Average main: 50 MP* ✉ *Calle Versalles 78, Juárez* ☎ *55/6842–0904* ⊕ *www.facebook.com/JoeGelatoMx* ⊘ *Closed Mon.* Ⓜ *Cuauhtémoc.*

Otro Café

$ | **Café.** On a hidden corner in Anzures, this chic café is pleasant for working and reading or just grabbing a cup of coffee to go. The selection of teas and infusions is impressive, and it's the only café with an underground, tucked-away vibe in the entire colonia. **Known for:** tranquil space in a tranquil neighborhood; one of the few cafés in Anzures; ideal for digital nomads and working from home days. *Average main: 35 MP* ✉ *Shakespeare 78, Anzures* ☎ *55/2624–3464* ⊕ *www.otrocafe.mx* ⊘ *Closed Sun.* Ⓜ *Metro Polanco, Chapultepec.*

SALVA Casa Niza

$$ | **Bakery.** This airy café entices from the street, where its baked goods are visible and whiffable from the outside. There's a plethora of beverages to choose from, such as coffee and juices, or grab a glass of wine and enjoy one of the massive vegetarian sandwiches prepared on house-made bread. **Known for:** Mexican craft beers in a lively setting; house-made breads and pastries; to-die-for breakfast chilaquiles. *Average main: 150 MP* ✉ *Calle Niza 15, La Zona Rosa* ☎ *55/5208–4232* ⊕ *www.salvecasaniza.com* Ⓜ *Cuauhtémoc.*

🍴 Dining

★ Alba

$$ | **Modern Mexican.** In a beautiful little jewel-box space, classic Mexican recipes are presented with colorful and flavorful contemporary twists—consider the lamb braised slowly in a pulque and ancho chile reduction and served with guacamole, pickles, fermented blueberries, and yogurt. This is some of the tastiest and most carefully thought-out cuisine in the city, yet at extremely approachable prices. **Known for:** thoughtful beverage program (especially the beer list); fried bananas with berry compote and cream for dessert; enchantingly boozy brunches. *Average main: 280 MP* ✉ *Calle Marsella 80, Juárez* ☎ *55/5207–3864* ⊕ *www.albacocinalocal.com* ⊗ *Closed Mon. No dinner Sun.* Ⓜ *Cuauhtémoc.*

Akarma

$ | **Vegetarian.** A pet-friendly vegan food stand, Akarma has the best of your health at heart, serving low-key healthy dishes. With just two stools and a bench at its sidewalk storefront, you quickly get intimate with the kitchen here. **Known for:** spicy lentil burgers so good you'll want the recipe; drool-worthy flor de calabaza (friend squash flower); locally made kombuchas featuring Mexican flavors like chile pepper and hoja santa. *Average main: 120 MP* ✉ *Lucerna 72a, Juárez* ☎ *55/6887–1036* ⊕ *www.facebook.com/AkarmaVegan* Ⓜ *Cuauhtémoc, Balderas.*

★ Amaya

$$ | **Modern Mexican.** At this elegant but unpretentious bistro, acclaimed chef Jaír Telléz presents a seasonally changing menu of internationally inflected contemporary Mexican dishes. Seafood figures prominently in the mix, both raw (in ceviche and aguachile) and

cooked (fried soft-shell crab, grilled octopus), and there are always a couple of robustly flavored game options, perhaps braised rabbit stew or lamb ribs. **Known for:** ceviches and aguachiles; impressive and diverse natural wine and craft beer list; creative desserts with housemade ice creams. *Average main: 250 MP* ✉ *Calle Gral. Prim 95, Juárez* ☎ *55/5592–5571* ⊕ *www.amaya-mexico.com* ⊗ *No dinner Sun.*

Bellinghausen

$$ | **Mexican.** This cherished Zona Rosa lunch spot has been in service for more than 100 years and its partially covered hacienda-style courtyard at the back, set off by an ivy-laden wall and fountain, is still a midday magnet for executives and tourists alike. A veritable army of waiters scurries back and forth serving tried-and-true Mexican favorites. Two slightly more luxe branches don't have the same historic charm, but the closest, Casa Bell (*Praga 14, Zona Rosa*), a courtyard restaurant ringed by dozens of caged chirping birds, is a must on a sunny afternoon. **Known for:** filete chemita (broiled steak with mashed potatoes) ; chamorro Bellinghausen (make-your-own tacos of minced lamb shank); high-end service without the price tag. *Average main: 185 MP* ✉ *Londres 95, at Niza, Juárez* ☎ *55/5207–6749* ⊕ *www.bellinghausen.mx* ⊗ *No dinner* Ⓜ *Cuauhtémoc.*

Bistrot Arlequin

$$ | **French.** Here you'll find everything you would expect from a petite bistro: an intimate environment open to the street, comforting food, good music that's not too loud, and excellent French wines. Start by ordering the house specialty, hailing from Lyon, France: fish quenelles with your choice of various sauces. **Known for:** traditional French bistro atmosphere; popular carne bourguignonne; clafoutis for dessert. *Average main: 180 MP* ⊠ *Río Nilo 42, at Río Panuco, Juárez* ☎ *55/5207–5616* ⊕ *www.facebook. com/BistrotArlequin* ⊘ *No dinner Sun.* Ⓜ *Sevilla.*

Cocina Lucio

$$ | Mexican. With a menu that is unassuming yet exploding with flavor, Lucio's is a local favorite of the neighborhood. Taco Tuesdays are inventive and feature a variety of fillings, from tongue and head to fish and squash flower while the *aguachile*, a spicy ceviche-style dish, is one of the best in the city. **Known for:** updated Mexican fare; stiff pours on mezcal and tequila cocktails; laid-back, hip, and artsy vibe. *Average main: 150 MP* ⊠ *Calle Versalles 92, Juárez* ☎ *55/3578–2499* ⊕ *www.facebook.com/doctorlucio1027* ⊘ *No dinner Sun., Mon., and Wed.* Ⓜ *Cuauhtémoc.*

Comedor Lucerna

$$ | International. This buzzy spot and communal eatery adorned with street art on the outside and vibrant colors on the inside is always busy. With four different kitchens to choose from (pizzas, hot dogs, hamburgers, or seafood) and a full-stocked bar, the offerings here would suit most people's palates and is great for trying a

variety of foods or for people who simply have different tastes than their dining companions. **Known for:** casual atmosphere and communal dining; funky decor by local artists; live music on Thursday. *Average main: 150 MP* ⊠ *Calle Lucerna 51, Juárez* ☎ *55/5535–8665* ⊕ *www. facebook.com/ComedorLucernaOficial* Ⓜ *Cuauhtémoc.*

El Dragón

$$ | Chinese. The former ambassador to China was so impressed by El Dragón's lacquered Beijing duck that he left behind a note of recommendation (now proudly displayed on one of the restaurant's walls) praising it as the most authentic in Mexico. The duck is roasted over a fruitwood fire and later brought to your table, where the waiter cuts it into thin, tender slices, though it's served with flour tortillas instead of the traditional Chinese steamed pancakes. **Known for:** a good place to splurge on a meal; a mix of regional Chinese cuisine, with a focus on Beijing; ideal location for a meal while out exploring. *Average main: 260 MP* ⊠ *Hamburgo 97, between Génova and Copenhague, Juárez* ☎ *55/5525–2466* Ⓜ *Cuauhtémoc.*

La Cuchara

$ | Mexican. At La Cuchara, you walk up creaky steps to an open dining area serving *comida corrida*, midday, multicourse meals at a cheap price. The homemade cuisine features Mexican specialties such as enchiladas and steak in salsa verde. **Known for:** lunch packages and breakfast specials; on-the-

DINING WITH FOOD ALLERGIES AND SENSITIVITIES

Mexican food has always been very meat heavy, but vegetarian and vegan options are becoming more widespread throughout Mexico City. While eating vegetarian here has long been pretty reasonable to do, even with street food, going vegan takes a little extra effort as most vegetarian dishes include dairy products and tortillas are sometimes prepared with small amounts of lard. But good news for those going gluten-free: the typical Mexican diet does not depend on a lot of bread.

One word to the wise, however: a lot of cooks use powdered chicken broth in their stews and soups (although not usually at vegetarian joints), so ask if they use *caldo de pollo en polvo* if you're trying to be a true vegetarian. For people with Celiac disease, this is also a must as it often contains gluten, too. For those with gluten sensitivity, the amount of gluten in said broth is not usually enough to cause problems.

Some restaurants in areas more frequented by foreigners will offer allergy information on their menus and will often have someone who speaks English on staff. Otherwise, you'll have to rely on at least decent Spanish to let a restaurant know that you have a specific allergy. Restaurants are generally as accommodating as they can be, though beware that most mole dishes are prepared with some kind of nut. If in doubt, say *"soy alérgico(a) a los mariscos"* for fish/shellfish, *las nueces* for a nut allergy, and *los lacteos* for dairy.

go meals; Mexican comfort food. *Average main: 60 MP* ⊠ *Londres 136, Juárez* ☎ *55/5207–6868* ⊘ *Closed weekends. No dinner* ⊟ *No credit cards* Ⓜ *Sevilla, Cuauhtémoc.*

Masala y Maiz
$$ | Fusion. Established in 2017 by wife-and-husband chefs Norma Listman (born in Mexico) and Saqib Keval (born in the U.S. to Indian farmers from East Africa), this intimate bistro presents an intriguing fusion menu of dishes that reflect the owners' diverse heritage. In the morning, you might try heirloom beans in a tamarind adobo sauce with a fried egg and puffy bhatura bread, while lunch favorites include the signature masala fried chicken with Indian and Mexican spices, cardamom sweet potato puree, and herb chutney. **Known for:** flavorful India-meets-Mexico cuisine; an exciting (but spendy) list of natural wines; leisurely weekend brunches. *Average main: 200 MP* ⊠ *Calle Marsella 72, Juárez* ☎ *55/1313–8260* ⊕ *www.masalaymaiz.com* ⊘ *Closed Tues. No dinner.*

Mikado
$$ | Japanese. Strategically positioned a few blocks west of the U.S. embassy and close to the Japanese embassy, this spot is notable for its varied sushi and teppanyaki options. A fine Japanese chef and a cheerful mix of Japanese embassy workers and young Mexicans also make Mikado a real treat. **Known for:** hibachi grills in view of diners;

plentiful vegetarian options; excellent yakimeshi, a fried-rice dish. *Average main: 200 MP ⊠ Paseo de la Reforma 369, at Río Guadalquivir, Juárez* ☎ *55/5525–3096* ⊘ *No lunch Sun.* Ⓜ *Sevilla.*

Nadefo
$$$ | Korean. Nestled close to busy Avenida Chapultepec, Nadefo is one of the many Korean restaurants in this part of southern Zona Rosa. Each table comes with a grill and the option to grill your meat right in front of you, and the dishes are varied, with popular Korean sides brought out as accompaniment. **Known for:** traditional Korean barbecue; gigantic ramen soup bowls; long waits if you come during peak hours. *Average main: 300 MP* ⊠ *Calle Liverpool 183, La Zona Rosa* ☎ *55/5525–0351* ⊕ *www.facebook. com/NadefoMX* Ⓜ *Sevilla.*

Niddo
$$ | Eclectic. This bustling café with a few sidewalk tables and an art deco aesthetic turns out tasty, globally influenced victuals throughout the day, including bagels and lox, eggs shakshuka, chilaquiles, and fluffy pancakes with a rotating array of toppings in the morning to a variety of creative sandwiches, pastas, and salads later in the day. There's also an impressive array of pastries, desserts, and espresso drinks as well as mimosas and other cocktails. **Known for:** first-rate espresso drinks; diverse breakfast and brunch fare; delicious brownies, cookies, and pastries. *Average main: 210 MP* ⊠ *Dresde 2,*

Juárez ☎ *55/5525–0262* ⊕ *www.niddo. mx* ⊘ *Closed Mon. No dinnner.*

Pan al Vapor
$ | Asian. This small diner isn't anything special from the outside, but upon entering, your eyes will immediately be drawn to the colorful steamed breads with animal faces that sit next to the cash register. Specializing in said bread, ramen lunch specials, and other Japanese and Korean delicacies, the food comes quick so it's a good stopping point for a bite to eat on a busy day of exploring. **Known for:** meal packages focusing on Japanese specialties; young and diverse crowd; cozy and welcoming atmosphere. *Average main: 100 MP* ⊠ *Estocolmo 24, La Zona Rosa* ☎ *55/5207–4554* ⊕ *www.facebook. com/Omandupanalvapor* Ⓜ *Sevilla, Cuauhtémoc.*

Pan Comido
$$ | Vegetarian. This bright space along one of Anzures's busiest roads is usually bustling, but not often crowded. As one of the neighborhood's only fully vegetarian and vegan eateries, it specializes in healthy options including fresh-squeezed juice, coffee, and gluten-free dining options. **Known for:** breakfast and lunch specials; digital nomad hangout; popular meeting place for friends and co-workers. *Average main: 200 MP* ⊠ *Leibnitz 117, Anzures* ☎ *55/6386–0192* ⊕ *www.facebook.com/elpancomido* Ⓜ *Chapultepec.*

⭐ Restaurante Emilia

$$$$ | Eclectic. A mindful and premium dining experience, Emilia serves omakase using seasonal Mexican ingredients in an intimate space that plays its elegance up against a somewhat gritty neighborhood. The food is adventurous and of high quality, with exchange rates favoring your chance of living like Mexico's one percent. **Known for:** elegant Japanese-Mexican fusion; alcoholic and nonalcoholic pairings; reservations required. *Average main: 2000 MP* ⊠ *Río Panuco 132, 2nd fl., Mexico City* ☎ *55/8662-0254* ⊕ *www. emilia.rest* ⊗ *Closed Sun.* Ⓜ *Sevilla.*

⭐ Rokai

$$ | Japanese. An immediate success since it opened on a quiet side street in Colonia Cuauhtémoc, tiny Rokai is perhaps the most authentic Japanese restaurant in a city where cream cheese, chipotle mayo, and bottled hot sauce adorn many a sushi roll. Japanese chefs Hiroshi Kawahito and Daisuke Maeda use immaculately fresh fish brought in daily from Mexico's various coasts, primarily Baja California and Oaxaca, and turn it into sushi and sashimi, as well as cooked dishes. There's also a ramen restaurant next door, bearing the same name and ownership. **Known for:** traditional omakase tasting menu that is a bargain for the quality; reservations typically needed; vegetarian ramen dishes. *Average main: 180 MP* ⊠ *Río Ebro 87, Juárez* ☎ *55/5207-7543* ⊗ *Closed Sun.*

⭐ Sobremesa Havre

$$$$ | Mexican. A true culinary experience, Sobremesa offers group cooking courses throughout the week with chefs and house staff in a renovated early 20th-century building. No industrial utensils, blenders, ovens, or other kitchenware is used, with the idea being to replicate home-cooking styles and recipes; guests are treated to a meal of their own creation in the school's beautiful dining room at the end of each three-hour course. **Known for:** cooking classes in a bright kitchen space; Mexican-style home cooking, with some diverse cuisines thrown in; entertaining and interactive dining option. *Average main: 1200 MP* ⊠ *Havre 70, Juárez* ☎ *55/5941-4521* ⊕ *www.sobremesa. mx* Ⓜ *Cuauhtémoc.*

⭐ Tamales Madre

$ | Mexican. If its building's divine design doesn't call to you immediately from the street, you will be enchanted as you take a step down, literally, into the sunken communal dining area, which also doubles as the kitchen where outstanding tamales are prepared before your eyes. The service is personalized, and the high ceilings make way for shelves to show off a number of beautiful artifacts from around Mexico as well as books about Mexico's almighty corn. **Known for:** sweet and savory vegetarian and vegan tamales (and one organic chicken option); surprisingly gourmet tamales; tasty hibiscus and tamarind juice. *Average main: 60 MP* ⊠ *Calle Liverpool 44a,*

Juárez ☎ 55/5705–3491 ⊕ *www. tamalesmadre.com* ⊘ *Closed Mon.* Ⓜ *Cuauhtémoc.*

Taquería El Califa

$ | Mexican. When you're craving a light bite or even a substantial meal late at night, this big and lively eatery hits the spot with its vast menu that goes well beyond tacos, including *costras* (addictive "tacos" with crispy shells made of grilled cheese), chicken pastor, and Hidalgo-style arrachera barbacoa. Open nightly until 4 am and with several other CDMX locations, Califa has table service, a clean and light dining room, and menus with detailed food descriptions, making it one of the city's more appealing—if slightly pricier—taquería experiences. **Known for:** several dishes with fried cheese; clean and attractive dining room; nice list of aguas frescas and craft beers. *Average main: 80 MP* ⊠ *Av. Paseo de la Reforma 382, Juárez* ☎ 55/5511–9424 ⊕ *www.elcalifa.com.mx.*

Tandoor

$$ | Indian. Indian and Pakistani cuisine are not easy to come by in Mexico City, much less of the high quality variety, but Tandoor is a welcome exception. The exquisitely decorated space, featuring items from India and Pakistan, is welcoming and intimate with plenty of space between tables. **Known for:** tandoor oven specialties; views overlooking a charming leafy street; natural mango lassis (without an excess of sugar). *Average main: 250 MP* ⊠ *Calle Copérnico 156, Anzures*

☎ 55/5545–6863 ⊕ *www.tandoor. mx* Ⓜ *Metro Polanco.*

Bars and Nightlife

Baby

Drawing a pretty gender-diverse crowd of mostly under-thirtysome-things, this wildly popular LGBTQ club offers up a varied menu of dance genres—anything from reggaeton to electronic. If you need a break from the pulsing crowds and intensely pink lighting within, head to the pleasant side patio. It's in Zona Rosa, but a few blocks east of the Calle Amberes bar strip. ⊠ *Londres 71, Juárez* ☎ *No phone.*

Bar Milán

The young and the hip favor this bar, a 10-minute walk northeast of Zona Rosa. Upon entering, you need to change pesos into *milagros* (miracles), which are notes necessary to buy drinks throughout the night. The trick is to remember to change them back before last call. ⊠ *Milán 18, at General Prim, Juárez* ☎ 55/5592–0031 ⊕ *www.barmilan. com.mx* Ⓜ *Balderas.*

Calle Genova

Closed off for pedestrians and lined with bars, this street is basically one long pub crawl, spanning several blocks and all kinds of different establishments. You'll be approached with menus by the hype people for various bars as you walk; feel free to take a quick look and move on to the next option if a place doesn't interest you (they're used to it). La Terraza and La Chelestial are particularly good for people-watching and drinks, although you're better off looking elsewhere for dining. ⊠ *Calle Genova, between Paseo de la Reforma and Calle Liverpool, Juárez* Ⓜ *Cuauhtémoc.*

★ Corazón de Tinto
This outdoor bar is the place to go if you want to learn about the plethora of delicious and underappreciated (at least internationally) Mexican wines. Service is intimate, friendly, and above all knowledgeable. More than 40% of the wines are Mexican, and not just from the Valle de Guadalupe. Live jazz music sets the vibe just right for a relaxing evening. ⊠ *Terminal Juárez, Calle Versalles 88, 2nd fl., Juárez* ⊕ *www.corazondetinto. com* Ⓜ *Cuauhtémoc.*

El Scary Witches Bar
A nod to international counterculture, with a special appreciation for everything goth, this bar is purposely dark and always bumping out industrial, metal, and rock tunes into the street. It's tight quarters and slightly confined, but you'll feel like you're part of a special, all-black-wearing club when you enter. Find a spot to squeeze in and wait for your server to come by with a menu that includes wine, mezcal, an impressive variety of international and artisanal Mexican beers, and cocktails served in skull-shape mugs. ⊠ *Oslo 3, La Zona Rosa* ☎ *55/5207–8416* ⊕ *www.facebook. com/elscarywitches* Ⓜ *Cuauhtémoc.*

★ Hanky Panky Cocktail Bar
If you're looking for it, you'll eventually find it, but you won't find it if you aren't looking for it. With a strict, secret location, Hanky Panky is one of Mexico City's few Prohibition-era-style speakeasies. Award-winning mixologists come and go from here to highlight their specialties abroad, while always bringing something back with them. Reservations are required, and when you arrive, you'll have to ask around (as in up and down the block) in order to find the entrance—it's part of the charm. Inside is dark, with leather booths and a 10-seat bar. Many cocktails are based on Mexican mixology magic, though there's plenty of international flavors as well; you won't be disappointed with something spicy. ⊠ *Calle Turín, between Calle Versalles and Abraham González, Juárez* ☎ *55/9155–0958* ⊕ *www.hankypanky. mx* Ⓜ *Cuauhtémoc.*

Nicho Bears & Bar
Zona Rosa's prime hangout for bearish gay guys and their admirers actually draws a pretty varied crowd. It acts as a generally more mature alternative to the more raucous crowds you'll find in many of the bars around the corner on Calle Amberes. It's open only Thursday through Saturday night. ⊠ *Calle Londres 182, Juárez* ⊕ *www.bearmex. com.*

★ Parker & Lenox
First you meet Parker, a classy diner with windowside black leather booths and an exquisite wooden

bar serving up gourmet pub fare. Then, at night, you meet Lenox, a tucked away, acoustically ideal live music venue with green leather booths and not a bad seat in the house. With live music throughout the week, including international acts and local tributes (think Quentin Tarantino night featuring your favorite soundtracks), locals love Lenox for its speakeasy vibe and chilled-out jazz club ambience. ⊠ *Calle Milán 14, Juárez* ☎ *55/7893-3140* ⊕ *www.facebook. com/parkerandlenox* Ⓜ *Cuauhtémoc, Balderas.*

Tokyo Music Bar

Across the hallway from ultrahip restaurant Emilia, this bar has a speakeasy vibe, phenomenal music, and an inventive cocktail list, including nonalcoholic options. They keep things super chill with vinyl records lining green marble-faced walls, and a DJ spins everything from current to old-school R&B hits. ⊠ *Río Panuco 132, Mexico City* ☎ *55/8662-4064* ⊕ *www.facebook. com/tokyomusicbar* Ⓜ *Sevilla.*

🎟 Performing Arts

Hojas de Té

Perhaps the best place to see flamenco in the city, this space doubles as a performance studio and school. With live performances and occasional dinners, a bar with wine, beer and mezcal, and performances hosted by the school's students as well as international performers, it's an intimate space that transports you from the clubs of Zona Rosa to the hills of Andalucia. Check the website for a full schedule. ⊠ *Oslo 7, Juárez* ☎ *55/5207-8416* ⊕ *www.hojasdete.org* Ⓜ *Cuauhtémoc.*

Teatro Milán

Intimate and affordable, Teatro Milán and its joint theater Foro Lucerna regularly present work by Mexican artists and feature local actors. From comedy to drama to ballet, the space changes nightly depending on the work it's showcasing. With 250 seats, everyone is entitled to a great view of the stage. Check the website for show dates and times. ⊠ *Calle Lucerna 64, Juárez* ☎ *55/5535-4178* ⊕ *www. teatromilan.com* Ⓜ *Cuauhtémoc.*

5

San Rafael and Santa María la Ribera

POLANCO

SANTA MARÍA LA RIBERA

SAN RAFAEL

ALAMEDA CENTRAL

CENTRO HISTÓRICO

BOSQUE DE CHAPULTEPEC

JUÁREZ AND ANZURES

ROMA

CONDESA

BENITO JUÁREZ

SAN ÁNGEL

COYOACÁN

Sightseeing ★★★☆☆ | Shopping ★★☆☆☆ | Dining ★★★☆☆ | Nightlife ★★★☆☆

Two of Mexico City's first official neighborhoods outside of the Centro Histórico, San Rafael and Santa María la Ribera have been considered well-located residential areas since the late 19th century. These neighboring colonias in the Cuauhtémoc borough have some similarities, but there's much that changes when you cross the Avenida Ribera de San Cosme.—*by Megan Frye*

First off, Santa María la Ribera is a lot busier than San Rafael. There are more restaurants, a coffee shop on seemingly every corner, and a number of beloved cantinas, and its activity is largely based around the late 19th-century Moorish Revival gazebo. The neighborhood has had its ups-and-downs over the years, but during the day, you'll see more parents picking up their children from school and elderly locals going about their daily business. Perhaps slightly rough around the edges for some, Santa María la Ribera feels like a small pueblo surrounded by a very large city.

Just south of Santa María la Ribera and north of Cuauhtémoc, San Rafael is mostly residential, with wide sidewalks, a few restaurants, classy cantinas and cafés, and its most famous offering: theaters. It's notably quieter than Santa María la Ribera, but equally as well situated to explore the city. San Rafael could be said to hide its secrets well: it's not flashy and there aren't as many young people or foreigners about (although with its relatively low rents that will likely change soon). But for now, it remains a storied neighborhood, with a history focused primarily on its number of theaters that have been in operation since the 1950s; some, like Cine Opera, have closed down but are in the process of renovation—an apt metaphor for San Rafael as a whole.

◉ Sights

★ Biblioteca Vasconcelos

With nearly 600,000 books, magazines, and international newspapers, this is the largest library in Mexico. It covers more than 410,000 square feet, with rows of catwalks leading up to its six-story ceiling. Opened officially in 2006, the space is regarded as having some of the most unique architecture of any public building in the city. An auditorium regularly hosts concerts, lectures, and other cultural events. Computers are available for public use, as is Wi-Fi. The massive building, which also houses the graffitied skeleton of a gray whale, is surrounded by gardens boasting palm trees and moonflowers. ⊠ *Eje 1, Santa María la Ribera ✛ North corner of Aldama* ☎ *55/9157–2800* ⊕ *www.bibliotecavasconcelos.gob.mx* Ⓜ *Buenavista.*

⭐ **Kiosko Morisco** (The Moorish Kiosk)

Built by Mexican architect José Ramón Ibarrola, the Moorish Kiosk was meant to serve as the Mexico Pavilion at the 1884 World's Fair in New Orleans. It was relocated to Mexico in 1910 and placed where it now stands, as a proud symbol of Santa María la Ribera. Designed in the Moorish Revival architectural style known as neo-Mudejar, which was popular at the time in Spain, it is made of wrought iron and wood painted in blue, red, and gold, and is topped with a glass cupola dome. It sits in the principal plaza of the colonia, and draws photographers and lovers (it's not uncommon to see a modeling shoot going on or a couple in a deep embrace) as well as families. Its sheer size is enough to accommodate even occasional dance classes and events. ✉ Kiosko Morisco de Santa María la Ribera, Santa María la Ribera ✛ Central park area of Santa María la Ribera Ⓜ Buenavista.

Mercado la Dalia

A classic Mexican market with labyrinth-like aisles, you'll find everything you could possible want for sale, from fresh produce to clothing and kitchenwares. Vendors are set up outside in front of the market, too. It's a great place to stop for a quick comida corrida, an affordable three-course midday meal, at any one of the market's stalls in the prepared food sections. This market is a little less hectic than others around the city, so it's worth checking out if crowds

GETTING HERE

About 3 km (2 miles) from the western edge of the Centro Histórico and bordering La Juárez, these residential neighborhoods are great for experiencing the city away from the tourist path while still being close to the action. Uber fares from the airport or city center run about MX$80–MX$150, depending on traffic. The neighborhoods are served by three subway lines (2, 8, and B). As the neighborhoods border Insurgentes, the main north–south artery of the city, they are also connected to the Metrobus line 1. You could cross both Santa María la Ribera and San Rafael by foot in less than an hour by walking along Jaime Torres Bodet in Santa María la Ribera, which connects to Miguel E. Schulz in San Rafael. While generally considered safe, it's a good idea to exercise caution in both neighborhoods if on a lonely street at night.

are not exactly your thing. ✉ Calle Sabino 225, Santa María la Ribera Ⓜ Buenavista.

Museo de Geología

Operated by the National Autonomous University of Mexico, the city's geology museum features multiple mammoth skulls and an entire hadrosaurid dinosaur fossil. Gems and minerals from around the world, but mostly Mexico, adorn impeccably preserved antique glass and wooden showcases. The large and expertly polished pieces of selenite from northern Mexico are particularly impressive, as is the architecture of the building itself, built in 1906. The beautiful colonial building enjoys a privileged location overlooking Santa María la Ribera's central park. ✉ *Jaime Torres Bodet 176, Santa María la Ribera* ☎ *55/5547-3948* ⊕ *www.geologia. unam.mx/igl/museo* ⊗ *Closed Mon.* Ⓜ *Buenavista.*

★ Museo Universitario del Chopo

This 603,000-square foot contemporary art space features several galleries of mostly Mexican visual and video artists, an auditorium for concerts, readings, and lectures, and a large rotating gallery space that features performance art. Operated by the National Autonomous University of Mexico, El Chopo is known for representing, honoring, and celebrating vast elements of contemporary culture and subcultures of Mexican society. ✉ *Calle Dr. Enrique Gonzalez*

Martinez 10, Santa María la Ribera ☎ *55/5546-3471* ⊕ *www.chopo. unam.mx* ⊗ *Closed Mon. and Tues.* Ⓜ *Revolucón.*

🛍 Shopping

Tienda Orgánica

Although its size and appearance is the same as most small corner stores in the city, Tienda Orgánica specializes in organic and local foods such as kombucha, coffee, dairy products, and even local tobacco rolled with medicinal flowers. It's a good spot to shop for delicious gifts to take home or, if you're staying a while, to do some quality grocery shopping. ✉ *José Antonio Alzate 46–B, Santa María la Ribera* ⊕ *www.facebook. com/organica.stamarialaribera* Ⓜ *Buenavista.*

☕ Coffee and Quick Bites

★ Alebrije

$ | International. Located in a renovated garage, Alebrije is loaded with plants, couches, and tables, good for working or chatting during the day and an ideal date spot in the evening. String lights and antique fixtures provide warm-toned light, dancing off the exposed brick as you eat sandwiches and drink hot chocolate, wine, or beer. **Known for:** bagels (hard to find in Mexico City!); eggplant and goat cheese chapatas; molletes (open-faced Mexican sandwiches). *Average main: 100 MP* ✉ *Santa María La*

Ribera 84, Santa María la Ribera
☎ 55/2630–2972 ⊕ www.facebook.
com/AlebrijeArteYCultura ⊘ Closed
Sun. ▭ No credit cards Ⓜ Buenavista.

Bello Café
$ | **Café.** Just around the corner
from the famed Moorish Kiosk,
this open-air coffee and tea spot
also specializes in fresh pastries.
Specializing in Mexican coffee, it's
also a place to go and buy a bottle
of mezcal, cacao, local honey, and
even artisanal Mexican beers.
Known for: bright, youth-friendly
atmosphere; 10 different ways to
brew your coffee; cocktails with
coffee, mezcal, and coffee-brewed
beer. *Average main: 50 MP* ⊠ *Manuel
Carpio 158, Santa María la Ribera*
☎ 55/4757–6046 ⊕ www.facebook.
com/BelloCoffee ▭ No credit cards
Ⓜ Buenavista.

★ Camino a Comala
$ | **Café.** Just a block from the busy
Avenida Ribera de San Cosme,
this quiet and elegantly designed
hideaway offers respite from the
crowds of nearby Metro San Cosme.
Decorated with antiques and
smelling of freshly roasted coffee,
it's the kind of place where you can
disappear for a quiet afternoon of
reading or a nice meal alone or with
a travel companion. **Known for:**
house-made bread and pastries,
baked fresh daily; serrano ham
or roast beef baguette; hand-
tossed pizzas. *Average main: 50 MP*
⊠ *Miguel E. Schultz 7, San Rafael*
☎ 55/5592–0313 ⊕ www.caminoa-
comala.com/menu Ⓜ San Cosme,
Revolución.

WORTH A TRIP

Originally started outside the Museo
del Chopo, El Chopo Cultural Market
is a *tianguis* (a Nahuatl, or Aztec,
word for regularly occurring outdoor
marketplaces) that has served as a
counterculture gathering space for
decades. Now located just outside
the Buenavista train station on
Saturday mornings, it's a favorite
for those looking to peruse vinyl
records, T-shirts, zines, and other
similar items. Find it at the corner of
Calle Juan Aldama and Calle Luna,
behind the Buenavista train station in
Colonia Buenavista, the neighboring
colonia from Santa María la Ribera.

★ Esquina Barragán
$$ | **Café.** Black-and-white tiles
give this bright space an impec-
cably clean and welcoming vibe.
With its own house mezcal, wines,
and beers, it can also be a place to
gather for a drink or grab a light
dinner. **Known for:** house-made
pastries; excellent molletes and
vegetarian chilaquiles; views of the
Jardin de Arte. *Average main: 150
MP* ⊠ *Miguel Schultz 146, San Rafael*
☎ 55/7651–9605 ⊘ Closed Mon. ▭ No
credit cards Ⓜ Revolución.

★ Estanquillo El 32
$ | **Mexican Fusion.** This is a place
where the neighborhood elders
gather during the day to eat their
tamales and drink their coffee, but
where you'll find mostly young,
artist types in the evenings. With a
wide variety of Mexican artisanal
beers and an impressive stock of
unique mezcals as well as Mexican

A TALE OF TWO NEIGHBORHOODS

Two of the first "suburbs" of Mexico City's center, both Santa María la Ribera and San Rafael faced disrepair and neglect in the late 1980s, some argue as a result of the deadly 1985 earthquake, which damaged a lot of the central area of the city and left people looking for more stable ground in other parts of the capital. Crime took over, especially in Santa María la Ribera. But one stroll down the streets of these neighborhoods today and it's clear they have since cleaned up their acts: Santa María la Ribera in particular has become a bohemian gathering space for those looking to escape the rising rents and high activity zones of more gentrified parts of the city.

The richness of San Rafael and Santa María la Ribera can be seen in the diversity and excellence of their architecture. Although less popular with visitors today, the building of these neighborhoods was clearly no afterthought. At once reflecting the city's Porfiriato architecture phase (referring to the dictatorship of Porfirio Díaz during the late 19th and early 20th centuries in which anything considered "European" was encouraged) and the folklore present in many of Mexico's most enchanting villages, it is not uncommon to see Baroque, European Gothic, Renaissance, and art deco buildings here side-by-side. Walking the calm streets of these neighborhoods is the best way to take in their architectural treasures.

coffee, the space is open to the street, like a former garage, and has a couple very well-behaved house dogs keeping everything in check. **Known for:** paté de conejo (rabbit paté) with herbs and tomato on rye bread; tamal de huitlacoche (corn fungus, a delicacy); relaxed atmosphere with books and magazines to browse. *Average main: 100 MP ⊠ Calle Dr. Enrique Gonzalez Martinez 32, Santa María la Ribera ☎ 55/5535-2310 ⊕ www.facebook. com/EstanquilloEl32 ⊗ Closed Sun. ⊟ No credit cards Ⓜ Revolución.*

La Vaca de Muchos Colores

$ | International. This is a small and comfy spot to stop in and grab a bite to eat or enjoy a beer, wine, or coffee. It feels immediately like

a good friend's (stylish) living room and is ideal for catching up with companions or coming in alone with a book. **Known for:** grasshopper and goat cheese chapatas; tasty frappuccinos; good Mexican beer menu. *Average main: 100 MP ⊠ Manuel María Contreras 52, San Rafael ☎ 55/5535-0233 ⊗ Closed Sun. ⊟ No credit cards Ⓜ San Cosme.*

MojiGato Café

$ | Café. A darling nook ideal for cat lovers, couches and cushions make for comfortable seating in a small, quiet space. You might have to duck your head to get in, but it serves as an espresso, tea, and coffee shop as well as a gift shop for all things cat-related. **Known for:** delicious, fresh croissants; adorable and affordable cat memorabilia; board games to play while you eat and drink (some of which are cat-themed). *Average main: 35 MP* ⊠ *Manuel Carpio 92, Santa María la Ribera* ☎ *55/5547–9993* ⊘ *Closed Tues.* ⊟ *No credit cards* Ⓜ *Buenavista.*

★ Panadería 220

$ | **Bakery.** Designed as a walk-up and take-out café, this locale is adored for its divine pastries. Despite its small space, the number of delicious beverages and baked goods they prepare is as impressive as they are delicious. **Known for:** guava bread (a pastry stuffed with marmalade); very small space with limited seating; tasty espressos or Americanos to go. *Average main: 50 MP* ⊠ *Manuel María Contreras 45, San Rafael* ⊕ *www.instagram.com/panaderia220* Ⓜ *San Cosme.*

★ Tacos El Güero

$ | **Mexican.** Although its name is barely visible on the sun-faded awnings, this neighborhood taquería is busy on most nights. It's a true local's spot and its bright lights are visible from the street; you'll know it from the number of people mostly patiently waiting to place their orders (food is available to go as well). **Known for:** excellent al pastor tacos; busy crowds and long lines on weekends; other Mexican favorites like suadero tortas and gringas. *Average main: 40 MP* ⊠ *Manuel María Contreras 59, San Rafael* ⊟ *No credit cards* Ⓜ *San Cosme.*

⅋ Dining

★ Cantina Salón París

$$ | **Mexican.** A large cantina with a sizeable lunch and dinner crowd, Salon París is an emblematic fixture of the neighborhood. A focused menu features Mexican bar food (think tortas, shrimp soup, and steaks) and varied liquor options (specifically Mexican beer, international rums, tequilas, and digestive liqueurs like Campari and Fernet). **Known for:** chamorro (braised pork shanks) on Thursday; tlacoyos (traditional corn masa stuffed with beans or cheese, cooked on a grill, topped with cheese and salsa); live music and soccer games on the television. *Average main: 150 MP* ⊠ *Jaime Torres Bodet 152, Santa María la Ribera* ☎ *55/5541–7319* ⊟ *No credit cards* Ⓜ *Buenavista.*

Cochinita Power

$$ | **Mexican.** It's not hyperbole to say that there are few interiors in the city as pink as the decor within this diner just near the San Cosme metro station. Cochinita Power specializes in Yucatecan food (read: pork and habanero salsas) with a set-up somewhere between a food cart and a restaurant, but without the hustle and bustle of standing and eating on the street. **Known for:** tasty and cheap pork-focused dishes from the Yucatan; guanabana juice; habanero pickled onions. *Average main: 150 MP* ⊠ *Ignacio Manuel Altamirano 19, San Rafael* ☎ *55/7589–6676* ⊕ *www.facebook.com/cochinitapowermx* ⊟ *No credit cards* Ⓜ *San Cosme.*

El Comedor de San Pascual Bailongo

$$ | Mediterranean. This intimate but elegant (for the neighborhood) diner has small tables in a quiet space with a reclaimed feel and appropriately minimalist decor. With juicy burgers, salmon carpaccio, and crunchy thin-crust pizza, the menu caters to a wide audience. **Known for:** fried barbacoa tacos; shrimp and linguine pasta; great tapas, including an excellent eggplant Parmesan. *Average main: 150 MP ⊠ Calle Sor Juana Ines de la Cruz 67, Santa María la Ribera* ☎ *55/2630-2227 ⊘ Closed Sun.* ⊟ *No credit cards* Ⓜ *Buenavista.*

El Corral del Chivo

$ | Mexican. A beloved family spot with indoor and outdoor seating overlooking Santa María la Ribera's main park, you can smell the *birria* (goat meat) from a block away. The service is quick and the menu is not entirely varied, but its specialties have kept people coming for years. **Known for:** excellent birria tacos; grilled meats and vegetables; great pozole, traditional Mexican stew. *Average main: 100 MP ⊠ Jaime Torres Bodet 152, Santa María la Ribera* ☎ *55/5547-5609* ⊟ *No credit cards* Ⓜ *Buenavista.*

★ El Guapo Grill

$$$ | Argentine. Mexico City is arguably the capital of all Latin America, and for that reason you'll see plenty of restaurants from immigrants of the region, especially South America. El Guapo Grill is Argentine to the max, so expect lots of meat and red wine. **Known for:** slightly upscale Argentine steak house; delicious choripan (chorizo sandwich); authentic jugo de carne. *Average main: 300 MP ⊠ Calle Eligio Ancona 207, Santa María la Ribera* ☎ *55/6718-7771* ⊕ *www.facebook. com/Guapogrill ⊘ Closed Mon.* Ⓜ *Buenavista.*

Kolobok

$$ | Russian. One of few Russian restaurants in the city, Kolobok showcases cuisine from Russian immigrants who came to Mexico after various Eastern European diasporas. A small space featuring just 10 wooden tables, the decor is homey with Russian music playing and murals depicting the Russian countryside, and the food is as authentic as it gets in Mexico. **Known for:** traditional Russian dishes like meat-stuffed cabbage rolls; a mean borscht; Baltika Russian beer. *Average main: 150 MP ⊠ Calle Salvador Díaz Mirón 87, Santa María la Ribera* ☎ *55/5541-7085* ⊕ *www.kolobok.com.mx* ⊟ *No credit cards* Ⓜ *Buenavista.*

★ La Oveja Negra

$$ | Mexican. Busy and stylish, this is a popular classic in the Santa María la Ribera neighborhood, located in an older building that has retained its original high ceilings and tile work. Known for having slightly higher prices than usual for the area, it's also recognized for excellent service, taste, and variety of traditional Mexican dishes. **Known for:** plato oveja (goat cheese, chorizo, and chicharrón); waits on weekends; great cocktails. *Average main: 250 MP ⊠ Calle Sabino 225, Santa María la Ribera ☎ 55/5643-4781 ⊘ Closed Mon.–Thurs. ⊟ No credit cards Ⓜ Buenavista.*

La Periquita Tacos Arabes

$ | Mexican. A popular lunch spot on a bustling corner of San Rafael, the *tacos arabes* (Arabic tacos) are always a delight here. With the pork cooked on a spit yelling distance from your table and pita bread replacing tortillas, it's a local and long-standing favorite of the neighborhood. **Known for:** late night eats; al pastor tacos; gigantic tortas. *Average main: 75 MP ⊠ Calle Maestro Antonio Caso 125, San Rafael ☎ 55/5546-0456.*

La Tía

$ | Mexican. In the residential neighborhood of San Rafael, La Tía is clearly a local favorite. Even with dozens of tables, it still doesn't match the demands of locals who crave the taste of homemade cooking and Mexican specialties such as *chile en nogada* (poblano chiles stuffed with picadillo) in August and September and less common cuisine for Mexico, such as mozzarella-and-spinach stuffed chicken breasts. **Known for:** always changing daily specials; quick service; weekday lunch crowds. *Average main: 85 MP ⊠ Manuel María Contreras 20, San Rafael ☎ 55/5546-0157 ⊕ www.facebook.com/LaTiaRestaurante ⊟ No credit cards Ⓜ San Cosme.*

★ María Ciento 38

$$ | Sicilian. Romantic and tucked away, María Ciento 38 is perhaps the most upscale eatery in the neighborhood. The authentic Sicilian cuisine is homemade and prepared fresh daily, which means the limited seats are in high demand and reservations are recommended. **Known for:** great weekend brunch; Sicilian-style pizzas; excellent wine selection. *Average main: 150 MP ⊠ Santa María La Ribera 138, Santa María la Ribera ☎ 55/7159-2039 ⊕ www.mariaciento38.com.mx ⊘ Closed Mon. Ⓜ Buenavista.*

Mercado Morisco

$$ | International. This hip space is a communal eatery featuring nine stalls with neon signs advertising everything from pulque (lightly alcoholic fermented agave nectar) to seafood tacos. Nestled among tortillerías, hardware stores, and apartments, it's easy to walk past it unless you happen to glance inward to spot the brightly decorated market and its picnic table–esque seating. **Known for:** wide variety of foods; pet-friendly location; hipster atmosphere. *Average main: 150 MP ⊠ Manuel Carpio 144, Santa María la Ribera ☎ 55/8190-9600 ⊕ www.facebook.com/morisco.mercado Ⓜ Buenavista.*

Naan

$ | Asian Fusion. One of the only purely vegan options in the area, this hidden spot serves more South Asian fusion rather than the traditional Indian fare that's advertised. Still, it's a great option for vegans, with very affordable prices, a lively color scheme featuring brightly painted peach and turquoise walls, and five white tables alongside the kitchen. **Known for:** vegan lassis; samosas with mango chutney; spinach croquets in tomato sauce. *Average main: 120 MP* ⊠ *Santa María La Ribera 12, Santa María la Ribera* ⊹ *Enter through Jardín Mascarones Park* 🕾 *55/6380–6168* ⊕ *www. naanmx.com* ⊙ *Closed Sun.* ▭ *No credit cards* Ⓜ *San Cosme.*

OaxacAquí

$$ | Mexican. If you've been dreaming about Oaxacan cuisine, but don't have the time to travel there, this authentic restaurant that serves up breakfast, lunch, and early dinners is the next best thing. Service can be a bit chaotic but always friendly, and the quality of the food makes up for any wait. **Known for:** horchata with fresh melon and walnuts; red and black moles; great tlayuda, a traditional Oaxacan dish. *Average main: 150 MP* ⊠ *Dr. Atl 207, Greater Mexico City* 🕾 *55/4150–7187* ▭ *No credit cards* Ⓜ *Buenavista.*

Pakaa

$$ | Portuguese. A charming little place perfect for lunch or early dinner, Pakaa specializes in Portuguese cuisine, though, of course, it's not uncommon to find a serrano pepper and some salsas on the table (this is Mexico after all). With a bright and welcoming atmosphere inside, it also has outdoor seating along a relaxed stretch of San Rafael. **Known for:** delicious

octopus and mussel dishes; nice sangria and wine lists; Portuguese bitoque. *Average main: 150 MP* ⊠ *Calle de Francisco Díaz Covarrubias 36-B, San Rafael* 🕾 *55/3783–7755* ⊕ *pakaarestaurante.wixsite.com/ jantaresreservas* ⊙ *Closed Sun.* Ⓜ *San Cosme.*

Patio María

$ | Mexican. As advertised on a plaque on the textured walled exterior, the building of Patio María is the former home of famed Cuban boxer Sugar Ramos and it does indeed feel like stepping into someone's front yard. Floral and Mexican artisan decor give it a cozy vibe as you sit under what is essentially a plastic roof in a space that once probably served as a makeshift garage. **Known for:** home-cooked Mexican breakfasts and lunches; vegetarian chile relleno; quiet and relaxed outdoor dining. *Average main: 100 MP* ⊠ *Calle Cedro 180, Santa María la Ribera* 🕾 *55/4341– 0192* ⊕ *www.facebook.com/patiomari- arestaurante* ⊙ *Closed Sun.* ▭ *No credit cards.*

Pollos Ray

$$ | Mexican. One thing you can always count on in Mexico City, and Mexico for that matter, is excellent roasted chicken. While popular with locals, the dish is often overlooked by foreigners in favor of flashy tacos, but you should visit this small, sidewalk eatery and try its delicious marinated chicken; there are also grilled vegetables and salsas to make your own tacos. **Known for:** local favorite; affordable chicken dishes; variety of salsas. *Average main: 150 MP* ⊠ *Manuel Carpio 158, Santa María la Ribera* ☎ *55/5640-5648* ⊕ *www.pollosray. com* Ⓜ *San Cosme.*

Restaurante Versalles

$ | Mexican. Featuring an ample dining area with an open kitchen, this is a breakfast and lunch specialty place in the tradition of Mexican comida corrida, a three-course meal that involves soup, rice or spaghetti, and a main course (a type of stew or grilled meat and tortillas). Expect dishes here to be homemade, affordable, and to arrive fast. **Known for:** molletes, a popular breakfast consisting of bread, bean spread, pico de gallo, and cheese; excellent chilaquiles; arrachera, flat-pounded marinated steak. *Average main: 75 MP* ⊠ *Calle Dr. Enrique Gonzalez Martinez 101, Santa María la Ribera* ☎ *55/6830-8826* ⊘ *No dinner* ⊟ *No credit cards* Ⓜ *Buenavista.*

San Cósmico

$$ | International. With sushi, tacos, and tarot readings, this chef-driven restaurant adds more variety to San Rafael's food scene. In addition to the eclectic culinary offerings, it's a space that also serves as a fresh vegetable market and art space (with art and Mexican-made jewelry for sale), which nicely complement the psychedelic artwork that adorns the small, deli-style space. **Known for:** chilaquiles with cochinita pibíl; funky, art-heavy atmosphere; weekly tarot card readings on Thursday and monthly

tarot classes. *Average main: 150 MP* ⊠ *Sadi Carnot 41, San Rafael* ☎ *55/7158-0242* ⊕ *www.facebook. com/Sancosmicosanrafael* ⊘ *Closed Sun.* ⊟ *No credit cards* Ⓜ *Revolución.*

 Bars and Nightlife

Don Fer's

More of a bar than a restaurant, it effectively functions as both. With live music on the weekends, it also has an open dance floor and a karaoke hall, depending on the night. The crowd is mostly locals and regulars, but it has a welcoming vibe to strangers as well. If you're hungry, try the flautas, beer specials, and *tacos de cochinita* (seasoned pork). ⊠ *Calle Sabino 245, Santa María la Ribera* ☎ *55/6363-2507.*

La Malquerida

Specializing in pulque, this is a traditional Mexico City type of pulquería. There's no bells or whistles here, just a nice variety of pulques (natural and flavored) to sample alongside other cocktails and beer. Its swinging doors open to a modest space, a clear locals' favorite. ⊠ *Jaime Torres Bodet 117, Santa María la Ribera* ☎ *55/1270-4119* Ⓜ *Buenavista.*

★ La Polar

This lively cantina is known for its barriga and mariachi performances as well as roving Norteño and cumbia bands that perform in the massive, two-story space under blinding lights. Since opening in 1934, La Polar has earned its status as a tradition in the San Rafael area and as one of the most beloved gathering spaces in the whole city. ✉ *Calle Guillermo Prieto 129, San Rafael* ☎ *55/5546–5066* Ⓜ *San Cosme, Normal.*

 Performing Arts

Teatro San Rafael
From cabarets and comedies to dramas and monologues, Teatro San Rafael (part of the greater Teatro Manolo Fabregas theater company) is one of the most beloved spots in the city to catch local talent onstage. An intimate theater space, it also offers acting classes and a variety of shows each weekend, and some during the week. ✉ *Virginia Fábregas No. 40, Santa María la Ribera* ☎ *55/5592–2142* ⊕ *www. manolofabregas.com.mx/teatro-san-rafael.html* Ⓜ *San Cosme.*

Polanco and Bosque de Chapultepec

GO FOR

Luxury shopping

Top museums

Fine dining

POLANCO

SANTA MARÍA LA RIBERA

SAN RAFAEL

ALAMEDA CENTRAL

CENTRO HISTÓRICO

JUÁREZ AND ANZURES

BOSQUE DE CHAPULTEPEC

ROMA

CONDESA

BENITO JUÁREZ

SAN ÁNGEL

COYOACÁN

Sightseeing ★★★★☆ | Shopping ★★★★☆ | Dining ★★★★★ | Nightlife ★★★☆☆

A neighborhood known primarily for its high-rise business hotels and fine-dining restaurants, Polanco offers a central location in the city along with a few key sights like the stupendous main branch of the Museo Soumaya. The area developed as an escape from the crowded city center for Mexico City's upper-middle class in the mid-20th century, rapidly urbanizing in the aftermath of the 1985 earthquake. Today, real estate in Polanco is some of the most expensive in the city.—*by Molly McLaughlin*

Polanco's main thoroughfare, Avenida Presidente Masaryk, is lined with upscale stores including Louis Vuitton, Gucci, and Tiffany & Co., as well as boutiques stocking local labels. In between Avenida Masaryk and Parque Lincoln, the Polanquito district is packed with restaurants and cafés. To the south, Polanco is bordered by Bosque de Chapultepec, named for the *chapu-lines* (grasshoppers) that populated it long ago. Chapultepec is the city's largest park, a great green refuge from concrete, traffic, and dust. It's also home to a castle, a lake, and five world-renowned museums.

You can easily spend an hour at each Bosque de Chapultepec museum, with the exception of the Museo Nacional de Antropología, which is huge compared to its sister institutions. There you can have a quick go-through in two hours, but to appreciate the fine exhibits, anywhere from a half day to a full day is more appropriate. Tuesday through Friday are good days to visit the museums and stroll around the park. On Sunday and on Mexican holidays they're often packed with families, and if you get to the Museo Nacional de Antropología after 10 am on a Sunday, you can expect to spend considerable time waiting. If you have time to visit only one of Bosque de Chapultepec's museums, make it the Museo Nacional de Antropología.

Bosque de Chapultepec

◉ Sights

Alberto Misrachi Gallery

This gallery in the lobby of the Hyatt Regency Mexico City is heavy on contemporary painting, with a smattering of sculptures by Mexican artists, many of them well-known. Some international artists are also represented. There is another branch of the gallery in the Santa Fe neighborhood. ✉ *Hyatt Regency Mexico City, Campos Elíseos 204, Polanco* ☎ *55/5281–5121* ⊕ *en.galeri-amisrachi.com* Ⓜ *Auditorio.*

★ Bosque de Chapultepec

This 1,600-acre green space, literally translated as Chapultepec Forest, draws hordes of families on weekend outings, along with cyclists, joggers, and horseback riders into its three sections, which are divided from east to west by major roads. The first section is the oldest and the most frequented, as it is closest to the city center and home to many museums and other attractions. The second section is much quieter, with plenty of space for recreational activities, while the third section is largely undeveloped and generally functions as an ecological reserve.

At the park's principal entrance, the *Monumento a los Niños Héroes* (Monument to the Boy Heroes) commemorates the young cadets who, it is said, wrapped themselves in the Mexican flag and jumped to their deaths rather than surrender during the U.S. invasion of 1847. To Mexicans, that war is still a troubling symbol of their neighbor's aggression: it cost Mexico almost half its territory—the present states of Texas, California, Arizona, New Mexico, and Nevada.

Other sights in the first section of Bosque de Chapultepec include a castle, three small boating lakes, a botanical garden, and the Casa

GETTING HERE

Polanco is notoriously hard to reach by public transport, with only one Metro stop serving the central section of the neighborhood (Auditorio Metro station and the Campo Marte Metrobus station also offer some coverage on its southern border). Ride-share apps like Uber, Beat, or Didi will likely be an easier choice, although some attractions can be reached on foot from Metro Polanco. For shorter distances, there are Ecobici stations nearby, as well as electric scooters that can be hired using an app. The Bosque de Chapultepec is similarly tricky to navigate, with three Metro stations dotted around its border. Get off at Metro Chapultepec for the castle and the Museo de Arte Moderno and the Auditorio station for the Museo Nacional de Antropología and Museo Tamayo. All museums are a 10- to 20-minute walk from the Metro stations.

del Lago cultural center. You'll also find Los Pinos, the ex-residential palace of the president of Mexico, which is now open to the public for the first time thanks to Mexico's current president, Andrés Manuel López Obrador. ⊠ *Bosque de Chapultepec* ⊕ *data.sedema. cdmx.gob.mx/bosquedechapultepec* 🖾 *Free* Ⓜ *Chapultepec, Auditorio, Constituyentes.*

★ Castillo de Chapultepec

The castle on Cerro del Chapulín (Grasshopper Hill) within Bosque de Chapultepec has borne witness to all the turbulence and grandeur of Mexican history. In its earliest form it was an Aztec palace, where the Mexica made one of their last stands against the Spaniards. Later it was a Spanish hermitage, gunpowder plant, and military college. French emperor Maximilian used the castle, parts of which date from 1783, as his residence, and his example was followed by various presidents from 1872 to 1940, when Lázaro Cárdenas decreed that it be turned into the Museo Nacional de Historia.

Displays on the museum's ground floor cover Mexican history from the conquest to the revolution. The bathroom, bedroom, tea salon, and gardens were used by Maximilian and his wife, Carlotta, in the 1860s. The ground floor also contains works by 20th-century muralists O'Gorman, Orozco, and Siqueiros, and the upper floor is devoted to temporary exhibitions, Porfirio Díaz's malachite vases, and religious art. From the garden and terrace, visitors can enjoy sweeping views of the city skyline. ⊠ Bosque de Chapultepec, Section 1, Bosque de Chapultepec ☎ 55/5256–5464 ⊕ mnh.inah.gob.mx ⊠ MX$75 ☉ Closed Mon. Ⓜ Chapultepec.

El Papalote, Museo del Niño

Six themed sections compose this excellent interactive children's discovery museum: My Body, Living Mexico, My Home and Family, My City, the Ideas Laboratory, and the Little Ones Zone, all together comprising more than 200 exhibits. There are also workshops, an

WORTH A TRIP

Bosque de Chapultepec is divided into three sections from east to west, with most of the park's attractions concentrated in the first, easternmost section. However, if you're looking for solitude or to enjoy some of the park's lesser-known wonders, consider stopping by the second section in the center of the park. This part is pet-friendly and home to the Papalote Museo del Niño, a great science, technology, and art museum for kids. At the Museo Jardín del Agua, a tribute to the city's water system, you can see murals and an impressive fountain created by Diego Rivera.

IMAX theater (note that tickets are discounted if purchased with museum tickets), a store, and a restaurant. Although exhibits are in Spanish, there are some English-speaking staff on hand. ⊠ Av. Constituyentes 268, Section 2, Bosque de Chapultepec ☎ 55/5237–1781 ⊕ www.papalote.org.mx ⊠ MX$199 Ⓜ Constituyentes.

Museo de Arte Moderno

The Modern Art Museum's permanent collection has many important examples of 20th-century Mexican art, including works by Mexican school painters like Frida Kahlo—her Las dos Fridas is possibly the most famous work in the collection—Diego Rivera, José Clemente Orozco, David Alfaro Siqueiros, and Olga Costa. There are also pieces by surrealists Remedios Varo and Leonora Carrington. ⊠ Bosque de

Chapultepec, Paseo de la Reforma,
Section 1, Bosque de Chapultepec
☎ 55/8647–5530 ⊕ mam.inba.gob.mx
💳 MX$70; free Sun. ⊘ Closed Mon.
Ⓜ Chapultepec.

Museo Jardín del Agua

Located in Chapultepec's second
section, this small museum
includes a fountain created by Diego
Rivera and the Cárcamo de Dolores,
part of Mexico City's hydraulic
system. The Cárcamo de Dolores
was designed by architect Ricardo
Rivas and built in 1951 to commemorate the completion of the Sistema
Lerma, an integral part of Mexico
City's water infrastructure. Inside,
you'll find an impressive mural, also
by Rivera, called El Agua, Origen
de la Vida (Water, Origin of Life).
The fountain is one of the park's
most interesting public art works,
depicting the formidable Tláloc,
the Aztec god of rain, in mosaic.
✉ Bosque de Chapultepec, Av. Rodolfo
Neri Vela, Bosque de Chapultepec
☎ 55/5515–0739 ⊕ www.chapultepec.
org.mx/actividad/jardin-del-agua-
museum 💳 MX$28, includes entry to
Museo de Historia Natural ⊘ Closed
Mon. Ⓜ Constituyentes.

★ Museo Nacional de Antropología

Architect Pedro Ramírez Vázquez's
outstanding design provides the
proper home for one of the finest
archaeological collections in the
world. Each salon on the museum's
two floors displays artifacts from
a particular geographic region or
culture. The collection is so extensive that you could easily spend a
day here, and even that might be
barely adequate.

The 12 ground-floor rooms treat
pre-Hispanic cultures by region,
in the Sala Teotihuacána, Sala
Tolteca, Sala Oaxaca (Zapotec
and Mixtec peoples), and so on.
Objects both precious and pedestrian, including statuary, jewelry,
weapons, figurines, and pottery,
evoke the intriguing, complex, and
frequently warring civilizations
that peopled Mesoamerica for the
3,000 years preceding the Spanish
invasion. Other highlights include a
copy of the Aztec ruler Moctezuma's
feathered headdress (the original
is now in Vienna); a stela from Tula,
near Mexico City; massive Olmec
heads from Veracruz; and vivid
reproductions of Mayan murals in
a reconstructed temple. Be sure to
see the magnificent reconstruction
of the tomb of 7th-century Mayan
ruler Pakal, which was discovered
in the ruins of Palenque. The nine
rooms on the upper floor contain
faithful ethnographic displays of
current indigenous peoples, using
maps, photographs, household
objects, folk art, clothing, and religious articles.

Explanatory labels have been
updated throughout, some with
English translations, and free tours
are available at set times from
Tuesday through Saturday, with a
prior reservation. You can reserve a
special tour (minimum five people)
with an English-speaking guide by
contacting the museum two weeks
in advance. Otherwise, opt for an

English audio guide or the English-language museum guide for sale in the bookshop. ⊠ *Basque de Chapultepec, Paseo de la Reforma at Calle Gandhi, Bosque de Chapultepec* ☎ *55/5553-6266* ⊕ *www.mna.inah. gob.mx* ▧ *MX$75* ⊘ *Closed Mon.* Ⓜ *Auditorio.*

Museo Tamayo Arte Contemporáneo

Within its modernist shell, the sleek Rufino Tamayo Contemporary Art Museum contains paintings by noted Mexican artist Rufino Tamayo as well as temporary exhibitions of international contemporary art. The selections from Tamayo's personal collection, which he donated to the Mexican people, form the basis for the museum's permanent collection and demonstrate his unerring eye for great art; he owned works by Picasso, Joan Miró, René Magritte, Francis Bacon, and Henry Moore. Guided tours (MX$140) in English are available if booked in advance. ⊠ *Bosque de Chapultepec, Paseo de la Reforma at Calle Gandhi, Bosque de Chapultepec* ☎ *55/4122-8200* ⊕ *www. museotamayo.org* ▧ *MX$70; free Sun.* ⊘ *Closed Mon.* Ⓜ *Chapultepec.*

Oscar Román Gallery

Works—mostly paintings with a contemporary edge—by Mexican artists pack this large gallery. Downstairs, the main gallery exhibits a different artist each month (including the likes of José Antonio Farrera, Francesca Dalla Benetta, and Carlos Marín) while an upstairs gallery holds the permanent collection. ⊠ *Julio Verne 14,*

Polanco ☎ *55/5280-0436* ⊕ *www. galeriaoscarroman.mx* ⊘ *Closed Sun.* Ⓜ *Campo Marte.*

Zoológico de Chapultepec

In the early 16th century, Mexico City's zoo in Chapultepec housed a small private collection of animals belonging to Moctezuma II; it became quasi-public when he allowed favored subjects to visit it. The current zoo opened in the 1920s, and has the usual suspects, as well as some superstar pandas. A gift from China, the original pair—Pepe and Ying Ying—produced the world's first panda cub born in captivity (much to competitive China's chagrin). Chapultepec is also home to a couple of California condors plus hippopotamus, giraffes, and kangaroos. The zoo includes the Moctezuma Aviary and is surrounded by a miniature train depot, botanical gardens, and two small lakes. You'll find the entrance on Paseo de la Reforma, across from the Museo Nacional de Antropología. ⊠ *Bosque de Chapultepec, Calz. Chivatito, Bosque de Chapultepec* ☎ *55/5553-6263* ⊕ *data.sedema.cdmx.gob.mx/zoo_ chapultepec* ▧ *Free* ⊘ *Closed Mon.* Ⓜ *Auditorio.*

 Shopping

Sergio Bustamante

The renowned artist's wild sculpture and jewelry are sold at this store and gallery within the Hotel InterContinental Presidente. ⊠ *Hotel InterContinental Presidente, Campos*

Elíseos 218, Polanco ☎ *55/5280–1605* ⊕ *www.coleccionsergiobustamante. com.mx* Ⓜ *Auditorio.*

☕ Coffee and Quick Bites

Amado
$$ | Bakery. Inside the Hyatt Regency Mexico City, one of the city's best *pastelerías* will satisfy even the most discerning sweet tooth. Here European-style chocolate tarts sit alongside all classic *pan dulce*as well as a selection of sweets, salads, and sandwiches.
Known for: elegant setting; experimental flavor combinations; magnificent cakes. *Average main: 180 MP* ⊠ *Hyatt Regency, Campos Elíseos 204, Polanco* ☎ *55/5083–1234* Ⓜ *Auditorio.*

🍴 Dining

Au Pied de Cochon
$$$ | French. Open around the clock inside the Hotel Presidente InterContinental, this fashionable bistro continues to seduce well-heeled chilangos with high-end French classics. The oysters are flown in from France as well as Baja California; the roasted leg of pork with béarnaise sauce is the signature dish; green-apple sorbet with Calvados is a delicate finish.
Known for: late-night atmosphere; extensive wine list; impressive breakfast menu. *Average main: 380 MP* ⊠ *Campos Elíseos 218, Polanco* ☎ *55/5327–7756* ⊕ *www.aupieddecochon.rest* Ⓜ *Auditorio.*

Chapulín
$$ | Mexican. Inside the Hotel Presidente InterContinental, chef Josefina López Mendez elevates traditional Mexican ingredients like *huitlacoche,* a type of fungus that grows on corn, and *chapulines,* or grasshoppers. If you visit for breakfast, order the blue corn chilaquiles for a nourishing start to the day.
Known for: leafy terrace seating; artistic presentation; authentic recipes. *Average main: 250 MP* ⊠ *Hotel Presidente InterContinental, Campos Elíseos 218, Polanco* ☎ *55/5327–7789* ⊕ *www.chapulin.rest* Ⓜ *Auditorio.*

★ El Bajío
$$ | Mexican. Carmen "Titita" Ramírez—a culinary expert who has been featured in various U.S. food magazines—has turned El Bajío into a true icon of traditional Mexican cuisine, with 19 locations throughout the city (the Polanco branch is likely to be most accessible to visitors). The *empanadas de plátano rellenas de frijol* (plantain turnovers filled with beans) are popular, as are the *tortas de huauzontles,* fritters of a Mexican green.
Known for: good value; traditional recipes; family-friendly atmosphere. *Average main: 210 MP* ⊠ *Alejandro Dumas 7, Polanco* ☎ *55/5281–8245* ⊕ *www.restauranteelbajio.com.mx* Ⓜ *Auditorio.*

El Mirador de Chapultepec
$$ | Mexican. Set in a handsome old building on a sliver of city blocks wedged between Parque Chapultepec and the Circuito

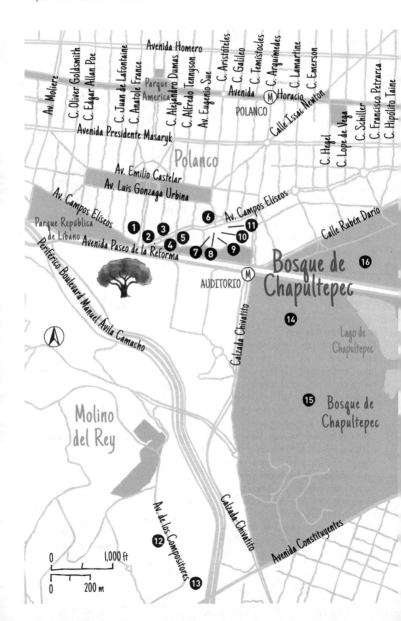

Bicentenario freeway (you may find it easier to Uber than walk here), El Mirador is a venerable old cantina that's been drawing a crowd of regulars since Porfirio Díaz was in office—1904 to be exact. In a dining room of paneled walls and white napery, well-dressed waiters whisk about with plates of pork tongue stewed in a rich chipotle-tomato sauce and tribilín, a flavorful dish of raw beef, fish, and shrimp marinated ceviche-style in olive oil, lime, onions, and roasted chiles. **Known for:** people-watching in the colorful side bar; slightly formal, clubby ambience; old-school traditional Mexican favorite. *Average main: 210 MP ⊠ Av. Chapultepec 606, La Condesa ☎ 55/5286-2161 ⊕ www. cantinaelmirador.com ⊗ No dinner weekends Ⓜ Chapultepec.*

Makoto

$$$$ | Japanese. With restaurants in Miami, Panama, and now Mexico City, Japanese chef Makoto Okuwa brings his energizing point of view to Mexico's rich culinary heritage. The dishes are beautifully presented; main dishes like the black cod miso and short rib maki offer a complex blend of flavors. **Known for:** edomae-style sushi; fresh local seafood; trendy interior. *Average main: 500 MP ⊠ Campos Elíseos 295, Polanco ☎ 55/5281-5686 ⊕ www. makoto-restaurant.com Ⓜ Auditorio.*

🍸 Bars and Nightlife

Karisma

This welcoming cantina, established in 1976, is an old-school hold-out in the neighborhood, with a traditional Mexican food menu, outdoor seating, and wine, beer, and spirits on offer. The prices are reasonable, considering the location near some of Polanco's top hotels; English menus are available. *⊠ Campo Elíseos 219, Polanco ☎ 55/5280-1872 ⊕ www.facebook.com/karismacantina Ⓜ Campo Marte.*

La No. 20

Part of a national chain, La No. 20 is an upscale cantina with slick decor and high-end mixology service. Mariachi bands roam the bar, while señores and young professionals dine on satisfying (if pricey) old-school Mexican cuisine. Try to nab a table on the terrace for the full experience. *⊠ Andrés Bello 10, Polanco ☎ 55/5281-3524 ⊕ www. cantina20.com Ⓜ Auditorio.*

Living Room Bar

At the W Hotel, Living Room is a lounge-style bar packed with intriguing design touches and creative cocktails. Living Room has a more happening ambience than your average hotel bar, thanks to resident DJs that spin starting at 10 pm, Wednesday through Saturday. *⊠ W Mexico City, Campos Elíseos 252, Polanco ☎ 55/9138-1800 ⊕ www. marriott.com/hotels/travel/mexwm-w-mexico-city Ⓜ Auditorio.*

Performing Arts

Danza de los Voladores
The mind-blowing Mesoamerican dance, the Danza de los Voladores, is performed outside the Museo Nacional de Antropología and looks more like skydiving. Four men are tied by their feet to a long pole which they then jump off, weaving through the air to the beat played by the Caporal standing on top. Although this fertility ritual is performed by several ethnic groups, it is often associated with the city of Papantla in Veracruz. Make sure to leave a donation if you enjoyed the show, which is performed almost continuously during museum hours every day except Monday. ⊠ *Grutas 770, Bosque de Chapultepec* ✛ *Outside Museo Nacional de Antropología* Ⓜ *Auditorio.*

Polanco

◉ Sights

Acuario Inbursa
This Mexico City attraction has been a hit since it opened, attracting long lines of people eager to see the largest aquarium in the country. A visit to the site starts four stories underground, at the "bottom of the ocean," and moves upward toward the surface. Thousands of species of fish, sharks, rays, eels, jellyfish, and more swim among the ruins of a sunken ship, vibrantly colored coral, and gracefully swaying kelp, all dramatically lit in huge tanks. The "rain forest" exhibit is home to reptiles and amphibians such as Mexico's endangered, curious-looking ajolote salamander. ⊠ *Av. Miguel de Cervantes Saavedra 386, Polanco* ☎ *55/5395–4586* ⊕ *www.acuarioinbursa.com.mx* 🎟 *MX$215* Ⓜ *San Joaquín.*

Galería Alfredo Ginocchio
Founded in 1988 by Alfredo Ginocchio as Praxis Mexico, this now-eponymous gallery promotes distinguished work from Mexico and elsewhere in Latin America. Its relatively small but interesting collection features a different artist every couple of months, alongside a variety of sculptures and paintings by familiar names including Santiago Carbonell and Alberto Aragón. ⊠ *Arquímedes 175, Polanco* ☎ *55/5254–8813* ⊕ *www.ginocchiogaleria.com* 🕙 *Closed Sun.* Ⓜ *Polanco.*

Juan Martín Gallery
This gallery opened in 1961 and made it's name representing the artists of the 1960s avant-garde "Ruptura" movement. In the 1970s it was an important champion of photography as fine art, representing such Mexican legends as Manuel Álvarez Bravo and Graciela Iturbide. Today it focuses on younger, mostly abstract artists, and occasionally exhibits established artists from around the globe. ⊠ *Dickens 33–B, Polanco* ☎ *55/5280–0277* ⊕ *www.galeriajuanmartin.com* 🕙 *Closed Sun.* Ⓜ *Campo Marte.*

Museo Jumex
Founded by an heir to the Jumex juice fortune, this contemporary art museum is located just across

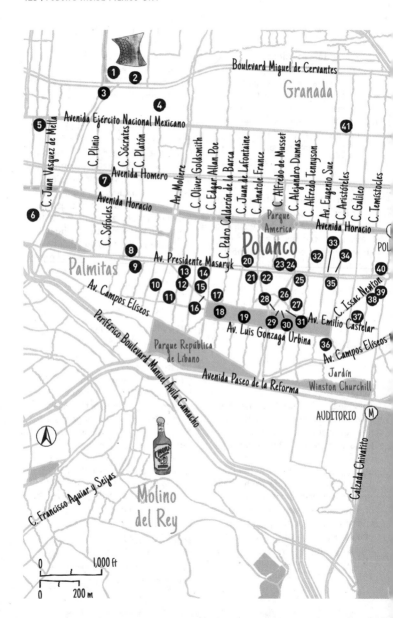

the way from the Museo Soumaya, and though the subdued travertine building that houses it is not as eye-popping as Carlos Slim's shiny silver cloud next door, the exhibition design of the Jumex is arguably superior. Shows draw from the museum's 2,700-strong collection, which includes boldfaced names like Jeff Koons, Damien Hirst, and Andy Warhol, as well as temporary exhibitions of work by international contemporary artists. There's also an on-site café and store. ⊠ *Blvd. Miguel de Cervantes Saavedra 303, Polanco* ☎ *55/5395–2615* ⊕ *www. fundacionjumex.org* ✉ *MX$50; free Sun.* ⊘ *Closed Mon.* Ⓜ *San Joaquin or Polanco.*

★ **Museo Soumaya Plaza Carso**
One of Mexico City's most well-known architectural icons, Museo Soumaya houses the valuable art collection of billionaire philanthropist Carlos Slim, as well as visiting exhibitions. The museum's Plaza Carso branch sits just beyond the edge of Polanco and contains sculptures by Rodin and Dalí and paintings from old masters to modernists and impressionists, including works from the likes of Leonardo da Vinci, El Greco, Tintoretto, Monet, and Picasso. But there are also many Mexican artists represented, including Diego Rivera. Each floor of the museum has a different layout, and you walk along curving ramps (not unlike those in the Guggenheim Museum in New York City) to get from one floor to another. Designed by the Mexican architect Fernando Romero, Slim's son-in-law, the $70 million building has a shape some have likened to a silver cloud, and is covered by thousands of hexagonal aluminum tiles. ⊠ *Blvd. Miguel de Cervantes Saavedra 303, Polanco* ⊕ *www.museosoumaya.org* ✉ *Free* Ⓜ *Polanco, San Joaquín.*

Parque Lincoln
This park offers a welcome respite in the center of Polanco, surrounded by buzzing shops and restaurants. It is named for its statue of Abraham Lincoln (there's also one of Martin Luther King Jr.), but its clock tower is equally recognizable as the logo for the neighborhood's Metro station. There's a small lake, a children's playground, an aviary, and the Teatro Ángela Peralta, an open-air theater. On Saturday, Parque Lincoln hosts Polanco's weekly *tianguis*, or local market. ⊠ *Emilio Castelar 163, Polanco* Ⓜ *Polanco.*

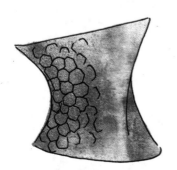

Shopping

Antara Polanco

One of only a few outdoor malls in the city, Antara Polanco has a collection of upscale stores that includes Carolina Herrera, Zara, Hugo Boss, and Tommy Hilfiger as well as branches of several luxury stores that are also found along the neighborhood's ritzy Avenida Presidente Masaryk; there are plenty of dining options, too. ⊠ *Ejército Nacional 843, Polanco* ☏ *55/4593–8870* ⊕ *www.antara.com. mx* Ⓜ *San Joaquín.*

Ikal

A large, upmarket concept store on Masaryk Avenue, Ikal aims to celebrate local independent labels. From luxury fashion and footwear to hard-to-find homewares and jewelry, the store curates a contemporary feel while maintaining a distinctly Mexican perspective. ⊠ *Av. Presidente Masaryk 340A, Polanco* ☏ *55/8436–9969* ⊕ *www.instagram. com/ikalstore* Ⓜ *Polanco.*

Lago DF

This sophisticated Latin American design store offers a collection of pieces from Peru, Colombia, Ecuador, Argentina, Brazil, and Mexico. Here you'll find leather goods, ceramics, clothing, and accessories from emerging and established brands including Zii Ropa, Colectivo 1050 Grados, Carla Fernandez, and Lorena Pestana. The two-story space itself is similarly impressive, with six huge windows facing out onto the street and creative product displays inside. ⊠ *Av. Presidente Masaryk 310, Polanco* ☏ *55/7261–9343* ⊕ *www. lagodf.com* Ⓜ *Polanco.*

Librería Porrúa

This branch of the popular Mexican bookseller is conveniently located in Bosque de Chapultepec and includes an open-air café. Although the selection of English books is limited, the store is beautifully designed with a panorama of the surrounding greenery and the lake. ⊠ *Bosque de Chapultepec, Paseo de la Reforma, Bosque de Chapultepec* ⊹ *Across from Museo Nacional de Antropología* ☏ *55/5212–2242* ⊕ *www. porrua.mx* Ⓜ *Chapultepec.*

★ Onora

In collaboration with artisans all over Mexico, Onora sells handmade homewares and textiles that you might recognize from the city's chicest boutique hotels. The store was founded in 2014, with a minimalist yet luxurious philosophy and a commitment to elevating fine Mexican design. You won't find bright colored *blusas* or kitschy jewelry here, instead neutral colors let the intricate handicrafts speak for themselves. ⊠ *Lope de Vega 330, Polanco* ☏ *55/5203–0938* ⊕ *www. onoracasa.com* Ⓜ *Polanco.*

Raquel Orozco

Known for her feminine color palette and extravagant silhouettes, Raquel Orozco is part of the new guard of Mexican fashion designers. This Polanco boutique is her flagship store, stocked with a full range of clothing and accessories. Pieces can also be found at the Palacio de Hierro department stores in Polanco and Santa Fe and at a second boutique in Pedregal. ⊠ *Emilio Castelar 227–B, Polanco* ☎ *55/5280–5081* ⊕ *www.raquelorozco. com* Ⓜ *Polanco, Campo Marte.*

Sandra Weil

Peruvian designer Sandra Weil opened this flagship Mexico City boutique in 2012. Combining traditional craftsmanship with high-quality fabrics, including pima cotton, alpaca wool, and silk, her bold designs have become a go-to for the capital's trendsetters. Weil's dresses and separates can be found at stores throughout Mexico, as well as in Miami and Houston, but this one has the most extensive collection. ⊠ *Emilio Castelar 185, Polanco* ☎ *55/5280–7597* ⊕ *www.sandraweil. com* Ⓜ *Polanco or Campo Marte.*

★ Tane

This store is a mine of perhaps the best silverwork in Mexico—jewelry, flatware, candelabras, museum-quality reproductions of archaeological finds, and bold designs by young Mexican silversmiths. The Masaryk shop is one of several in the city, including locations in the Four Seasons and Presidente InterContinental hotels and in the upscale Centro Santa Fe. Outside this Polanco branch, you'll find an Instagram-famous bright pink wall with a neon sign that sums up most visitors' sentiments: *Mexico mi amor.* ⊠ *Av. Presidente Masaryk 430,*

Polanco ☎ *55/5282–6200* ⊕ *www.tane. com.mx* Ⓜ *Polanco, Campo Marte.*

🍵 Coffee and Quick Bites

★ Caffe Biscottino

$ | Café. This cozy café on the corner of Parque Lincoln pours the best espresso in the neighborhood, with a simple yet satsifying breakfast menu and homemade pastries (including vegan, gluten-free, and kosher options). The coffee is sourced from Chachaxtla in Veracruz, and always freshly roasted. **Known for:** excellent sourdough bread; specialized coffee; blue corn scones. *Average main: 125 MP* ⊠ *Luis G. Urbina 4, Polanco* ☎ *55/5280–2155* ⊘ *Closed Sat.* Ⓜ *Auditorio.*

★ El Turix

$ | Mexican. Polanco's most beloved taquería serves up tacos, tortas, and *panuchos* of *cochinita pibíl*, the Yucatecan specialty of achiote-marinated pork. People from all walks of life, from hipsters to construction workers to businesswomen, line up throughout the day for a quick fix, topped with the habanero salsa and pickled red onion (and Montejo beer) typical of the Yucatán. **Known for:** authentic atmosphere; no-nonsense

FINE DINING IN MEXICO CITY

Polanco has been the hub of Mexico City's fine-dining scene since at least the year 2000, when Enrique Olvera redefined Mexican food with the opening of his beloved restaurant Pujol. Quintonil, Mexico's second entry (after Pujol) on the World's 50 Best Restaurants list, can also be found here, headed up by power couple Alejandra Flores and Jorge Vallejo. While tacos do occasionally feature on these upscale menus, Mexican haute cuisine is varied, modern, playful, and gorgeously plated.

Generally, Polanco's affluent residents tend to favor seafood, steak, and locally sourced greens, and the dress code at these places is often more relaxed than similar establishments in the United States. The neighborhood's fine dining restaurants also buck the nationwide trend of closing in the early evening (after the day's most important meal, lunch), with most staying open until 11 pm or midnight. While Polanco may lack Condesa's youthful cool, its eateries deliver on taste, sophistication, and quality every time.

service; best cochinita pibíl in the neighborhood. *Average main: 100 MP* ⊠ *Emilio Castelar 212, Polanco* ☎ *55/5280–6449* Ⓜ *Polanco, Campo Marte.*

Joselo
$ | Café. The coffee at Joselo is great, as is the location, in the center of stylish Polanquito. The sandwiches and sweets are tasty, but you'll be lucky if you snag an outdoor table during meal times, so you may prefer to get your caffeine fix to go and enjoy it across the road in Parque Lincoln. **Known for:** consistently delicious espresso; outdoor seating; late hours for a café. *Average main: 100 MP* ⊠ *Emilio Castelar 107, Polanco* ☎ *55/5281–0849* ⊕ *www.facebook.com/joselocafe* Ⓜ *Auditorio.*

Klein's
$$ | Mexican Fusion. This popular deli has been serving up affordable Mexican-Jewish fusion in Polanco since 1962. You'll find hotcakes, waffles, and chili dogs on the menu alongside chilaquiles and enchiladas, all topped with a large range of house-made salsas. **Known for:** family atmosphere; diner classics; extensive menu. *Average main: 150 MP* ⊠ *Av. Presidente Masaryk 360B, Polanco* ☎ *55/ 5281–0862* ⊕ *www. kleins.mx* Ⓜ *Polanco.*

Los Villanos Taquería
$ | Mexican. Condesa and Roma may be full of hipster taquerías, but in sophisticated Polanco they are surprisingly few and far between. Los VIllanos fills that niche, serving up classic al pastor tacos alongside more unusual versions like *picaña* (sirloin cap). **Known for:** taco deals; fun atmosphere; unique flavors. *Average main: 100 MP* ⊠ *Horacio 400,*

Polanco ☏ *55/8848–5582* ⊘ *No dinner Sun.* Ⓜ *Polanco.*

Maison Belen

$$ | French Fusion. A colorful French-Mexican fusion café, Maison Belen offers pastries and hearty breakfasts. The space itself is small, but the outdoor seating provides an excellent opportunity for people-watching over a pain au chocolat. **Known for:** glorious eggs Benedict; freshly baked bread; warm decor. *Average main: 250 MP* ⊠ *Galileo 31, Polanco* ☏ *55/5280–3756* Ⓜ *Auditorio.*

Peltre Lonchería

$$ | Mexican. One of seven branches across the city, Peltre is an easy budget option in ritzy Polanco. Like traditional *loncherías*, this modern version has an extensive menu covering everything from chilaquiles negros to sopa Aguascalientes. **Known for:** best pan de muerto relleno (a type of pastry) in the city; contemporary design; great coffee and juices. *Average main: 150 MP* ⊠ *Francisco Petrarca 253, Polanco* ☏ *55/7824–2010* ⊕ *www.bullandtank. com/peltre* Ⓜ *Polanco.*

Signora Mariola

$$ | Mexican. If you find yourself in the north of Polanco (visiting Museo Soumaya, Museo Jumex, or the aquarium), Signora Mariola is the perfect spot for a quick coffee or a casual meal. The croissants and bread are to die for, and the Mexican breakfasts are tasty and light. **Known for:** trendy decor; great weekend brunch; impressive pour-over coffee. *Average*

main: 150 MP ⊠ *Lago Tanganica 75, Polanco* ⊹ *Corner of Ejército Nacional* ☏ *55/8437–0070* Ⓜ *San Joaquín.*

★ Tortas Royalty

$ | Mexican. Chilangos (as Mexico City's residents are often known) are notorious for putting everything in a sandwich, even going as far as to create the carb-heavy *guajolota*, or *torta de tamal*. Convenient, filling, and cheap, tortas are the perfect fuel for a day of sightseeing and Royalty, Polanco's favorite sandwich shop, offers excellent versions of them. **Known for:** freshly baked bread; delicious consomé de pavo (turkey); fast service. *Average main: 50 MP* ⊠ *Horacio 227, Polanco* ☏ *55/5250–2118* Ⓜ *Polanco.*

🍴 Dining

Belifore

$$ | Italian. Quite a few CDMX restaurants do upscale Italian food well, but this romantic, warmly lighted trattoria stands out for serving some of the finest pizzas around. Each thin-crust pie is crisped to perfection in the wood-fired oven on view at the front of the dining room—the pie layered lavishly with burrata and prosciutto is worth the splurge. **Known for:** wood-fired pizzas with premium toppings; extensive Italian wine list; classic Italian desserts. *Average main: 290 MP* ⊠ *Av. Pdte. Masaryk 514, Polanco* ☏ *55/5282–0413* ⊕ *www. belfiore.com.mx* ⊘ *No dinner Sun.* Ⓜ *Auditorio.*

⭑ Blanco Castelar

$$$ | International. The architecture here is just as impressive as the food, with the restaurant housed inside a California colonial-style mansion built in 1940. Diners can choose from an international menu with Mexican flourishes (like the tacos de lechon confit) accompanied by a sour Castelar, the house cocktail. **Known for:** park views; dramatic dishes; trendy crowd. *Average main: 375 MP* ⊠ *Emilio Castelar 163, Polanco* ☎ *55/ 5027-0322* ⊕ *www.blancocastelar.com.mx* Ⓜ *Campo Marte.*

Cabanna

$$ | Mexican. This laid-back seafood eatery brings the beach to Mexico City. Try the fresh taco Gobernador or tostada Punta Mita accompanied by a michelada. **Known for:** fast service; good for groups; Sinaloa-style seafood. *Average main: 150 MP* ⊠ *Av. Presidente Masaryk 134, Polanco* ☎ *55/5545-2225* ⊕ *www.cabanna.com.mx* Ⓜ *Polanco.*

Caldos D'Leo

$ | Mexican. A stalwart of north-western Polanco since 1966, this traditional restaurant offers a taste of home-style Mexican fare. Choose from a menu of hot breakfasts, soups, moles, and enchiladas, then enjoy the efficient service and simple yet satisfying flavors. **Known for:** wholesome chicken soup; long lunches; great value Mexican classics. *Average main: 100 MP* ⊠ *Av. Ejército Nacional 1014 B, Polanco* ☎ *55/5557-6760* ⊕ *www.grupoleos.com.mx* Ⓜ *Polanco.*

Cambalache

$$$$ | Argentine. This beef-lover's dream (with three additional locations in Mexico City, as well as branches in Cancún and Toluca) is popular with everyone from businessmen to young families. Everything is grilled, from the Argentine beef and Australian lamb to the whitefish in a mild chili sauce. **Known for:** generous portions of classic Argentine cuisine; passionate staff; high-quality ingredients. *Average main: 500 MP* ⊠ *Alejandro Dumas 122, Polanco* ☎ *55/5280-2080* ⊕ *www.cambalacherestaurantes.com* Ⓜ *Auditorio.*

⭑ Comedor Jacinta

$$ | Mexican. Inspired by his mother's cooking, chef Edgar Núñez (of Sud777 fame) opened the unpretentious Comedor Jacinta in 2016. Like most *comedores* , Jacinta offers a typical *comida corrida*, or set lunch menu, alongside a fully vegetarian option. **Known for:** regional seafood dishes; homey feel; convenient location. *Average main: 200 MP* ⊠ *Virgilio 40, Polanco* ☎ *55/5086-6965* ⊕ *comedorjacinta.com* Ⓜ *Polanco.*

Dulce Patria

$$$ | Modern Mexican. Don't let the slightly fussy ambience of this dignified eatery inside the exclusive Las Alcobas Hotel mislead you; the cuisine of renowned chef Martha Ortiz is bold, bright, and cleverly presented, each dish a photo-worthy work of art. Ortiz creatively interprets regional Mexican cuisine, from her pork loin swimming in a silky yellow mole sauce with ginger and mango to a simple-sounding quesadilla sampler plate brought to new heights thanks to handmade multicolored tortillas and flavorful fillings like huitlacoche with goat cheese and squash blossoms with pine nuts. **Known for:** playfully presented dishes; refined service; wildly imaginative desserts. *Average main: 375 MP* ⊠ *Las Alcobas, Anatole France 100, Polanco* ☎ *55/3300–3999* ⊕ *www.marthaortiz.mx* ⊗ *No dinner Sun.* Ⓜ *Polanco.*

Emilio

$$$ | European. Emilio is a popular all-day eatery in Polanquito, combining Italian, Mexican, and Spanish influences. The sidewalk seating is matched with a casual menu of imaginative share plates and cocktails (try the tacos *de pato confitado*) while a classic European menu is served on the pleasant terrace upstairs. **Known for:** weekly specials; elevated tacos; park views. *Average main: 400 MP* ⊠ *Emilio Castelar 107, Polanco* ☎ *55/5280–5877* ⊕ *www.emiliorestaurante.com* Ⓜ *Auditorio.*

Farina

$$ | Italian. With a focus on wood-fire pizzas and veggie-packed salads, Farina delivers uncomplicated Italian food. The outdoor terrace makes for a cozy and romantic meal, including a full bar. **Known for:** exquisite tiramisu; friendly vibe; good Italian wine list. *Average main: 200 MP* ⊠ *Av. Isaac Newton 53–1, Polanco* ☎ *55/7825–9921* ⊕ *www.facebook.com/FarinaPolancoF4* Ⓜ *Polanco.*

Garum

$$$ | Mediterranean. Spanish chef Vicente Torres puts together a creative, seasonal menu of Mediterranean-style dishes made with Mexican ingredients. The foie gras and *bacalao negro* (salted cod) are stellar, as are the cocktails. **Known for:** imaginative desserts; understated elegance; locally sourced ingredients. *Average main: 325 MP* ⊠ *Av. Presidente Masaryk 513, Polanco* ☎ *55/5280–2715* ⊕ *garumrestaurante.com* ⊗ *No dinner Sun.* Ⓜ *Campo Marte.*

Hacienda de los Morales

$$$$ | Mexican. Built in the 17th century on the site of a mulberry farm, this hacienda has been transformed into one of Mexico's most elegant dinner spots. The atmosphere outclasses even the food, which consists of both Mexican classics and more experimental dishes that incorporate Spanish and Mediterranean influences. **Known for:** gorgeous colonial architecture; creative flavor combinations; a variety of live music while you dine. *Average main: 500 MP* ⊠ *Juan Vázquez de Mella 525, Polanco* ☎ *55/5283–3055* ⊕ *www.haciendadelosmorales.com* Ⓜ *Campo Marte.*

Ivoire

$$$ | Modern French. The epitome of Polanquito chic, Ivoire brings a touch of France to Mexico. The interior is reminiscent of a Parisian bistro, complete with cane chairs and indoor plants, and the menu features fondue, escargot, and artichokes. **Known for:** delicate

French dishes; Instagram-friendly aesthetic; group-friendly terrace overlooking the park. *Average main: 300 MP* ⊠ *Emilio Castelar 95, Polanco* ☎ *55/5280–0477* ⊕ *www.ivoirepolanco.com* Ⓜ *Polanco.*

La Barra de Fran

$$$ | Spanish. This contemporary Spanish tavern plates up Mexico City's top tapas, alongside paella and other delicacies. The *jamon serrano* is freshly carved and the red wine is full bodied; both are made to be shared. **Known for:** local crowds; imported meats and cheeses; small space so reservations are smart. *Average main: 300 MP* ⊠ *Av. Emilio Castelar 185, Polanco* ☎ *55/5280–6650* ⊕ *www.labarradefran.com* ⊙ *Closed Mon.* Ⓜ *Campo Marte.*

La Buena Barra

$$$$ | Mexican. One of Polanco's most upscale cantinas, La Buena Barra is popular with meat-lovers, thanks to its Monterrey-style steaks and convivial atmosphere. The upstairs terrace offers an impressive panorama of the city skyline. **Known for:** delightfully rich desserts; outstanding service; generous portions. *Average main: 450 MP* ⊠ *Aristóteles 124, Polanco* ☎ *55/5280–6699* ⊕ *www.grupobarra.com* Ⓜ *Polanco.*

Lur

$$$ | Spanish. From the team behind Biko (a Basque restaurant in Polanco that was regularly ranked as one of the world's best but closed in 2017), Lur is a relaxed Spanish restaurant with a sunny terrace overlooking Polanco's main avenue. The menu is simple and inspired, incorporating seasonal ingredients and unexpected textures. **Known for:** home-style cooking; exceptional seafood; worthwhile five-course tasting menu. *Average main: 300 MP* ⊠ *Av. Presidente Masaryk 86, Polanco* ☎ *55/5545–6802* ⊕ *www.restaurantelur.com* ⊙ *No dinner Sun.* Ⓜ *Polanco.*

★ Nativo

$$$ | Modern Mexican. With views of Parque Lincoln, Nativo bills itself a *taller gastronómico* (gastronomic workshop), thanks to a focus on slow food and house-made bread and salsas. The wood fire-grilled octopus is the stand-out, using a traditional cooking technique from the state of Nayarit. **Known for:** innovative tacos; parkside people-watching; dancing and great cocktail menu on weekends. *Average main: 300 MP* ⊠ *Emilio Castelar 135, Polanco* ☎ *55/5280–0023* ⊕ *www.facebook.com/nativopolanco* Ⓜ *Campo Marte.*

Noso

$$$ | Mexican Fusion. Up-and-coming chefs Sandra Fortes and Miguel Hidalgo have been creating nostalgic and beautiful Spanish-Mexican fusion since 2017, with a menu of small shared plates, plus seafood and meat mains. There's also a delectable eight-course tasting menu (with a vegetarian option available). **Known for:** friendly service; show-stopping desserts; striking interior design. *Average main: 350 MP* ⊠ *Av.*

Presidente Masaryk 311, Polanco ☎ *55/5801-0338* ⊕ *www.noso.com.mx* ☾ *Closed Mon.* Ⓜ *Polanco.*

Porfirio's

$$ | Modern Mexican. Named after the Mexican dictator whose 31-year reign sparked the Mexican Revolution, Porfirio's does classic Mexican steak and seafood dishes very well. The service and atmosphere are fittingly dignified during the day, with DJs taking over after dark. **Known for:** extensive wine list; top-notch service; traditional chile relleno. *Average main: 250 MP* ⊠ *Av. Presidente Masaryk 214, Polanco* ☎ *55/5280-1494* ⊕ *www.porfirios. com.mx* Ⓜ *Polanco.*

★ Pujol

$$$$ | Mexican. The internationally acclaimed chef at Pujol, Enrique Olvera, continuously reinvents traditional Mexican dishes and their presentation, and is largely responsible for the country's gastronomic revolution. The dining experience here can be as educational as it is hedonistic, and the two seven-course menus are designed to create a holistic flavor experience. **Known for:** exquisite local flavors; best set menu in town; surprisingly low-key atmosphere for such haute cuisine. *Average main: 2400 MP* ⊠ *Tennyson 133, Polanco* ☎ *55/5545-4111* ⊕ *www.pujol.com.mx* ☾ *Closed Sun.* ☞ *Children under 12 discouraged* Ⓜ *Polanco.*

★ Quintonil

$$$$ | Modern Mexican. Chef-owner Jorge Vallejo cut his teeth at Pujol before opening Quintonil (named after a wild green herb often found in *milpas*, a Mesoamerican crop-growing system) in 2012. Vallejo eschews fussiness to let the ingredients shine: smoked trout from nearby Zitácuaro or a salad of greens and herbs from the floating gardens of Xochimilco. **Known for:** accessible fine dining; thoughtful ingredient pairings; local ingredients, including from rooftop garden. *Average main: 460 MP* ⊠ *Isaac Newton 55, Polanco* ☎ *55/5280-1660* ⊕ *www.quintonil.com* ☾ *Closed Sun.* ☞ *Children under 12 discouraged* Ⓜ *Polanco.*

Royal India

$$ | Indian. Royal India is the real deal: flavorful curries and biryani in a welcoming setting. The tandoor oven delivers mouthwatering chicken appetizers, but vegetarians and vegans will also find plenty of options. **Known for:** authentic spices; crispy chicken pakora; live dance performances last Friday of each month. *Average main: 250 MP* ⊠ *Homero 1500, Local 2, Polanco* ☎ *55/8751-6987* ⊕ *www.royalindia. com.mx* Ⓜ *Campo Marte.*

Sagardi

$$$$ | Basque. Inside a grand old house on Avendia Masaryk, Sagardi serves uncompromising and interesting Basque food. Head chef Iñaki López de Viñaspre is a food anthropologist, spearheading authentic Basque restaurants in seven cities worldwide. **Known for:** Txuleton aged beef steak; rooftop cocktail bar; good value pintxos bar. *Average main: 500 MP ⊠ Av. Presidente Masaryk 183, Polanco* ☎ 55/5250–0881 ⊕ www.sagardi.com.mx Ⓜ *Polanco.*

Thai Gardens
$$ | Thai. This is the best—indeed, one of the only—places in Mexico City for upscale Thai food. The atmosphere is tranquil with a lovely indoor garden, and the menu is reasonably extensive and well executed. **Known for:** hard-to-find Thai dishes; generous tasting menu; Thai fusion cocktails. *Average main: 225 MP ⊠ Moliere 44, Polanco* ☎ 55/6650–4155 ⊕ www.thaigardenspolanco.com ✆ No dinner Sun. Ⓜ *Campo Marte.*

 Bars and Nightlife

Fiebre de Malta
With 36 beers on tap and a knowledgeable staff, Fiebre de Malta is an ideal place to start your Mexican craft beer education. Ask the bartender for a recommendation to match your selection from the pub-style food menu of tacos, wings, and burgers. Another branch can be found in Cuauhtémoc, near the Ángel de la Independencia on Avendida Reforma. ⊠ *Av. Presidente Masaryk 42, Polanco* ☎ 55/5531–6828 ⊕ www.fiebredemalta.com Ⓜ *Polanco.*

Habita
The Habita Hotel rooftop showcases a magnificent view of the city from its hip open-air bar and terrace.

The lounge area and its fireplace is a great place to chill out without catching a chill. Sipping a selection from the range of mezcals on offer will also do the trick. ⊠ *Av. Presidente Masaryk 201, at Lamartine, Polanco* ☎ 55/5282–3100 ⊕ www.hotelhabita.com.

★ Handshake Speakeasy
Inspired by 1920s Chicago, this small speakeasy features black and gold Prohibition-era decor and international guest bartenders that make the bar feel luxurious yet welcoming. Order an Old Fashioned at the bar and settle in for an evening of house beats and good conversation. Reservations can only be made via the bar's Instagram page (@handshake_bar). ⊠ *Av. Presidente Masaryk 393, Polanco* Ⓜ *Polanco.*

★ Jules Basement
This iconic speakeasy kicked off a nationwide trend when it opened its doors in 2012 (actually, a commercial refrigerator door in the kitchen of a nondescript restaurant, to be precise). The well-balanced cocktails are the main focus, enhanced by ultramodern and monochromatic decor and live DJs on Friday and Saturday night. Arrive before 9 pm to beat the lines. ⊠ *Julio Verne 93, Polanco* ☎ 55/5280–1278 ⊕ www.julesbasement.com Ⓜ *Polanco.*

Panic Botanic
This sprawling, neon-lit bar is a favorite of Polanco's young professionals, who drop by for after-work drinks. Later in the night, you'll find

a DJ (reggaetón, of course), experimental cocktails, and a fashionable crowd. ⊠ *Av. Presidente Masaryk 353, Polanco* ☎ *55/4390–4924* ⊕ *www. facebook.com/PanicBotanicMasaryk* Ⓜ *Polanco.*

★ Terraza Fortuna

This spot adds some much-needed fun to Polanco, with colorful cocktails, seafood tacos, and a warm, green interior that goes well with an espresso martini. In the back, a red lightbulb indicates live music is underway in a second part of the venue, a hidden speakeasy called Felicha. To reach this tropical paradise, ask at the We Love Burgers eatery downstairs. ⊠ *Alejandro Dumas 71, Polanco* ☎ *55/2120–4770* Ⓜ *Polanco.*

GO FOR

Trendy dining
and drinking

Grand mansions

Hip shopping

SANTA MARÍA
LA RIBERA

POLANCO

SAN
RAFAEL

ALAMEDA CENTRAL

CENTRO
HISTÓRICO

BOSQUE DE
CHAPULTEPEC

JUÁREZ AND
ANZURES

ROMA

CONDESA

BENITO
JUÁREZ

SAN ÁNGEL

COYOACÁN

Although it contains only a handful of small museums and cultural attractions, Roma has become one of the Mexico City's essential destinations, especially since its rapid gentrification throughout the 2010s. This is the neighborhood where you're most likely to hear the voices of foreigners as you amble about, exploring the area's main draws: shopping, gallery-hopping, dining, and drinking. The neighborhood is divided into Roma Sur and Roma Norte, and most of the action is in the latter district, which is also the much larger of the two (Calle Coahuila is the dividing line). Exceedingly trendy, Roma's rapid rise has led to both newfound respectability and soaring rents, but restaurants and shops here still, by and large, offer better values than comparable establishments in Polanco and other high-end districts in the city.—*by Andrew Collins*

....

Like its western neighbor Condesa, Roma was developed in the early 1900s on a huge tract of land owned previously by two Spanish countesses; the area was turned into an aristocratic enclave of stately homes, many of which still stand. By the 1940s and 1950s, many of the city's wealthiest residents began moving to newer and fancier developments farther west and south. Roma—far more than even Condesa—became better known for its rough-and-tumble cantinas, pool halls, dance clubs, and nightspots of questionable repute. The neighborhood's nadir followed the 1985 earthquake, but the rock-bottom rents of the 1990s and early 2000s—along with an amazing stock of grand beaux-arts and art nouveau mansions—helped spur its transformation into a center of edgy fashion, avant-garde art, innovative dining, and cleverly themed bars catering to a mix of styles, ages, and orientations.

The lower portion of Roma borders Condesa along Avenida Insurgentes Sur. At Calle Guanajuato, however, Roma Norte leaps across Insurgentes and follows a rather meandering border with Condesa for several blocks to the west. In this area, even many locals don't know (and likely don't care) whether they're in Condesa or Roma Norte, and there's little discernible difference between the look and feel of either district. Busy and wide Avenida Chapultepec forms Roma's northern border with Juárez, and similarly busy Avenida Cuauhtémoc separates the neighborhood from Doctores, to the east.

Roma North of Av. Álvaro Obregón

⊙ Sights

Avenida Álvaro Obregón

Roma's main east–west boulevard is wide and tree-lined, with a central promenade that's studded with sculptures and fountains. With dozens of restaurants, bars, cafés, and shops lining either side, Álvaro Obregón is an ideal place to stroll and take in occasional cultural exhibitions and events like classic car shows and public art displays. ⊠ Av. Álvaro Obregón, between Avs. Cuauhtémoc and Sonora, Roma Norte Ⓜ Insurgentes.

Casa Lamm Cultural Center

Inside this imposing early 20th-century mansion and its connected buildings, artists are nurtured and browsers are welcomed to the three exhibition spaces, a library, a bookstore, a wide range of courses, a café, and a swanky restaurant called Nueve Nueve that serves upmarket contemporary Mexican and international cuisine. All of the spaces surround a beautiful courtyard, and the restaurant—set inside a modern glass-walled addition—offers particularly nice views. ⊠ Av. Alvaro Obregón 99, Roma Norte ☎ 55/5525–0019 ⊕ www.casalamm.com.mx ☜ Free Ⓜ Insurgentes.

Fuente de Cibeles

This striking fountain anchors the busy traffic circle in Roma Norte's northwestern quadrant, an exact copy of the neoclassical Plaza de

GETTING HERE

Roma is easily reached by Uber and Metro as well as walkable from the hotels on or near Paseo de la Reforma. Roma consists of two halves: the quieter and more prosaic Roma Sur and the trendier and much larger Roma Norte, which is divided by one of the city's most prominent north–south thoroughfares, Avenida Insurgentes. Two other major streets, Avenida Cuauhtémoc and Avenida Chapultepec, form Roma's eastern and northern borders, respectively. This is generally a safe neighborhood for strolling, but take a little extra care when walking closer to the border with Colonia Doctores. Roma has several metro stations, all on its borders, including the Sevilla, Insurgentes, and Cuauhtémoc stops on the 1 line, the Hospital General stop on the 3 line, and the Centro Médico stop on both the 3 and 9 lines.

Cibeles fountain found in Madrid (which depicts the Roman goddess of fertility, Cybele, in a carriage pulled by lions). The surrounding traffic circle is officially called Plaza Villa de Madrid, although most locals just called it Plaza Cibeles. Six streets intersect here, and there's a lively flea market, Mercado Cibeles, held on weekends on the narrow lane running southeast to Avenida Insurgentes (Calle El Oro). There are a number of prominent restaurants on or within a few steps of the circle, including the famously sceney seafood eatery, Contramar, and branches of the popular coffee-pizza eateries, Cancino and La Ventanita, which have large swaths of sidewalk tables curving around the northwestern arc of the circle. ⊠ Plaza Villa de Madrid, at Av. Oaxaca and Calle de Durango, Roma Norte Ⓜ Insurgentes.

★ Galería OMR

Set within a typical-looking Roma house with an early 20th-century stone facade, Galería OMR has been a leader in the city's contemporary arts scene since it opened in 1983. It contains dramatic, light-filled exhibit spaces on two levels as well as an art library, a bougainvillea-filled courtyard, and a roof-deck with grand views of the neighborhood. The gallery also has a strong presence in international art fairs and art magazines. ⊠ Calle Córdoba 100, Roma Norte ☎ 55/5207–1080 ⊕ www.galeriaomr. com Ⓜ Insurgentes.

MAIA Contemporary Gallery

An essential stop on any gallery stroll through Roma, MAIA occupies one of the more striking mansions on elegant Calle Colima, the Porfirian-era Casa Basalta. The galleries are connected by a long, columned veranda, and there's a dramatic modern addition at the back with a sleek, curving wooden staircase. The gallery represents a mix of up-and-coming and more established contemporary talents, and exhibits make great use of the dramatic space. ⊠ Calle Colima 159, Roma Norte ☎ 55/8434–9599 ⊕ www.maiacontemporary.com Ⓜ Insurgentes.

★ MODO (Museo del Objeto de Objeto)

Literally the Museum of the Object of the Object, MODO presents fascinating rotating exhibits from an immense collection of some 150,000 objects dating back to the early 19th century, all with some relationship to design. The building itself is a series of relatively compact gallery spaces inside a gracious Porfirian art nouveau mansion on one of Roma's prettiest streets. This trove of objects was donated by collector Bruno Newman, the museum's founder, and it's really intended to celebrate prosaic objects of everyday use that aren't often celebrated in museums: recent exhibitions have featured vintage sneakers, household appliances, political posters and propaganda, beer and liquor bottles, erotica, lucha libre memorabilia, and rock music. The little gift shop is terrific, too, filled with original, captivating items, large and small, practical and whimsical. ⊠ Calle Colima 145, Roma Norte ☎ 55/5533–9635 ⊕ www. elmodo.mx ☑ MX$50 ⊙ Closed Mon. Ⓜ Insurgentes.

MUCA Roma (Museo Universitario de Ciencias y Artes Roma)

This small, free art space operated by Universidad Nacional Autónoma de México (UNAM) occupies three floors of a Porfirian-era town house on a prominent corner in Roma Norte. The exhibits rotate throughout the year, and the contemporary installations generally relate to technology and science and are often quite imaginative. Be sure to make your way up to the roof-deck, which is a relaxing place for a break and offers nice views of the many pretty surrounding buildings. ✉ *Tonalá 51, Roma Norte* ☎ *55/5511–8867* ⊕ *www. mucaroma.unam.mx* ⊗ *Closed Mon.* Ⓜ *Insurgentes.*

Museo Soumaya–Casa Guillermo Tovar de Teresa

The newest addition to Carlos Slim's growing collection of cultural holdings that operate—always with free admission—under the aegis of Soumaya Museum, this classic late 19th-century Porfirian mansion was formerly owned by the late historian and art collector Guillermo Tovar de Teresa. The grand, if imposingly formal, home is filled with priceless antiques and artwork, including an important painting of Archangel San Rafael by noted religious painter Miguel Cabrera, fine porcelain and glassworks from both Europe and Spanish Colonial Mexico, and Tovar de Teresa's huge library of historic books. Walking amid the Oriental rugs, gilt-framed mirrors and paintings, and sweeping drapes give a nice sense of what it might have felt like to live in one of the city's grandest homes, but the real treat here is visiting the romantic, cloistered garden, with its huge ferns, flowering plants, and curving pathways—it's a peaceful little green treasure in the heart of a bustling neighborhood. ✉ *Calle Valladolid 52, Roma Norte* ☎ *55/1103–9800* ⊕ *www. museosoumaya.org* Ⓜ *Sevilla.*

★ Plaza Río de Janeiro

Perhaps the most picturesque—and oft-photographed—of Roma's several public squares, this large rectangular plaza was laid out as part of the neighborhood's formal development into an upper-class residential district in 1903. Near the neighborhood's northern border and the more frenetic Gloria de los Insurgentes traffic circle, the Plaza attracts dog walkers, joggers, shoppers, and passersby of all stripes. The fountain, anchored by a bronze replica of Michelangelo's *David*, is the square's social focal point, and you'll find a handful of inviting cafés on the north side, including Cafe Toscano (the very same wine-and-coffee eatery with a branch on Plaza Cabrera) and Buna. Ornately detailed early 20th-century mansions fringe the plaza, the most famous being the redbrick *Casa de las Brujas* (Gouse of the Witches), so named for its soaring conical

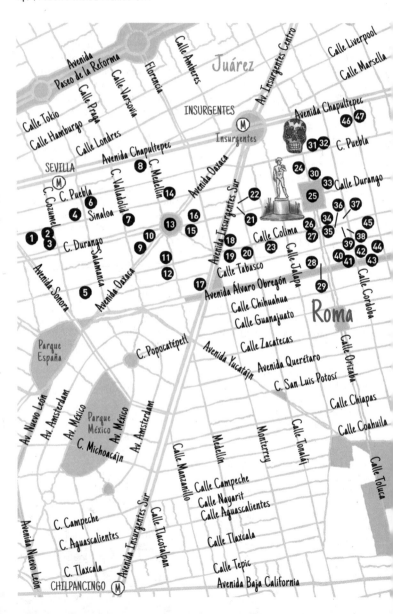

SIGHTS

Avenida Álvaro
Obregón 43
Casa Lamm
Cultural Center 40
Fuente de Cibeles 13
Galería OMR 42
MAIA Contemporary
Gallery 34
MODO (Museo del
Objeto de Objeto) 37
Museo Soumaya–
Casa Guillermo
Tovar de Teresa 7
MUCA Roma (Museo
Universitario
de Ciencias
y Artes Roma)........... 20
Plaza
Río de Janeiro 25
Proyectos
Monclova 49
Romita 52

SHOPPING

Córdoba 25 32
Dulcería de Celaya .. 24
180º........................ 27
Roma Quince
Concept Store 11
Sangre de
mi Sangre 28
Tuza 45
Vértigo Galería 54
Viriathus 47

COFFEE & QUICK BITES

Caravanserai............ 29
Glace Helado 23
Helados Cometa 36
Raku Café 1
Taquería Orinoco 17

DINING

Contramar 10
Corredor
Salamanca................. 6
El Roma Bistrot 33
Fonda Fina 12
Huset 19
Kura Izakaya.............. 5
La Docena................ 48
La Tecla 15
Lorea......................... 4
Loup Bar 21
Meroma 39
Peltre Lonceria 41
Rosetta 26
Sartoria 30
Sepia 2
Trattoria Lingua
Franca...................... 51

BARS & NIGHTLIFE

Bar Oriente............... 16
Blanco Colima...........35
Casa Franca 44
Covadonga................ 31
Gin Gin 9
Hotel Casa Awolly.... 14
Jardín
Chapultepec 8
La Bodeguita
del Medio 3
Maison Artemisia..... 22
Multiforo Alicia 53
Patrick Miller 46
Pulqueria Los
Insurgentes 18
Traspatio 38

PERFORMING ARTS

Centro Cultural
Teatro 1 y 2...............50

STROLLING AROUND OLD-WORLD ROMITA

A ramble through the northeastern corner of Roma, centered around the prehistoric village of Romita, offers visitors a laid-back experience that is still relatively free of the gentrification that characterizes the rest of neighborhood. Start by visiting the narrow lanes that lead away from **Plaza Romita** and its nearly 500-year-old church, Rectoria San Francisco.

From there, meander a few blocks south to **Jardín Pushkin,** a pretty swath of greenery that's popular with dog walkers and contains one of the better playgrounds in Roma. On Sunday, it also hosts a bustling flea market. The stretch of Colima bordering Jardín Pushkin contains an interesting mix of shops that reflect Roma's eclecticism, from a ukulele store to prestigious Vértigo Galería, and just around the corner, the legendary punk bar, Multiforo Alicia.

Diagonal from Jardín Pushkin to the northeast, across wide Avenida Cuauhtémoc and on the edge of the steadily gentrifying but still somewhat sketchy Doctores neighborhood, another pleasant spot to go for a stroll is **Jardín Dr. Ignacio Chávez,** which was created following the destruction of several buildings in the 1985 earthquake. It's fringed by towering pine trees, and on weekends, it's the site of Tianguis de Antigüedades, a popular antiques market. If you're in the mood to haggle, the vendors here have a reputation for price flexibility, especially if you're willing to buy more than one item from the same seller.

Back at Plaza Romita, one last patch of benches and trees lies just a block north at **Plaza Morelia,** a small, semicircular pocket park with a lush canopy of greenery. There are no markets here, and the pace is sleepy, but it's still a nice spot for dog-walkers and families. From just a half-block south of here, you can follow Calle Puebla back into Roma's trendy heart.

turret's resemblance to a witch's hat. ⊠ *Calle Orizaba, at Calle de Durango, Roma Norte* Ⓜ *Insurgentes.*

Proyectos Monclova

Established in 2005, this gallery in a nondescript-looking garagelike structure on Calle Colima describes its mission as furthering "dialogues between Mexican and international artists from different generations." The wide, white-walled space with a vaulted ceiling is essentially a blank canvas, which makes it ideal for exhibiting the often large-scale, abstract works in which the gallery specializes. ⊠ *Calle Colima 55, Roma Norte* ☎ *55/5525–9715* ⊕ *www.proyectosmonclova.com* Ⓜ *Cuauhtémoc.*

★ Romita

Before real estate developers established most of Roma as a fashionable residential neighborhood in the early 1900s, this small quadrant of narrow lanes thrived as an off-the-beaten-path village for centuries. Originally occupying one of the many small, low islands of massive Lake Texcoco, the area was inhabited by Aztecs well before the arrival of Spaniards. As the city and then Roma and neighboring Juárez and Doctores districts grew up around it, Romita retained a distinct—and decidedly more working-class—personality and independence that it continues to retain, to a degree, to this day. Its name is said to derive from its resemblance during the mid-1700s to a neighborhood in Rome, Italy, that was similarly rife at the time with large trees. To get a feel for the neighborhood, walk along one of its narrow lanes to Plaza Romita, a tranquil tree-shaded courtyard with park benches and a central fountain that's flanked on its eastern side by the small, 1530s Rectoria San Francisco Javier Church. The neighborhood's liveliest street, Real de Romita, has a few shops and cafés, including the noteworthy Trattoria Lingua Franca, Cafe Romita, and Ramen Mogra; down another lane you'll find the headquarters (with very limited hours) of the fast-emerging craft bewery, Cru Cru. ⊠ *Cjon. de Romita 24, Roma Norte.*

 Shopping

Córdoba 25
This small cluster of art- and design-related spaces includes a bookshop specializing in art (Casa Bosques Librería) and a notable contemporary gallery (Machete). There are also cool fashion sources like Apartment 25 for men's and women's pop-art-inspired outer-wear and club gear (including pieces from Mexican-Japanese designer 1/8 Takamura) and Naked Boutique for arresting women's wear by local and international designers. ⊠ *Córdoba 25, Roma Norte* ⊕ *www.facebook.com/ Cordoba25* Ⓜ *Insurgentes.*

★ Dulcería de Celaya
Part of the fun of visiting this vener-able Mexican candymaker that's been in business since 1874 is admiring the hand-painted *calaveras* (sugar skulls) and Elvis figurines that are especially popular around the Día de Muertos celebrations. These are to be admired rather than eaten, but Celaya also features long glass cases filled with delicious edibles, including candied fruits, *polvorones de canela* (Mexican wedding cookies), *puerquitos* (pig-shape gingerbread cookies), colorful marzipan, *jamoncillo de leche* (similar to fudge), and traditional *dulces de coco* (coconut candies) in a wide range of flavors. ⊠ *Calle Orizaba 37, Roma Norte* ☎ *55/5514–8438* ⊕ *www.dulceriadecelaya.com* Ⓜ *Insurgentes.*

180°
This boutique carries modish fashion for the city or the beach, much of it by young, Latinix talents. You can browse slick sunglasses by Mexican-born Miami designer Sunny Patoche, Mónica Márquez chunky women's boots, stylish Paruno men's shoes, and the store's own print tote bags and playful Leyenda Urbana "Urban Legend" T-shirts. There's an interesting selection of skateboards too, as well as books and other whimsical gifts. ⊠ *Calle Colima 180, Roma Norte*

☎ 55/8436–1026 ⊕ www.180grados.mx Ⓜ Insurgentes.

★ Roma Quince Concept Store

This tastefully restored Porfirian-era mansion just a block from the fray of Fuente de Cibeles is an aptly stunning setting for displaying gorgeous accessories, furnishings, and fashion for the home. The wares are created by a roster of carefully selected designers and boutique owners, most of them already well established in San Miguel de Allende. Within these same lovely walls, you can celebrate your purchases (or consider new ones) over a leisurely lunch in the swank bistro and wine bar, Carlota & Emilia. ✉ Calle Medellín 67, Roma Norte ☎ 55/5207–8682 ⊕ www.facebook.com/romaquinceconceptstore Ⓜ Sevilla.

Sangre de mi Sangre

Artist Mariana Villarreal creates one-of-a-kind jewelry in this small boutique on the ground floor of the stately beaux-arts Balmori Mansion near Casa Lamm Cultural Center. Stop in and browse her collections of silver and gold earrings, necklaces, and rings, often with inlaid precious stones. Naturalistic, neo-Gothic motifs—skulls, bumblebees, stars, leaves—figure prominently in her whimsical designs. ✉ Calle Orizaba 101, Roma Norte ☎ 55/5511–8599 ⊕ www.sdemis.com Ⓜ Insurgentes.

Tuza

In addition to carrying owner Suzzan Atala's jewelry, handbags, and women's clothing, all of it made in Mexico City, this boutique also carries fashionable accessories and women's clothing from Carla Fernández, Héctor de la Peña, Macaria, and other Mexico luminaries. Tuza also has a boutique in New York City. ✉ Calle Colima 124, Roma Norte ☎ 55/7159–4960 ⊕ www.tuzatuzatuza.mx Ⓜ Insurgentes.

Vértigo Galería

This terrific little gallery is more a destination for every day art buyers than many of the other big-name international art spaces in the neighborhood. Here you'll find not only cool pop-art-inspired decorative items, ceramics, toys, and one-of-a-kind gifts, but also a nice selection of art, architecture, and design books, and a selection of eye-catching silk-screen and graphic tees. There's also a gallery space that stages rotating exhibits, and occasionally it presents live acoustic music. ✉ Calle Colima 23, Roma Norte ☎ 55/5207–3590 ⊕ www.vertigogaleria.com Ⓜ Cuauhtémoc.

★ Viriathus

In this rambling, historic Roma Norte town house, two brothers and business partners with a passion for collecting one-of-a-kind historical memorabilia and antiques sell their treasures to the public. Just walking through each room is great fun—more so, really, than touring some of the city's somberly baroque house-museums. You'll find expensive and rare items (a 1790s map of the Americas, a 1930s oak credenza) along with a number of smaller and more affordable pieces, including model ships, vintage valises, fine books, and framed artwork. ⊠ *Calle Mérida 10, Roma Norte* ☎ *55/2624-3553* ⊕ *www. viriathus.com.mx* Ⓜ *Insurgentes.*

☕ Coffee and Quick Bites

Caravanserai

$ | Café. This Paris–meets–Silk Road–inspired teahouse on a lively street corner along Avenida Álvaro Obregón is a wonderful spot to sip interesting hot and iced teas (nearly 200 blends are available, from spicy chais to delicate white teas) while watching passersby from a sidewalk table or cozied up in one of the warmly furnished interior rooms. French-Asian desserts are offered, too, including green tea cakes and tarte tatin. **Known for:** intimate and inviting space; tea blends in a vast range of flavors; tarte tatin and other desserts. *Average main: 75 MP* ⊠ *Calle Orizaba 101, Roma Norte* ☎ *55/1134-6758* ⊕ *www.caravanserai. com.mx* Ⓜ *Insurgentes.*

★ Glace Helado

$ | Café. The acclaimed artisan Centro Histórico ice-cream shop has opened this fun little satellite branch inside a hip bazaar of sustainable maker goods. Browse the clothing, jewelry, housewares, and mezcal while enjoying a bowl of rose-chile, brie-zarzamora (blackberry), or pan de elote (corncake) ice cream. **Known for:** location in a cool little bazaar; highly original artisan ice-cream flavors; tasty affogato. *Average main: 60 MP* ⊠ *Calle Colima 220, Roma Norte*

☎ *55/6363-6683* ⊕ *www.glacehelado. mx* Ⓜ *Insurgentes.*

Helados Cometa

$ | Café. Pop inside this tiny café for first-rate ice cream and sorbets in interesting flavors like ginger-hibiscus, chocolate-mint, and raspberry-green tea. There are a few stools and two little tables, but the best plan is to take your purchase to enjoy by the fountain at Plaza Río de Janeiro. **Known for:** gourmet sorbets and ice creams; cute, cozy space; short walk to Plaza Río de Janeiro. *Average main: 60 MP* ⊠ *Calle Colima 162, Roma Norte* ⊕ *www. heladoscometa.com* Ⓜ *Insurgentes.*

Raku Café

$ | Café. This itty-bitty, modern café turns out some of the finest Kyoto-sourced matcha green tea in the city as well as exceptional house-roasted coffee drinks, which are served in beautiful hand-thrown ceramic mugs. Have a seat on one of the little benches fashioned out of tree trunks. **Known for:** matcha tea; intimate, tranquil ambience; well-crafted espresso drinks and cold brew. *Average main: 55 MP* ⊠ *Calle Sinaloa 188, Roma Norte* ⊕ *www. rakucafe.com* Ⓜ *Insurgentes.*

Taquería Orinoco

$ | Mexican. There are few more satisfying experiences after a night of dancing and drinking than devouring a plate of tacos in this taqueria on the border between Roma and Condesa. Fillings include *trompo* (al pastor), chicharrón with spicy house-made salsa, and beef; a side of the crunchy fried *papas orinoco* potatoes is a must. **Known for:** late-night tacos; great people-watching; guayaba popsicles. *Average main: 80 MP ⊠ Av. Insurgentes Sur 253, Roma Norte* ☎ *55/5514-6917* ⊕ *www.taqueriaorinoco.com* Ⓜ *Insurgentes.*

🍴 Dining

⭐ Contramar

$$$ | Seafood. Come before 1 pm or make an online reservation to avoid the long wait at this airy seafood haven, a power-lunch spot for the creative and celebrity sets since it opened in 1998 (there's often less of a wait for the casual outside tables). While the people-watching is prime, your attention will be on the food: start with the famed tuna tartare tostadas, then try some fish cooked al pastor or a bowl of clam chowder, minced soft-shell crab or octopus tacos, or the huge butterflied pescado Contramar with red chile. **Known for:** see-and-be-seen crowd lunch spot; some of the freshest seafood in Mexico City; octopus aguachile. *Average main: 365 MP ⊠ Calle Durango 200, Roma Norte* ☎ *55/5514-9217* ⊕ *www.contramar.com.mx* ☽ *No dinner* Ⓜ *Sevilla.*

Corredor Salamanca

$ | Eclectic. This modern open-air mercado draws a young-ish crowd who appreciate its variety of social features such as beer pong, televisions airing sports games, a DJ spinning tunes, and a pet-friendly terrace. The craft beer selection is impressive (about 45 options are available), and the 16 different eating options tend toward elevated comfort food, like fries, burgers, sausages, ice cream, and the like. **Known for:** huge craft beer selection; ping-pong bar; fun, loud, and social ambience. *Average main: 100 MP ⊠ Calle Salamanca 32, Roma Norte* ☎ *55/1689-0142* ⊕ *www.corredorsalamanca.mx* Ⓜ *Sevilla.*

El Roma Bistrot

$$ | Cuban. This dapper bistro with seating overlooking the pretty greenery of Plaza Río de Janeiro serves a modern French twist on the Caribbean food of chef Joaquín Cardoso's Cuban *abuela*, with a particularly strong emphasis on seafood. A good plan is for friends to share a selection of fresh tuna crudo, fish croquettes, and skewers (eggplant with peanut-adobo sauce or calamari with habanero oil), before moving on to some of the larger plates, such as grilled fish of the day with citrus butter or noodles with lobster tail. **Known for:** artful desserts (rum cake and passionfruit tart among them); great spot for breakfast and brunch; late-night dining and drinking. *Average main: 290 MP ⊠ Plaza Río de Janeiro 52, Roma Norte* ☎ *55/7822-9800* ⊕ *www.elromabistrot.com* ☽ *No dinner Sun.* Ⓜ *Insurgentes.*

Fonda Fina

$$ | Modern Mexican. Partly owned by Quinonil's celebrity chef Jorge Vallejo, step into Fonda Fina for a lunch or dinner of modernly interpreted Mexican classics, such as raw tuna tostadas with citrus oil and a gaujillo-chile vinaigrette, or a casserole of beef cheeks braised in a green mole sauce with smoked cauliflower. One popular way to choose your meal here is to mix and match your protein (rib-eye, octopus, and pork among them) with any of several vegetable garnishes and about 10 salsa options—the servers are happy to recommend tasty pairings. **Known for:** casually chic dining room; regional Mexican fare with a modern twist; creative cocktails. *Average main: 285 MP* ⊠ *Calle Medellín 79, ·Roma Norte* ☎ *55/5208–3925* ⊕ *www. fondafina.com.mx* ⊙ *No dinner Sun.* Ⓜ *Insurgentes.*

★ Huset

$$$ | Contemporary. You can opt for either of the two distinct experiences in this stylish Calle Colima restaurant: dining in the early 20th-century town house that overlooks the busy street below or sitting in the much more casual and social covered outdoor section with a green living wall. The menu changes seasonally but might feature crab tostadas with grapefruit, ginger, and arugula or fillet of beef with pureed potatoes and a soy-carmel emulsion. **Known for:** two distinct (romantic versus social) dining areas; sophisticated wood-fired cuisine; innovative cocktails. *Average main: 320 MP* ⊠ *Calle Colima 256, Roma Norte* ☎ *55/5511–6767* ⊕ *www.huset.mx* ⊙ *Closed Mon. No dinner Sun.* Ⓜ *Insurgentes.*

★ Kura Izakaya

$$ | Japanese. Savor deftly crafted modern Japanese fare—yakitori skewers, oden and ramen bowls, tempura, udon noodle, raw shell-fish, and sushi and sashimi—in this inviting, contemporary space with a variety of seating options, including private tatami rooms. The menu stand-outs are many, including a serrano-wagyu beef roll and okonomiyaki topped with roasted Brussels sprouts. **Known for:** huge menu designed for sharing; attractive dining areas with ample natural light; diverse alcohol menu. *Average main: 250 MP* ⊠ *Calle Colima 378, Roma Norte* ☎ *55/7989–3102* ⊕ *www. kuramexico.com* Ⓜ *Sevilla.*

La Docena

$$ | Seafood. This boisterous, upmarket seafood spot is an especially fun late-night option, but also popular for weekend brunch. The menu blends Mexican and American (especially New Orleans) seafood traditions and features several kinds of po'boys, aguachile and sashimi, grilled soft-shell crab, and a pretty good variety of steaks and meatier items. **Known for:** lively, chatter-filled dining room; oysters on the half shell and other raw-bar items; serving food until very late at night. *Average main: 280 MP* ⊠ *Av. Álvaro Obregón 31, Roma Norte* ☎ *55/5208–0833* ⊕ *www.ladocena. com.mx* Ⓜ *Insurgentes.*

La Tecla

$$ | Modern Mexican. This popular veteran of the city's modern Mexican culinary scene is still a mainstay for reasonably priced, consistently well-prepared dishes like huitlacoche risotto with corn and poblano chiles, and grilled prawns with a sweet-spicy tamarind-guajillo reduction. The space is refined, relaxed, and ideal for conversation, and there are a few tables on the sidewalk overlooking Plaza Villa de Madrid and Fuente de Cibeles. **Known for:** refined, quiet dining room; excellent selection of Mexican wines; artfully plated contemporary fare. *Average main: 280 MP* ⊠ *Calle de Durango 186A, La Roma* ☎ *55/5525–4920* ⊘ *No dinner Sun.* Ⓜ *Insurgentes.*

Lorea

$$$$ | **Modern Mexican.** Meals in this minimalist dining room are among the most refined and romantic culinary adventures in Roma. Local chef-owner Oswaldo Oliva spent years abroad honing his craft at some of Spain's most hallowed restaurants, and he shares his farm-to-table approach here in the form of 9- or 14-course tasting menus (with optional wine pairings) of exquisitely plated, ethereal bites that change daily according to what's fresh, but you can expect a number of Mexico-centric ingredients, such as huitlacoche, tomatillos, and honeycomb. **Known for:** beautifully plated farm-to-table cuisine; prix-fixe multicourse dinners; carefully planned drink pairings. *Average main: 1600 MP* ⊠ *Calle Sinaloa 141, Roma Norte* ☎ *55/9130–7786* ⊕ *www.lorea.mx* ⊘ *Closed Sun. and Mon. No lunch* Ⓜ *Sevilla.*

Loup Bar

$$ | **Wine Bar.** This cozy wine-cave-like space, located beneath the wildly popular cocktail-piano bar Artemisia, stands out from the city's growing clutch of vino bars for its devotion to natural bottles, from German orange wines to heady, bold Rhône blends (nearly all are priced over MX$1,000—and many are much costlier—so budget accordingly). But there's also a quite reasonably priced menu of tasty French-inspired bar fare, including a savory Wagyu beef tartare with piquillo chiles, Roquefort-and-avocado salad, and lamb couscous with olives and preserved lemon. **Known for:** impressive natural wine list; tasty French bar fare; hip and intimate setting. *Average main: 175 MP* ⊠ *Calle Tonalá 23, Roma Norte* ☎ *55/5514–6983* ⊕ *www.loupbar.mx* ⊘ *Closed Sun.* Ⓜ *Insurgentes.*

★ Meroma

$$$ | **Contemporary.** The mid-century-modern design of this fashionable, trendy, and yet somehow still unpretentious restaurant feels distinct from its grandiose Porfirian neighbors, and so does the seasonally inspired small-plate-focused cuisine, which is heavy on fresh vegetables, hand-made pastas, and seafood. A foie gras terrine is served with a zesty apple-shiso-rhubarb-port sauce, while tender, slow-roasted lamb is served with mashed plantains, cilantro pesto, and a lamb-coffee reduction. **Known for:** house-made pastas tossed with seasonal ingredients; distinctive mid-century-modern aesthetic; noteworthy cocktail, beer, and wine list. *Average main: 355 MP* ⊠ *Calle Colima 150, Roma Norte* ☎ *55/5920–2654* ⊕ *www.meroma.mx* ⊘ *Closed Mon. No dinner Sun.* Ⓜ *Insurgentes.*

Peltre Lonchería

$ | Mexican. This rather elegant mid-century-modern lunchroom offers a contemporary take on classic Mexican and American comfort fare, like ham-turkey-gouda sandwiches with a fried egg on top, cochinita pibíl, and beef milanesa tortas with salsa verde. There's nothing fancy about this place, but it's great for a light in-between meal, late-night snack (it's open till 11 pm), or breakfast, which features a similarly extensive variety of favorites, from huevos rancheros to French toast slathered in berries and agave honey. **Known for:** hearty sandwiches and tortas; house-made jams, snacks, and peltre (pewter) kitchenware for sale; good coffee drinks (including cold brew with horchata). *Average main: 110 MP* ⊠ *Av. Álvaro Obregón 86, Roma Norte* ☎ *55/3716-5849* ⊕ *www.bullandtank. com/peltre* Ⓜ *Insurgentes.*

★ Rosetta

$$$ | Modern Italian. Chef-owner Elena Reygadas worked for years at London's Michelin-starred Italian restaurant Locando Locatelli before moving back to her hometown in 2011 to open Rosetta in a stunning early 1900s belle epoque mansion. Despite the perfect risottos and handmade pastas in varying shapes, what her cuisine primarily takes from Italy is reliance on local and seasonal ingredients (the olive oil is from Baja California, the burrata cheese made in the town of Atlixco)—but much of the food has a creative Mexican heart. **Known for:** superb modern Italian fare; fresh baked goods from the adjacent bakery, Panadería Rosetta; rosemary ice cream over herbs for dessert. *Average main: 410 MP* ⊠ *Calle Colima 166, Roma Norte* ☎ *55/5533-7804* ⊕ *www.rosetta.com. mx* ☾ *Closed Sun.* Ⓜ *Insurgentes.*

Sartoria

$$$ | Modern Italian. This uber-hip osteria with a cool arched dining room overlooking Plaza Río de Janeiro is justly famous for the fresh handmade pastas of internationally renowned chef Marco Carboni—think gnocchi with a 12-hour ragu of beek cheek, lamb, sausage, and pork leg, or tagliolini tossed with lobster, lemon, tarragon butter, and fish roe. Portions are a bit small, so consider ordering a side or two of the marvelous Creole tomatoes with burrata, pesto, and preserved lemon. **Known for:** artisanal handmade pastas; fine coffees in adjoining Buna café; gorgeous, chicly modern dining room. *Average main: 310 MP* ⊠ *Calle Orizaba 42, Roma Norte* ☎ *55/7265-3616* ⊕ *www. sartoria.mx* ☾ *No dinner Sun.* Ⓜ *Insurgentes.*

Sepia

$$$ | Modern Italian. This chic restaurant is a scene-y destination for sumptuous modern Italian fare, much of it featuring sustainably sourced seafood. Consider starting out with a plate of grilled oysters with fine herbs and grated fresh grana padano or a rich saffron-shellfish soup, before tucking into a plate of braised octopus caponata or risotto with Patagonian shrimp. **Known for:** creatively prepared

modern Italian seafood; cheese-charcuterie plates; astoundingly extensive wine list. *Average main: 360 MP* ⊠ *Calle Sinaloa 170, Roma Norte* 🕾 *55/7827-9395* ⊕ *www.cocinasepia.mx* ⊘ *No dinner Sun.* Ⓜ *Sevilla.*

Trattoria Lingua Franca
$$ | Fusion. Set down one of quaint Romita's narrow little side streets, this inviting restaurant with a large central courtyard dining area is the brainchild of the team behind wildly popular Mog Bistro—only here in this cheerful space, you'll encounter a menu that features neighborhood Italian, Japanese ramen, and a few dishes that fuse recipes from both cultures. Perhaps start with a plate of burrata and anchovies or Japanese steamed rice with eel and foie gras, before considering one of the thin-crust pizzas, linguine with soft-shell crab, or chashu ramen. **Known for:** ramen and spaghetti Bolognese on the same menu; pretty courtyard dining area; notable craft beer selection. *Average main: 220 MP* ⊠ *Real de Romita 13, Roma Norte* 🕾 *55/4398-4084* ⊘ *Closed Tues.* Ⓜ *Cuauhtémoc.*

🍸 Bars and Nightlife

⭐ Bar Oriente
Bright lighting and a bold color scheme create a striking vibe for singing karaoke, watching live bands, sipping craft cocktails, and nibbling on Japanese-Mexican-fusion bar snacks in this quirky space that draws a mix of artists, club kids, and style-makers. Music tends toward the playful and accessible—think trash disco, alternative, reggae, and pretty much anything that gets the diverse crowd moving. Oriente's two private karaoke rooms are great for small parties (they hold up to 30 guests). ⊠ *Calle de Durango 181, Roma Norte* 🕾 *55/3239-9887* ⊕ *www.oriente.bar* Ⓜ *Insurgentes.*

⭐ Blanco Colima
Ensconced within one of the most opulent Porfirian mansions in Roma, this urbane bar is a dramatic setting for well-crafted cocktails and tasty tapas. Located in the mansion's former courtyard, the bar is just one element of the building's rambling series of dining spaces (which also includes an Asian-inflected oyster bar and a more formal high-end farm-to-table restaurant), but it's also arguably the most delightful of the venues to pass time in. ⊠ *Calle Colima 168, Roma Norte* 🕾 *55/5511-7527* ⊕ *www.blancocolima.com.mx* Ⓜ *Insurgentes.*

Casa Franca
The glow of flickering candles welcomes visitors to this swish Parisian-style bar that presents live jazz bands several days a week, along with a menu of designer pizzas, Mediterranean tapas, wine, and cocktails. It's a popular spot on weekends, and reservations are recommended if you want a table. Around the corner, sister restaurant Franca Bistro serves a more extensive food menu and has a similarly classy but laid-back air about it. ⊠ *Calle Mérida 109, Roma Norte* 🕾 *55/5208-2265* ⊕ *www.*

facebook.com/Lacasamerida109
Ⓜ Insurgentes.

★ Covadonga

This grand, cavernous 1940s-era cantina has a long antique bar to one side and a kitchen serving up tasty Asturian Spanish fare. It's filled nightly with the sounds of the *tercera edad* (a polite phrase for the elder generation) playing exuberant games of dominoes and millennials chatting about their adventures at Roma's latest gallery opening. ⊠ *Calle Puebla 121, Roma Norte* ☎ *55/5533-2922* ⊕ *www.banquetescovadonga.com.mx.*

Gin Gin

You'll find some of the city's most esteemed mixologists slinging drinks in this swanky cocktail bar in a grand old house off of Cibeles. The menu changes regularly, but you might try El Viejo Reyes with Ancho Reyes (a poblano and ancho-chile liqueur from Puebla), Siete Misterios Doba-Yej mezcal, Angostura bitters, and flaming orange oil, or Gin Gin's take on a mule with Tanqueray, ginger, yerba buena, cane syrup, lime, and soda. There are tasty food options, too. There are additional locations in Polanco and Santa Fe, but this one has the most inviting ambience. ⊠ *Av. Oaxaca 87, Roma Norte* ☎ *55/5248-0911* ⊕ *www.gingin.mx* Ⓜ *Sevilla.*

★ Hotel Casa Awolly

Duck into this bar and restaurant set inside an elegant Porfirian town house with a three-story wall decorated with abstract murals, a ravishing second-floor salon with green velvet chairs and gilt mirrors, and several different seating areas. The talented mixologists use house-made bitters and shrubs as well as fresh-squeezed juices in its inventive cocktails. It's one of the swankier—and pricier—venues in the city for drinks, and the food is every bit as tantalizing. ⊠ *Calle Sinaloa 57, Roma Norte* ☎ *55/5086-2820* ⊕ *www.instagram.com/hotel-casaawolly* Ⓜ *Insurgentes.*

Jardín Chapultepec

On Roma's northern border with Colonia Juárez, this long and narrow order-at-the-bar beer garden is populated by picnic tables and lushly landscaped, making it surprisingly easy to forget the traffic noise outside (especially if you snag a seat near the back). The beer selection is vast, and you'll find plenty of notable brews from Mexico's up-and-coming artisanal brewers. There's burgers, sandwiches, and other pub fare, too, along with a selection of cocktails. ⊠ *Av. Chapultepec 398, Roma Norte* ☎ *55/7097-1302* Ⓜ *Insurgentes.*

La Bodeguita del Medio

At this welcoming, lively Cuban joint set in a fadingly grand mansion that wouldn't look the least out of place in Havana, every surface is splashed with graffiti. Inspired by the original Havana establishment where Hemingway once lapped up mojitos, La Bodeguita also serves inexpensive Cuban food and sells Cuban cigars. Much of the time, live salsa, timba, and rumba bands provide entertainment. ⊠ *Calle Cozumel*

37, Roma Norte ☎ *55/5553–0246* Ⓜ *Sevilla.*

★ Maison Artemisia

A small group of French and Mexican friends have created this inviting, cosmopolitan bar with a top-flight mixology program that features local botanicals and bitters as well as a house-brand Absinthe distilled in Paris. The relatively short cocktail menu changes weekly but always features some novel creations. There's live jazz, blues, soul, and other music once or twice a week. Downstairs, you'll find sister establishment, Loup Bar, which specializes in natural wines. ✉ *Calle Tonalá 23, Roma Norte* ☎ *55/6303–2471* ⊕ *www.maisonartemisia.com* Ⓜ *Insurgentes.*

Multiforo Alicia

This old-school music club with a colorful mural on the upper front facade headlines foreign and local indie bands playing punk, ska, surf, and garage music. In true punk-rock fashion, the space is poorly ventilated, and the sound system leaves much to be desired, but it offers a cheap night out and a thoroughly entertaining scene. ✉ *Cuauhtémoc 91–A, Roma Norte* ☎ *55/5511–2100* ⊕ *www.multiforoalicia.blogspot.com.*

Patrick Miller

At this long-standing, high-energy, Friday-only "danceteria," DJs spin 1980s pop classics, disco, and techno while the flamboyant patrons, a fairly even mixture of gays and straights, compete in theatrical dance-offs. Prepare to sweat. ✉ *Calle Mérida 17, Roma Norte* ☎ *55/5511–5406* ⊕ *www.facebook.com/PatrickMillerMX.*

★ Pulqueria Los Insurgentes

Behind the colorful—almost garish—facade of this wildly popular pulqueria, you'll find three floors to enjoy plain and flavored (blackberry, guayaba, mamey, apricot, mango) versions of the milky millennia-old beverage distilled from the fermented sap of the very agave plants that give us mezcal and tequila. The most popular seating area, especially on warm evenings, is the expansive roof-deck. And if you're not much for pulque, fear not: there's a full selection of liquor and beer, plus nachos, tacos, burgers, and the like. ✉ *Av. Insurgentes Sur 226, Roma Norte* ☎ *55/5207–0917* ⊕ *www.facebook.com/pulqueriainsurgentes* Ⓜ *Insurgentes.*

Traspatio

This cool backyard-garden space with a retractable roof to protect from the elements is a great place to hang out with friends on a warm afternoon or evening. It's part of the Milagrito del Corazón mezcal group, and sure enough, there's a good variety of cocktails featuring the spirit. Plus, there's a decent selection of pub grub, including vegetarian options. There's a slightly quieter upper-level terrace if you prefer a bit more privacy. ✉ *Calle Córdoba 81, Roma Norte* ☎ *55/7678–3937* ⊕ *www.milagrito.com* Ⓜ *Insurgentes.*

Performing Arts

Centro Cultural Teatro 1 y 2

A diverse range of concerts, theatrical performances, and other entertainment are presented at these two big venues in the northeastern Romita section of the neighborhood. ⊠ *Av. Chapultepec at Calle Guaymas, Roma Norte* ☎ *55/4000–5631* ⊕ *www.carteleradeteatro.mx* Ⓜ *Cuauhtémoc.*

Roma South of Av. Álvaro Obregón

◉ Sights

Huerto Roma Verde

This eco-minded organic urban farm is one of the more unusual spaces in the city center—it occupies an expansive corner lot beside Roma Sur's attractive, wooded Jardín Ramón López Velarde Park. Built largely from repurposed materials, the farm is easy to spot from the giant temple-like structure by its entrance, made up of hundreds of blue plastic water bottles with a palm tree growing through the center. The center offers workshops and classes open to the public on sustainability, recycling, organic and hydroponic gardening, yoga, dance, jewelry-making, slow-food cooking, and much more. And there are regular eco-markets featuring a wide range of sustainable products. Visitors are welcome to saunter around the property, admiring the eclectic artwork, patting the many friendly and free-ranging cats

(most of which are up for adoption through the farm), and spotting a bounty of potted plants and leafy gardens. ⊠ *Calle Jalapa 234, La Roma* ☎ *55/5564–2210* ⊕ *www.huertoromaverde.org* 🕓 *Closed Mon.* Ⓜ *Hospital General.*

Plaza Luis Cabrera

Designed around the same time and in a somewhat similar style to Plaza Río de Janeiro, which is a few blocks due north, this stately plaza centered on an elliptical reflecting pool and fountain is one of the most enchanting spots in Roma to sit with a cup of coffee and soak up the streetscape. Art installations are regularly set up around the pool's tree-shaded perimeter, and the streets flanking the eastern and western sides of the plaza contain several imposing Porfirian mansions, some of which now house restaurants and cafés. If you'd rather frequent a more locally grown business than the ubiquitous, albeit attractive, Starbucks on the northwest corner, try Cafe Toscano, at the southwest end of the plaza, which makes a nice break for coffee and cake or a glass of wine and a sandwich. ⊠ *Calle Orizaba, between Calles Guanajuato and Zacatecas, Roma Norte* Ⓜ *Insurgentes.*

★ Terreno Baldío Arte

This prestigious gallery repre-sents acclaimed artists like Emilio Rangel, known for his playful and sometimes erotic depictions of pop cultural icons like Miss Piggy and Elvis; Javier Marín—whose massive sculptures, such as *Cabeza Vainilla* (Vanilla Head) have been installed in a number of prominent spaces around the world; and about a dozen other diverse talents. The gallery itself occupies an imposing mansion whose interior has been given a striking, light-filled contem-porary redesign. ⊠ *Calle Orizaba 177, Roma Norte* ☎ *55/2454-4013* ⊕ *www.terrenobaldio.com* Ⓜ *Hospital General.*

 ## Shopping

Global Comics Noveno Arte

This flashy-looking space carries one of the best selections of comic books and graphic novels in the city, including a number of hard-to-find titles. ⊠ *Calle San Luis Potosí 109, Roma Norte* ☎ *55/5913-1318* ⊕ *www. globalcomics.com.mx* Ⓜ *Hospital General.*

Kameyama Shachuu

Both serious and amateur chefs are drawn to this shop for its radiant Sakai Takayuki knives. Available in a wide range of designs and types of handles, they are hand-forged on-site using a style that's been carefully maintained in Osaka for 800 years. ⊠ *Av. Álvaro Obregón 230, Roma Norte* ☎ *55/1866-2362* ⊕ *www.kameyamashachuu.com.mx* Ⓜ *Insurgentes.*

La Increíble Librería

Small but with a well-chosen selec-tion of books, this fun and free-spirited bookstore puts an emphasis on art and architectural titles. It also has a central table and benches where you can enjoy a cup of coffee while you peruse any books you're thinking about purchasing. There's a nice assortment of decorative gifts and knickknacks for sale, too. ⊠ *Calle Jalapa 129, Roma Norte* ☎ *55/5564-8943* ⊕ *www.facebook. com/Laincrelibre* Ⓜ *Insurgentes.*

★ Mercado Medellín

Inside this colorfully painted brick market building that's officially named Mercado Melchor Ocampo, you'll find rows and rows of stalls stocked with sausages, bacalao, nopales, candies, spices, nuts, mole pastes, and sauces of every kind, plus small restaurants selling tasty street-food bites like pozole, arrachera, chile rellenos, Cuban ice cream, and Colombian coffee. It's one of the better organized and less chaotic of the city's many traditional mercados, and it stands out for having vendors hawking goods from a number of other Latin American countries. It's an excellent place to shop for snacks as well as other kinds of gifts, from locally made crafts to household goods. There's also an enormous section devoted to flowers. ⊠ *Calle Campeche 101, Roma Sur* Ⓜ *Chilpancingo.*

Retroactivo

One of a few shops around Roma where you can find vinyl LPs, this funky little shop has an especially impressive selection, including hard-to-find treasures from Latin America and Europe. And you can listen before you buy on a handful of turntables in the store. Prices are fair, and the cheerful staff is very helpful. ⊠ *Calle Jalapa 125, Roma Norte* ☎ *55/7158–5701* Ⓜ *Insurgentes.*

🍽 Coffee and Quick Bites

Casa Cardinal

$ | Café. A lovely, inviting spot for a light meal, Casa Cardinal employs a team of well-trained baristas devoted to producing some of the finest coffee drinks in the neighborhood, using the method of your choice (Aeropress, Japanese siphon, Chemex pour-over, and a few others—plus very good mochas). There's always cool music playing, and you can dine inside or out at one of the sidewalk tables. **Known for:** well-crafted coffee drinks; hip but unpretentious vibe; sandwiches and stroopwaffles. *Average main: 65 MP* ⊠ *Calle Córdoba 132, Roma Norte* ☎ *55/6721–8874* ⊕ *www.casacardinal. mx* Ⓜ *Insurgentes.*

⭐ Casa Tassel

$ | Café. When you're seeking a calm break from the bustle of the big city, have a seat in this dainty and diminutive tearoom with white painted walls, a brick ceiling, and shelves piled high with beautiful teacups, kettles, and bins of tea. You'll find an impressive array of tea blends as well as yerba mate, and a staff who prepares every drink with great care—in fact, the shop offers classes in tea tasting. **Known for:** tea cakes and baguette sandwiches; knowledgeable and friendly staff; extensive and quirky selection of teaware. *Average main: 70 MP* ⊠ *Calle Córdoba 110, Roma Norte* ☎ *55/5264–3313* ⊕ *casatassel. business.site* Ⓜ *Insurgentes.*

⭐ Churrería El Moro

$ | Café. This festive and always packed spot has been a mainstay for sweet tooths since 1935. The best plan is to share an order or two of long, crispy churros with at least two dipping sauces (condensed milk, chocolate, and—maybe the best—cajeta are your options), along with a churro ice-cream sandwich. **Known for:** churros with sweet dipping sauces; churro ice-cream sandwiches; Spanish and Mexican

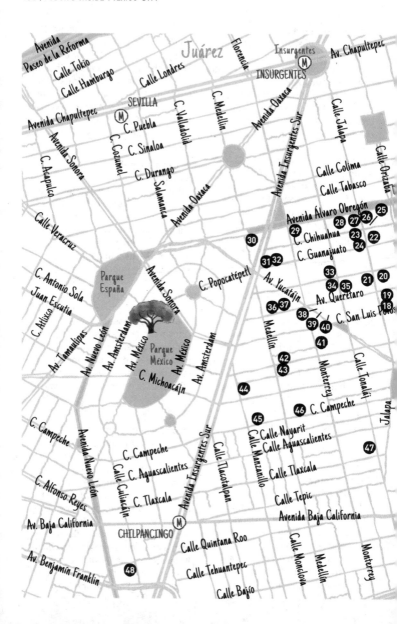

hot chocolate. *Average main: 50 MP* ⊠ *Calle Frontera 122, Roma Norte* ⊕ *www.elmoro.mx* Ⓜ *Cuauhtémoc.*

★ **El Auténtico Pato Manila**
$ | Asian Fusion. Tucked inside a little nook beneath MAIA Contemporary, this offbeat Asian-Mexican-fusion taqueria features duck in every one of its handful of dishes, all of them addictively good. In addition to both Mexican- and Asian-style taco preparations (the Peking duck–inspired "Kim" version is especially tasty), you can enjoy ginger-duck-filled wontons and spring rolls as well as duck tortas. **Known for:** Asian Peking-duck tacos; interesting house-made Asian-Mexican salsas; cozy location beneath a prestigious art gallery. *Average main: 85 MP* ⊠ *Calle Colima 159, Roma Norte* ☎ *55/9130–0610* Ⓜ *Insurgentes.*

Eno
$$ | Modern Mexican. World-famous Pujol mastermind Enrique Olvera is the talent behind Eno, a smart-casual bakery and café on a lively Roma Norte street corner (there's another location in Polanco). The airy brick-ceilinged spot with a handful of sidewalk tables is great for a light meal, dessert, coffee, or atole (a warm Mesoamerican corn drink) from early morning until late at night, with breakfast especially popular. **Known for:** delicious egg and veggie breakfast dishes; fresh-baked cookies and pastries; Mesoamerican drinks, like atole and amaranto. *Average main: 185 MP* ⊠ *Calle Chihuahua 139, Roma Norte*

☎ *55/7576–0919* ⊕ *www.eno.com.mx* Ⓜ *Insurgentes.*

Forte
$ | Café. Although this cozy, discrete café is in Roma Norte, it's at the southern end of the less frenetic neighborhood, making it a nice option for a relaxed coffee break or a light snack. The artisan house-baked goods here are superb, from sourdough pizzas (usually available Friday and Saturday nights only) to flaky croissants and other French pastries. **Known for:** stellar coffee drinks (and coffee-infused craft beer on tap); house-baked pastries; sourdough pizza nights on weekends. *Average main: 55 MP* ⊠ *Calle Querétaro 116, Roma Norte* Ⓜ *Hospital General.*

Tres Galeones
$ | Seafood. The hip, tiny Mexico City location of the popular seafood spot in Tulum has just a handful of tables inside and on the sidewalk. It's a perfect stop for a light snack—try the pibíl-style octopus or pastor-style fish tacos, a ceviche tostada, or a heartier garlic-shrimp burrito. **Known for:** seafood tacos and burritos; ceviche tostadas; ice-cream sandwiches. *Average main: 75 MP* ⊠ *Calle Jalapa 117, Roma Norte* ☎ *55/5564–3121* ⊕ *www.facebook. com/TresGaleones* ☉ *No dinner* Ⓜ *Insurgentes.*

Tsubomi
$ | Bakery. This cozy bakery with Edison bulbs illuminating just a handful of small wooden tables is a source of singularly delicious Japanese and European treats, both

savory and sweet. Matcha cakes, orange pastries, and perfectly crafted baguettes and sandwiches are among the top options. **Known for:** baguette and rustic-bread sandwiches; matcha tea cakes; colorfully frosted cakes and pastries. *Average main: 80 MP* ⊠ *Calle Jalapa 161A, Roma Norte* ☎ *55/5204–3818* ⊕ *www.tsubomimexico.com* Ⓜ *Insurgentes.*

🍴 Dining

⭐ Bar El Sella

$$ | Spanish. This old-time cantina a block from the eastern edge of Roma opened in 1950 and continues to attract crowds of both locals and tourists-in-the-know. There's nothing fancy about the brightly lit dining room, but the authentic Spanish food is up there with the best in the city and includes slow-cooked octopus, chorizo with cabrales cheese, Spanish omelets with asparagus, and *chamorro* (a fall-off-the-bone pork shank braised in a heady achiote sauce). **Known for:** no-frills old-fashioned cantina ambience; pork chamorro; authentic Spanish fare. *Average main: 210 MP* ⊠ *Calle Dr. Balmis 210, Doctores* ☎ *55/5578–2001* ⊕ *www.barelsella.com.mx* ⊗ *Closed Sun. No dinner Mon.* Ⓜ *Hospital General.*

Broka Bistrot

$$ | Modern Mexican. You'll find one of Roma's prettiest dining rooms—with high brick walls and lush greenery set around a two-story interior courtyard with plenty of natural sunlight—in this moderately upscale and somewhat unassuming restaurant that turns out excellent globally influenced bistro fare. Consider the Vietnamese shrimp dumplings in a fragrant soy-shiitake sauce or tuna tartare tostadas to start, before choosing among the soft-shell-crab tacos, grilled Pacific snapper, or rabbit carnitas among the mains. **Known for:** soft-shell crab tacos; lovely light-filled courtyard dining room; good cocktails. *Average main: 285 MP* ⊠ *Calle Zacatecas 126, Roma Norte* ☎ *55/4437–4285* ⊕ *www.brokabistrot.com* ⊗ *No dinner Sun.* Ⓜ *Insurgentes.*

Cafebreria El Péndulo

$$ | Eclectic. The grand, three-story Roma location of this local chain of stunningly designed bookstore-cafés is a wonderful destination for brunch, cocktails, or late-night snacking, either on the breezy roof-deck or seated on one of the comfy lounge chairs inside. Try the pancakes with bananas and blueberries early in the day, or one of Roma's top burgers later in the day, and don't overlook the extensive dessert selection. **Known for:** weekend brunch; lots of veggie options; huge selection of books to browse before or after you eat. *Average main: 170 MP* ⊠ *Av. Álvaro Obregón 86, Roma Norte* ☎ *55/5574–7034* ⊕ *www.pendulo.com* Ⓜ *Insurgentes.*

Chetito

$ | Mexican. This relaxed spot for gourmet tacos and empanadas offers a refreshingly classy ambience compared to most of the no-frills, brashly lit taquerias in Mexico City. On a quiet block just off Avenida Insurgentes, Chetito is an appealing place to linger over empanadas filled with mushrooms, caramelized onions, mozzarella, and goat cheese, or tacos packed with *chistorra* (a cured Spanish sausage), spicy peanut salsa, and lettuce, and maybe one of the several varieties of Clamato-based cocktails. **Known for:** tacos and empanadas with creative fillings; late-night dining; hip, dimly lit space. *Average main: 85 MP* ⊠ *Calle Guanajuato 239, Roma Norte* ☎ *55/6798-1360* ⊕ *www.facebook.com/chetitomx* ⊗ *Closed Mon. No dinner Sun.* Ⓜ *Insurgentes.*

⭐ **Chico Julio**
$$ | Seafood. For all the buzzy seafood restaurants in Roma, not one serves a better aguachile than this casual, affordable spot decorated like an old fishing shanty, with mermaid wall sconces, mounted fish, and seaside bric-a-brac. Everything here—including fish and chips, smoked-marlin tostadas, octopus-chorizo tacos, and salmon burgers—is fresh and boldly flavored, and you can add even more spice by choosing a few salsas from the extensive condiment bar (some of these are *muy picantes*, so ask for advice if you're wary). **Known for:** aguachile and ceviche; variety of grilled-fish tacos; big selection of house-made salsas. *Average main: 150 MP* ⊠ *Jalapa 126, Roma Norte* ☎ *55/2124-5276* ⊕ *www.chicojulio.com* Ⓜ *Insurgentes.*

Delirio Mónica Patiño
$$ | Mediterranean. This gourmet market, artisan bakery, and sidewalk café with a prime location on

Álvaro Obregón is a top destination for any meal, but especially breakfast and brunch, when you might try French toast with whipped cream and fresh fruit or Greek-style baked eggs with jocoque, olives, tomato sauce, and grilled pita. The rest of the day, the eclectic but slightly Mediterranean-leaning menu features tortas and toasts (like the one with smoked trout, pickled beets, and capers) as well as lasagna, lamb moussaka, and other heartier dishes. **Known for:** savory and sweet baked goods; leisurely breakfasts and brunches; gourmet house-made jams, oils, and other goodies to take home. *Average main: 165 MP* ⊠ *Calle Monterrey 116, Roma Norte* ☎ *55/5584-0870* ⊕ *www.delirio.mx* Ⓜ *Insurgentes.*

El Hidalguense
$$ | Mexican. This laid-back restaurant has been serving Hidalgo-style lamb *barbacoa* to grateful Mexico City residents since the 1990s. Friday through Sunday afternoons only, fresh lamb from owner Moisés Rodríguez's Hidalgo farm is roasted for 12 hours over mesquite and oak in an underground pit, then served in charred agave leaves. **Known for:** excellent lamb barbacoa tacos; informal, local scene; variety of pulques. *Average main: 185 MP* ⊠ *Calle Campeche 155, Roma Sur* ☎ *55/5564-0538* ⊟ *No credit cards* ⊗ *Closed Mon.–Thurs. No dinner* Ⓜ *Chilpancingo.*

El Parnita
$ | Mexican. The logo says "tradición desde 1970," but in fact El Parnita is a more recent addition to Roma's

lunch scene: a hip, updated take on the simple family-owned fonda. The menu consists of *antojitos* (snacks like tacos, tostadas, and ceviches), from recipes culled from the family's travels throughout the country, such as *rellenito*, a chipotle chile stuffed with cheese and beans in a sauce of *piloncillo* (unrefined brown sugar) from Zacatecas; and tacos *viajeros*, homemade tortillas piled with pork loin and leg long cooked in citrus, from Michoacán. **Known for:** boisterous people-watching scene; affordable regional Mexican fare; great micheladas. *Average main: 120 MP* ⊠ *Av. Yucatán 84, Roma Norte* ☎ *55/5264-7551* ⊕ *www.elparnita. com* ⊘ *No dinner. Closed Mon.* Ⓜ *Insurgentes.*

★ Expendio de Maiz Sin Nombre

$ | **Mexican.** The owners of this tiny Roma kitchen with volcanic-rock floors and walls are devoted to preserving Mexico's ancient culinary traditions, including the *nixtamalización* process of grinding corn into tortilla dough, which is used to create exquisite yet simple breakfast and lunch fare that changes day to day, according to what's in season. You might enjoy anything from corn tacos filled with fresh cheese, *hoja santa* (a peppery Mexican herb), and squash blossom, to a blue-corn tortilla topped with avocado, ants, and salsa. **Known for:** corn tortillas produced following centuries-old Mesoamerican traditions; seasonally changing breakfast and lunch fare; covered sidewalk seating. *Average main: 85 MP* ⊠ *Av. Yucatan 84, Roma Norte*

☎ *55/2498-9964* ⊕ *www.expendiode-maiz.com* ⊘ *Closed Mon. No dinner* Ⓜ *Insurgentes.*

Farina

$$ | **Modern Italian.** In this unassuming hole-in-the-wall pizza place, you'll find a generous selection of excellent thin-crust pizzas and handmade pastas, plus a good variety of cocktails and wines. The pizzas come with red or white bases, with the truffle oil, gorgonzola, and wild-mushroom pie being a favorite among the latter, and the pie with Brie, mozzarella, pepperoni, and cherry tomatoes standing out among the "rosso" pies. **Known for:** creative thin-crust pizzas; good selection of wines by the glass; late-night hours. *Average main: 210 MP* ⊠ *Calle Chihuahua 139, Roma Norte* ☎ *55/7589-0520* Ⓜ *Insurgentes.*

★ Galanga Thai Kitchen

$$ | **Thai.** Fans of Thai food who were frustrated by the lack of options in the capital rejoiced when this stellar restaurant moved from its previous tiny home into a dramatic, spacious 19th-century mansion in 2019. The artfully prepared dishes here can hold their own with any you'll find in North America—it's best to share a few dishes, such as duck in a red curry of pineapple, eggplant, and lychee; a southern-style pad thai with soft-shell crab, tamarind sauce, and coconut milk; and the dessert of fried bananas with house-made chrysanthemum ice cream. **Known for:** inventive, boldly flavored Thai cuisine; beautiful dining room in a gracious Roma house; rich desserts with homemade ice cream. *Average main: 285 MP* ⊠ *Calle Monterrey 204, Roma Norte* 🕿 *55/6550-4492* Ⓜ *Insurgentes.*

Kiin Thai-Viet Eatery
$$ | Thai. This younger sibling to Galanga offers a more varied menu that includes both Thai and Vietnamese fare at slightly lower prices, but as with the original restaurant, the food is flavorful, expertly prepared, and delicious. The solarium-style space creates the feel of dining in an art nouveau birdcage, and there's outdoor seating on a side patio as well. **Known for:** beautiful, plant-filled dining room; creative desserts with house-made ice creams; mix of contemporary Thai and Vietnamese dishes. *Average main: 220 MP* ⊠ *Calle Orizaba 219, Roma Sur* 🕿 *55/7095-7421* ⊕ *www.kiin-thai. com* ⊘ *Closed Mon. No dinner Sun.* Ⓜ *Hospital General.*

Lalo!
$$ | Contemporary. The walls are decked with cartoon figures and bursts of color at this lively space differs from its more sophisticated night-time sister restaurant, Bistrot Maximo. Come in the morning to feast on smoked-salmon bagels with poached eggs, acai bowls with seasonal fruit, and croque monsieur sandwiches, while afternoons are the time for gourmet pizzas, pastas, ceviche, roasted chicken, and other satisfying fare. **Known for:** gourmet pizzas; contemporary breakfast fare; artisanal beer. *Average main:*

205 MP ⊠ *Calle Zacatecas 173, Roma Norte* 🕿 *55/5564-3388* ⊕ *www.eat-lalo.com* ⊘ *Closed Mon. No dinner* Ⓜ *Insurgentes.*

La Pitahaya Vegana
$ | Vegetarian. Although the availability of vegan cuisine has come a long way in Mexico City in recent years, few restaurants are devoted exclusively to it, but this small café produces some of the tastiest and most beautifully plated plant-based fare in town. Tortillas at La Pitahaya are as bright pink as the walls (they're dyed with beet juice—the tortillas, that is), and they come with equally bright, fresh fillings like cauliflower with coconut cream and pineapple, and pastor-style oyster mushrooms. **Known for:** bright-pink tortillas with creative vegan fillings; chia pudding with cashew milk, cardamom, and agave syrup for dessert; house-brewed kombucha. *Average main: 90 MP* ⊠ *Calle Querétaro 90, Roma Norte* 🕿 *55/7159-2918* ⊕ *www.lapitahay-avegana.mx* Ⓜ *Hospital General.*

Lima 700
$$$ | Peruvian. The name of this upscale Peruvian restaurant located within a sumptuous Porfirian-era mansion is a nod to 700 years of Incan and European culinary tradition. This tradition informs the menu of brightly acidic ceviches and tiraditos, *anticuchos* (beef-heart skewers), wok-sautéed *tacu tacu* (rice and beans with marinated sliced steak), and mushroom risotto with cheese, wild mushrooms, and aji amarillo. **Known for:** excellent pisco sours; charming rooftop

terrace; contemporary Peruvian fare. *Average main: 360 MP* ⊠ *Calle Tonalá 144, Roma Norte* ☎ *55/5264–1769* ⊕ *www.lima700.com* ⊗ *No dinner Sun. and Mon.* Ⓜ *Insurgentes.*

Maíz de Cacao

$ | Mexican. Part of the city's rapidly growing embrace and advocacy of Mesoamerican culinary traditions, this diminutive café with Mexican folk art on the walls specializes in dishes made with—as the name suggests—corn and chocolate. Tuck into a plate of blue-corn tamales with mildly spicy pork rib meat, eggs grilled with chiles in banana leaf, or cheese gorditas, washing everything down with corn atole or indigenous chocolate drinks (all of which are also available in the form of refreshing *paletas*, or popsicles). **Known for:** corn tortillas and tamales made with Mesoamerican nixtamalization practices; cute, cheerful dining space with an open kitchen; traditional indigenous corn and chocolate drinks (and popsicles). *Average main: 100 MP* ⊠ *Calle Córdoba 148, Roma Norte* ☎ *55/5584-9638* ⊗ *Closed Mon.* Ⓜ *Hospital General.*

★ Máximo Bistrot

$$$ | Modern French. Of the capital's most sought-after dining experiences, this surprisingly unassuming bistro is also one of the most accessible and reasonably priced, especially as it doesn't involve a multicourse tasting menu or require reservations weeks in advance (although booking a few days ahead, especially on weekends, is advisable). Chef Eduardo García

crafts complex, locally sourced French-Mediterranean dishes like butterfish in a white miso broth and flat-iron steak au jus with potato puree and porcini mushrooms—nothing outlandish, and always perfectly executed. **Known for:** stone crab, lobster, and other seafood fare; decadent desserts; pleasant sidewalk seating. *Average main: 390 MP* ⊠ *Calle Tonalá 133, Roma Norte* ☎ *55/5264-4291* ⊕ *www.maximobistrot.com.mx* ⊗ *Closed Mon. No dinner Sun.* Ⓜ *Insurgentes.*

★ Mercado Roma

$ | Eclectic. More than 60 vendors offering everything from elevated short-order street food to rather refined farm-to-tables victuals operate out of this trendy food hall with a popular artisan beer bar, the Biergarten, on the third-floor rooftop space. The first floor features stalls and a patio seating area, and a smaller mezzanine offers still more options; all told you'll find outposts of several popular CDMX eateries—including El Moro Churreria, Butcher & Sons burgers, Que Bo! artisan chocolates, and Cafe Emir coffee—plus stands doling out paella, mezcal, boozy paletas, and French crepes. **Known for:** plenty of to-go options; different food choices for every taste; lively and fun rooftop beer garden. *Average main: 120 MP* ⊠ *Calle Querétaro 225, Roma Norte* ☎ *55/5564-1396* ⊕ *mr.mercadoroma.com* Ⓜ *Insurgentes.*

★ Mog Bistro

$$ | Asian Fusion. This rambling, seemingly always-packed restaurant is one of the city's pioneers in genuinely sophisticated, authentic modern Asian (mostly Japanese) cuisine. The food, which is artfully presented in small plates, bowls, and bamboo steamers, spans Thailand, Japan, and China, with highlights being several varieties of ramen, shimp pad thai, hamachi sashimi, sushi rolls, and Chinese sausage. **Known for:** colorful tropical cocktails; creative sushi rolls; about a dozen varieties of ramen. *Average main: 220 MP ⊠ Calle Frontera 168, Roma Norte ☎ 55/5264–1629 ⊕ www.facebook.com/Mogbistro* Ⓜ *Hospital General.*

Páramo

$$ | Modern Mexican. Depending on the time of day and your mood, this buzzy warren of smartly designed nooks can be a fun options for drinks after lunch at El Parnita cantina (downstairs) or for a late-night feast of ceviche and tacos with creative fillings like hibiscus flowers, seared tuna, and longaniza sausage. Keep in mind that it gets packed here on weekends, so scoring a table and receiving your order can be slow, but everything here—from the food to the drinks—is delicious. **Known for:** cool, trendy vibe; delicious, creatively prepared tacos; big crowds and relatedly iffy service on weekend nights. *Average main: 180 MP ⊠ Av. Yucatan 84, Roma Norte ☎ 55/5941–5125 ⊕ www.facebook.com/ParamoRoma ⊗ No lunch* Ⓜ *Insurgentes.*

Parcela

$$ | Mexican Fusion. You enter this magical little compound through a lush garden with a cute play area for kids, which leads to an expansive, open-air dining room—from inside, you can almost imagine you're deep in the heart of the Yucatán. The healthy seasonally inspired Mexican fare is well-prepared—try the tacos with roasted cauliflower, traditional *fideo seco* (lightly spicy Mexican noodles), or rib-eye steak. **Known for:** lush and tranquil garden ambience; fresh juices and smoothies; healthy, locally sourced cuisine. *Average main: 185 MP ⊠ Calle Querétaro 217, Roma Norte ☎ 55/7822–3319 ⊕ www.facebook. com/ParcelaRoma ⊗ No dinner Sun.* Ⓜ *Insurgentes.*

Porco Rosso

$$ | Barbecue. Blaring rock music, hanging plants, and picnic tables laden with hot sauces are hallmarks of this trendy, open-air spot overlooking Plaza Cabrera and specializing in American-style barbecue. If you're not convinced that it's possible to find truly tender and flavorful fall-off-the-bone barbecue outside the United States, you may be surprised—these guys turn out legitimately tasty pulled pork, beef brisket, baby-back ribs, and smoked sausage, along with brisket ramen and lo mein, and a cornucopia of sides and sandwiches. **Known for:** smoked brisket (on its own and in ramen); lively outdoor dining space; great selection of classic and Mexican-inspired BBQ sides. *Average main: 210 MP*

✉ *Calle Zacatecas 102, Roma Norte* ☎ *55/7822-3310* ⊕ *www.porcorossobbq.com* Ⓜ *Hospital General.*

Taquería El Jarocho

$ | Mexican. This old-time neighborhood institution has weathered Roma's booms and busts since 1947 and is today far more than a taqueria, although tacos de guisados (filled with rich, stewed ingredients) are still the restaurant's main draw. Try authentic fillings like *moronga* (ground blood sausage with onions and chiles), beef tongue in a olive-tomato Veracruz sauce, or traditional lamb barbacoa. **Known for:** famous tacos de guisados; big, inexpensive portions; refreshingly untrendy ambience. *Average main: 75 MP* ✉ *Calle Tapachula 94, Roma Norte* ☎ *55/5574-5303* ⊕ *www.taqueriaeljarocho.com.mx* Ⓜ *Chilpancingo.*

Bars and Nightlife

Bar Félix

A favored fixture along the voguey nightlife row that is Avenida Álvaro Obregón, Félix is a popular, dimly lit cocktail bar at first glance. Head down the side hallway to the back, however, and you'll find a chatter-filled garden pizzeria that rakes in sizable crowds until late into the evening—the pies here are pretty tasty too. ✉ *Av. Álvaro Obregón 64, Roma Norte* ☎ *55/5160-1791* Ⓜ *Insurgentes.*

Departamento

Meant to evoke the inviting, laid-back trappings of a friend's (very large) *departamento*—or apart-ment—this often packed lounge has DJs spinning trancy tunes on turntables. It's a fun place to chill and mingle before going clubbing, or a place to enjoy while the night is winding down. Some nights there's live music. ✉ *Av. Álvaro Obregón 154, Roma Norte* ☎ *55/2855-9154* ⊕ *www.facebook.com/departamentostudiobar* Ⓜ *Insurgentes.*

Jazzatlán Capital

The Mexico City branch of a famous Latin swing jazz club in the historic town of Cholula (just outside Puebla), this energetic spot has a few different areas, including the live music area where bands perform both traditional and contemporary tunes. On other levels, there's a tap room serving craft beers and a full restaurant with gastropub fare. ✉ *Calle Guanajuato 239, Roma Norte* ☎ *55/5459-2840* ⊕ *www.jazzatlan.club* Ⓜ *Insurgentes.*

La Chicha

A low-key neighborhood hangout with kitschy decor, string lights, and reasonably priced craft beers, cocktails, and globally inspired tapas, La Chicha is a few blocks south of Roma Norte's flashier and more crowded Álvaro Obregón bar strip. It's a much more mellow place to meet locals and a generally easy spot to find a table. There's another location at Cineteca Nacional in Coyoacan. ✉ *Calle Orizaba 171, Roma Norte* ☎ *55/5574-6625* Ⓜ *Hospital General.*

★ Licorería Limantour

Much-lauded and regularly named among the world's 10 best bars by a panel of drink-industry experts, Limantour looks nevertheless remarkably approachable—a narrow, neatly designed space with one of the city's first truly serious mixology programs (hence its phenomenal reputation). The surprisingly affordable drinks, like the herbal Green Park (with gin, celery bitters, basil, lime, and egg white) and the Machete (San Cosme mezcal with tangerine liqueur, grapefruit and lime extract, agave syrup, and spearmint), delight the senses and explain why ardent cocktail aficionados flock here. You'll find tasty bar snacks too. ⊠ *Av. Álvaro Obregón 106, Roma Norte* ☎ *55/5264-4122* ⊕ *www.limantour.tv* Ⓜ *Insurgentes.*

Riviera del Sur

You might not guess this lively cantina has been around for generations. A mid-2010s makeover designed to give it broader appeal to a younger clientele has indeed given the venerable Roma Sur institution fresh currency, as has the exceptionally well-prepared Yucatecan food (don't pass up the cochinita pibíl). Thankfully, the crowd remains diverse and unpretentious, a mix of ages and backgrounds. There are several sidewalk tables, too. ⊠ *Calle de Chiapas 174, Roma Norte* ☎ *55/5264-1552* ⊕ *www.facebook. com/cantinariviera* Ⓜ *Chilpancingo.*

Tasting Room

This laid-back, simply decorated bar on the ground floor of Roomies Hostel in Roma Sur is a mecca for craft-beer lovers. The menu features around two dozen rotating taps, about three-quarters of them from smaller, notable Mexican breweries and the rest generally from the United States. Cocktails and light pub food are on offer as well. ⊠ *Calle de Chiapas 173, Roma Norte* ☎ *55/7159-8388* ⊕ *www.facebook. com/TastingRoomMX* Ⓜ *Chilpancingo.*

Vinamore

This charming, tiny spot with modern wooden tables and white brick walls has quickly become a go-to for its thoughtfully curated selection of wines. You can also build your own cheese-charcuterie board to accompany your sipping, and cannoli are available for a sweet ending. ⊠ *Calle Guanajuato 78, Roma Norte* ☎ *55/8437-4062* ⊕ *www.facebook. com/vinamorecdmx* Ⓜ *Insurgentes.*

🎭 Performing Arts

★ Cine Tonalá

Three or four indie and foreign films show daily at this terrific little arthouse cinema in Roma Sur. The space also contains myriad places to hang out before or after your movie, including a roof terrace with occasional live entertainment, a bookstore, and a café with good pizzas, burgers, and other casual pub fare. ⊠ *Calle Tonalá 261, Roma Sur* ☎ *55/5264-4101* ⊕ *www.cinetonala.mx* Ⓜ *Centro Médico.*

SANTA MARÍA LA RIBERA

ALAMEDA CENTRAL

POLANCO

SAN RAFAEL

JUÁREZ AND ANZURES

CENTRO HISTÓRICO

BOSQUE DE CHAPULTEPEC

ROMA

CONDESA

BENITO JUÁREZ

SAN ÁNGEL

COYOACÁN

Sightseeing ★★★☆☆ | Shopping ★★★★☆ | Dining ★★★★★ | Nightlife ★★★★☆

A bundant with striking 1920s and 1930s architecture, tree-lined streets, and a wealth of hip and trendy bars and eateries, Condesa is usually mentioned in the same breath as its similarly cool neighbor, Roma. Many people treat the two areas as one large district, but Condesa retains its own subtly distinct history and personality, and it generally feels a little more established and less hipsterized than Roma. It also has a considerable supply of tiny parks and promenades, many on crescents and down hidden lanes, all with lush greenery, especially its two most famous parks, España and México.—*by Andrew Collins*

Condesa is a trove of grand, artful architecture—much of it historic, but you'll also find a number of eye-catching modern buildings, few of them rising higher than five or six stories. As you walk around, be sure to look up, as grand balconies and sweeping roof-decks are part of the visual picnic. Angular art deco structures with expansive casement windows mingle beside ornate and slightly curvier art nouveau beauties, while many of the newer structures have sheer glassy facades and huge terraces decked with ferns, flowers, and shrubs. Condesa sustained heavy damage following the massive earthquake of September 19, 1985, and many of the neighborhood's newer buildings replaced those that had collapsed or been condemned. Exactly (to the day) 32 years later, the 2017 earthquake caused further destruction; even today it's possible to detect cracks in building facades and extra structural supports. For the most part, however, Condesa looks and feels enchanting, with a slightly faded elegance and a decidedly bohemian vibe.

Condesa's grandeur dates back generations. It's named for Spanish contessa (or *condesa*) Miravalle, who owned the land (as well as Roma and much of Tacubaya) throughout the city's colonial era. In the early 1900s, the contessa's vast property had been sold and subdivided, and it quickly became a desirable place to live among wealthy supporters of Mexico's aristocratic Porfirio Díaz regime, which ended in 1911. The neighborhood's grand avenues, lush parks, and glorious art nouveau and art deco buildings were developed over the next three decades. Like Roma, Condesa experienced a downturn during the latter half of the 20th century that was greatly exacerbated by the '85 earthquake. Following this period and well into the 1990s, the neighborhood began to attract artists and countercultural types drawn to its gorgeous old buildings and newfound affordability.

Today the neighborhood vibe spans youthful, monied, LGBTQ, touristy, hipster, entrepreneurial, and artsy, and this diverse blend results in some of the best people-watching in the city. Condesa has one of Mexico City's most eclectic dining and drinking scenes, with an abundance of everything from cheap old-school taquerias and casual international restaurants to voguish bistros and darkly lit craft-beer bars and mezcalerias. Much of the action is along the broad Avenidas Tamaulipas, Michoacán, and Nuevo León, along with elliptical Avenida Amsterdam—all of these streets have gracious, landscaped medians down their centers. The neighborhood's dense green foliage is alluring any time of year, but late winter (mid-February to mid-April), it's especially gorgeous as the neighborhood's many jacaranda trees bloom with lavender flowers.

Condesa East

◉ Sights

★ Avenida Amsterdam
An elliptical avenue that feels like it could be in Paris or Madrid minus the unusually lush semi-tropical foliage, Amsterdam was designed in the early 1900s as the outer perimeter of a racetrack that would eventually become Parque México. Today it ranks among the best streets in the city for a stroll. The two lanes of auto traffic are divided by a landscaped median with a paved sidewalk, old-fashioned street lamps, and a smattering of

GETTING HERE

La Condesa is easy to reach and navigate by Uber, metro, or on foot. It's just south of Avenida Paseo de la Reforma, and it's flanked by two other important roads, Aveninda Insurgentes and the Circuito Bicentenario freeway. One of the city's safest neighborhoods for strolling, it's within walking distance of Roma and Parque de Chapultepec as well as the Sevilla, Chapultepec, and Juanacatlán Metro stops on the 1 line, and Chilpancingo and Patriotismo stops on the 9 line. To get from upper Condesa to the outer sections covered in this chapter, such as Escandón and outer San Miguel Chapultepec, it's a 30- to 45-minute walk—consider Uber or take the metro to the Tacubaya or Constituyentes stop.

art noveau tiled benches. There are three roundabouts connecting Amsterdam, each named for one of the city's cloud-scraping peaks: Popocatépetl, Iztaccihuatl, and Citlaltépetl. This is also one of the best streets for admiring the neighborhood's distinctive residential architectural, from ornate art deco and art nouveau beauties to strikingly contemporary mid-rise towers. Although predominantly residential, the ground floors of many of these buildings contain hip coffeehouses, ice cream shops, bistros, and bars, along with a handful of noteworthy boutique shops. The avenue completely encircles Parque México, and at the northwestern side of the ellipse, you can walk from Parque

México just two blocks along restaurant-lined Avendia Parras to reach Parque España. ⊠ *Av. Amsterdam, La Condesa* Ⓜ *Chilpancingo.*

Parque España

Like nearby Parque México, this slightly smaller but no less alluring 16½ acre urban oasis was laid out in the early 1920s by architect José Luis Cuevas, who was also responsible for planning much of the surrounding Hipódromo section of the Condesa neighborhood. It opened officially in September 1921, during the centennial celebrations of the Mexican War of Independence. A focal point of Parque España is the dramatic, modern sculpture and fountain installed in 1974 in honor of statesman and Mexican Revolutionary General Lázaro Cárdenas. It's a figurative depiction of the outstretched palm of then President Cárdenas, welcoming Republican refugees of the Spanish Civil to Mexico during the late 1930s. Both the statue and the park in general is a popular place to sit

BACK IN THE DAY

As you walk along two of the neighborhood's most picturesque streets, avenidas Amsterdam and México, you may wonder about their distinctive elliptical shapes. In fact, Avenida México sits atop a former racetrack—in which Parque México formed the center—where both horse and auto races took place in the 1910s; Avenida Amsterdam forms an outer perimeter "ring road" encircling it.

with a book or watch locals strolling with their dogs. It's filled with flower beds, native shrubs, a small pond, and a playground. ⊠ *Av. Nuevo León at Av. Sonora, La Condesa* Ⓜ *Sevilla.*

★ Parque México

Condesa's other green lung, the 22-acre Parque México lies just southeast of its slightly smaller and slightly older sister, Parque España. Among its many enchanting features, you'll find a gracious duck pond, a large children's playground, fountains, a strikingly ornate art deco iron clocktower, and dozens of footpaths passing by emerald gardens, topiary shrubs, and towering specimen trees. The park was constructed in 1927 on the site of a former racetrack, which explains the circular road, Avenida México, looping its perimeter and the name of the colonia in which its officially located, Hipódromo (hippodrome) Condesa. The park is lined with handsome buildings, including some of the best examples of art deco in the city. Dozens of cafés, taquerias, and healthy markets are within a couple of blocks of the park, making it a great spot to enjoy a casual bite to eat. ⊠ *Av. Michoacán at Av. México, La Condesa* Ⓜ *Sevilla.*

 Shopping

Buck House
This tiny little shoe boutique stocks an impressively big selection of beautifully crafted leather sneakers, sandals, boots, Oxfords, and loafers. They've been making fine leather shoes in Mexico City since 1955. ⊠ *Av. Tamaulipas 38, La Condesa* ☎ *55/5162-7532* ⊕ *www.buckhouse. com.mx* Ⓜ *Chilpancingo.*

Carmen Rion
Linen dresses by this Mexican designer are done in palettes and patterns that bring to mind (and sometimes incorporate) traditional Mexican textiles, embroidery, and lace. The draping and layering, however, are very contemporary. Skirts and wraps that flow elegantly—often in vertical lines—are juxtaposed with structured, sometimes architectural bodices and tops. Ties, fastenings, and jewelry are equally tantalizing, the latter often combining wood, silver, and seedpods. Rion has been recognized not only for her unique designs, but also for her ethical practices, which have included working with Mexican artisans to create her garments. ⊠ *Av. Michoacán 30–A, La Condesa* ☎ *55/5264-6179* ⊕ *www.carmenrion. com* Ⓜ *Chilpancingo.*

★ Librería del Fondo de Cultura Económica
Located within the strikingly white Cultura Económica Rosario Castellanos cultural center and containing more than 250,000 books on exhibit, this outstanding bookstore with a dramatically illuminated black-and-white ceiling and plenty of comfy armchairs also contains a café and art gallery. One of Condesa's hubs of intellectualism, the center regularly presents films, lectures, readings, and other events. ⊠ *Av. Tamaulipas 202, La Condesa* ☎ *55/5276-7110* ⊕ *www. fondodeculturaeconomica.com* Ⓜ *Patriotismo.*

★ Tout Chocolat
Owner and chocolatier Luis Robledo, who trained with Daniel Boulud in New York and at the prestigious L'école de Grand Chocolat in Paris, was named best pastry chef in Latin America in a República del Cacao competition. In his light and cheerful boutique on Avendia Amsterdam, you can shop for exquisite bonbons in intriguing flavors (passionfruit-vanilla, calamansi, mezcal-sea salt, and pineapple-ginger), or have a seat and sip a lusciously rich hot chocolate or mocha. There's also a selection of cakes, cookies, and French macarons. ⊠ *Av. Amsterdam 154, La Condesa* ☎ *55/5211-9840* ⊕ *www. toutchocolat.mx* Ⓜ *Chilpancingo.*

VOID
A pink neon "Come In We're Closed" sign beckons bargain hunters and fashionistas alike to enter the Void, a big vintage clothing

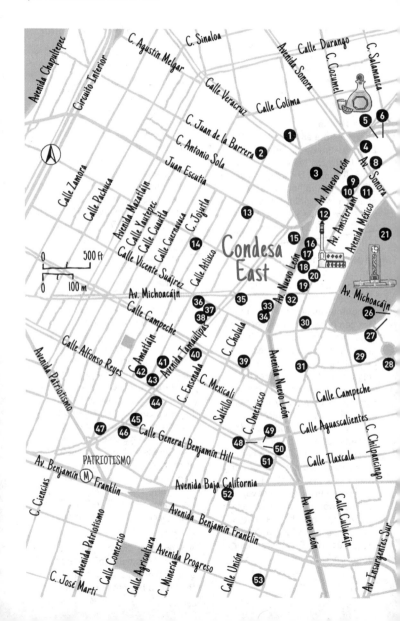

emporium set over two floors. You'll find an impressive selection of upmarket men's and women's boots, clubwear, designer threads, and accessories. There's a second location in Roma. ⊠ *Calle Parral 5, La Condesa* ☎ *55/9130–8319* ⊕ *www. voidmx.com* Ⓜ *Chapultepec.*

 Coffee and Quick Bites

Chiquitito Café
$ | Café. For a refreshing caffeine pick-me-up in the southern reaches of Condesa, pop into this cute and cozy third-wave espresso bar that serves delicious breakfasts and sandwiches too. Students and free-lancers work away on their laptops in the triangular white-brick interior space, while you're more likely to spy friends gabbing at the sidewalk tables. **Known for:** tasty baguette sandwiches; cakes and pastries; artisanal coffee drinks. *Average main: 75 MP* ⊠ *Calle Alfonso Reyes 232, La Condesa* ☎ *55/5211–6123* ⊕ *www.chiquititocafe.com* ⊘ *No dinner Sun.* Ⓜ *Chilpancingo.*

El Farolito
$ | Mexican. A neighborhood favorite since 1962, this spacious taqueria with a striking black awning and red-and-white color scheme offers up hefty platters of delicious tacos and other classics. Try the *costras crujientes,* in which the meat is wrapped in fried cheese before being wrapped in a tortilla, or any of the *alambres al carbón* with bacon, onions, chile poblano, and any number of fillings. **Known for:** costras crujientes (tacos enveloped

in fried cheese); horchata, jamaica, tamarindo, and other juices; churros with cajeta, chocolate, and condensed milk. *Average main: 110 MP* ⊠ *Calle Altata 19, La Condesa* ☎ *55/5515–2380* ⊕ *www.taqueriasel-farolito.com.mx* Ⓜ *Chilpancingo.*

El Tizoncito
$ | Mexican. You shouldn't leave this sprawling, casual place without trying one the tacos al pastor, which come in a variety of styles—long-running El Tizoncito claims to have invented the now iconic dish. This festive spot also serves excellent pozole, tacos *choriquesos* (grilled chorizo slathered in melted mozza-rella), marinated *huesitos* (ribs) with guacamole, and plenty of other street-food-style options. **Known for:** famous tacos al pastor; mari-nated huesitos (ribs); elote (corn) cake for dessert. *Average main: 100 MP* ⊠ *Av. Tamaulipas 122, La Condesa* ☎ *55/5286–7321* ⊕ *www.eltizoncito. com.mx* Ⓜ *Patriotismo.*

Enhorabuena Café
$ | Café. From morning through early evening, this casual, contem-porary café that opens to a quiet, tree-lined street near Parque España welcomes a mix of regulars and tourists with bountiful plates of Mexican and international breakfast dishes, soups, salads, and sand-wiches. The menu tends toward healthy and fresh, with mango-granola bowls, toasted ham-and-gruyere brioche sandwiches, green juices, and fine teas and lattes. **Known for:** chilaquiles verdes; house-made sodas, juices, and sipping chocolates; relaxing ambi-

ence for work or socializing. *Average main: 110 MP* ⊠ *Calle Atlixco 13, La Condesa* ☎ *55/9155-6654* ⊕ *www.facebook.com/enhorabuenacafe* Ⓜ *Chapultepec.*

Frëims

$ | **Café.** Although there's a small indoor dining room, the big draw here is the expansive patio with a retractable glass roof, tall ivy-covered walls, and tables of varying sizes. It's a great place to relax or work on your laptop for a few hours, and there are enough tasty pressed-sandwich, salad, and soup options to make a meal of it. **Known for:** late-night dining; waffles and waffle sandwiches; well-crafted coffee drinks. *Average main: 145 MP* ⊠ *Amsterdam 62-B, La Condesa* ☎ *55/9130-8449* ⊕ *www.freims.mx* ⊗ *Closed Mon.* Ⓜ *Sevilla.*

★ Molino El Pujol

$ | **Modern Mexican.** Legendary chef and Enrique Olvera, a devoted practitioner of making tortillas according to tradition and with only the highest-quality ingredients, has opened this hole-in-wall shop and café, in part to supply his world-famous Polanco restaurant to the masses. The short menu is basically an ode to maíz, featuring elote and esquites, *enmoladas* (chicken mole enchiladas), quesadillas, huitla-coche tamales, and other perfectly prepared botanas (for breakfast and lunch)—you can even sip a glass of *atole* (a thick and warm masa-based beverage with Mesoamerican roots). **Known for:** house-made tortillas, salsas, and mole to go; tamales with creative fillings; long waits

so coming early is smart. *Average main: 80 MP* ⊠ *Gral. Benjamín Hill 146, La Condesa* ☎ *55/5271-3515* ⊕ *www.pujol.com.mx* ⊗ *No dinner* Ⓜ *Patriotismo.*

Neveria Roxy

$ | **Café.** Throughout the day, Condesa's traditional Mexican ice-cream parlor—and its several other locations around the city—packs in kids and hipsters alike with its *nieve* (sorbet) flavors like *maracuyá* (passionfruit) and *tuna* (prickly pear cactus fruit), and its *helado* (ice-cream) flavors, including *rompope* (eggnog) and macadamia. It's distinctly old school, with its teal vinyl chairs, white tables, and bright fluorescent lights, but the quality is first-rate. **Known for:** old-school ambience; lots of regional Mexican fruit flavors; ice-cream sundaes. *Average main: 40 MP* ⊠ *Fernando Montes de Oca 89, La Condesa* ☎ *55/5286-1258* ⊕ *www.neveriaroxy.com.mx.*

Nómada

$ | **Café.** This modern, pet-friendly ice-cream parlor is a perfect stop for sweet break while ambling along Avendia Amsterdam. The smooth, not-overly sweet ice cream comes in such intriguing flavors as cardamom, chia-cucumber, and vanilla-mezcal. **Known for:** interesting flavors of artisanal ice cream; ice-cream sandwiches and milk shakes; cupcakes and cookies. *Average main: 60 MP* ⊠ *Av. Amsterdam 297, La Condesa* ☎ *55/6830-6912* ⊕ *www.nomadahela-deria.com* Ⓜ *Chilpancingo.*

★ Ojo de Agua

$$ | **Café.** This fast-expanding Mexican chain of health food café-markets has one of its busiest but prettiest locations in Condesa, over-looking one of Avenida Amsterdam's most photographed fountains. Choose from an extensive array of combination juices and smoothies, plus excellent, if somewhat pricey, salads and sandwiches, like roasted turkey with manchego and ginger sauce. **Known for:** delicious smoothies in numerous flavors; fresh produce and healthy snacks to go; prime location overlooking a grand fountain. *Average main: $205* ⊠ *Citlaltépetl 23–C, La Condesa* ☎ *55/6395–8000* ⊕ *www.grupoojo-deagua.com.mx* Ⓜ *Chilpancingo.*

Orígenes Orgánicos

$ | **Café.** Although on a pretty, tree-shaded street corner overlooking Plaza Popocatépetl, this bustling café and gourmet natural market doesn't have a ton of atmosphere. The draw here is the extensive selection of healthy eats, like quinoa burgers with broccoli and Asian noodles, and match-tea hotcakes topped with seasonal fresh fruit. **Known for:** organic groceries and produce; sidewalk seating with pretty views; fresh-squeezed juices and smoothies. *Average main: 140 MP* ⊠ *Plaza Popocatépetl 41–A, La Condesa* ☎ *55/5208–6678* ⊕ *www. origenesorganicos.com* ⊘ *No dinner weekends* Ⓜ *Sevilla.*

★ Qüentin Café

$ | **Café.** Generally less crowded than the original location in Roma, this buzzy third-wave coffeehouse is every bit as inviting, from its peaceful setting on leafy Avendia Amsterdam to its comfy seating and plant-filled interior. The baristas are knowledgeable and profes-sional, whether crafting a *carajillo* (a refreshing cocktail with iced espresso and Licor 43, a fragrant herbal liqueur), a *cascara* (a tea brewed with coffee cherries), or a single-origin pour-over. **Known for:** carefully sourced small-batch coffees from around the world; artisanal chocolates and pastries; coffee-based cocktails. *Average main: 60 MP* ⊠ *Av. Amsterdam 67a, La Condesa* ☎ *55/7312–6188* Ⓜ *Sevilla.*

★ Tacos Hola

$ | **Mexican.** This simple, tiny taqueria on Avendia Amsterdam is a favorite standby for tacos *guisados,* a completely addictive style with stewed and richly seasoned braised meats like *higado* (beef liver topped with avocado), chicken mole, and a tuna-sardine blend. Hola stands out from the pack for its variety of vege-tarian and vegan options, including squash, Swiss chard, nopales, and *quelites,* a distinctive Mexican herb that's commonly used in soups and stews. **Known for:** excellent tacos guisados (with stewed fillings); plenty of fresh vegetarian selec-tions; fillings displayed in attractive stone bowls on the counter. *Average main: 85 MP* ⊠ *Av. Amsterdam 135, La Condesa* ☎ *55/8669–8455* ⊘ *No dinner Sun.* Ⓜ *Chilpancingo.*

Taquería El Greco
$ | Mexican. At this no-frills, old-fashioned take-out taquería, shaved meat rotates enticingly on a spit before an open flame, practically daring you not to try a plate of the Árabe-style (wrapped in grilled pita bread) tacos al pastor, plus tortas, grilled meats, and a long menu of other short-order snacks. It's a great, cheap Condesa option when you're hungry and on the run, and it's open until 4 am on weekends. **Known for:** late-night snacking; flan and key lime pie; tacos Árabes. *Average main: 70 MP* ⊠ *Av. Michoacán 54, La Condesa* ☎ *55/3934-0040* ☉ *Closed Sun* Ⓜ *Chilpancingo.*

Yolkan Barra de Cafe
$ | Café. This cool coffeehouse set down a quiet street just a block off bustling Avendia Tamaulipas serves up well-prepared coffees using Chemex, Aeropress, and other high-standard brewing practices, along with lattes and other espresso sippers. The small pink-walled room in back is a good place to get work done, and there's a selection of baked goods and sweets, too. **Known for:** colorful art on the walls; top-notch house-roasted coffee beans; friendly staff. *Average main: 55 MP* ⊠ *Calle Salvador Alvarado 186-A, La Condesa* ☎ *55/7822-0728* ⊕ *www.facebook.com/Yolkancafe* ☉ *No dinner* Ⓜ *Patriotismo.*

Yume
$$ | Café. Part cute vintage store (with clothing, housewares, jewelry, and antique toys) and part café, this homey spot in Escandón is the sort of place you want to linger. The all-day breakfast menu features a number of hearty dishes, including the house dish: poached eggs over ham, bacon, and roast beef with hollandaise sauce; plus, there's a good selection of pastas, sandwiches, and other tasty fare available later in the day. **Known for:** quirky, living room–esque vibe; hearty breakfasts served all day; antiques for sale. *Average main: 155 MP* ⊠ *Calle Sindicalismo s/n, at Av. Progreso, Mexico City* ☎ *55/2614-2376* ☉ *No dinner Sun.* Ⓜ *Chilpancingo.*

🍴 Dining

Alphi Pizzería Artesanal
$$ | Pizza. Opened in 2019 by a graduate of New York's Culinary Institute of America, this smart but simple eatery with sidewalk tables and a massive brick pizza oven serves up heavenly Neapolitan-style pies with blistered thin crusts and ethereal toppings. Try the one with guanciale, spicy salami, and Italian chorizo, or the white pizza with clams and salsa verde. **Known for:** wood-fire grilled Neapolitan pizzas with inventive toppings; small wine list; dessert pizzas. *Average main: 280 MP* ⊠ *Aguascalientes 237, La Condesa* ☎ *55/9627-8527* ⊕ *www.facebook.com/alphipizzeria* ☉ *Closed Mon. No dinner Sun.* Ⓜ *Chilpancingo.*

Asian Bay
$$ | Chinese. Hanging orange globes, rattan chairs and tables, and potted palms lend a tropical air to this popular Chinese-fusion spot along the busy Avendia Tamaulipas's

restaurant strip. Consider a few starters, like crab wontons and spring rolls, before venturing on to the larger plates, such as bok choy sautéed with garlic; stir-fried pork with ginger, chile oil, and Sichuan peppers; or kicky kung pao shrimp with chiles de árbol, peanuts, and carrots. **Known for:** great selection of bao, dumplings, and other dim sum; impressive Peking duck; matcha tea flan. *Average main: 225 MP* ⊠ *Av. Tamaulipas 95, La Condesa* ☎ *55/5553–4582* ⊕ *www.asian-bay. com* Ⓜ *Patriotismo.*

★ Azul Condesa

$$$ | Mexican. When it comes to authentic Mexican food, chef and food historian Ricardo Muñoz Zurita literally wrote the book with his *Diccionario Enciclopédico de la Gastronomía Mexicana* (*Encyclopedia of Mexican Food*). Here in his art-filled, elegant Condesa restaurant, you can sample some of his superb regional Mexican dishes, such as beef drizzled in a smoky Oaxacan mole that takes three days to make, Veracruz-style fish, or ancient Mayan dishes from the Yucatán. **Known for:** cochinita pibíl; authentic Mexican breakfasts; chocolate dessert tamales. *Average main: 360 MP* ⊠ *Av. Nuevo León 68, La Condesa* ☎ *55/5286–6380* ⊕ *www.azul.rest* ⊗ *No dinner Sun.* Ⓜ *Sevilla.*

Cafe Toscano

$$ | Italian. Among the most inviting locations of this small chain of Italian neighborhood cafés (the one on Plaza Cabrera in Roma is also lovely), Toscano sits at a quiet street corner overlooking Parque

México and is a cheerful option for reliably good egg dishes in the morning and sandwiches, salads, pastas, and pizzas later in the day. It's also a good bet simply to pause and sip coffee or wine while you watch the world go by. **Known for:** outdoor seating with park views; tasty Mexican and Italian breakfast fare; guayaba cheesecake and other sweets. *Average main: 190 MP* ⊠ *Av. Michoacán 30–A, La Condesa* ☎ *55/5584–3681* ⊕ *www.cafetoscano. com.mx* Ⓜ *Chilpancingo.*

Fat Boy Moves

$$ | Korean Fusion. Bathed in pink neon and with an industrial-chic look, this tiny, trendy hole in the wall is a great choice for satisfying your Korean food fix. The chalkboard menu is limited, but everything—kimchi-fried rice, fried chicken with a tangy honey dipping sauce, bibimbap, short ribs braised with sweet potatoes, carrots, and kumquats—is delicious. **Known for:** Korean fried chicken; Soju and kombucha; taiyaki (fish-shape) sweet waffles topped with ice cream. *Average main: 165 MP* ⊠ *Av. Tamaulipas 147, La Condesa* ☎ *55/5086–8192* ⊕ *www.facebook. com/fatboymoves* ⊗ *No dinner Sun.* Ⓜ *Patriotismo.*

La Guerrerense

$ | Seafood. Fans of Baja-style seafood flock to this bustling counter inside the Parián Condesa food hall for fresh, delicious crab tostadas, *caracol* (snail) ceviche, oysters and clams on the half shell, and shrimp and octopus cocktails. Enjoy your food at one of the casual tables, imagining you're at the beach in Ensenada, where the original La Guerrerense (which was much lauded by Anthony Bourdain) is located. **Known for:** raw shellfish and ceviche; seafood tacos; impressive range of house-made salsas. *Average main: 140 MP* ⊠ *Av. Nuevo León 107, La Condesa* ☎ *55/8434–0407* ⊕ *www.laguerrerense.com* ⊙ *Closed Tues.* Ⓜ *Chilpancingo.*

La Vinería

$$ | **Mediterranean.** This cozy, old-fashioned restaurant and wine bar is ideal for conversation and lingering over a light meal from the eclectic menu that shows Mexican, Spanish, and Italian influences. Try the wild mushrooms and goat cheese in pastry with brandy sauce, the fish of the day with artichokes and white wine, and the cajeta crepes for dessert. **Known for:** low-key, quiet ambience; excellent Eurocentric wine list; interesting mix of new-world and old-world cuisine. *Average main: 210 MP* ⊠ *Av. Fernando Montes de Oca 52–A, La Condesa* ☎ *55/5211–9020* ⊕ *lavineria. com.mx* ⊙ *No dinner Sun.*

Le Bon Bistro

$$$ | **Bistro.** One of the newer and decidedly modern French restaurants that abound and, indeed, fit in perfectly amidst Condesa's vaguely Parisian vibe, this dapper bistro is a charming option when you're seeking a slightly fancy but still unpretentious dinner out. You'll find all the classics here, well-prepared and artfully plated, including salade niçoise, steak au poivre, duck leg confit, and beef bourguignonne.

Known for: attractive sidewalk seating on Avenida Amsterdam; beautiful desserts (especially the chocolate mousse); thoughtful and attentive service. *Average main: 315 MP* ⊠ *Av. Amsterdam 225, La Condesa* ☎ *55/5087–2132* ⊕ *www.lebonbistro. mx* ⊙ *No dinner Sun.* Ⓜ *Chilpancingo.*

★ Merkavá

$$ | **Israeli.** In this sleek, narrow dining room, the best strategy for enjoying some of the city's best Israeli fare is to order the selection of 7 or 14 *salatim* (cold dishes), which include tomatoes with eggplants and honey, tamarind-cured beets, baba ghanoush, labneh with zaatar, and a host of other easily shared delectables. From the oven, you can't go wrong with the roasted cauliflower with mint yogurt, potato latkes with sour cream (and optional caviar), or grilled whole chicken with fried artichokes. **Known for:** halva for dessert in a variety of flavors; shrab al loz (an almond drink sweetened with rose water and pistachio); great creative cocktail list. *Average main: 225 MP* ⊠ *Av. Amsterdam 53, La Condesa* ☎ *55/5086–8065* ⊕ *www. bullandtank.com* ⊙ *Closed Mon. No dinner Sun.* Ⓜ *Sevilla.*

Merotoro

$$$ | **Modern Mexican.** The esteemed team behind Roma's Contramar also operates this glitzy see-and-be-seen bistro specializing in a rarefied take on the contemporary cuisine of Baja California. The oft-changing menu veers toward rich and beautiful, with dishes like sea urchin–cream rice with crispy soft-shell crab, preserved beef tartare with serrano chile aioli and chapulines, and braised lamb with creamy potatoes, turnips, and bok choy. **Known for:** refined Baja California cuisine; sophisticated service; dessert cheese plate with caramelized fig. *Average main: 420 MP* ⊠ *Av. Amsterdam 204, La Condesa* ☎ *55/5564-7799* ⊕ *www.merotoro.mx* ⊙ *No dinner Sun.* Ⓜ *Chilpancingo.*

⭐ Pasillo de Humo

$$ | Modern Mexican. Located upstairs at the bustling Parián Condesa, an arcade mostly of food stalls, Pasillo de Humo and its gorgeous atrium-style space is at once sophisticated but easygoing. The kitchen produces flavorful, authentic Oaxacan fare, including tlayudas with grasshoppers, chorizo, strips of chile, and other traditional toppings, plus octopus grilled with a *hauchimole* (guaje-seed mole) sauce and pork belly with fruit mole, plantains, sweet potato puree, and roasted pineapple. **Known for:** tlayudas with a variety of toppings; authentic Oaxacan fare; house-made ice creams with unusual flavors. *Average main: 285 MP* ⊠ *Av. Nuevo León 107, La Condesa* ☎ *55/5211-7263* ⊕ *www.facebook.com/pasillodehumo* ⊙ *No dinner Sun.* Ⓜ *Chilpancingo.*

Patagonia

$$ | Argentine. Dine at one of the sidewalk tables here when you're craving first-rate Argentinean-style steaks and other expertly prepared grills, such as grilled veal osso buco, pork shoulder with caramelized sweet potatoes, and sous vide confit of octopus with roasted potatoes and aioli. There's an excellent Argentina-focused wine list, and the desserts (including a cardomom-lemon crème brûlée) are impressive. **Known for:** attractive sidewalk seating; perfectly prepared Argentinean-style steaks; late-night dining. *Average main: 280 MP* ⊠ *Campeche 345, La Condesa* ☎ *55/5211-8032* Ⓜ *Chilpancingo.*

Ramen Sairi

$$ | Ramen. About a dozen styles of ramen are offered at this lively little Japanese restaurant, from traditional shoyu style with pork or chicken to thick curry ramen to a fragrant seafood broth brimming with shrimp, calamari, and clams. The optional ramen add-ons are many and include kimchi, hard-boiled egg, seaweed, char-siu pork, and several others, and there's also a short menu of gyoza, bao, and rice dishes. **Known for:** authentic ramen; gyoza and yakimeshi combination meals; on-site market with Japanese cookware and groceries. *Average main: 180 MP* ⊠ *Calle Alfonso Reyes 139, La Condesa* ☎ *55/1106-5962* ⊕ *www.facebook.com/ramen-sairi2019* Ⓜ *Patriotismo.*

Rojo Bistrot

$$ | Bistro. The bright-red vintage neon sign and mustard-hue facade of this corner bistro overlooking Avenida Amsterdam will have you feeling as though you've stumbled into Paris's Latin Quarter. The short chalkboard menu changes nightly but might feature grilled salmon with an orange-star anise sauce or beef fillet with olives, sundried

tomatoes, and roasted potatoes.
Known for: warm Parisian-
style vibe; classic French bistro
fare; views of charming Avenida
Amsterdam. *Average main: 265 MP*
✉ *Av. Amsterdam 71, La Condesa*
☎ *55/5211-3705* ⏱ *No dinner Sun.*
Ⓜ *Sevilla.*

Specia
$$$ | Polish. The famous roasted
duck with an apple-based stuffing,
mashed potatoes, and a baked apple
bathed in blueberry sauce has made
Specia a wildly popular destination,
but the refined Polish restaurant
with 1920s-inspired Jazz Age
artwork serves a number of other
tasty dishes, too. Consider the lamb
goulash, seasoned with paprika and
tomato, or the slow-grilled rabbit
loin with cabbage and beets. **Known
for:** apple-stuffed roasted duck;
refined Polish food; elegant art-
filled dining room. *Average main: 380
MP* ✉ *Amsterdam 241, La Condesa*
☎ *55/5564-1367* ⏱ *No dinner Sun.*
Ⓜ *Sevilla.*

 Bars and Nightlife

Antolina
This stylish mezcaleria has a
smartly decorated tile-floor interior
as well as plenty of sidewalk tables.
In addition to artisanal mezcal
and cocktails, there's a great
wine selection and well-prepared
modern Mexican food to snack on.
✉ *Aguascalientes 232, La Condesa*
☎ *55/5211-6845* ⊕ *www.antolina.mx*
Ⓜ *Chilpancingo.*

⭐ Baltra
This snug and stylish hideout just
off Avenida Amsterdam is decorated with framed butterflies and
bird illustrations and offers up an
enticing list of innovative cocktails—try the Old George Sour with
Altos Plata tequila, cardamom, and
cucumber, or any of the several fine
mezcal elixirs. The tight space with
just a handful of seats can get busy
on weekends, but if you can snag a
table, it's a lovely place to chat with
friends or mingle with new ones. It's
owned by the same team behind the
Roma's famed Licorería Limantour.
✉ *Iztaccihuatl 36D, La Condesa*
☎ *55/5264-1279* ⊕ *www.baltra.bar*
Ⓜ *Chilpancingo.*

Doméstico
This lively cocktail bar can get loud
and crowded, but good DJs keep
everybody moving and in an upbeat
mood. The pick-up-scene mood
shifts on Sunday afternoon, when
from 1 until 7 pm Doméstico hosts
an always interesting dog-friendly
retail bazaar, Bazar Condesa MX,
with jewelry, housewares, food,
and other maker-movement goods.
✉ *Av. Nuevo León 80, La Condesa*
☎ *55/5211-5833* ⊕ *www.facebook.
com/DomesticoMX* Ⓜ *Chilpancingo.*

Drunkendog
With more than 35 beers on tap
and more seating than nearby beer
haven El Trappist, this is another
of the city's best bets for sampling
unusual beers from around the
world (or purchasing cans and
bottles to go). It's dog-friendly, too.

✉ *Av. Nuevo León 4A, La Condesa* Ⓜ *Sevilla.*

El Centenario
This traditional 1940s cantina in the heart of Condesa serves up tasty Spanish- and Mexican-style tapas, inexpensive drinks, and loads of atmosphere. Tables go fast, so prepare to saddle up to the bar. ✉ *Av. Vicente Suarez 42, La Condesa* ☎ *55/5553-5451.*

★ El Trappist
This diminutive bar along nightlife-rich Avenida Álvaro Obregón is further evidence of Mexico City's fervent embrace of craft beer. As the name suggests, it has a partic-ular soft spot for Belgian beers, but you'll find a little bit of everything here, including some bottles from smaller, culty brewers around the world, as well as one of the most current selections of up-and-coming Mexican producers. The friendly bartenders really know their stuff, too. ✉ *Av. Álvaro Obregón 298, La Condesa* ☎ *55/5916-4260* ⊕ *www.facebook.com/ElTrappistBarBieres* Ⓜ *Sevilla.*

Felina
There's no signage outside this darkly seductive bar with blue-and-gold velvet seats and an intentionally distressed exterior, but everyone from postgallery-goers to hipster cocktail enthusiasts make their way here, five nights a week (they're closed Sunday and Monday). The atmosphere is low-key, and the kitchen turns out pretty good bar food. ✉ *Calle Ometusco*

87, *La Condesa* ☎ *55/5277-1917* Ⓜ *Patriotismo.*

★ Hotel CondesaDF
One of the most fashionable cocktail venues in the neighborhood, this contemporary open-air rooftop bar is perched atop the chic Hotel ConsdesaDF. Hang with friends beneath a white umbrella on one of the wide arm chairs or snag a table overlooking the lush foliage of Parque Espana. In addition to well-crafted drinks, there's a menu of tasty sushi and other Japanese-fusion snacks. ✉ *Av. Veracruz 102, La Condesa* ☎ *55/5241-2600* ⊕ *www.condesadf.com* Ⓜ *Chapultepec.*

La Botica
This lively mezcaleria played a big role in launching the mezcal boom when it opened in 2005, and it continues to stock a care-fully curated selection of mezcals sourced directly from producers in Oaxaca. Try the *pechuga* (distilled with fruit and a chicken breast), the *añejo* (aged), or the *cremas* (liqueurs). There are additional loca-tions in Hipódromo Condesa, Roma, Juárez, El Centro, and Coyoacán. ✉ *Calle Alfonso Reyes 120, La Condesa* ☎ *55/5212-1167.*

★ La Clandestina
A womblike, intimate space with shelves adorned with countless bottles of mezcal, La Clandestina is one of four establishments in Roma and Condesa operated by Mezcales Milagrito, an artisanal distiller in Oaxaca (La Lavandería, El Palenquito, and Traspatio are the others). The fun here is in sampling

some of the many different varieties, ideally straight up so that you can taste the different complexities. There's also an extensive list of creative cocktails as well as tlayudas and other light bar snacks. ✉ *Av. Álvaro Obregón 298, La Condesa* ☎ *55/5212-1871* ⊕ *www.milagrito. com* Ⓜ *Sevilla.*

Salón Malafama

This long bustling bar ranks among the city's hippest pool halls. Since there's often a wait for the tables (it's two-for-one games before 4 pm), the bar area is a popular gathering spot. ✉ *Michoacán 78, La Condesa* ☎ *55/5553-5138* ⊕ *salonmalafama.com.*

Tom's Leather Bar

A dark back room and naked, muscular, bar-top dancers make for a cruise-y atmosphere at this long-popular Condesa gay bar. It doesn't attract as much leather gear anymore, but is a favorite of otters, bears, and guys who favor Scruff as their favorite hookup app. ✉ *Av. Insurgentes Sur 357, La Condesa* ⊕ *www.toms-mexico.com.*

Xampañería

A wall of windows allows the fashionable patrons of this posh champagne bar to enjoy views of lush Parque España. Inside, beneath a coffered ceiling and vintage light fixtures, you can sip bubbly or any number of well-poured cocktails while noshing on upscale bar fare. ✉ *Av. Nuevo León 66, La Condesa* ☎ *55/4432-4073* Ⓜ *Chilpancingo.*

 Performing Arts

El Plaza Condesa

This massive 1,900-seat concert hall books top touring pop, alternative, rock, and jazz acts. Recent headliners have included Kamasi Washington, Nine Inch Nails, Kacey Musgraves, and Cut Copy. ✉ *Calle Juan Escutia 4, La Condesa* ☎ *55/5211-0044* ⊕ *www.elplaza.mx* Ⓜ *Chapultepec.*

Un Teatro

Check the website of this small theater space with a cute seafood restaurant (Bob Marlin) to see what's on. The options include a wide range of performances—modern dance, experimental theater, spoken word, and other generally incisive and often funny material. ✉ *Av. Nuevo León 46, La Condesa* ☎ *55/2623-1333* ⊕ *www. unteatro.org* Ⓜ *Sevilla.*

Condesa West

 Sights

Archivo Diseño y Arquitectura

Contemporary Mexican design and architecture intersect in this cultural center set inside the striking 1952 modernist home created by prominent architect Arturo Chávez Paz, located next to land formerly owned by Luis Barragán. Barragán, in fact, designed the archive's beautiful little garden. Archivo Diseño y Arquitectura contains both the library of del Moral and an impressive collection of some

1,500 international and Mexican design objects. In 2012, current and renowned architect Fernando Romero and his wife Soumaya Slim (the daughter of billionaire industrialist and art patron Carlos Slim; Romero was the lead architect on Slim's iconic Museo Soumaya building in Polanco) founded this organization and established the space, which also contains a gallery that hosts rotating exhibits. Other features include an outstanding shop that carries artfully designed everyday objects and architectural books, and a small café in the garden serving lunch and coffee. ⊠ *Calle General Francisco Ramírez 4, La Condesa* ☎ *55/2614–1063* ⊕ *www. archivo.design* ⊘ *Closed Sat.–Mon.* Ⓜ *Juanacatlán.*

Casa Gilardi

Located just a few blocks from Casa Estudio Luis Barragán, you'll find the famed architect's final design project. This narrow, deep house looks modest from the street, but its light-pink facade hints at something interesting within. Indeed, a tour of this house that Barragán constructed in 1976, well after he'd retired professionally, reveals many of the trademark features that characterize his design approach:

boldly colored walls, geometrically shaped windows that allow light to filter in at interesting angles, and a stunning back patio anchored by a jacaranda tree. There's also an almost miragelike indoor swimming pool. A visit here is a must for devotees of Barragán, but anyone with an interest in design will enjoy a tour. Because the occupants of the house still reside here (their son gives the tours), visiting does require a little effort: advance reservations are required (you must call or email), and tours are offered only twice a day on weekdays and once on Saturday mornings. ⊠ *Calle Gral. Antonio León 82, La Condesa* ☎ *55/5271–3575* ⊕ *www.casagi-lardi.mx* ⊠ *MX$300* ⊘ *Closed Sun.* Ⓜ *Juanacatlán.*

★ Casa Luis Barragán

Bold colors, lines, and innovative designs are among the most ubiquitous features of Mexico City architecture, and this modernist approach can in large part be traced to Luis Barragán, who lived and worked in this home—now designated as a UNESCO World Heritage Site—from the year he built it (1947) until his death in 1988. The architect's singular aesthetic is apparent throughout the house—in the angular staircases, sharp angles, ample natural light, and bold-colored accent walls. Visits are strictly by guided tours, which are available by advance reservation several times a day on weekdays and twice on weekend mornings. Book online or by calling, and keep in mind that tour slots often fill

LUIS BARRAGÁN AND MEXICO CITY MODERNISM

Arguably Mexico's most famous architect, Luis Barragán (1902–88) designed some of the most striking and recognizable structures in the city, although his output was greatly limited by how selectively he accepted work. He also greatly influenced illustrious architects like Tadao Ando and Frank Gehry, along with his most important Mexican protege, Ricardo Legoretta. Barragán espoused clean lines, bright colors, and geometric shapes and angles that infused his designs with ample light and interesting shadows. Like Frank Lloyd Wright, he also pioneered the integration of his building designs with their natural settings. In addition to visiting Barragán's home studio and neighboring Casa Gilardi, there are a number of places in greater Mexico City where you can view works he either created.

One must-visit is **Jardines del Pedregal,** a residential subdivision that Barragán developed in the late 1940s in the desolate, volcanic lava-strewn foothills south of San Ángel. Here you can see one of the first homes he ever built, **Casa Pedregal,** and its former stable, **Tetetlán,** which is now a restaurant, architectural library, yoga studio, and boutique shop. Tours of the pink rectilinear home, which was fully restored in 2016, can be arranged by appointment.

If you're a true fan, you might consider driving 16 km (10 miles) out to see the **Torres de Satélite,** which rise some 170 feet above the highway that leads into the white-collar, mid-century suburb for which they're named. Along with artists Jesús Reyes Ferreira and Mathias Goeritz, Barragán created the 1957 sculptural cluster of five narrow obelisks painted in primary blue, red, yellow, and white. It's another 19 km (12 miles) north to visit one of Barragán's most extensive intact designs, **Cuadra San Cristobal Los Clubes,** a sprawling equestrian hacienda the artist created in 1968 (tours of the stables, the Fuentes de los Amantes, and the landscaped gardens can be arranged by emailing cuadrasancristobal@gmail.com).

up a few weeks in advance, so try to plan your visit early. ⊠ *General Francisco Ramírez 12–14, La Condesa* ☎ *55/5515–4908* ⊕ *www.casaluisbarragan.org* ⊠ *MX$400* Ⓜ *Constituyentes.*

★ Kurimanzutto

Renowned architect Alberto Kalach (of Biblioteca Vasconcelos fame) converted this former lumber yard into an internationally acclaimed contemporary art gallery in San Miguel Chapultepec, using polished wood, cement floors, and a curving metal-plated spiral staircase to set a dramatic stage for the well-attended exhibits. Often ranked among Latin America's most influential art spaces, Kurimanzutto represents about three dozen established and emerging talents and has a second location on New York City's Upper East Side. ⊠ *Calle Gobernador Rafael Rebollar 94, La Condesa* ☎ *55/5256–2408* ⊕ *www.kurimanzutto.com* Ⓜ *Constituyentes.*

LABOR

About 20 esteemed contemporary artists show at this spacious, airy gallery across the street from both Casa Estudio Luis Barragán and Archivo Diseño y Arquitectura. Like its neighbors, the gallery is a prominent work of Mexican modernist design, having been built in 1948 by functionalist architect Enrique del Moral, who resided here for many years. Both solo and group shows usually run for a couple of months, and the openings always draw a cadre of big names in the art world. The adjoining gardens, with benches and tables, are a relaxing spot to take a break from art viewing. ⊠ *Gral. Francisco Ramírez 5, La Condesa* ☎ *55/6304–8755* ⊕ *www.labor.org.mx* Ⓜ *Constituyentes.*

Museo Casa de la Bola

Although open only on Sunday and located a 10- to 20-minute walk south of Condesa in Miguel Hidalgo, this magnificent 16th-century villa that belonged to San José de Tacubaya is worth a visit to admire the 13 ornately decorated rooms, filled with fine European (predominantly French) tapestries, finery, decorative objects, and furniture that dates over the past few centuries. Give yourself an hour or so to take it all in, and be sure to spend some time in the grand gardens. ⊠ *Calle Parque Lira 136, La Condesa* ☎ *55/2614–0164* ⊕ *www.museoshaghenbeck.mx* ⊠ *MX$30* ⊙ *Closed Mon.–Sat.* Ⓜ *Tacubaya.*

 Shopping

Galería de Arte Mexicano (GAM)

Founded in 1935, the GAM was the first place in Mexico City dedicated full-time to the sale and promotion of art. It's played an important role in many Mexican art movements since then and continues to support the country's most important artists. GAM has also published noteworthy books, which are available at the gallery's bookstore. ⊠ *Gob. Rafael Rebollar 43, La Condesa* ☎ *55/5272–5529* ⊕ *www.galeriadeartemexicano.com* Ⓜ *Constituyentes.*

Hydra + Fotografía

In this building painted in boldly colored abstract designs, shutterbugs and admirers of art photography can take classes and workshops, view contemporary gallery shows, and peruse the extensive selection of photography books. ⊠ *Calle Tampico 33, La Condesa* ☎ *55/6819–9872* ⊕ *www.hydra.lat* Ⓜ *Chapultepec.*

Sabrá Dios

With a superb selection of small-batch mezcals, this tiny shop is a must if you're looking for a great sippable Mexican souvenir or gift. The staff is extremely knowledgeable and helpful, and you'll find (and can sample) some truly special, and spendy, bottles here, but others are more in the 400 to 500 pesos range. You'll also find a few other specialty food items, such as Oaxacan coffee and *sal de gusano*, salt with ground agave-fattened worms. ⊠ *Av. Veracruz 15, La Condesa*

☎ 55/5211-7623 ⊕ www.sabra-dios. net Ⓜ Chapultepec.

Coffee and Quick Bites

Deli Lou

$ | Café. A cheerful bakery-café near Parque Chapultepec and San Miguel Chapultepec's art galleries, Deli Lou serves exceptionally good baguette sandwiches with distinctive toppings (turkey with pistachios, goat cheese, Camembert, jamón serrano, and the like), plus fresh-baked cakes, brownies, and cookies. There's also a small selection of jams, wines, artisan bottled juices and teas, and other gourmet goodies, plus a variety of espresso drinks. **Known for:** phenomenal baguettes and sandwiches; delicious cakes and brownies; picnic supplies for visiting Parque Chapultepec. *Average main: 85 MP* ⊠ *Calle Gobernador Gregorio V. Gelati 78, La Condesa* ☎ 55/4444-6334 ⊕ *www.delilou.com.mx* ⊘ *Closed Sun. No dinner Sat.* Ⓜ *Constituyentes.*

⑪ Dining

★ Café Milou

$$ | Bistro. There's usually a slight wait for one of the marble tables in this chic, intimate wine bar on the border with Roma Norte—it has a loyal following among the city's trendier residents. Enjoy a glass of Muscadet or Grenache-Carignan—or perhaps an espresso and pan au chocolate in the morning—while enjoying deftly prepared modern French tapas, like pork rillettes, spicy pickled sardines, asparagus with spring peas and sage, and bouillabaisse with sea bass, white clams, confit potatoes, and aioli. **Known for:** eggs Benedict and scrambled eggs with gravlax for breakfast; late-night dining and drinking; well-curated French wine list. *Average main: 205 MP* ⊠ *Av. Veracruz 38, La Condesa* ☎ 55/7098-1422 ⊕ *www.cafemilou. com* Ⓜ *Chapultepec.*

Cancino San Miguel

$ | Italian. Near several art spaces in San Miguel Chapultepec (and across the street from famed Kurimanzutto), this upbeat, stylish Italian restaurant has a lovely brick patio that fills with creative types after gallery openings. The roasted potatoes with truffle oil and Parmesan is a worthy starter, and there are some nice pasta and salad options, but the real star is the pizza, including a distinctly Mexican-style pie topped with huitlacoche, Oaxacan cheese, corn, and jalapeños. **Known for:** affordable thin-crust pizzas; sangria, clericot, and other wine-based cocktails; on-site coffeehouse and breakfast spot, La Ventanita. *Average main: 130 MP* ⊠ *Gobernador Rafael Rebollar 95, La Condesa* ☎ 55/4333-0770 ⊕ *www. archipielagomx.com/los-cancinos* Ⓜ *Constituyentes.*

Chinaloa

$$ | Asian Fusion. Set in a snazzy second-floor space with hanging rice-paper lanterns and umbrellas, a retractable roof, and patterned plates and bowls, this colorful restaurant is one of the more

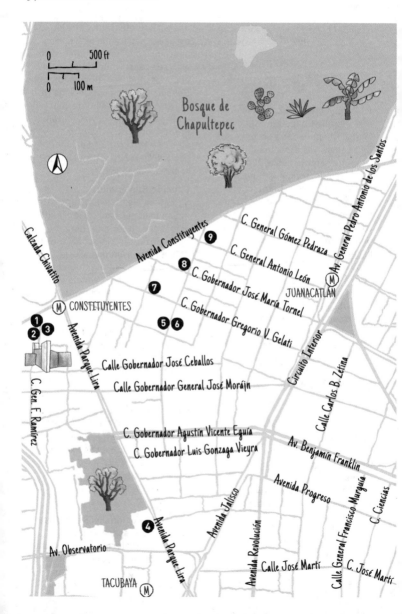

0 500 ft
0 100 m

Bosque de Chapultepec

Calzada Chivatito

Avenida Constituyentes

C. General Gómez Pedraza

C. General Antonio León

Av. General Pedro Antonio de los Santos

9

8

7

C. Gobernador José María Tornel

JUANACATLÁN

Ⓜ CONSTITUYENTES

5 6

C. Gobernador Gregorio V. Gelati

1

2 3

Avenida Parque Lira

Calle Gobernador José Ceballos

Calle Gobernador General José Moráin

C. Gen. F. Ramírez

C. Gobernador Agustín Vicente Eguía

C. Gobernador Luis Gonzaga Vieyra

Circuito Interior

Calle Carlos B. Zetina

Av. Benjamín Franklin

Avenida Progreso

4

Avenida Parque Lira

Av. Observatorio

TACUBAYA Ⓜ

Avenida Jalisco

Avenida Revolución

Calle José Martí

Calle General Francisco Murguía

C. Ciencias

C. José Martí

inviting venues in town for fusion-y Chinese-American-Mexican fare that's very popular in the country's northern border cities, like Tijuana and Mexicali (the chef's hometown). Here you can tuck into side-by-side plates of Mazatlán-style shrimp aguachile and LA Chinatown-style chop suey, while washing everything down with colorful cocktails. **Known for:** warm, bold decor; Mexicali-style fusion Chinese food; aguachile and ceviche. *Average main: 220 MP* ⊠ *Calle de Durango 359, La Condesa* ☎ *55/3099-4961* ⊕ *www.facebook. com/chinaloamx* ⊘ *No dinner Sun.* Ⓜ *Chapultepec.*

★ Lardo

$$ | **Mediterranean.** At this more casual and free-wheeling sibling to famed Rosetta restaurant and bakery, sit at one of the cozy café tables in the sun-filled, shabby-chic dining room and fill up on exceptional grilled, panfried, and oven-baked modern Mediterranean fare served on whimsical antique china. Highlights from the extensive menu include grilled rustic bread topped with tomato and anchovies, blistered-crust pizzas topped with eggplant and ricotta, and rabbit liver ravioli with a rabbit ragù. **Known for:** creative, contemporary Mediterranean cuisine; stunning desserts, some featuring home-made ice cream; baked goods and light fare available from the take-out window. *Average main: 290 MP* ⊠ *Calle Agustín Melgar 6, La Condesa* ☎ *55/5211-7731* ⊕ *www.lardo.mx* ⊘ *No dinner Sun.* Ⓜ *Chapultepec.*

Osteria 8

$$ | **Modern Italian.** A modern, warmly lit neighborhood spot, Osteria 8 uses mostly organic, regional ingredients in its hand-made pastas and thin-crust pizzas. The pie topped with jamón Serrano and fresh arugula is a favorite, while pappardelle with a cured Italian sausage and a creamy tomato sauce and wild mushroom risotto with guanciale shine among the pastas. **Known for:** handmade pastas; fresh burrata with a balsamic drizzle; noteworthy Italian wine selection. *Average main: 210 MP* ⊠ *Calle Sinaloa 252, La Condesa* ☎ *55/5212-2008* ⊕ *www.facebook.com/Osteria8* ⊘ *Closed Mon* Ⓜ *Chapultepec.*

🎫 Performing Arts

★ Foro Shakespeare

On a quiet street in the north-western corner of the neighborhood, this highly regarded performing arts nonprofit presents dozens of plays and other kinds of shows—film, music, dance—throughout the year. Although the name may have you expecting classic Elizabethan fare, Foro Shakespeare is devoted to diversity and social impact, and often presents edgy and provocative material. The organization collaborates with a number of noteworthy partners, including La Compañía de Teatro Penitenciario, which aims to help inmates reintegrate through art and culture. ⊠ *Calle Zamora 7, La Condesa* ☎ *55/5256-0014* ⊕ *www.foroshakespeare.com* Ⓜ *Chapultepec.*

GO FOR

Leafy
boulevards

Walkable
neighborhoods

Hidden gems

SANTA MARÍA
LA RIBERA

SAN
RAFAEL

POLANCO

ALAMEDA CENTRAL

JUÁREZ AND
ANZURES

CENTRO
HISTÓRICO

BOSQUE DE
CHAPULTEPEC

ROMA

CONDESA

BENITO
JUÁREZ

SAN ÁNGEL

COYOACÁN

Named in honor of Mexico's first indigenous president, Benito Juárez is one of Mexico City's 16 alcaldías, or boroughs (which cover a larger space than its colonias, or neighborhoods). Covering more than 41 square km (16 square miles) of the central city, Benito Juárez is primarily residential with the exception of the bustling business district that lines Insurgentes Avenue, an area that includes the World Trade Center and a number of international financial and engineering institutions.

—by Megan Frye

Blessed with ample green parks, wide sidewalks, and charming mom-and-pop *tiendas de abarrotes* (corner stores) and restaurants, its 43 colonias are about as relaxed as you can get this close to the action in Mexico City. Every corner of the borough is well connected to the city's public transport system, including the subway, the metrobus, the trolleybus, and a deluge of other buses in varying degrees of decrepitation—the smaller ones are known as combis, or *peseros*. Each neighborhood has its age-old cantina (some classier than others) and its favorite coffee shops, many of which have been there for decades.

Certain neighborhoods, such as the Narvartes and Del Valles, are seeing a plethora of new restaurants and bars geared to the young and hip. Meanwhile, big-block movie theaters, malls filled with international brands, multifloor apartment buildings, microbreweries, organic coffee shops, and foreign cuisine restaurants are springing up next to the little cafés and houses that have been passed down through the generations. In general, walking or biking through Benito Juárez is the best way to get to know its neighborhood-on-the-verge charm.

 Sights

Alberca Olímpica Francisco Márquez

If you've ever wanted to swim in an Olympic-size pool, this one from the 1968 Olympic games (and the largest pool in all of Mexico) might be your best option. Created just for the 1968 games, today it serves as a neighborhood pool that offers open swim for all levels. Water polo and scuba diving are also options in the pool area, while the neighboring Gimnasio Olímpico Juan de la Barrera hosts volleyball and basketball pick-up and league games, tae kwon do classes, and other sports. ✉ *División del Norte 2333, Benito Juárez* ✛ *Colonia General Anaya* ☎ *55 /5604–8344* Ⓜ *Eje Central.*

Parque de los Venados

This 25-acre park represents one of the best of Mexico City's outdoor spaces. With more than 10,000 trees, a fountain, kids' carnival rides and games, a dog park, and food trucks, it can make for a whole day of fun and people-watching. Weekdays see the park filled with dog-walkers, people exercising, and kids on carnival rides after school. Weekends turn into a full-on spectacle, packed with people lining its Talavera-tiled benches and snacking at the many different food stands. Though popular, it maintains its neighborhood friendly vibe and provides a lot of shade and oxygen to an otherwise not heavily treed zone. ✉ *Miguel Laurent between Av. Division del Norte and Dr. José María Vertiz, Santa Cruz Atoyac, Benito Juárez* Ⓜ *Parque de los Venados.*

★ **Parque Hundido**

Known as the "sunken park" in Spanish, this 22-acre green space is exceedingly quiet, especially considering that it lies on busy Insurgentes Avenue. With jogging and walking paths that curve through the lush greenery, fountains, and statues, the park is a good place to escape the city and its stresses. When you descend into the park via the ramp or steps, the temperature always seems to drop about 10 degrees: an excellent antidote for a hot day. ✉ *Av. Insurgentes between Av. Porifirio Díaz and Calle Millet, Extremadura Insurgentes, Benito Juárez* Ⓜ *Insurgentes Sur.*

Poliforum Siqueiros

The history of Poliforum Siqueiros has been and remains turbulent, but it still remains one of the city's most beloved cultural treasures. The cultural space was first opened in 1971 and features the largest mural of the world, "The March

GETTING HERE

Sitting about 4 km (2½ miles) south of Centro Histórico, the borough of Benito Juárez spans more than 26 square km (10 square miles), with the northeastern edge bordering Roma Sur. Uber fares from the airport or the city center run about MX$120–MX$180. Due to the size of the delegation, there are four subway lines that cross through it (2, 3, 7, and 12) and two lines of the Metrobus (1 and 2). Benito Juárez is largely safe to explore on foot, and there's usually a subway or Metrobus line close to major points of interest. To cross the entire delegation, you could walk the length of División del Norte, one of its main north–south arteries, in 1½ hours (it's just over 5 km [3 miles]). Street parking is common and most establishments have parking available for their customers.

of Humanity" painted by Mexican muralist and political dissenter David Siqueiros. The interior mural covers more than 93,646 square feet and depicts the struggle of humanity across four sections, narrated by the late artist himself as a rotating platform carries visitors on a journey through the mural. The space also features galleries and a

TACUBAYA

Condesa

Roma

Avenida Jalisco

Av. Progreso

C. José Martí

Av. Patriotismo

Viaducto Presidente Miguel Alemán

Av. Revolución

Calle la Morena

SAN PEDRO DE LOS PINOS

Viaducto

C. Filadelfia

C. Dakota

9

10

8

11

7

C. Pennsylvania

C. Nebraska

C. Nueva York

Avenida Insurgentes Sur

C. Pedro Romero de Terreros

Calle Luz Saviñón

Calle Torres Adalid

13

Manuel Ávila Camacho

Avenida Patriotismo

1 SAN ANTONIO

Av. Colonia del Valle

14

Avenida San Antonio

Calle Eugenia

Benito

Juárez

Calle San Borja

Ángel Urraza

Av. División del Norte

C. Tintoreto

Avenida Revolución

Avenida Patriotismo

2

MIXCOAC

Calle Matías Romero

Avenida Insurgentes Sur

5

6

16

17

18

19

Calle Pilares

15

C. Moras

C. Adolfo Prieto

Coyoacán

Gabriel Mancera

Avenida Cuauhtémoc

Félix Cuevas

ZAPATA

Deprimido Mixcoac

4

Calle Parroquia

20 DE NOVIEMBRE

José María Rico

Avenida Universidad

Avenida Revolución

3

Calle Minería

Deprimido Mixcoac

C. José María Olloqui

COYOACAN

20

San Ángel

Avenida México-Coyoacán

Circuito Interior

0 ——— 2,000 ft

0 ——— 400 m

theater. The facade, a dodecahedron by design, brings Siqueiros' art to the outside world. Over the years, numerous groups have worked to restore the building, now officially declared as part of the city's cultural heritage. ⊠ *Insurgentes Sur 701, Benito Juárez* ☎ *55/5536–4520* ⊕ *www.facebook.com/www.polyforumsiqueiros.com.mx.*

World Trade Center Mexico City

Originally built to be a hotel, Mexico City's World Trade Center now stands as the third tallest building in the city and hosts a number of office spaces, functioning as a grand-scale meeting place and convention center. Construction began in 1966, and while it never lived its life as a hotel due to financial and bureaucratic troubles, it opened officially as a world commerce building in 1995. Atop the 52-story glass and aluminum building sits what Guinness World Records calls the largest rotating restaurant in the world, the pricey Bellini, which specializes in views of the city and Italian food. Also within the WTC are a number of cafés, a cinema, a concert venue, and several restaurants. ⊠ *Montecito 38, Benito Juárez* ☎ *55/9000–6000* ⊕ *www.wtcmexico. mx* Ⓜ *San Pedro de los Pinos.*

Zona Arqueológica de Mixcoac

Located relatively close to the city center in the San Pedro de los Pinos colonia, relatively near San Ángel and Del Valle, this important archaeological site is on what centuries ago was the southwestern shore of Lake Texcoco, an area fed by streams from the western moun-

tains. Its name, which in the Nahuatl language of the Aztecs who resided here means "viper of the cloud," is believed to refer to the swirl of stars above that we call the Milky Way. The physical structure preserved at this site is relatively young, having been inhabited from around AD 900 to 1521. One of Mexico's smallest archaeological sites (it's just under 2 acres), Mixcoac only opened to the public for visits in summer 2019, under the aegis of Instituto Nacional de Antropología e Historia (INAH). Visitors can tour the remaining structures, which include a central courtyard surrounded by east and west platforms, with a ceremonial plaza, residential rooms, and other spaces. ⊠ *Calle Pirámide 7, Greater Mexico City* ⊕ *www.inah.gob.mx* Ⓜ *San Antonio.*

Shopping

Torre Manacar

What Benito Juárez might lack in boutique shops, it certainly makes up for with international fashion brands within this 29-story skyscraper. Expect the normal stores you'd find in the United States, but with a few upscale additions like Mango, Uterqüe, Massimo Dutti, and Julio (a Mexican clothing brand). There's also a cinema and a number of restaurants, all of which are international or Mexican chains. ⊠ 1457 Av. de los Insurgentes Sur, Benito Juárez ⊕ www.manacarmx.com Ⓜ Hospital 20 de Noviembre.

☕ Coffee and Quick Bites

Almanegra Café

$ | Café. As its name would suggest (it translates to "black soul"), you'll find lots of brooding music and black attire here. With two locations in Benito Juárez, the Narvarte Poniente spot was the first and is still the coziest, with just a small coffee counter and a few benches outside to sit along Avenida Universidad. **Known for:** a rotating menu of Mexican coffee from different states; fast service; good people-watching. *Average main: 40 MP* ⊠ Av. Universidad 420–A, Benito Juárez ⊹ Narvarte Poniente ☎ 55/4162–5899 ⊕ www.almanegra-cafe.mx Ⓜ Eugenia.

★ Bajo Sombra Café & Vinyl

$ | Café. While it specializes in espresso, pour-overs, and other hipster coffee-lover delights, this café has more of a neighborhood vibe than many of its counterparts. Mexican coffee is its specialty, though it occasionally features standout imports as well. **Known for:** house-made tea infusions; herbal soda waters; mezcal and coffee-based Mexican craft beer. *Average main: 40 MP* ⊠ Diagonal San Antonio 1507, Benito Juárez ⊹ Narvarte Oriente ☎ 55/5530–8216 ⊕ www.facebook.com/bajosombra-cafe ⊘ Closed Sun. Ⓜ Etiopía/Plaza de la Transparencia.

Costra

$ | Café. Fresh-baked bread, doughnuts, muffins, and croissants are eye-catching from the display just inside the window at Costra. With only a few seats inside, it is a cozy spot to catch up on some work or with a friend. **Known for:** house-made baked goods; varieties of tea; friendly service. *Average main: 50 MP* ⊠ Av. Universidad 371, Benito Juárez ⊹ Narvarte Poniente ☎ 55/7457–2240 ⊕ www.costra.mx Ⓜ Eugenia.

El Vilsito

$ | Mexican. With its quirky setting inside a large industrial building that also houses an auto repair shop, this Colonia Narvarte Poniente hot spot was featured on Netflix's *Tacos Chronicles* and is a serious contender in the city's crowded battle for al pastor primacy. Overflowing with happy eaters into the wee hours of the night, Vilsito serves pastor tacos with or without cheese along with a good variety of the usual suspects (tacos choriqueso, tortas Cubanas). **Known for:** tacos al pastor;

refreshing horchata; crowded but festive scene. *Average main: 55 MP* ⊠ *Av. Universidad, Benito Juárez* ☎ *55/5682-7213* ⊘ *No lunch.*

La Divina Culpa

$ | **Mexican.** This perpetually packed sidewalk diner offers the quintessential quick bite experience in Mexico City. Serving breakfast and lunch, it's popular for the daily *comida corrida* (three-course meal); tables turn over fast. **Known for:** mole enchiladas stuffed with chicken; lunch deals including a three-course option; exceedingly delicious pozole (a Mexican soup made with hominy and pork). *Average main: 60 MP* ⊠ *Eje Central Lázaro Cárdenas 514, Benito Juárez* ⊹ *Portales Sur* ☎ *55/5605-3019* ⊘ *No dinner* ⊟ *No credit cards* Ⓜ *Xola.*

★ Mimo Café Bueno

$ | **Café.** Serving up caffeinated beverages in a variety of forms from all over the country, this attractive space maintains a chill vibe and attracts passersby looking for a beverage on the go. Sit at one of the three tables inside or two by the sidewalk, where you can expect to be serenaded by wandering buskers. **Known for:** varieties of Mexican coffee, served several different ways; shots of carajillo (espresso with Licor 43); relaxed atmosphere. *Average main: 40 MP* ⊠ *Amores 1403, Benito Juárez* ⊹ *Del Valle Centro* ☎ *55/7826-6900* ⊕ *www. facebook.com/MimoCAFEBUENO* Ⓜ *Hospital 20 de Noviembre.*

Pan de Nube

$ | **Bakery.** There is always something in the oven at Pan de Nube, a quiet nook near the lovely Parque Mariscal Sucre. Daily breakfast and brunch specials range from housemade granola and yogurt to quiches and Spanish tortillas. **Known for:** pastries and sweets prepared fresh daily; cozy atmosphere; clientele with a refreshing lack of laptops. *Average main: 70 MP* ⊠ *Diagonal San Antonio 922, Benito Juárez* ⊹ *Narvarte Poniente* ☎ *55/5687-3949* ⊘ *Closed Sun. No dinner* ⊟ *No credit cards* Ⓜ *Etiopía/Plaza de la Transparencia.*

★ Té Cuento

$ | **Café.** Looking out on vibrant Parque Tlacoqueméctal, this cozy, bright teahouse and eatery is run by an Argentine journalist and specializes in dozens of teas and infusions. It also doubles as a cultural space in the evenings, offering workshops on topics such as film and literature. **Known for:** mouthwatering baked goods; house-made organic foods; excellent tea menu. *Average main: 80 MP* ⊠ *Corner of Adolfo Prieto and Tlacoquemécatl, Benito Juárez* ☎ *55/7589-9210* ⊕ *www.facebook. com/TeCuentoCasadeTe* Ⓜ *Hospital 20 de Noviembre.*

Village Café

$ | **International.** Facing Parque Hundido with a view of nothing but trees (okay, and some parked cars and an EcoBici stand), Village Café is a great place to unwind and take in a bit of tranquillity in one of the busier parts of the city. Massive windows open to the sidewalk, where diners take their time on sandwiches, coffees, and pastries. **Known for:** lovely views of the park; tasty bagel sandwiches; peaceful atmosphere. *Average main: 120 MP* ⊠ *Av. Colonia del Valle 603, Benito Juárez* ✢ *Noche Buena* 🕾 *55/1107–6072* ⊕ *www.villagecafe.com.mx* ☽ *Closed Sun.*

🍴 Dining

⭐ Banneton Bistro

$ | International. A cozy corner diner specializing in vegetarian cuisine often with a Middle Eastern flair, Banneton Bistro faces the public park Plaza de las Naciones Unidas and has an intimate vibe, with usually only the chef/owner and one other person working. The menu changes daily according to the whims of chef Carlos Guillén Santos and the availability of the freshest products. **Known for:** very reasonable prices; rotating, plant-based menu; personalized service. *Average main: 120 MP* ⊠ *La Quemada 9, Benito Juárez* ✢ *Narvarte* 🕾 *55/4140–5686* ⊕ *www.facebook. com/bannetonmx* ☽ *Closed Tues.* ▬ *No credit cards* Ⓜ *Etiopía/Plaza de la Transparencia.*

Bellini

$$$ | Eclectic. Revolving slowly on the 45th floor of the World Trade Center, Bellini maintains a formal, reserved character. While it's definitely known less for its food than the views (romantically twinkling city lights at night and a pair of volcanoes on a clear day), it's still worth the dining experi-

ence, especially for its beloved osso buco and French onion soup. **Known for:** pricey international cuisine; panoramic views of the city; excellent lobster. *Average main: 300 MP* ⊠ *Torre WTC (World Trade Center), Montecito 38, 45th fl., Nápoles* 🕾 *55/9000–8305* ⊕ *www.bellini.com. mx* Ⓜ *Metro San pedro de los Pinos.*

Branca Parilla

$$ | South American. Sitting on a quiet corner on a residential street, Branca Parilla is stunning both inside and out. It's snazzy enough to dress up a bit, but casual enough not to worry about it if you're not. **Known for:** pasta and steaks; nice variety of wine by the glass or bottle; romantic outdoor seating. *Average main: 250 MP* ⊠ *Av. Universidad 626, Benito Juárez* ✢ *Narvarte Oriente* 🕾 *55/6550–0644* ⊕ *www.brancapar-rilla.com.mx* Ⓜ *División del Norte.*

⭐ Cantina La Valenciana

$$ | Mexican. While one side of the cantina speaks more to drinking, party-heavy crowds and the other to family outings focused on watching soccer, they merge as one on evenings and weekends with live cumbia and salsa. The building has been on this popular stretch of Narvarte for more than 100 years, with more than 50 years under the same ownership, making it a true neighborhood cantina. **Known for:** thick, juicy steaks; dancing on the weekends; hefty cocktail and liquor list. *Average main: 250 MP* ⊠ *Av. Universidad 48, Benito Juárez* ✢ *Narvarte Oriente* 🕾 *55/3330–7505* ⊕ *www.facebook.com/CantinaLaVale* ▬ *No credit cards* Ⓜ *Xola.*

CHANGING DEMOGRAPHICS

Benito Juárez has long been considered one of Mexico City's most residential delegations. Since the era of Porfirio Diaz's dictatorship era in the late 19th and early 20th century and its park-building extravaganza aimed at making the city more European, it has attracted people from both high society and from the working class. When the financial and international business sectors took up shop on Insurgentes in the late 20th century, it became an even more desirable place to live.

As rents have risen over the past decade in areas like Roma and Condesa, much of the artistic community that called those colonias home has shifted south of the Viaducto Alemán in search of more ample, affordable, and quiet living. This movement started to incorporate more young expats following the devastating September 19, 2017, earthquake that rocked Roma and Condesa particularly hard and left many buildings there uninhabitable. As a result, new restaurants, cafés, and bars have popped up in Benito Juárez in order to cater to these migrations of mostly young and single professionals.

While Benito Juárez largely remains a place to call home more than a place to work, sightsee, or party, the changing vibe of its neighborhoods is noticeable and only expected to evolve as the years pass.

★ Charcutería Hinojosa y Baguetería

$ | **Deli.** This charming, European-style charcuterie is one of few in the city. With a couple of outdoor seats and a bar where you can watch all the action, sandwiches are served on fluffy or crunchy baguettes and feature smoked cheeses and sausages. **Known for:** neighborhood charcuterie catering to locals; excellent price-to-quality ratio; lovely sidewalk seating. *Average main: 100 MP* ⊠ *Dr. José María Vertiz 1251, Benito Juárez* ✛ *Vertiz Narvarte* ☎ *55/5601–1181* ⊕ *www.facebook. com/CharcuteriaHinojosayBaguetteria* ⊟ *No credit cards* Ⓜ *Parque de los Venados.*

★ Fonda Dakota

$ | **Mexican.** Nestled among the city's most bustling financial and business institutions, a restaurant like Fonda Dakota should naturally have plenty of competition, but it remains perhaps the best eatery in the neighborhood. Office workers, known colloquially as *godínez*, form lines outside during the lunch hour, although breakfast is usually packed as well. **Known for:** delicious breakfast chilaquiles; chile en nogada (a seasonal stuffed poblano pepper dish); long lines and quick service. *Average main: 80 MP* ⊠ *Dakota 55, Nápoles* ☎ *No phone* ☉ *Closed weekends. No dinner* ⊟ *No credit cards.*

★ Fonda Margarita

$ | **Mexican.** Everyone from post-clubbing revelers to early morning workers to ardent foodies (the late

Anthony Bourdain was a big fan) wait in line for a chance to feast on the hearty guisados served in this legendary breakfast joint. Come with a big appetite, and try a few specialties, such as *refritos huevos* (eggs whipped with refried beans), chilaquiles with salsa verde, and eggs stewed with longaniza sausage. **Known for:** stick-to-your-ribs breakfast fare; no-frills dining room with communal seating; early closure at 11:30 am so get here early. *Average main: 70 MP* ⊠ *Adolfo Prieto 1364B, Benito Juárez* ☎ *55/5559–6358* ⊘ *Closed Mon. No lunch or dinner* Ⓜ *20 de Noviembre.*

La Secina
$$ | Mexican. On the northwest edge of La Narvarte, this ample-size restaurant is great for big parties and sitting out on the terrace in the evening. The menu is specific: cecina (cured beef) in all of its mighty forms, including an appetizing ceviche. **Known for:** upscale Mexican fare focusing on cured beef; craft beer and cocktails; outdoor dining in the evenings. *Average main: 200 MP* ⊠ *Calzada Obrero Mundial 305, Benito Juárez* ✛ *Narvarte Poniente* ☎ *55/6730–2462* ⊘ *Closed Mon. No dinner Sun.* Ⓜ *Centro Médico.*

Las Sirenas del Pacífico
$$ | Seafood. With a charming terrace and breezy indoor seating, this exquisite seafood restaurant carries a vibe from Mexico's west coast, from where the day's catch is flown. More pricey than other neighborhood restaurants, the flavor and service make up for it.

Known for: Mexico City's freshest seafood; wine pairings; shaded patio dining. *Average main: 250 MP* ⊠ *Av. Universidad 273, Narvarte Poniente, Benito Juárez* ☎ *55/5536–8330* ⊕ *www.lassirenasdelpacifico.com.mx* Ⓜ *Eugenia.*

★ Los Chamorros de Tlacoquemécatl
$$ | Mexican. A bustling restaurant with no frills, but plenty of flavor, Los Chamorros is dark, hot, and popular. In business since 1974, the restaurant offers an array of Mexican specialties that take diners on a gastronomic voyage into Mexico's countryside. **Known for:** chamorro (juicy, butter-soft pork knuckle); huazontles (native herbs) battered and stuffed with cheese and doused in pasilla chili sauce; hearty soups like sopa de haba (lima bean soup). *Average main: 150 MP* ⊠ *Calle Tlacoquemécatl 177, Del Valle Centro, Benito Juárez* ☎ *55/5575–1235* ⊘ *No dinner* Ⓜ *Insurgentes Sur, Hospital 20 de Noviembre.*

Mazurka
$$ | Polish. The glowing reputation of this long-standing Polish restaurant shone even brighter after people got word that the establishment had served Pope John Paul II on several of his visits to Mexico City; the generous *Degustación del Papa* (Pope's Menu) includes small portions of various entrées served to the pope. Its best days might be behind it, but it's an interesting slice of the city's diverse culinary history, and still a source for terrific duck dishes. **Known for:** the best kielbasa for miles; impressive international

BULLFIGHTING IN MEXICO CITY

Fair warning: the topic of the legality and morality of bullfighting in Mexico City might bring out stronger opinions than talking about Mexican politics. That said, Mexico is one of only eight countries in the world where bullfighting is legal, and Mexico City is home to the biggest bullfighting ring in the world. The Plaza de Toros opened in 1946 with stands that are designed to fit over 40,000 spectators and today it still draws quite a crowd of those who come to imbibe, listen to live mariachi, and watch what those in favor of bullfighting call tradition, and what others would call pure brutality.

Bills to ban bullfighting (in which, spoiler, the bull always dies), especially in Mexico City, have been routinely introduced and then rejected by a majority of city officials. As it stands, animal rights activists are still tirelessly trying to stop the events, while those who are neutral turn a blind eye and those who are passionate spectators line up to buy tickets, especially for the novice matador show in November and the largest of the city's bullfighting events, La Temporada Grande, in February.

wine collection; pierogi with piano accompaniment. *Average main: 290 MP* ⊠ *Nueva York 150, between Calles Texas and Oklahoma, Benito Juárez* ☎ *55/5543–4509* ⊕ *www.mazurka. com.mx* ⊘ *No dinner Sun. and Mon.* Ⓜ *San Pedro de los Pinos.*

★ **Piloncillo y Cascabel**
$ | **Mexican.** On a verdant corner in Narvarte, this neatly decorated space has plenty of room and a quickly rotating lunch crowd. Known for its lines down the block, diners come for an updated take on traditional Mexican cuisine and reasonable prices. **Known for:** casual gourmet Mexican dishes; lunch specials; charming outdoor space. *Average main: 100 MP* ⊠ *Torres Adalid 1263, Narvarte Poniente, Benito Juárez* ☎ *55/3330–2121* ⊕ *www.facebook.com/piloncilloycas-cabel* ⊘ *Closed Sun.* Ⓜ *Eugenia.*

Pimienta Gorda
$ | **Vegetarian.** This hidden eatery along bustling Cuauhtémoc Avenue is at the heart of the Narvarte neighborhood. With seven tables inside pushed up next to the open kitchen, it feels a bit like dining at your hippie relative's house, thanks to the extensive menu of vegan and vegetarian dishes. **Known for:** creative vegan and vegetarian lunch specials; relaxed, unhurried vibe; famous garbanzo burger. *Average main: 80 MP* ⊠ *Av. Cuauhtémoc 841, Narvarte Poniente, Benito Juárez* ☎ *55/5264–3137* ⊘ *No dinner* ▭ *No credit cards* Ⓜ *Eugenia.*

★ **Pizza Local**
$$ | **Pizza.** Most visitors to Mexico City don't come here in search of New York–style pizza, but that's not to say a fine pie isn't appreciated in the city. Mexican pizza is typically light on the sauce, but Pizza Local

is the rare exception with thin-crust options such as roasted tomato and garlic or classic, charcuterie-style pepperoni (also a rarity in the city). **Known for:** pizza that even a New Yorker could love; thin-crust pies; pretty patio for outdoor dining. *Average main: 250 MP* ✉ *Uxmal 88, Benito Juárez* ☎ *55/4632-1669* ⊕ *www.pizzalocal.mx* ⊙ *Closed Mon.* ▭ *No credit cards* Ⓜ *Etiopía/Plaza de la Transparencia.*

★ Tortas Jorge
$ | Mexican. Covering nearly a whole city block, this corner bar has been around since 1950. Still selling its famous sandwiches (thin-cut, breaded beef known as milanesa, with pickled, spiced vegetables on the side) for just 27 pesos, this place hasn't changed much since the old days: neighborhood troubadours still play traditional Mexican songs in the evenings to crowds sipping on beers and cocktails. **Known for:** live music from local artists; incredible, old-school lunch specials; kitschy retro vibe. *Average main: 30 MP* ✉ *Diagonal San Antonio 1699, Benito Juárez* ⊕ *Narvarte Poniente* ☎ *55/5519-7559* ⊕ *www.facebook.com/tortasjorgeoficial* ⊙ *Closed Mon.* ▭ *No credit cards* Ⓜ *Etiopía/Plaza de la Transparencia.*

⏳ Bars and Nightlife

Bulldog Café
This spot north of Coyoacán books mostly rock acts on weekend nights. The cover charge varies depending on the headline band; expect to pay at least MX$350 if a well-known group is playing. ✉ *Rubens 6, at Av. Revolución, Benito Juárez* ☎ *55/5611-8818* ⊕ *www.bulldogcafe.com* Ⓜ *Estacion Mixcoac.*

Kaito Bar Izakaya
This small bar serves up some of the best sushi in Del Valle as well as inventive cocktails featuring Mexican and international liquors. Dark and intimate, the space relies heavily on a Japanese industrial aesthetic, with concrete, stainless steel, and wood all put to good use. ✉ *Calle J. Enrique Pestalozzi 1238, Colonia del Valle Centro, Benito Juárez* ☎ *55/5605-6317* ⊕ *www.facebook.com/kaitodelvalle* Ⓜ *División del Norte.*

La Maraka
Many locals consider the merengue and salsa music played at this dance hall, southeast of Colonia Roma, to be some of the city's best. It also offers dance classes and live music. ✉ *Mitla 410, at Eje 5, Benito Juárez* ☎ *55/5682-0636* ⊕ *www.lamaraka.com.mx* Ⓜ *Eugenia.*

★ La Paloma Azul
Specializing in one thing and one thing only (pulque), this bar is decorated with wall paintings of Mexico's pre-Columbian past. The pulque comes in a variety of flavors to sample, and be sure to enjoy the ever-revolving cast of characters here, including students, neighborhood fixtures, and older folks. ✉ *Av. Popocatépetl 154D, Benito Juárez* ⊕ *Portales Sur* ☎ *55/5688-5662* ⊕ *www.facebook.com/Palomaazuloficial* Ⓜ *Eje Central.*

RR Live

Known for hosting rock cover bands and the occasional touring act, this small concert hall has a larger-than-life stage, table service, and a 1980s metal club vibe. It hosts live music four nights per week, and there's usually costumed cover bands (think KISS and the Rolling Stones), plenty of tequila, and traditional pub fare. Depending on the act, it can be quite packed as the hall itself is small. ⊠ *Luz Saviñon 1315, Narvarte Poniente, Benito Juárez* ☎ *55/6363-2823* ⊕ *www.facebook.com/bar.rrlive.*

Taberna Calacas

Serving Mexican and imported artisanal beer, including three brands brewed on-site (you'll be engulfed by the scent of malt while you imbibe), seating at this small bar is mostly communal and against dark walls with tattoo-style art. Snacks (including charcuterie plates and guacamole with grasshoppers and pork rinds) are served each afternoon, with a special brunch menu on Sunday. ⊠ *Eje. Central Lazaro Cardenas 409, Portales Sur, Benito Juárez* ☎ *55/1381-4359* ⊕ *www.facebook.com/TabernaCalacas* Ⓜ *Portales.*

Performing Arts

★ Cineteca Nacional

Since 1984, the Cineteca Nacional (or National Film Archive) has been one of the highlights of Mexico City's contemporary offerings, hosting local and foreign films as well as film classes. The massive 41,172 square-foot complex houses coffee shops, restaurants, bars, bookstores, 10 viewing rooms (including three auditoriums), and more than 15,000 film titles. An outdoor viewing amphitheater invites filmgoers to take in movies on the grass at the entrance, a popular date activity. Affordable prices and edgy titles make it popular among youths, while the overall variety keeps it interesting for all ages. ⊠ *Av. México Coyoacán 389, Xoco, Benito Juárez* ☎ *55/4155-1200* ⊕ *www.cinetecanacional.net* Ⓜ *Coyoacán, Eje Central.*

Teatro Insurgentes

With a Diego Rivera mural covering 5,920 square feet of space above its entrance, this 1,000-seat theater intrigues from its stately location along Insurgentes Avenue. Opened in 1953, it regularly hosts theatrical works, concerts, and even the occasional sporting event. Even if you don't get a chance to see a performance in this historic theater, even just glimpsing it from the street invites its own fair share of drama as the Rivera mural represents the theatrics of Mexico, from Aztec rituals to scenes of the Mexican Revolution and 20th-century film stars. Check the website for upcoming shows. ⊠ *Av. de los Insurgentes Sur 1587, San José Insurgentes, Benito Juárez* ☎ *55/5611-4253* ⊕ *www.carteleradeteatro.mx/teatro/sur/teatro-de-los-insurgentes* Ⓜ *Barranca Del Muerto.*

SANTA MARÍA
LA RIBERA

SAN
RAFAEL

POLANCO

JUÁREZ AND
ANZURES

ALAMEDA CENTRAL

CENTRO
HISTÓRICO

BOSQUE DE
CHAPULTEPEC

ROMA

CONDESA

BENITO
JUÁREZ

SAN ÁNGEL

COYOACÁN

Sightseeing ★★★★☆ | Shopping ★★★☆☆ | Dining ★★★★☆ | Nightlife ★★★★☆

Founded by Toltecs in the 10th century and later settled by Aztecs, then Spanish conquistador Cortés, and then—over the past century or so—by a steady stream of artists, writers, intellectuals, and creative spirits, Coyoacán is as much a mood as a physical place. About 12 km (7 miles) south of Centro Histórico, this colonial neighborhood of quiet tree-lined streets feels like its own little village, and indeed, until it was officially incorporated a part of Mexico City in 1857, it functioned as a distinct—and quite rural—municipality. It's a wonderful place for strolling and people-watching, especially around its festive central squares (or zócalo), Plaza Hidalgo and Jardín Centenario; it's also home to one of the country's most popular attractions, Casa Azul, where painter Frida Kahlo resided.—by Andrew Collins

In fact, Coyoacán has been the home of many illustrious residents considered part of Mexico's rich and intellectual elite, including artists David Alfaro Siqueiros and Diego Rivera; directors Luis Buñuel and Emilio "El Indio" Fernández; actors Dolores del Río, Mario Moreno, and Diego Luna; singer Lila Downs; and writers Octavio Paz, Laura Esquivel, Jorge Ibargüengoitia, and Salvador Novo. It's also the neighborhood where the exiled Leon Trotsky met his violent death. The neighborhood's bohemian spirit is still palpable, and during the day, its artsy cafés, shaded parks and plazas, and bounty of cultural centers and excellent, often under-rated museums (Museo Frida Kahlo is by no means the only game in town) overflow with both locals and tourists.

Bear in mind that Coyoacán is both one of Mexico City's 16 official delegaciónes (comparable to boroughs) and the name commonly used to refer to the much smaller historic neighborhood that's covered in this chapter. When most Chilangos (residents of Mexico City) refer to Coyoacán, they mean this small historic core (also known as Colonia del Carmen) that's home to Museo Frida Kahlo, Avenida Francisco Sosa, Plaza Hidalgo, and Jardín Centenario. The delegación of Coyoacán spans well beyond this historic center and is home to some 650,000 residents; the major attractions in the delegación outside the historic core—such as Museo Anahuacalli, Universidad Nacional Autónoma de México (UNAM), and Estadio Azteca—are farther afield and thus covered in the Greater Mexico City chapter of this book.

Historic Coyoacán lacks the self-conscious coolness factor of Roma and Condesa, and its relatively out-of-the-way location insulates it—to a degree—from the faster pace and urban sprawl that characterizes much of the rest of the city. As popular as it is for breakfast, coffee, and daytime exploring, it quiets down a bit in the evening, except for the handful of locals-oriented cantinas and bars around the always buzzing zócalo. Even compared with its southern neighbor San Ángel, unpretentious Coyoacán lacks foodie-driven restaurants—it's more a place to come as you are, eat traditional food, and mingle with locals.

Although lacking hotels, the neighborhood is rife with charming Airbnbs and a handful of commercial inns. It's a perfect hub if you're seeking a relatively tranquil base for exploring the city, and you don't mind having to Uber or take the Metro to more central neighborhoods. Many who stay here combine their visit with a few days closer to the city center, which is a nice strategy for experiencing two very distinct sides of Mexico City. The most ardent devotees of Coyoacán's artsy vibe and manageable pace can't imagine staying, or living, anywhere else in the city.

⊙ Sights

★ Avenida Francisco Sosa

One of the prettiest historic streets in the city, this narrow tree-lined thoroughfare paved with stone is a delightful destination for a short stroll or (if you're feeling a bit more ambitious) as the most scenic way

GETTING HERE

Along with its neighbor San Ángel, Coyoacán is one of the city's southern neighborhoods—the center of the neighborhood is about 9 km (6 miles) south of Roma and Condesa and 12 km (7 miles) south of Centro Histórico. Uber fares from the airport or the city center run about MX$90–MX$150. By Metro, you can take the 3 line to the Coyoacán, Viveros, or Miguel Ángel de Quevedo stops or the 2 line to General Anaya, but none of these stations are in the center of the neighborhood, so expect a 15- to 25-minute walk to most points of interest (Coyoacán is very safe for walking). From San Ángel, it's a quick Uber ride (around MX$50) or picturesque 45- to 60-minute walk via Avendia Francisco Sosa. The neighborhood also has a fair amount of free street parking as well as several inexpensive and secure lots.

to walk between the historic centers of Coyoacán and San Ángel. From Jardín Centenario, it runs west for just under 2 km (a little over a mile), ending at Avendia Universidad beside the tiny and historic San Antonio de Padua Chapel. Along the route you'll pass grand 19th-century mansions hidden behind, or towering over, colorfully painted walls. The surrounding neighborhood has been home to various celebrities over the years, from Dolores del Río, Luis Buñuel, and Octavio Paz to, more recently, actor Diego Luna, singer Lila Downs, and *Like Water for Chocolate* novelist Laura Esquivel. The sidewalks become narrower the farther west you walk, and ancient tree roots have in places pushed up and broken the pavement to an almost comical degree (it can feel more like bouldering than walking in a couple of spots).

The plaza surrounding 16th-century Santa Catarina Chapel is especially picturesque, hung with strings of colorful papel picado and dotted with stone benches and pretty trees. Across the street, the shaded, peaceful grounds of Casa de Cultura Jesús Reyes Heroles are also lovely to walk around, and you may witness a dance or crafts class taking place in one of the cultural center's workshops. Up and down Sosa, and especially closer to Jardín Centenario, you'll pass by inviting cafés and boutiques. There are a few attractions of note on or near this street, such as Fonoteca Nacional and Museo Nacional de la Acuarela Alfredo Guati Rojo. The narrow lanes that intersect with Francisco Sosa are also quite pretty, especially the allegedly haunted and oft-photographed Callejon Aguacate, reached via a quick turn south onto Calle Tata Vasco. To reach San Ángel, cross Universidad where Francisco Sosa ends and continue west on Calle Arenal and Avenida de la Paz (past Parque de la Bombilla); without stops, it's about a one-hour stroll from Jardín Centenario to San Ángel's Plaza del Carmen. ⊠ *Av. Francisco Sosa, Coyoacán* ✚ *Between Jardin Centenario and Av. Universidad* Ⓜ *Viveros.*

Casa Municipal *(Casa de Cortés)*
The place where the Aztec emperor Cuauhtémoc was held prisoner by Cortés is often alleged to have been rebuilt in the 18th century from the stones of the conquistador's original house, although historians agree that Cortés himself lived not here but several blocks away by La Conchita Church. Topped by two coyote figures, this long, single-story building on the north side of Plaza Hidalgo houses Coyoacán's municipal government offices and a small tourism visitor center (as well as the local library in the adjacent building). You can wander through the wide arches to see the handsomely tiled courtyard. ⊠ *Plaza Hidalgo 1, Coyoacán* Ⓜ *Viveros.*

★ **Fonoteca Nacional de México**
On the western end of picturesque Avendia Francisco Sosa, this grand mansion with a dramatic facade was built in the Moorish and Andulusian style in the 18th century and eventually became the home of Mexican Nobel poet Octavio Paz, who lived here in the late 1990s until his death in 1998. In 2008, the building—known as Casa Alvarado—became the home of Mexico's national sound archive. Today, visitors can explore the archives and, in the listening rooms, hear digitized recordings from the archive's immense collection, which includes Frida Kahlo, Álvaro Obregón, and dozens of other historical figures. There's also an extensive library of books related to music and sound, and you can saunter through the gracious gardens and grounds, which are

a perfect spot to relax with a book or rest your feet for a bit. Fonoteca also hosts a rich array of lectures, concerts, and other events—check the online calendar for details. ✉ *Av. Francisco Sosa 383, Coyoacán* ☎ *55/4155–0950* ⊕ *www.fonotecanacional.gob.mx* ⊘ *Closed Sun.* Ⓜ *Viveros.*

⭐ Jardín Centenario and Plaza Hidalgo

These infectiously festive plazas function as Coyoacán's zócalo and are barely separated from each other by a narrow, slow-moving street. The Jardín, with its shading trees, an oft-photographed fountain with two snarling coyotes, and a fringe of lively patio bars and restaurants (of varying culinary repute), is the more commercial—but also arguably the prettier—of the two.

The larger Plaza Hidalgo hosts children's fairs, musical and dance performances, clowns, bubble blowers, and cotton candy and balloon sellers, especially on weekends and holidays. It's anchored by an ornate old bandstand and the impressive Parroquia de San Juan Bautista, one of the first churches to be built in New Spain. Each afternoon of September 15, before the crowds become suffocating at nightfall, these delightful plazas are perhaps the best place in the capital to enjoy Independence Day celebrations. More recently, they've become the city's must-go for Día de Muertos in early November, with throngs of people of all ages cavorting about in costume and face paint. Both plazas are filled with landscaped courtyards, public art installations, and dozens of park benches, and they're a memorable destination for people-watching. You'll see passersby of all ages and backgrounds, from multigenerational families and young couples of all sexual orientations cuddling, kissing, and holding hands, to tourists from all over the world, and locals walking their dogs (who are often gussied up in sweaters and bows). ✉ *Coyoacán* ⊹ *Bounded by Calle Centenario and Calle Ignacio Allende* Ⓜ *Viveros.*

Monumental Casa de Emilio el "Indio" Fernández

Although open only on weekends, this palatial former home of Emilio "El Indio Fernández"—one of the greatest directors in Mexican cinematic history—is well worth a visit any time of year, but is especially a must-see during the weeks around Día de Muertos, when its rooms and gardens abound with remarkably extensive and colorful *ofrendas* (altars). The fortresslike home, built in the 1940s of volcanic rock with a design influenced by prehistoric temples, is filled with movie memorabilia, and vendors sell crafts, food, and other goods in the house's tree-shaded front courtyard. ✉ *Ignacio Zaragoza 51, Coyoacán* ☎ *55/1924–7477* ⊕ *www.facebook.com/MonumentalCasaIndioFdez* 🎫 *MX$70* ⊘ *Closed weekdays* Ⓜ *Viveros.*

⭐ Museo Casa de Leon Trotsky

From the house's original entrance on Calle Morelos (around the corner from the current museum entrance) with its forbidding high walls and turrets for armed guards, you get a sense of just how precarious life was for its final resident, Leon Trotsky, one of the most important figures of the Russian Revolution. Living in exile, Trotsky moved his family here in 1939 at the behest of his friends Diego Rivera and Frida Kahlo (whose own Casa Azul is just a few blocks away). Less than a year later, he would be assassinated. The house and adjoining exhibit galleries make for an eerily fascinating glimpse of Trotsky's later life and death. As you walk through the house, which looks largely as it did the day of his death, you'll see bullet holes still in the walls from the first assassination attempt, in which the muralist David Alfaro Siqueiros was implicated. The rooms include his bedroom, his wife's study, the dining room and kitchen, and the study where assassin Ramón Mercader (a man of many aliases) drove a pickax into Trotsky's

head. On his desk, cluttered with writing paraphernalia and an article he was revising in Russian, the calendar is open to that fateful day: August 20, 1940. ⊠ *Río Churubusco 410, Coyoacán* ☎ *55/5658–8732* ⊕ *www.museotrotsky.com* 🖃 *MX$40* 🕙 *Closed Mon.* Ⓜ *Coyoacán*.

★ Museo Frida Kahlo

The Casa Azul (Blue House), where the iconic artist was born in 1907 (not 1910, as she wanted people to believe) and died 47 years later, is both museum and shrine. Kahlo's astounding vitality and originality are reflected in the house itself, from the giant papier-mâché skeletons outside and the *retablos* (small religious paintings on tin) on the staircase to the gloriously decorated kitchen and the bric-a-brac in her bedroom. The house displays relatively few of Kahlo's original paintings, but you can admire her early sketches, diary entries, tiny outfits, and wheelchair at her easel, plus her four-poster bed fitted with a mirror above, and in a separate exhibit space across the garden, a collection of her dresses presented in the context of her physical disabilities. The relaxing garden also has a small but excellent gift shop and café. The museum has become astoundingly popular in recent years and carefully limits ticket sales to avoid the house becoming too crowded at any given time—you'll be thankful for this once you're inside, but perhaps less thrilled when you encounter the line to get into the building, which extends down and sometimes around the block daily, especially on weekends. It's highly advisable that you purchase your tickets online in advance, or arrive as early as possible on a weekday. ⊠ *Londres 247, Coyoacán* ☎ *55/5554–5999* ⊕ *www.museofridakahlo.org.mx* ✉ *MX$230 weekdays, MX$250 weekends (includes admission to Museo Diego Rivera–Anahuacalli)* ⊘ *Closed Mon.* Ⓜ *Coyoacán.*

Museo Nacional de Culturas Populares

A huge *arbol de la vida* (tree of life) sculpture stands in the courtyard of this museum devoted to popular culture and regional arts and crafts and located just a few steps from Plaza Hidalgo. Its exhibitions and events are nicely varied, including children's workshops, traditional music concerts, and dance performances. On certain weekends the courtyard becomes a small crafts-and-sweets market with some worthwhile exhibitors from throughout the country displaying their wares. The museum shop stocks art books and high-quality crafts. ⊠ *Av. Hidalgo 289, Coyoacán* ☎ *55/4155–0920* ⊕ *museoculturaspopulares.gob.mx* ✉ *MX$15* Ⓜ *Viveros.*

Museo Nacional de la Acuarela Alfredo Guati Rojo

Founded in 1964 by the late artist Alfredo Guati Rojo, this museum devoted entirely to watercolor painting makes for an enjoyable detour if you're strolling along nearby Avendia Francisco Sosa. Admission is free, and the two-story white house that contains the galleries is surrounded by pretty flower gardens and hedges, which you can admire from the terrace of the small museum café. The art includes dozens of works by Rojo and his wife, plus galleries devoted to watercolor paintings by Mexican, international, and contemporary artists; a separate building across the garden stages temporary exhibits. ⊠ *Calle Salvador Novo 88, Coyoacán* ☎ *55/5554–1801* ⊕ *www.acuarela.org.mx* Ⓜ *Viveros.*

★ Museo Nacional de las Intervenciones

Surrounded by a park with mature trees and greenery, cannons, and a towering statue of General Anaya, this fascinating museum in San Diego Churubusco—just east of Coyoacán's historic center—may just be the city's best museum you've never heard of. It's devoted to relating the surprisingly lengthy and storied history of Mexico's wars, dating from the 1810–1821 War of Independence to the Mexican Revolution a century later. The exceptionally well-executed exhibits within the building's many galleries provide an impressive explanation of how exactly Mexico became, well, Mexico. But you don't need to be a history buff to appreciate the building, which occupies the former Nuestra Señora de los Angeles de Churubusco monastery, a glorious structure built in the late 1600s and converted into an ad-hoc military fort in 1847 during the Mexican-American War. In the exhibits, history is told through displays of uniforms, guns, flags, paintings, and

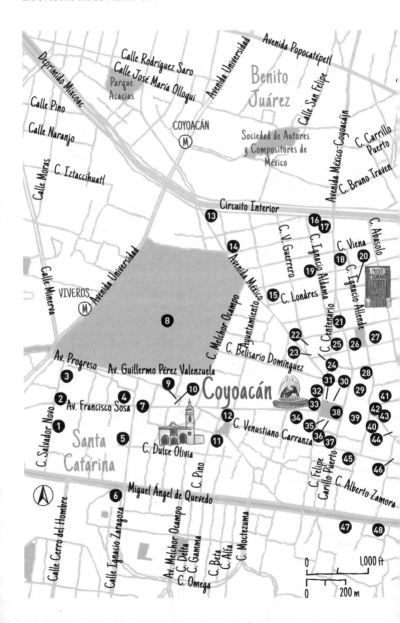

other artifacts, including a diorama of the Battle of Churubusco and photos of Pershing's 1914 punitive expedition in search of the elusive Pancho Villa. The museum also contains a remarkable collection of original frescoes, religious paintings, and ex-votos from the building's period as a monastery. In addition, there's a tranquil community garden as well as galleries that host rotating shows. Part of the fun of touring the museum is observing the building's well-preserved sloping floors, beamed ceilings, fine tile work, and ancient arches. ⊠ *20 de Agosto s/n, at Calle Xicoténcatl, Coyoacán* ☎ *55/5604–0699* ⊕ *www. intervenciones.inah.gob.mx* ⊠ *MX$75* ⊙ *Closed Mon.* Ⓜ *General Anaya.*

Parque Xicoténcatl
This less-visited but beautiful little park is in the San Diego Churubusco neighborhood, just east of Coyoacán's historic center and en route to the excellent Museo Nacional de las Intervenciones. The 1.5-acre patch of lush gardens is fenced in (and open only during the day). There's a central kiosk and fountain, a huge statue of Cortés, stone and brick paths, a couple of children's playgrounds, and plenty of benches to relax on. The tranquil oasis is a perfect spot for a picnic. ⊠ *Calle Xicoténcatl s/n, east of Av. División del Norte, Coyoacán* Ⓜ *General Anaya.*

Parroquia de San Juan Bautista
One of the earliest churches built in New Spain, this huge and striking church dates to 1527, although construction wasn't completed until 1550, and it's been rebuilt and extensively remodeled at various times—presently, work continues on repairing the spire, which was badly damaged in the city's 2017 earthquake. The interior is quite spectacular, with priceless artwork and gorgeous vaulted ceiling. Next door, the cloister of the former convent is a peaceful spot to relax and reflect. ⊠ *Centenario 8, Coyoacán* ☎ *55/5554–8142* ⊙ *Closed Wed.* Ⓜ *Viveros.*

Plaza de La Conchita
Connected to the neighborhood's other central plazas by café-lined Calle Higuera, this tree-shaded plaza with red-painted cement benches and pretty gardens is anchored by a little chapel known officially as La Chapel of the Immaculate Conception Church—although everyone calls it by its nickname, "La Conchita." The twin-spired, relatively modest structure has an impressive pedigree: it stands on the site of a pre-Hispanic ceremony ground, and it was built by none other than Spanish conquistador Hernán Cortés in 1525

(although, like so many of the city's ancient structures, it was extensively rebuilt later—in this case sometime around the late 1600s). Cortés, incidentally, is said to have had a home overlooking the church. The interior is closed indefinitely for renovations, but you can admire the striking facade of the *tezontle* (volcanic stone) that's so common in this part of the city. Before you leave, stroll across Calle Fernández Leal to peaceful Parque Frida Kahlo, a pretty little slice of greenery that contains life-size bronze statues of the artist and Diego Rivera. ⊠ *Calle Fernández Leal 74, Coyoacán* Ⓜ *Viveros.*

★ Viveros de Coyoacán

Officially this 96-acre swath of greenery is a nursery that was developed around 1913 to grow tree seedlings to be transplanted to the forests in and around Mexico City, but today Viveros functions for visitors as a glorious park (it has, in fact, been an official national park since 1938). A 2.2-km (1.4-mile) gravel walking and jogging trail laces the perimeter of the property, and a series of narrow trails crisscross the park, each one lined with specimen trees that are planted around the city: acacia, sweet gum, jacaranda, cedar, and so on. There are five entrances around the park—the southwest one is closest to Viveros metro, but the northeast one is better if you're walking over from elsewhere in Coyoacán or from the Coyoacán metro stop. Each entrance is staffed by security, and although admission is free, the gates shut to the public promptly at 6 pm and don't reopen until the next morning at 6 am. This is one of the most enjoyable (and popular) spots in the city for jogging, but throughout Viveros you'll also find benches, rows of ornamental plants, hundreds of colorful and friendly black and gray squirrels, swatches of grass to set up picnic blankets, and a central plaza that's often the site of small groups informally practicing fencing, yoga, dancing, and the like. Unless you glimpse the two unfortunately bland high-rise towers that went up in 2019 on the neighborhood's northern border, you can easily imagine that you're miles from urban civilization while relaxing in this enchanting urban sanctuary. Near the northeast entrance, an actual nursery sells plants and flowers of every imaginable kind. ⊠ *Av. México and Calle Madrid, Coyoacán* Ⓜ *Viveros.*

 Shopping

★ Centro Cultural Elena Garro

Named for the late novelist and screenwriter Elena Garro, this huge bookstore occupies a early-20th-century mansion that's been enclosed within a stunning contemporary glass-walled, two-story addition. You'll find a terrific selection of literary and artistic titles as well as concerts, lectures, children's events (from puppet shows to storytelling), and other cultural programming. There's also a café with an enchanting garden seating area. ⊠ *Calle Fernández Leal 43, Coyoacán*

FRIDA AND DIEGO'S MEXICO CITY

Arguably the two most recognized figures in Mexican art, Frida Kahlo and Diego Rivera enjoy an almost fanatical following among visitors to the capital, which is where they lived (in both San Ángel and Coyoacán) and where much of their work can be viewed today. The two larger-than-life personalities were married from 1929 through Kahlo's death, at age 47, in 1954—except for a one-year gap in 1929–1930, when the pair divorced. Their tumultuous relationship endured numerous affairs by both parties, but they also remained a joint artistic and political force—both were committed to leftist causes—until the end.

Rivera enjoyed greater fame as a painter, especially for his murals, during their lifetimes, but Kahlo's deeply personal paintings began to earn wider acclaim during the final decade of her life. And by the 1990s—as she became a symbol of feminist, LGBTQ, indigenous, and Mexican-American

rights—Kahlo surpassed Rivera as the better recognized of the two. Ironically, the rejection of more commercial artistic styles that cost Kahlo financial success during her life is in part what fuels her vaunted reputation today. It's a painting by Rivera, however—which fetched $9.76 million in 2018—that holds the current record price for a work by a Latin American artist. It broke the previous record, which a Frida Kahlo painting had set two years prior.

Although you'll find works by Frida Kahlo and Diego Rivera throughout the city center (especially Palacio Nacional and Palacio de Bellas Artes for his murals and Museo de Arte Moderno for her paintings), their art is best explored in the south of the city, which is home to four key attractions: **Museo Frida Kahlo**, **Museo Casa Estudio Diego Rivera y Frida Kahlo**, **Museo Anahuacalli**, and **Museo Dolores Olmedo**.

☎ *55/3003-4081* ⊕ *www.educal.com. mx/elenagarro* Ⓜ *Viveros.*

HomoHabilis

At this small boutique, artisans hand-craft gorgeous, stylish leather products, including backpacks, computer bags, wallets, purses, journals, and aprons. The level of quality is superb, and the goods have a timeless look. ⊠ *Cjon. Belisario Domínguez 25, Coyoacán* ☎ *55/7156-7112* ⊕ *www.homohabilis. mx* Ⓜ *Viveros.*

Mayolih Arte Mexicano

Set on a quiet residential street a bit away from the more crowded parts of the neighborhood, this unassuming boutique carries an impressive, well-priced selection of authentic regional Mexican folk art and crafts. The quality is far better than most of the gifts you'll find on and around Jardín Centenario and Plaza Hidalgo. Many items come from the southern states of Chiapas, Oaxaca, and the Yucatán. Look especially for good deals on colorful guayabera shirts, colorful *tenango*-style embroidered pillows, ornately carved pine boxes, and fantastical *alebrijes*—the brightly painted animal figurines carved from copal wood in San Martín Tilcajete, Oaxaca. ⊠ *Ignacio Aldama 74, Coyoacán* ☎ *55/5658-5588* ⊕ *www.mayolih.com* Ⓜ *Coyoacán.*

★ Mercado de Coyoacán

Although it's not as big as some of the city's other markets, this lively mercado just a couple of blocks from Frida Kahlo's house is one of the most popular with visitors, in large part because of the famous food stalls at its center doling out plates of delicious ceviche, octopus, shrimp, chicken tinga, picadillo, and other fillings for about MX$30 to MX$40 per portion. But you'll also find aisles of the usual fresh juices, produce, spices, candies, and other goodies typical of Mexican markets as well as a number of souvenir and homeware vendors (mostly near the northwest entrance) as well as many other food vendors. Arguably even better than the tostadas are the quesadillas sold from a tiny little stand at the west entrance, directly across from pretty Jardín Allende, a small landscaped park with benches and pathways; on weekends, artists sell their wares in the park, too. ⊠ *Calles Ignacio Allende and Xicoténcatl, Coyoacán* ☎ *55/4072-1596* Ⓜ *Coyoacán.*

Pladi

Since 1981, Martha García has been creating beautiful experimental works in silver and other natural materials as jewelry, sculpture, and in other forms. ⊠ *Francisco Javier Mina 29, Coyoacán* ☎ *55/5658-5192* ⊕ *www.pladi.com.mx* Ⓜ *Coyoacán.*

★ Taller Experimental de Cerámica

At this tree-shaded compound founded in 1964 and situated midway between Museo Frida Kahlo and Jardín Centenario, exquisite Japanese-inspired bowls, plates, vases, tea sets, and other ceramics are produced and sold at quite reasonable prices. Daylong ceramics workshops are offered as well, and as you're browsing the wares, you can say hello to the owners' friendly cadre of xoloitz-cuintlis (the distinctive hairless dogs that have been a part of Mexican culture for more than 3,500 years). ⊠ *Centenario 63, Coyoacán* ☎ *55/5554-6960* ⊕ *www.ceramicadi-azdecossio.com* Ⓜ *Coyoacán.*

🍵 Coffee and Quick Bites

★ Café Avellaneda

$ | Café. One of the few spots in Coyoacán with the hip factor that you might expect to see in Roma, this tiny artisan roaster turns out some of the best, and most interesting, coffee drinks in city as well as selling connoisseur-worthy beans to go. The classics, including single-origin pour-overs and lattes, are superb, but you'll also find tasty iced drinks, like the refreshing Greench (green tea, kefir, and soda water) and the soothing Trago Tranquila with coffee, coconut cream, pineapple, and tonic water. **Known for:** carefully sourced and roasted coffee beans;

creative iced coffee and tea elixirs; meticulous brewing techniques. *Average main: 40 MP* ⊠ *Calle Higuera 40-A, Coyoacán* ☎ *55/6553-3441* ⊕ *www.facebook.com/Avellanedakf* Ⓜ *Viveros.*

Café El Jarocho

$ | **Café.** About a block from Plaza Hidalgo, this old-time café whose name translates to "native of Veracruz" has a nearly fanatical following. It has stood at this prime street corner in 1957—many evenings the line for coffee, hot chocolate, mochas, and doughnuts extends down the block well past midnight. **Known for:** hot chocolate and mochas; colorful people-watching; crafts vendors selling their wares out front. *Average main: 50 MP* ⊠ *Cuauhtémoc 134, Coyoacán* ☎ *55/5554-5418* ▭ *No credit cards* Ⓜ *Viveros.*

★ Café El Olvidado

$ | **Café.** Detour just a block off Francisco Sosa to find this inviting, light-filled café that offers up gorgeous breakfast and lunch fare as well as exquisite cakes and pastries based on recipes from the owner's British grandmother, including scones with jam and *nata* (clotted cream), trifle, and cardamom cakes. Other menu options include eggs Benedict; smoked salmon, ricotta, and egg croissants; and roast beef, gouda, Dijon mustard, and caramelized onion sandwiches on rustic bread. **Known for:** fine black teas and organic coffee drinks; modern takes on classic British baked goods and breakfasts; artful, minimalist decor. *Average main: 120 MP* ⊠ *Calle Pdte. Carranza 267, Coyoacán* ☎ *55/7095-6125* ⊕ *www.elolvidado. com* Ⓜ *Viveros.*

Café Negro

$ | **Café.** This stylish, plant-filled contemporary café and artisanal bakery is just a few steps from Jardín Centenario and is one of the top spots in the neighborhood for fresh, healthy sandwiches, salads, and devilishly good desserts (the chocolate-covered pretzels and flaky chocolatínes are particularly notable). Stop for a light meal or a quick snack and flat white or mocha—the coffee beans here are sourced from organic farms in Guerrero, Veracruz, and Chiapas. **Known for:** first-rate espresso drinks; fresh-baked cakes and pastries; creative sandwiches and salads. *Average main: 100 MP* ⊠ *Av. Centenario 16, Coyoacán* ☎ *55/5554-4514* ⊕ *www.cafenegrocoyoacan.com* Ⓜ *Viveros.*

Il Vicolo Panaderia

$ | **Bakery.** A friendly family with Italian and Mexican roots operates this tiny artisan bakery that's tucked in a historic alleyway near Jardín Centenario and open only Thursday through Sunday, from mid-morning until they sell out (usually by 1 pm or so). You'll find crisp-but-chewy shallot-garlic and cranberry-walnut-fennel baguettes, flaky scones, soft and chewy amaretto and orange pastries, and lusciously gooey chocolate-banana cakes. **Known for:** savory and sweet breads made with simple, natural ingredients; baguettes in several flavors; delicious sweets. *Average main: 50 MP* ⊠ *Av. Francisco Sosa 32, Coyoacán* ☎ *55/3100-7638* ⊕ *www.facebook.com/ilvicolopanaderia* ⊗ *Closed Mon.–Wed. No dinner* Ⓜ *Viveros.*

★ Mercado de Antojitos Mexicanos

$ | Mexican. Just a few steps down Calle Higuera from Plaza Hidalgo, this covered, open-air market with about a dozen stalls is home to some of the best street food in the neighborhood: barbacoa tacos, squash-blossom quesadillas, fresh-squeezed juices and smoothies, and plenty more, all of it at rock-bottom prices. There's nothing trendy about this bustling space where you may have to jostle a bit for a seat, but young buskers often entertain the crowds with great music. **Known for:** inexpensive, old-school street food; great people-watching; excellent quesadillas at Las Dietetics. *Average main: 60 MP* ⊠ *Calle Higuera 10, Coyoacán* Ⓜ *Viveros.*

Pastelería Caramel

$ | Bakery. Skip the more touristy bakeries near Coyoacán's main plazas and head to this cute traditional shop on tree-lined Calle Londres, a short walk from Museo Frida Kahlo. The chocolatines, cinnamon rolls, and almond pastries are fresh, delicious, and generously portioned, and you'll also find savory poblano and other breads. **Known for:** affordable, generously sized pastries and cakes; locals snacking on the white iron benches out front; coffee or juices available from the bakery's adjacent beverage counter. *Average main: 50 MP* ⊠ *Corina 117, Coyoacán* ☎ *55/5601-3472* ⊕ *www.pasteleria-caramel.mx* Ⓜ *Coyoacán.*

Picnic Helados

$ | Café. This simple take-out window on a quiet but central side street serves the best hand-crafted ice cream and sorbet in the neighborhood, always featuring just a handful of flavors that change regularly but might include coffee-cardamom, plum–goat cheese, guava-cinnamon, and tangerine. Picnic also sells a few kinds of delicious cookies and brownies too. **Known for:** interesting flavors, often with seasonal fruits; cute take-out window (but no seating); chocolate brownies. *Average main: 50 MP* ⊠ *Calle Malintzin 205–2, Coyoacán* ☎ *55/5510-9209* ⊕ *picnic-helados.negocio.site* ⊗ *Closed Mon.* Ⓜ *Coyoacán.*

Super Tacos Chupacabras

$ | Mexican. Open all night and drawing a particularly spirited crowd during the wee hours, this no-frills taco stand named for the vampire-ish "goat sucker" of Latin American folklore serves up joyously messy, overstuffed pastor, chorizo, beef, cecina, and other meaty tacos for around just MX$15 apiece. There's now a branch in Roma, too, but it's hard to beat the festive camaraderie of dining at the original, which has a seating area with several metal picnic tables. **Known for:** generous array of free fixings (potatoes, grilled onions, jicama, salsas, and more); late-night dining; steps from Centro

Coyoacán mall and Coyoacán metro. *Average main: 50 MP* ⊠ *Av. México Coyoacán s/n, Coyoacán* ⊹ *Beneath Av. Río Churubusco highway overpass* ☎ *618/163–6247* Ⓜ *Coyoacán.*

🍴 Dining

Alverre Café Bistró
$ | Café. A cute, unpretentious local favorite, Alverre has the sort of extensive international menu that's perfect when you and your friends aren't exactly sure what you're hungry for. Excellent bets here include the bountiful jamón serrano salad with arugula and goat cheese, the oven-baked lasagna with Bolognese sauce, and enchiladas suizas with chicken, but you'll also find crepes, omelets, empanadas, pizzas, and sandwiches. **Known for:** hearty breakfasts; remarkably extensive and varied menu; good selection of artisanal Mexican beers and kombuchas. *Average main: 120 MP* ⊠ *Calle Gómez Farias 42, Coyoacán* ☎ *55/5658–9027* ⊕ *alverre-cafe-bistro.business.site* Ⓜ *Viveros.*

⭐ Café Ruta de la Seda
$ | Café. Named for the Silk Road, this handsome café with an especially enchanting outdoor patio overlooking tranquil Parque Santa Catarina does indeed draw its culinary inspiration from both East and West, serving up delectable kimchi omelets, Cuban sandwiches, soba noodle and toasted sesame salads, and anise–avocado leaf cakes. Most of the fair-trade ingredients, from the coffee beans and teas to the whole grains and flours used

in the artisan breads and pastries, are sourced organically. **Known for:** matcha cakes and lattes; extensive list of organic Asian teas; close proximity to pretty Avendia Francisco Sosa. *Average main: 100 MP* ⊠ *Calle Aurora 1, Coyoacán* ☎ *55/3869–4888* ⊕ *www.caferutadelaseda.com* Ⓜ *Viveros.*

⭐ Corazón de Maguey
$$ | Modern Mexican. A stylish bi-level bistro and mezcal bar with a prime views across Jardín Centenario, Corazón de Maguey is a prime setting for artfully presented regional Mexican fare and creative cocktails. You could easily put together a meal of several starters—the guacamole with chapulines and shrimp-and-octopus burrito among them—or opt for one of the substantial main dishes, such as Mazatlán-style grilled whole fish of the day with a fresh chile-soy-lime marinade, or tender Yucateca cochinita pibíl. **Known for:** superb cocktails using the acclaimed Alipús house brand mezcal; great views of Jardín Centenario; lemon merengue with house-made lemon ice cream. *Average main: 230 MP* ⊠ *Parque Centenario 9A, Coyoacán* ☎ *55/5554–7555* ⊕ *www.corazondemaguey.com* Ⓜ *Viveros.*

El Beneficio Café
$ | Mexican. This dapper all-day café with white-brick walls, colorful peltre dishware, and fresh flowers on every table is in a semi-residential section of Coyoacán, well-removed from the crowds and an easy stroll from Museo Frida Kahlo. The owner uses organic

coffees and, as much as possible, locally sourced ingredients in the European-influenced Mexican fare, which includes superb chilaquiles (order them with both the green and red sauces), panfried potatoes with paprika and chipotle aioli, and turkey-and-panela baguette sandwiches. **Known for:** wide assortment of fresh-baked pastries and desserts; fresh fruit plates (with honey and granola); bright and cheerful space. *Average main: 140 MP* ⊠ *Calle Valentín Gómez Farías 85, Coyoacán* ☎ *55/6724–9536* Ⓜ *Coyoacán.*

El Entrevero
$$$ | Argentine. Although a Uruguayan owns this fashionable eatery on Coyoacán's lively Jardín Centenario, the menu will be familiar to fans of Argentine cuisine: the superb *provoleta* (grilled provolone cheese with oregano), for example, and the stellar steaks. Uruguay's Italian heritage appears on the menu as well, with good pizzas and gnocchi with a creamy gorgonzola sauce. **Known for:** prodigiously aged steaks; clericot (a classic Argentine drink of red wine, sugar, lemon juice, and soda water); dulce de leche imported from Uruguay. *Average main: 360 MP* ⊠ *Jardín Centenario 14, Coyoacán* ☎ *55/5659–0066* ⊕ *www.grupoentrevero.com* Ⓜ *Viveros.*

El Sheik
$$ | Middle Eastern. The flavorful Lebanese cuisine—including baked eggs, raw kibbeh, falafel, grilled kofta, dolmas, and cucumber salad—at this charming restaurant with amiable servers is perfect for filling up before or after a stroll or run in nearby Viveros park. If you're not sure what to order, the best approach is the extensive sampler platter, or dine here on the weekend, when there's a huge buffet offering. **Known for:** boldly flavored mint tea, Turkish coffee, and lassi drinks; generous weekend buffet offering a huge sampling of dishes; scrumptious Arabic cookies and other desserts. *Average main: 160 MP* ⊠ *Calle Madrid 129, Coyoacán* ☎ *55/5659–3311* ⊕ *www.elsheik.com.mx* Ⓜ *Coyoacán.*

★ El Tajín
$$ | Mexican. Named after El Tajín pyramid in Veracruz state and a longtime proponent of the "slow food" movement, this elegant lunch spot inside Jardin Cultural Del Centro Veracruzano sizzles with pre-Hispanic influences. Innovative appetizers include *chilpachole*, a delicate crab-soup with epazote and macha chile paste, while main dishes might include rabbit in a guajillo mole sauce and octopus cooked in its own ink with red wine, olives, and almonds. **Known for:** lovely setting overlooking a garden courtyard; impressive wine list; artfully prepared pre-Hispanic Mexican cuisine. *Average main: 210 MP* ⊠ *Jardin Cultural Del Centro Veracruzano, Av. Miguel Ángel de Quevedo 687, Coyoacán* ☎ *55/5659–5759* ⊕ *www.eltajin.com.mx* ⊘ *No dinner* Ⓜ *Viveros.*

Flor de Viento
$ | Vegetarian. Woven-basket lamps, hanging plants, high glass ceilings, and a tree growing up through the dining room set the tone for this airy restaurant's healthy approach to international food. Offering an extensive list of smoothies and juices, this space produces flavorful fare, some of it vegetarian—pancakes with coconut butter and house-made fruit compote or grilled portabello mushroom–nopales sandwiches— and some featuring sustainably procured proteins, from ahi poke bowls to surprisingly decadent organic cheeseburgers with heirloom tomatoes. **Known for:** interesting drink selection, from artisan beer to cold-pressed juices; breakfast toasts with avocado and gravlax; passionfruit cheesecake with mango sorbet. *Average main: 140 MP* ⊠ *Calle Pdte. Carranza 82–B, Coyoacán* ☎ *55/9154–8987* ⊕ *flor-de-viento-health-food-coyoacan.negocio. site* Ⓜ *Viveros.*

Green Corner
$ | Eclectic. Attached to the health food market that bears its name and specializes in organic, sustainable, and gourmet goods, this airy two-level eatery with a spacious garden seating area serves dishes that exemplify the company's green approach. Think coconut-yogurt bowls and quinoa with eggs in the morning, and falafel-mushroom sandwiches, chicken tinga tostadas, and beet carpaccio salads later in the day. **Known for:** meat and vegetarian burgers; certified-organic (in about 95% of all cases) ingredients; attractive dining room and outdoor seating. *Average main: 110 MP* ⊠ *Av. Miguel Ángel de Quevedo 733, Coyoacán* ☎ *55/6723–0313* ⊕ *www. thegreencorner.org* Ⓜ *Viveros.*

★ **La Barraca Valenciana**
$ | Spanish. This casual Spanish restaurant is known both for traditional tapas like *tartar de atún con ajillo*, *croquetas de jamón serrano*, and *patatas bravas*, and for its Iberian take on tortas, the classic Mexican sandwich. The tortas are among the best in the city, some with Mexican touches—like the *secretaria* (pork leg, chorizo, and cheese)—but the specialties are the *calamar* (chopped baby squid in chimichurri sauce) and *vegetariana* (a hearty stack of roasted eggplant and melted cheese). **Known for:** anything with squid or octopus (including tortas and tapas); house-brewed artisanal beers (available by the bottle); a pretty good wine list. *Average main: 95 MP* ⊠ *Av. Centenario 91–C, Coyoacán* ☎ *55/5658–1880* ⊕ *www.labarracava-lenciana.com* Ⓜ *Viveros.*

La Pause
$$ | European. Set along picturesque Avendia Francisco Sosa, this charming neighborhood bistro stands out for its peaceful, inviting courtyard with flowers, tall hedges, and tables set beneath red umbrellas—an especially nice spot for breakfast. The kitchen produces beautifully plated Mexican-meets-continental cuisine, such as *huevos albañil* (eggs, red chile sauce, and panela served bubbling hot in a

molcajete) at breakfast, and grilled salmon with saffron sauce and chicken stuffed with artichokes for lunch or dinner. **Known for:** charming patio; decadent Mexican pastries at breakfast; leisurely breakfasts. *Average main: 280 MP* ✉ *Av. Francisco Sosa 287, Coyoacán* ☎ *55/5658-6891* ⊕ *www.lapausec-oyoacan.com* ⊗ *No dinner Sun.* Ⓜ *Viveros.*

★ **Los Amantes Café & Bistro**
$ | Café. Stroll just a block south of Jardín Centenario's inevitable crowds to find this little gem with simple red-and-white-checked tablecloths and a front window lined with tantalizing displays of fresh-made cakes and pies. Indeed, sweets—as well as finely curated teas and well-crafted espresso drinks—are the specialty here, but you'll also find excellent breakfast, lunch, and dinner options, ranging from vegetable frittatas and mollettes with beans and ham in the morning to spinach-and-artichoke casserole and salmon burgers later in the day. **Known for:** enticing cakes, cookies, and brownies; unpretentious dining room with endearingly quirky decor; generous portions. *Average main: 125 MP* ✉ *Calle Felipe Carrillo Puerto 19, Coyoacán* ☎ *55/7576-0946* ⊗ *No dinner Fri.–Sun.* Ⓜ *Viveros.*

Los Danzantes
$$$ | Modern Mexican. Although fancy and a bit expensive for the neighborhood, this venerable outpost of the famed Mexican fusion restaurant in Oaxaca opened in a handsome two-story space overlooking Jardín Centenario in 1995 and has been a destination for foodies ever since. Artfully plated dishes like *guajolote* (organic wild turkey) smothered in mole poblano and negro sauces, and achiote-marinated *huachinango* (Gulf red snapper) with plantains, avocado, and cotija cheese reflect the kitchen's considerable talents, although service can be a tad stiff, especially for laid-back Coyoacán. **Known for:** regional Mexican cuisine with an emphasis on Oaxaca; charming setting overlooking Jardín Centenario; impressive wine and mezcal lists. *Average main: 300 MP* ✉ *Parque Centenario 12, Coyoacán* ☎ *55/6585-2477* ⊕ *losdanzantes.com/ los-danzantes-coyoacan* Ⓜ *Viveros.*

Mercado Roma Coyoacán
$ | Eclectic. The hip Mercado Roma has replicated its success on a slightly smaller scale with this attractive, bi-level food hall a block from both Avendia Francisco Sosa and from the swanky Oasis Coyoacán shopping mall and cinema. You'll find a remarkable variety of options, including mini outposts of several notable restaurants around town (Porco Rosso, Butcher & Sons, Kura Izakaya), serving everything from sushi and burgers to tortas and gourmet *paletas* (popsicles). **Known for:** fun, lively ambience; great variety of cuisine types; some excellent beer and wine stalls. *Average main: 150 MP* ✉ *Av. Miguel Ángel de Quevedo 355, Coyoacán* ☎ *55/2155-9435* ⊕ *www.mrc.mercadoroma.com* Ⓜ *Miguel Ángel de Quevedo.*

Merendero Las Lupitas

$ | Mexican. Eclectic paintings of Mexican scenes, colorful tilework and papel picado banners, and ladderback rush-seated chairs capture the traditional vibe of this cozy restaurant that opened here in 1959 on a lovely corner of Avenida Francisco Sosa. The charming setting is the top reason to dine here, but home-style machaca with eggs, chorizo gorditos, carne asada, and other Norteño-style dishes are affordable and tasty. **Known for:** Northern Mexico–style ("Norteño") comfort food; historic setting overlooking a famous church; atole (a traditional Mesoamerican corn-masa beverage served warm). *Average main: 120 MP* ⊠ *Calle Jardín Sta Catarina 4, Coyoacán* ☎ *55/5554–3353* ⊕ *www.merenderolaslupitas.com.mx* Ⓜ *Viveros.*

Restaurante Frida

$$ | Mexican. This attractive open-air restaurant is set within the small campus of modern buildings and lovely gardens that make up the Centro del Patrimonio Inmobiliario Federal (Federal Real Estate Heritage Center), on a quiet lane between Avendia Francisco Sosa and Viveros Park. It's an excellent spot to sample large portions of well-prepared classic Mexican fare, including chilaquiles, hand-made *huaraches* (masa flatbread with various toppings), and *albóndigas* (Mexican meatballs in a hearty tomato stew). **Known for:** enmoladas (chicken enchiladas smothered in mole sauce); beautiful garden setting; monthly changing

menus dedicated to different regions of Mexico. *Average main: 170 MP* ⊠ *Centro del Patrimonio Inmobiliario Federal, Calle Salvador Novo 8, Coyoacán* ☎ *55/5563–2699* ⊕ *restaurantefrida.com* Ⓜ *Viveros.*

🍸 Bars and Nightlife

Centenario 107

Midway between Coyoacán's plazas and the Cineteca Nacional film center, this spacious, conversation-filled bar and tavern stands out for its extensive selection of both Mexican and international craft beers on tap and by the bottle. But there's also a big all-day-and-night food menu featuring pretty tasty pizzas, burgers, pastas, sandwiches, and the like. ⊠ *Centenario 107, Coyoacán* ☎ *55/4752–6369* ⊕ *www. centenario107.com* Ⓜ *Coyoacán.*

El Convento
Stop by this restaurant-bar set in dramatic former 16th-century convent for drinks on the cloistered central patio. It's especially lovely around dusk and a great option for a pre-dinner drink, whether you opt to stay and dine here or wander elsewhere. There's live music some evenings, too. ⊠ *Fernández Leal 96, Coyoacán* ☎ *55/5554–4065* ⊕ *www.facebook.com/ElConventoDF* Ⓜ *Viveros.*

El Hijo del Cuervo
Students and hip intellectuals of all ages pack "the Raven's Son," thanks to an interesting mix of rock, jazz, and other live music performances as well as intriguing art shows on the walls. Set on the northwest corner of Jardín Centenario, it's also a nice spot to enjoy a beer or a light bite to eat on the patio. It stages occasional theater shows, too. ⊠ *Jardín Centenario 17, Coyoacán* ☎ *55/5658–7824* ⊕ *www.elhijodelcuervo.com.mx* Ⓜ *Viveros.*

★ Júpiter Cervecería
This softly lit, stylish craft-beer bar stands out among the usual array of crowded cantinas in Coyoacán for its exceptionally varied selection of bottled—as well as six draft—craft beers, most of them Mexican. There's also a great menu of elevated tacos, tortas, and other bar food, plus ping-pong and live music some evenings. ⊠ *Calle Higuera 22, Coyoacán* ☎ *55/7261–0855* Ⓜ *Viveros.*

La Bipo
A trendy, youthful crowd congregates in this always-busy bar co-owned by actor Diego Luna and decorated with pop-art murals. You can sometimes catch alternative and rock bands performing, and there's better-than-average bar food (burgers, Jamaica quesadillas, etc.) along with an extensive selection of mezcal and other top-shelf booze. ⊠ *Calle Malintzin 155, Coyoacán* ☎ *55/5484–8230* ⊕ *www. labipo.com.mx* Ⓜ *Viveros.*

★ Laca Laca
Talented mariachis, a long drinks list, and very tasty (though slightly expensive for the neighborhood) contemporary Mexican food are among the draws of this trendy modern cantina across the street from Jardín Centenario. But the biggest boast is the gracious setting: the main dining and drinking area is in a scenic courtyard with giant trees and a glass roof. There's a cozier bar upstairs, and next to the entrance, the Laca Laca has a cute little shop that sells fun gifts, crafts, and artwork. ⊠ *Av. Centenario 2, Coyoacán* ☎ *55/5554– 7652* ⊕ *restaurant-bar-lacalaca. business.site* Ⓜ *Viveros.*

La Coyoacana
A few steps from Plaza Hidalgo, this venerable cantina has been a neighborhood fixture for years. It's nothing fancy, but the food and drink

are inexpensive, and mariachis perform on the cheerful covered patio out back. ⊠ *Calle Higuera 14, Coyoacán* ☎ *55/5658–5337* ⊕ *www. lacoyoacana.com* Ⓜ *Viveros.*

Mezcalero

As the name suggests, the considerable selection of mezcal is the big draw at this very popular cocktail bar behind San Juan Batista Church. If you're not sure what you'd like, try a flight of three or five one-ounce pours. DJs spin good music later in the evening, and there's pretty tasty bar food to pair with your sips. ⊠ *Calle Caballocalco 14, Coyoacán* ☎ *55/5554–7027* ⊕ *lacasadelmezcal. negocio.site* Ⓜ *Viveros.*

 Performing Arts

La Titería

Also known as Casa de las Marionetas, or House of Puppets, this small kids-oriented cultural center and theater uses (you guessed it) puppets in its theater and music performances but also shows films and offers other kinds of family-friendly programming. ⊠ *Calle Vicente Guerrero 7, Coyoacán* ☎ *55/5662–6952* ⊕ *www.latiteria.mx* Ⓜ *Coyoacán.*

★ Teatro Bar El Vicio

Since 2005, this fabulous little cabaret theater and bar has been delighting crowds with irreverent, original shows, often with a decidedly queer and provocatively political bent. ⊠ *Calle Madrid 13, Coyoacán* ☎ *55/5659–1139* ⊕ *www. elvicio.com.mx* Ⓜ *Coyoacán.*

★ Teatro La Capilla

Founded in 1953 by the gay playwright and poet Salvador Novo, who's sometimes referred to as Mexico's Oscar Wilde, this intimate theater hosts a wide range of mostly contemporary indie plays. Productions rotate often, and there's something going on virtually every night of the week. It's one of the best small theaters in the city, and many performances are geared to kids and teens. There's also a bar and restaurant attached. ⊠ *Calle Madrid 13, Coyoacán* ☎ *55/5658–6285* ⊕ *www. teatrolacapilla.com* Ⓜ *Coyoacán.*

Teatro Santa Catarina UNAM

Situated just off Avendia Francisco Sosa across the courtyard from beautiful Santa Catarina Chapel, this fairly intimate black box theater operates through the acclaimed drama program at UNAM (Universidad Nacional Autónoma de México). It's the site of often experimental and contemporary works. Although small, its productions are top-notch. ⊠ *Jardín Sta Catarina 10, Coyoacán* ⊹ *Corner of Av. Francisco Sosa and Av. Progreso* ☎ *55/5658–0560* ⊕ *www.teatrounam. com* Ⓜ *Viveros.*

SANTA MARÍA LA RIBERA

SAN RAFAEL

POLANCO

JUÁREZ AND ANZURES

ALAMEDA CENTRAL

CENTRO HISTÓRICO

BOSQUE DE CHAPULTEPEC

ROMA

CONDESA

BENITO JUÁREZ

SAN ÁNGEL

COYOACÁN

Sightseeing ★★★☆☆ | Shopping ★★★★☆ | Dining ★★★★☆ | Nightlife ★★☆☆☆

A small colonial enclave of cobblestone streets, stone walls, stately pastel houses, lush foliage, blooming jacaranda trees, and gardens drenched in bougainvillea, San Ángel is one of the city's most inviting outlying neighborhoods. Its historic core is abundant with boutiques, design shops, arts and crafts galleries, and both casual and fashionable restaurants. It's an especially popular destination on Saturday, when its famed Bazaar Sábado draws legions of shoppers.—by Andrew Collins

Many who come to San Ángel combine their adventure with adjacent Coyoacán, which can be an effective strategy if you're short on time. But there are several excellent museums and some stellar upscale restaurants here in San Ángel, so if you can, consider setting aside a full day to shop, dine, and take your time exploring the three most noteworthy attractions: Museo del Carmen, Museo Casa Estudio Diego Rivera y Frida Kahlo, and Museo de Arte Carrillo Gil.

Like Coyoacán, this community functioned as its own distinct, agrarian municipality from the precolonial Aztec era to its settlement in the late 1500s by the Spaniards—who constructed the San Jacinto and El Carmen monasteries that came to define the area—

to the early 20th century, when San Ángel became fully part of Mexico City. The construction in the 1950s of sprawling Ciudad Universitaria to the south as well as two wide and modern (if not especially pleasant) north-south boulevards, Avenida de los Insurgentes and Avenida Revolución, spurred the area's rapid urbanization. Today you'll find a number of high-rise office buildings, residential towers, and shopping malls on the busy streets just beyond San Ángel's charming and historic core.

Enamored of the area's pleasant climate, rural character, and striking setting atop fields of volcanic rock, Mexico City's wealthy elite built lavish haciendas and mansions in San Ángel during the late 18th and 19th centuries to use as country homes. The neighborhood has maintained a reputation for affluence ever since. The grandest of these homes have been converted into high-end restaurants or shopping arcades. On either sides of Avenidas Revolución and Insurgentes, however, you'll also discover block after block of narrow cobblestone lanes flanked by gorgeous old houses. When you need a break from the hubbub of retail activity around the main plazas, take a stroll through these tranquil, picturesque residential districts, which lie immediately west and north of Plaza San Jacinto and south and east of Parque de la Bombilla.

◉ Sights

Centro Cultural Isidro Fabela

This 1681 mansion, which contains both a cultural center and Museo Casa del Risco, is one of the prettiest houses facing the Plaza San Jacinto. The huge 18th-century Risco Fountain—exploding with colorful porcelain tiles, shells, and mosaics—dominates the eastern wall of the enclosed courtyard. Inside, the upper galleries contain a splendid if slightly somber collection of 17th- and 18th-century European baroque and colonial Mexican paintings and furnishings, all donated by the house's last owner, statesman and politician Isidro Fabela, who died in 1964. Fabela also donated books and magazines to a small library behind the museum (by way of a lovely patio) that is open to the public. Events and rotating art exhibits are staged throughout the year. ⊠ *Plaza San Jacinto 15, San Ángel* ☎ *55/5616–2711* ⊕ *www.isidrofabela.org.mx* ⊠ *Free* Ⓜ *M. A. de Quevedo.*

GETTING HERE

Along with neighboring Coyoacán, San Ángel is in the city's southern section; it's about 9 km (6 miles) south of Roma and Condesa and 12 km (7 miles) south of Centro Histórico. Uber fares from the airport or the city center run about MX$90–MX$150. By Metro, you can take the 3 line to Coyoacán, Viveros, or Miguel Ángel de Quevedo or the 7 line to the final stop Barranca del Muerto, but none of these stations is in the center of the neighborhood, so expect a 15- to 25-minute walk to most points of interest (the area is very safe for walking). From Coyoacán, it's a quick Uber ride (around MX$50) or picturesque 45- to 60-minute walk via Avendia de la Paz, Calle Arenal, and Avendia Francisco Sosa. The neighborhood also has a fair amount of free street parking as well as several inexpensive but secure lots.

★ Museo Casa Estudio Diego Rivera y Frida Kahlo

This small museum compound is where Diego and Frida lived, painted, loved, and fought (they divorced briefly in 1939) from 1934 to 1940; its three angular red and blue buildings with large multipane windows and a cacti-filled courtyard is stylistically the antithesis of the traditional Spanish Colonial Museo Frida Kahlo just a few miles away in Coyoacán. In the red main house, some of Rivera's final paintings rest on easels, and you can see his denim jacket and shoes on a wicker chair with his modest little bed and side table made up as though the artist might return at any moment. In the building's studio you can view giant papier-mâché sculptures (some of the pre-Hispanic pottery that Rivera collected) and other curious figurines and colorful folk art. The buildings' unusual, and at the time highly avant garde, design are a big part of what makes a visit here so interesting. Architect Juan O'Gorman, who devised these buildings in 1931, was a close friend of Rivera's and lived on the property in a third structure that today, like the blue house that Frida resided in, contains rotating exhibits.

Interesting architectural features include several curving concrete exterior and interior staircases, and a bridge that connects the rooftops of Diego's and Frida's homes—a convenient passageway that allowed the two simultaneous access to and space from one another. ⊠ *Calle Diego Rivera, at Av. Altavista, San Ángel* ☎ *55/8647-5470* ⊕ *estudiodiegorivera.bellasartes.gob.mx* 🖾 *MX$35; free Sun.* ⊘ *Closed Mon.* Ⓜ *Barranco Del Muerto.*

★ Museo de Arte Carrillo Gil

This cube-shape art museum built in 1972 by businessman and collector Dr. Alvar Carrillo Gil is one of the top venues in the city for viewing vanguard art. Rotating exhibits showcase contemporary art in a wide range of media, often by young, emerging artists. At times you can also view portions of the immense permanent collection, which consists of more than 2,000 works, about 1,400 of which Gil collected himself. These include more than 50 murals and paintings by José Clemente Orozco as well as important pieces by Rivera, Siqueiros, Klee, and Picasso. ⊠ *Av. Revolución 1608, San Ángel* ☎ *55/8647-5450* ⊕ *www.museodeartecarrillogil.com* 🖾 *MX$50; free Sun.* ⊘ *Closed Mon.* Ⓜ *M. A. de Quevedo.*

★ Museo del Carmen

Erected by Carmelite friars with the help of an Indigenous chieftain between 1615 and 1628, this church—with its domes, frescoes, vaulted archways, fountains, and gardens—was never actually a convent, despite its name. Though some locals might tell you otherwise, nuns never actually lived here. The church still operates (you can enter it for free from a separate entrance next door), but part of it has been converted into Museo del Carmen, with a fine collection of 16th- to 18th-century religious paintings and icons. Much of the religious art (along with a captivating collection of photos that depict San Ángel and the southern portions of the city during the early 20th century) is on the second floor of the adjoining Casa de Acueducto, which overlooks another courtyard fringed by an interesting ancient aqueduct. It's also worth visiting the dozen-or-so mummified corpses tucked away in the crypt—a creepy but fascinating sight, for sure. For a perhaps much-needed breath of fresh air, saunter out to the gracious rear garden, with its shady trees and benches. There's usually an excellent temporary exhibit as well, typically touching on some element of Mexico City history and culture. ⊠ *Av. Revolución 4, San Ángel* 🕾 *55/5616-2816, 55/5616-1177* ⊕ *www.elcarmen.inah.gob.mx* 🎫 *MX$60* 🕙 *Closed Mon.* Ⓜ *M. A. de Quevedo.*

Museo Soumaya Plaza Loreto

The Plaza Loreto branch of the famed art museum in Polanco contains several huge exhibition rooms set inside the upper level of a colonial-era warehouse building that now houses shops and restaurants. It's a bit south of the heart of San Ángel, and not necessarily worth a trip all on its own, but the rotating exhibits can sometimes be quite interesting, and admission is free. ⊠ *Rio de la Magdalena at Av. Revolución, San Ángel* 🕾 *55/5616-3731* ⊕ *www.museosoumaya.org* 🎫 *Free* 🕙 *Closed Tues.* Ⓜ *M. A. de Quevedo.*

Parque de la Bombilla

At the eastern edge of the neighborhood, not far from the border with Coyoacán, this handsome park is anchored by a striking art deco obelisk monument to Álvaro Obregón, the much-lauded general of the Mexican Revolution and 39th president of Mexico. In 1928, shortly after his reelection to the presidency, Obregón was assassinated while dining in La Bombilla restaurant, which stood exactly where the monument and park stand today—they opened seven years after his death, in 1935. A long, shallow reflecting pool frames the monument, which is illuminated dramatically at night, and is surrounded by beautifully tended gardens and rows

of trees. Rife with benches, the park is a perfect place to enjoy a picnic or relax with a book; it also makes a nice break if you're strolling to or from Coyoacán via Avendia Francisco Sosa. Along Avendia de la Paz, which forms the park's northern border, you'll find a series of well-stocked, bargain-filled used-book stalls. The streets immediately south of the park, a neighborhood known as Chimalistac, are lined with lovely old homes and gardens. ⊠ *Av. de los Insurgentes Sur at Av. de la Paz, San Ángel* Ⓜ *M. A. de Quevedo.*

Parroquia de San Jacinto

With its ancient dome and roof line rising above the shops that flank the west edge of Plaza San Jacinto, this church built by Dominican friars during the 16th and 17th centuries is best viewed from its gracious courtyard. From the beautiful gardens, you can take in the view of the church's distinctive facade of volcanic stone and chipped and faded salmon-pink stucco. It's a peaceful spot to relax and catch your breath after shopping around San Ángel, and the interior—with its ornate Spanish Rococo–style retablo behind the altar—is stunning. ⊠ *Plaza San Jacinto 18 Bis, San Ángel* 🕾 *55/5616-2059.*

Parroquia San Sebastián Mártir

Built in the mid-1500s and containing a remarkably ornate, 18th-century altarpiece, this small oft-photographed church with high, timber-beam ceilings anchors a small plaza in a quiet section of the charmingly historic Chimalistac neighborhood. More intimate than many of the city's noteworthy places of worship, the church is unusual for having a sanctuary that's much wider than it is deep. ⊠ *Plaza Federico Gamboa 11, San Ángel* ☎ *55/5661-6041* Ⓜ *M. A. de Quevedo.*

Plaza de Los Arcángeles
From Plaza San Jacinto, it's a leisurely 10-minute stroll through an elegant neighborhood of cobblestone streets to reach this tiny, tranquil park that few people, except for the residents of its surrounding homes, ever see. The verdant sliver of dense shrubbery, specimen trees, bougainvillas, and flower beds is laced with flagstone pathways and contains several statues as well as three ornate stone benches named for the three *arcángeles* for whom the little park is dedicated: San Miguel, San Gabriel, and San Rafael. Virtually free of car traffic, it's an idyllic place to sneak away from the crowds of weekend shoppers and briefly imagine life as a resident of this historic neighborhood. ⊠ *2a Frontera 37, Mexico City* Ⓜ *M. A. de Quevedo.*

★ Plaza San Jacinto
This picturesque plaza lined with palatial 18th- and 19th-century homes as well as a number of galleries, boutiques, and restaurants constitutes the heart of San Ángel. On the north side of the plaza, the excellent arts-and-crafts market Bazaar Sábado is held all day Saturday, and just west up Calle Benito Juarez there's an additional covered market on weekends where you can find cheaper knickknacks and goods. Continue a block down

the hill along shop-lined Calle Madero to reach Plaza del Carmen, a smaller park with pathways and benches where still more artists sell their works on Saturday. A memorial plaque on Plaza San Jacinto's west side lists the names of about 50 Irish soldiers from St. Patrick's Battalion who helped Mexico during the "unjust North American invasion" of 1847. These men had been enticed to desert the ranks of U.S. General Zachary Taylor by appeals to the historic and religious ties between Spain and Ireland, siding with the Mexicans in the Mexican-American War. Following their capture by U.S. forces, all were hanged (16 of them on Plaza San Jacinto). ⊠ *Plaza San Jacinto, San Ángel* Ⓜ *M. A. de Quevedo.*

 Shopping

Avenida Altavista
Once of the fanciest retail destinations in Mexico City outside Polanco and Lomas de Chapultepec, this six-block thoroughfare is lined

with swanky furniture and design shops, scene-y restaurants (such as Farina, La Buena Fe, and Tori Tori), and tony boutiques. Along here you'll find local branches of MaxMara, Carolina Herrera, Salvatore Ferragamo, and other acclaimed designers. If you're in the market for housewares, this is a good place to spend an afternoon—standouts include GAIA, Dupuis, and Muebles Pergo Altavista. The luxe shopping continues, rather jarringly, right up to the modernist complex that houses Museo Casa Estudio Diego Rivera y Frida Kahlo, which is about 100 feet from a Starbucks (thankfully when you're at the museum, you can't actually see all these shiny new shops). Altavista is just a 15-minute walk from Plaza San Jacinto, but is itself weirdly pedestrian-unfriendly and designed more with cars in mind. ⊠ Av. Altavista, San Ángel ✛ Between Av. Revolución and Calle Diego Rivera Ⓜ Barranca Del Muerto.

⭐ El Bazaar Sábado

It's worth visiting San Ángel on a Saturday just to visit the upscale artisan market that's been going strong there since 1960. Before you even make it into the grandiose colonial mansion, you'll encounter dozens of vendors selling crafts, wood carvings, embroidered clothing, leather goods, wooden masks, beads, *amates* (bark paintings), and trinkets at stalls just outside and around Plaza San Jacinto and adjacent Calle Benito Juárez. Inside, on two levels that encircle a beautiful courtyard, are the (generally) better-quality—and higher-priced—goods, including *alebrijes* (painted wooden animals from Oaxaca), glassware, pottery, jewelry, fashion, furniture and housewares, and a smattering of gourmet goods and beauty products. There's also a decent traditional Mexican restaurant in the courtyard, which has a massive tree looming over it. The bazaar is open only on Saturday, but if you're unable to visit in person, check out the website, where you can purchase many of the goods online (shipping is free in Mexico City for orders over MX$799 and can be arranged for international deliveries). ⊠ *Plaza San Jacinto 11, San Ángel* ☎ *55/5616–0082* ⊕ *www.bazaarsabado.com* Ⓜ *M. A. de Quevedo.*

Librería Octavio Paz

This huge contemporary bookstore that's part of the nonprofit Fondo de Cultura Económica is named for the Mexican poet and diplomat who lived the final years of his life in nearby Coyoacán. Inside you'll find a huge inventory of titles as well as a small café. ⊠ *Av. Miguel Ángel de Quevedo 115, San Ángel* ☎ *55/5480–1801* Ⓜ *M. A. de Quevedo.*

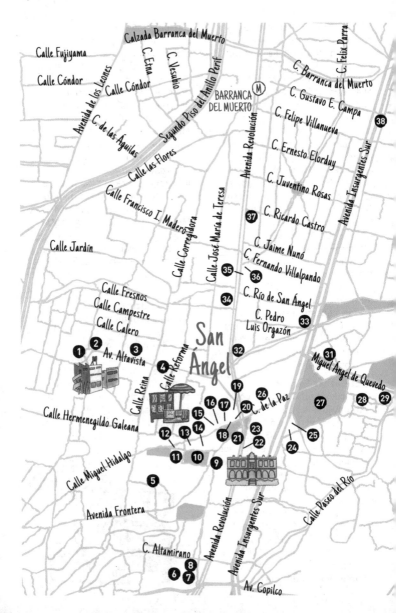

Calle Fujiyama

Calle Cóndor

Avenida de los Leones

C. de las Águilas

C. Etna

C. Vesubio

Calzada Barranca del Muerto

Calle Cóndor

Segundo Piso del Anillo Perif

BARRANCA
DEL MUERTO Ⓜ

C. Felix Parra

C. Barranca del Muerto

C. Gustavo E. Campa

C. Felipe Villanueva

Avenida Revolución

C. Ernesto Elorduy

C. Juventino Rosas

38

Avenida Insurgentes Sur

Calle las Flores

Calle Francisco I. Madero

Calle Jardín

Calle Correguidora

Calle José María de Teresa

C. Ricardo Castro

37

C. Jaime Nunó

C. Fernando Villalpando

35

36

C. Río de San Ángel

34

C. Pedro
Luis Orgazón

C. Pedro Luis Orgazón

33

Calle Fresnos
Calle Campestre
Calle Calero

**San
Ángel**

32

31

Miguel Ángel de Quevedo

❶ ❷

❸

Av. Altavista

Calle Reina

Calle Reforma

❹

19

26

27

28

29

Calle Hermenegildo Galeana

15

16 **17**

20

C. de la Paz

25

12 **13** **14**

18 **21**

23

22

24

❺

❶❶

❶0

❾

Calle Miguel Hidalgo

Avenida Frontera

C. Altamirano

❽

❻ ❼

Avenida Revolución

Avenida Insurgentes Sur

Calle Paseo del Río

Av. Copilco

★ Local México

Offering top-quality, fair-trade goods (much of it made in Chiapas), this small compound between Plaza and Parroquia San Jacinto contains six different enterprises, one of which is entirely devoted to Día de Muertos figures and artwork. Other highlights include the artists' co-op Jolom Mayaetik for beautifully designed apparel, Fou Fou Chat for jewelry and gifts, Maestras Artesanas for home textiles, and Maka México for leather jewelry boxes and handbags. ⊠ *Calle Benito Juárez 2, San Ángel* ☎ *55/1702-2850* Ⓜ *M. A. de Quevedo.*

Tienda de Antiguedades

The faded elegance of this pale-blue single-story colonial mansion overlooking Plaza del Carmen hints at the several rooms of antique treasures contained within. The front parlors mostly showcase smaller decorative items, drinking glasses, tableware, crafts, and smaller artworks. As you venture toward the back, you'll find larger furniture, including an interesting selection of antique mirrors, chairs, framed paintings, and other pieces that look as though they once inhabited some of the neighborhood's stately old homes. ⊠ *Calle Plaza del Carmen 6, San Ángel* Ⓜ *M. A. de Quevedo.*

Uriarte Talavera

Inside a small shopping arcade just off Plaza del Carmen, this is one of two retail showrooms in Mexico City for the Uriate workshop, one of the oldest and largest producers of Puebla's famously ornate Talavera pottery. Uriate began in 1824, and this small shop carries tiles, vases, bowls, and other decorative works. The company has another shop in Polanco. ⊠ *Calle de la Amargura 17, San Ángel* ☎ *55/5550-3293* ⊕ *www. uriartetalavera.com.mx* Ⓜ *M. A. de Quevedo.*

☕ Coffee and Quick Bites

Borola Café

$ | **Café.** Drop by this cheerful café on the eastern side of Plaza San Jacinto for a cold brew or well-crafted latte to go or to enjoy at one of the handful of tables. Borola also serves sandwiches, pastries, and other light fare. **Known for:** central location steps from San Ángel shopping; well-crafted espresso drinks; friendly staff. *Average main: 50 MP* ⊠ *Plaza San Jacinto 12, San Ángel* ☎ *55/2559-7618* ⊕ *www.borola.mx* Ⓜ *M. A. de Quevedo.*

Oveja Negra

$ | **Café.** You'll find cozy Oveja Negra immediately on your left as you enter trendy Mercado del Carmen—it's separate from the main food hall and thus a bit more intimate and peaceful. The baristas here produce a wide array of hot and iced espresso drinks along with some interesting cocktails infused with coffee, including a cookies-and-cream *carajillo* (a Spanish hot coffee drink) that'll warm your soul on a rainy day. **Known for:** intimate seating away from the main mercado food hall; iced lattes and cold brews; coffee-infused cocktails. *Average main: 90 MP* ⊠ *Calle de la*

MEAL TIMES IN MEXICO CITY

Traditionally, in Mexico the most substantial meal of the day is *la comida,* and it happens roughly between 1:30 and 4:30 pm. Breakfast is usually available in restaurants starting around 8 am, while Mexicans tend to prefer eating light at night, often enjoying a simple dinner (*la cena*) at around 9 or 9:30.

These customs sometimes confound visitors used to lunching around noon and saving their largest meal for dinnertime. But in diverse and cosmopolitan Mexico City, you'll find plenty of restaurants that serve meals at times that suit both visitors and locals, not too mention countless cafés, taquerías, and street vendors doling out tacos and other quick bites throughout the day. Just keep in mind that some establishments—especially more traditional ones—may not open for lunch until 1 pm, and if you show up for dinner before 8, you may encounter a fairly empty dining room. Also note that on Sunday, even many trendy international restaurants close by 6 pm.

Although not many restaurants in Mexico City specifically offer "brunch" menus, you'll find plenty of places that offer late-morning and early-afternoon dining that's very typical of what might be called brunch in other parts of the world. Think expansive menus featuring a mix of breakfast and lunch dishes, along with free-flowing cocktails and a charming setting—there may even be live music. Especially in affluent neighborhoods like Polanco and San Ángel, wonderfully inviting brunchlike experiences abound on weekends and even at some restaurants during the week.

Finally, if you're a fan of the morning meal, take comfort in knowing that breakfast (*el desayuno*) is highly popular in Mexico City, and typically a great value. Many restaurants offer package deals (*paquetes*) that include your main dish, coffee, fresh fruit or fresh-squeezed juice, and—best of all—a decadently delicious pastry of your choosing.

Amargura 5, San Ángel ☎ *55/3516-8718* Ⓜ *M. A. de Quevedo.*

Tierra Garat
$ | Café. With an airy design, comfortable seating, good Wi-Fi, and large windows that let in plenty of light, this branch of the popular local coffee franchise is ideal for meeting up with friends, getting some work done on your laptop, or grabbing a quick snack or meal. Tierra Garat offers an extensive range of espresso drinks but particularly excels with its sweet chais, flavored hot chocolates, and frozen drinks—it's a favorite of sweet tooths. **Known for:** inviting atmosphere for reading or working; hot chocolates, chais, and other dessert drinks; late hours. *Average main: 80 MP* ✉ *Av. de los Insurgentes Sur 1722, San Ángel* ⊕ *www.tierragarat.mx* Ⓜ *Barranca Del Muerto.*

🍴 Dining

Bistro 83

$$$ | Modern Mexican. Set in the back of a small but posh contemporary shopping arcade overlooking a tranquil formal garden just off Plaza del Carmen, chic Bistro 83 is a go-to for lavish contemporary Euro-Mexican fare, such as escargot sautéed in garlic butter, grilled salmon with pureed beets and polenta, and tuna tartare tostadas with a soy-ginger marinade. During the day, enjoy a drawn-out feast on the classy patio. **Known for:** views of lush green gardens; perfectly grilled steaks and burgers; weekend brunch. *Average main: 370 MP* ✉ *Calle de la Amargura 17, San Ángel* ☎ *55/5616–4911* ⊕ *www.bistro83. com.mx* ⊘ *No dinner Sun.* Ⓜ *M. A. de Quevedo.*

⭐ Cafebrería El Péndulo

$ | Eclectic. Located beside Centro Cultural Helénico, this latest branch of the chainlet of stylish bookstore-restaurants contains three levels designed with massive glass windows, loft mezzanines, and wide bridges and staircases—it's basically a modern treehouse for hungry booklovers. The encyclopedic menu of creatively conceived food and drink includes Mexican, American, and European staples, from burgers to breakfast sandwiches to macadamia-nut cheesecake, but what makes this place special is the artful aesthetic. **Known for:** well-prepared gastropub fare; seating placed throughout a well-stocked bookstore; late-night dining.

Average main: $135 ✉ *Av. Revolución 1500, San Ángel* ☎ *55/3640–4540* ⊕ *www.pendulo.com* Ⓜ *Barranca del Muerto.*

⭐ Carlota

$$$ | Modern Mexican. With its soaring ceilings, uncluttered interior, and marvelous back terrace overlooking a leafy courtyard and the 17th-century domes of the former Del Carmen convent, this chic temple to modern Mexican cuisine feels cloistered from the bustle of Avendia Revolución. The menu features a mix of creatively rendered classics (think tacos de lechón and tiradito of tuna and purslane) and contemporary dishes like braised short ribs with wild mushrooms and a sweet potato puree. **Known for:** extensive, global wine list; tranquil outdoor patio overlooking a garden; gracious but unpretentious service. *Average main: 360 MP* ✉ *Plaza, Del Carmen 4, San Ángel* ☎ *55/5550–0072* ⊕ *www. restaurantecarlota.com* Ⓜ *M. A. de Quevedo.*

⭐ El Cardenal

$$ | Mexican. Although not as historic as the original in El Centro (there are four locations in all), this beloved outpost of one of the city's most highly regarded traditional Mexican restaurants occupies a courtly redbrick mansion with high ceilings and expansive terraces, a setting that's ideal for a leisurely weekend brunch before shopping around nearby Plaza San Jacinto. The menu is extensive and includes consistently well-executed renditions of such regional specialties as chilaquiles rojo with cecina, Oaxacan-style chicken mole, pan de elote with clotted cream, and chiles en nogada (in September). **Known for:** exceptionally thoughtful and knowledgeable servers; grand, elegant setting; weekend brunch or dinner. *Average main: 220 MP* ✉ *Av. de la Paz 32, San Ángel* ☎ *55/5550–0293* ⊕ *www.restauranteelcardenal. com* ⊘ *No dinner* Ⓜ *M. A. de Quevedo.*

El Rincón de la Lechuza
$ | **Mexican.** This decidedly untrendy, old-school restaurant whose name means "the owl's hideout" opened in 1971 and was reputedly a favorite of Nobel Laureate Octavio Paz, who lived nearby. Open past midnight most evenings, it's a great option for enormous tacos packed with chorizo, chuleta, mushroom, poblano, melted cheese, and other classic fillings, plus seriously delicious tortilla soup. **Known for:** house-made tortillas; hefty portions; late-night dining. *Average main: 110 MP* ✉ *Av. Miguel Ángel de Quevedo 34, San Ángel* ☎ *55/5661-5911* ⊕ *www.elrincondelalechuza.mx* Ⓜ *M. A. de Quevedo.*

Eloise
$$$ | **Modern French.** A swanky spot for celebrating a special meal or simply savoring artful plates of opulent modern French fare— including crème brûlée de foie gras, truffled asparagus with Parmesan, and flank steak–frites Béarnaise— Eloise could be faulted only for its slightly ho-hum decor. The food is consistently excellent, right down to the indulgent desserts and globally representative wine list. **Known for:** dressy, special-occasion ambience; eight-hour-braised short ribs bourguignonne; outstanding wine list. *Average main: 380 MP* ✉ *Av. Revolución 1521, San Ángel* ☎ *55/5550–1692* ⊘ *Closed Mon. No dinner Sun.* Ⓜ *Barranca del Muerto.*

Gruta Ehden
$$ | **Lebanese.** Established in 1976 by owners whose grandparents emigrated from Lebanon to Mexico in 1930, this casual spot with red tiles and hammered-tin light fixtures serves some of the most authentic and flavorful Middle Eastern food in the city. A rewarding way to approach a feast here is to share a variety of smaller and larger plates—kibbeh, jocoque, baba ghanoush, fattoush, shawarma, and alambre-style grilled shrimp among them. **Known for:** flavorful hummus and other Middle Eastern dips; welcoming service; wide range of grilled and raw meat dishes. *Average main: 175 MP* ✉ *Calle Pino 69, San Ángel* ☎ *55/5661-1994* ⊕ *www.grutaehden. com.mx* Ⓜ *Coyoacán.*

Hunan
$$$ | **Chinese.** By far the fanciest Chinese restaurant in Mexico City, Hunan occupies a cavernous, solarium-style dining room overlooking a peaceful garden set back from the street. The long and varied menu tends toward lavish, traditional fare like crispy and spicy whole trout or sea bass with a fragrant garlic-chili-ginger sauce, and Peking duck served with house-made crepes and a rich plum sauce.

Known for: grand, art-filled dining room; refined, traditional Chinese cuisine; formal, attentive service. *Average main: 420 MP ⊠ Calle Pedro Luis Ogazón 102, San Ángel* ☎ *55/5661–6414* ⊕ *www.hunan.com. mx* ⊗ *No dinner Sun.* Ⓜ *Viveros.*

La Taberna del León

$$$ | **Modern European.** Set in a pretty 1920s chalet-style house, this dignified destination for sophisticated modern European–Mexican cuisine is surrounded by the historic redbrick buildings of the Plaza Loreto shopping center. Once you're seated on the shaded side patio or old-world dining rooms—supping on beef tartare with caviar, roasted duck with a mango sauce and wild rice, or seaball grilled with pistachios in a vermouth reduction— it's easy to feel like you've been transported to a wealthy friend's hideaway in the French Alps. **Known for:** solicitous, slightly formal service; refined old-world ambience; beautifully presented cuisine. *Average main: 420 MP ⊠ Antonio Plaza, Altamirano 46, San Ángel* ☎ *55/5616–2110* ⊕ *www.tabernadel-leon.rest* ⊗ *No dinner Sun.* Ⓜ *M. A. de Quevedo.*

★ **Loretta Chic Bistrot**

$$$ | **Mediterranean.** With a chic terrace upstairs and a modern white-on-white interior space on the ground floor, Loretta is one of the few restaurants in the southern half of the city that consistently makes it onto critics' top dining lists. Celebrated chef Abel Hernández presents contemporary takes on classic Provençal, Tuscan, Greek, and Middle Eastern dishes, like pork belly confit–and–heirloom tomato crostini, followed by creative pastas, steaks, moussakas, seafood grills, and a generous selection of vegetable sides. **Known for:** knowledgeable, efficient service; superb pan-Mediterranean wine list; creatively prepared vegetable sides that could be combined into a full meal. *Average main: 400 MP ⊠ Av. Revolución 1426, San Ángel* ☎ *55/5550–1692* ⊕ *www.loretta.rest* ⊗ *No dinner Sun.* Ⓜ *Barranca del Muerto.*

Maque Café

$$ | **Café.** This charming little café and bakery opens onto a glass-roof courtyard anchored by a giant central tree—it's set in the back of a small shopping arcade, away from the traffic noise of ritzy Avendia Atlavista, which makes it less of a scene than most of the restaurants nearby. Breakfast is the favorite meal here, with ham-manchego omelets and *machaca* (shredded dry beef) with eggs among the best bets, along with plenty of juice, pastries, espresso, and fresh fruit options. **Known for:** omelets with a variety of fillings; fresh-baked goods; inviting courtyard. *Average main: $155 ⊠ Av. Altavista 131, San Ángel* ☎ *55/5550–5863* Ⓜ *Barranca del Muerto.*

★ **Mercado del Carmen**

$ | **Eclectic.** One of the most beautifully designed and eclectic of the city's many contemporary food hall–style mercados, this bustling complex occupies a stylishly converted colonial home off Plaza del Carmen. The front contains hip boutiques selling sophisticated gourmet goodies, designer sunglasses, and mod housewares, and the open-air rear section is anchored by a bi-level seating area with a retractable roof that's fringed with trendy food stalls dispensing elevated pork buns, burgers, tortas, pizzas, tacos, and a range of wine, craft beer, and cocktail options. **Known for:** wide variety of cuisine and drink options; beautiful open-air dining area; trendy shops to browse while you wait for your food. *Average main: 110 MP* ✉ *Calle de la Amargura 5, San Ángel* ☎ 55/5256–4005 ⊕ *www.facebook. com/MercadodelCarmenSanÁngel* Ⓜ *M. A. de Quevedo.*

Restaurante San Ángel Inn

$$$ | **Mexican.** Dark mahogany furniture, crisp white table linens, exquisite blue-and-white Talavera place settings, and refined service strike a note of restrained opulence at this 18th-century estate whose dining rooms surround a central courtyard with fragrant gardens and a circular fountain. Although you'll find European-influenced classic fare like chateaubriand for two and crispy calves' brains in brown butter, the Mexican delicacies are the stars—consider the crepes of huitlacoche, or a jewel-like dish of *escamoles* (ant larvae) panfried in butter and herbs. **Known for:** gorgeous indoor and outdoor dining areas; weekend brunch; elaborate dessert cart. *Average main: 385 MP* ✉ *Calle Diego Rivera 50, San Ángel*

☎ 55/5616–1402 ⊕ *www.sanangelinn. com* Ⓜ *Barranca del Muerto.*

Taro

$$$ | **Japanese.** A bit south of San Ángel on the main street leading to UNAM, this clean and simple restaurant has been serving some of the finest Japanese food in the city since it opened in 1980. Sushi and sashimi prepared exactly as it is in Japan is a highlight, but you'll also find an extensive menu of izakaya-style dishes: gyozas, chicken karaage, seafood teppanyaki, tempura vegetables, beef katsu curry, and a variety of udon and soba noodle dishes. **Known for:** authentic sushi and sashimi; beef and seafood teppanyaki; extensive soba and udon noodle menu. *Average main: 370 MP* ✉ *Av. Universidad 1861, San Ángel* ☎ 55/5661–4083 ⊕ *www.restaurantetaro.com* Ⓜ *M. A. de Quevedo.*

Zohe China Gourmet

$$$ | **Chinese.** Reasonably priced and generally authentic Cantonese, Sichuan, and other Chinese dishes are the draw at the spacious Zohe China Gourmet and its soaring atrium-style dining room. Specialties include hand-pulled noodles, duck soup, pork dumplings, black-peppercorn beef, and honey-sesame chicken. **Known for:** authentic Chinese hand-pulled noodles; lavish lobster and king crab dishes; dishes from several notable regions of China. *Average main: $320* ✉ *Av. de los Insurgentes Sur 2108, San Ángel* ☎ 55/5661–6789 ⊕ *www.zohe.com.mx* Ⓜ *M. A. de Quevedo.*

Bars and Nightlife

El Depósito

A bustling branch of Mexico City's self-proclaimed world beer store, this dark and otherwise nondescript bar and bottle shop stands out for its vast selection of both Mexican and international craft beers. There are about a dozen other branches around the city, and light pub fare is available as well. ⊠ *Av. Insurgentes Sur 2098A, San Ángel* ☎ *55/5647–8015* ⊕ *www.eldeposito.com.mx* Ⓜ *M. A. de Quevedo.*

La Barra del Patrón

One of a handful of bars in the inviting and seemingly always busy Mercado del Carmen, La Barra sits right at the entrance to the communal food hall and is a great spot for creative cocktails and artisanal mezcal. You can drink at the bar or enjoy your libations with food at one of the hall's communal tables. ⊠ *Mercado del Carmen, Calle de la Amargura 5, San Ángel* ☎ *55/4515–3842* ⊕ *www.facebook. com/labarradelpatron* Ⓜ *M. A. de Quevedo.*

 Performing Arts

★ Centro Cultural Helénico

One of the most stately performance spaces in Mexico City, the Hellenic Cultural Center was constructed in 1954 using portions of a Spanish cloister and chapel from the 12th and 14th centuries as well as a baroque Guanajuato facade from the 17th century. The stately building became a cultural center in 1973 and showcases a wide range of popular plays, musicals, and festivals. It adjoins the handsome bookstore and café, Cafebrería El Péndulo. ⊠ *Av. Revolución 1500, San Ángel* ☎ *55/4155–0919* ⊕ *www.helenico.gob.mx* Ⓜ *Barranca del Muerto.*

Centro Cultural San Ángel

A variety of plays, musicals, concerts, and other events are presented in this elegant performance hall built in 1887 as a municipal palace and later used as the government offices of President Álvaro Obregón. ⊠ *Av. Revolución s/n, San Ángel* ☎ *55/5616–1254* ⊕ *www. cultura.cdmx.gob.mx* Ⓜ *M. A. de Quevedo.*

Cinemanía Loreto

In the same converted historic building that houses Museo Soumayo in Plaza Loreta, this inviting indie cineplex shows a steady roster of indie films and retrospectives. ⊠ *Rio de la Magdalena at Av. Revolución, San Ángel* ☎ *55/5616-4836* ⊕ *www.cinemanias.com.mx* Ⓜ *M. A. de Quevedo.*

12

Greater Mexico City

Fascinating archaeology

Destination eats

Charming neighborhoods

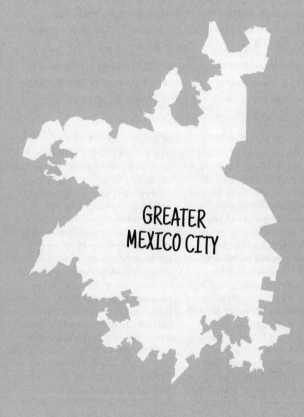

GREATER MEXICO CITY

Sightseeing ★★★★★ | Shopping ★★★☆☆ | Dining ★★★★☆ | Nightlife ★★☆☆☆

T hose who venture beyond the city's immediate central neighborhoods, and even beyond popular Coyoacán and San Ángel to the south, will be rewarded with the opportunity to visit some fascinating attractions, including the country's most important archaeological sites (with the pyramids of Teotihuacán leading the way), several charming historic neighborhoods (such Tlalpan Centro and Xochimilco, with its extensive canal network and gondolalike boats), and a selection of both inexpensive and high-end restaurants and shops. In the north, in addition to Teotihuacán, there's the iconic Basílica de Guadalupe, a gigantic church dedicated to Mexico's patron saint, as well as the small, historically significant Spanish colonial city of Tepotzotlán. CDMX's western mountains are also home to Mexico's first national park, alpine-aired Desierto de los Leones, as well as the futuristic edge city of Santa Fe, with its forest of contemporary skyscrapers.—by Andrew Collins

Many of the top sites worth visiting are located in the south of the city, a large district of lava-covered foothills and slopes that include not just Tlalpan Centro and Xochilmilco, but also a number of interesting parks, restaurants, and museums. There's also the picturesque and culturally rich main campus of National Autonomous University of Mexico (UNAM), which was constructed in the 1950s on a particularly scenic patch of lava—now known as Ciudad Universiteria (University City)— and contains some truly superb museums and performing arts venues; the campus is one of four UNESCO World Heritage Sites in the metro region. Finally, you'll also find a couple of key Frida Kahlo and Diego Rivera sites in this part of the city: Museo Anahuacalli and Museo Dolores Olmedo.

How to best balance your time while exploring Greater Mexico City depends a lot on your particular interests and your tolerance for potentially dense traffic, which can be wearying whether you're the driver or a passenger in this sprawling metropolis. Most of the sites on the city's immediate periphery can be reached without too much effort by public transportation or a short Uber ride. To fully appreciate Teotihuacán or Xochimilco, give yourself at least a half-day, and perhaps consider combining your trips to these places with others nearby (like visiting a museum and having dinner in Tepotzotlán following a trip to Teotihuacán, and doing the same in Tlalpan after visiting Xochimilco). Exploring Desierto de los Leones pairs nicely with lunch, dinner, or a movie in Santa Fe, and if you're visiting the outstanding Museo Universitario Arte Contemporáneo (MUAC) at UNAM, consider dining on campus at Azul y Oro and perhaps seeing a performance in one of the adjacent performance halls. If you're in Mexico City for at least four full days, it's well worth setting aside at least a day to embark on some of these side trips. Many travelers who do make the effort to venture farther afield discover some of their favorite attractions or meals of the trip.

Greater Mexico City North

◉ Sights

Estadio Alfredo Harp Helú
Thanks to batter-friendly thin air, baseball fans here are often treated to slugfests at Diablos Rojos games in this dramatic stadium near the airport. The season for the Mexican League pro team (they play at roughly the caliber of U.S. MLB Triple A minor league teams) runs from April to August, with play-offs lasting into September. ⊠ *Av. Viaducto Rio de la Piedad Ciudad de los Deportes Magdalena Mixihuca, Granjas México, Greater Mexico City* ☎ *55/8751–8081* ⊕ *www.diablos.com. mx* Ⓜ *Puebla.*

La Villa de Guadalupe
La Villa—the local moniker of the site of the two basilicas of the Virgin of Guadalupe, about 7 km (4 miles) north of the Zócalo—is Mexico's holiest shrine. Its importance derives from the miracle that the

GETTING HERE

The attractions and businesses in this chapter are spread throughout the greater Mexico City area, some of them relatively close to the city center and reachable via metro, Metrobus, or a short Uber ride. Others are well outside the range of public transportation and are best visited by Uber or a hired driver, or by renting a car and driving yourself. As crowded and potentially confusing as Mexico City is for drivers, it's really not any more difficult to navigate than any other big, sprawly North American metropolis—if you're comfortable driving in Los Angeles, you'll probably be fine here. Renting a car for just a day or two to hit the farther-afield sites is fairly cost-effective compared with multiple long taxi or car-share rides. You'll find specific directions and transportation tips in many of the individual listings in this chapter.

devout believe occurred here on December 12, 1531: an Aztec named Juan Diego received from the Virgin a cloak permanently imprinted with her image so he could prove to the priests that he had experienced a holy vision. Although the story of the miracle and the cloak itself have been challenged for centuries, they are hotly defended by clergy and laity alike. Every December 12, millions of pilgrims arrive, many crawling on their knees for the last few hundred yards, praying for divine favors.

Outside the **Antigua Basílica** (Old Basilica) stands a statue of Juan

Diego, who became the first indigenous saint in the Americas when he was canonized in 2002. The canonization of Juan Diego was wildly popular among Mexican Catholics, although a vocal minority of critics (both in and out of the Church) argued that, despite the Church's extensive investigation, the validity of Juan Diego's existence is suspect. Many critics see the canonization of this polarizing figure as a strategic move by the Church to retain its position among Mexico's indigenous population. The old basilica dates from 1536; various additions have been made since then. The altar was executed by sculptor Manuel Tolsá. The basilica now houses a museum of ex-votos (hand-painted depictions of miracles, dedicated to Mary or a saint in gratitude) and popular religious, decorative, and applied arts from the 15th through 18th centuries.

Because the structure of the Antigua Basílica had weakened over the years and the building was no longer large enough or safe enough to accommodate all the worshippers, Pedro Ramírez Vázquez, the architect responsible for Mexico City's splendid Museo Nacional de Antropología, was commissioned to design a shrine, which was consecrated in 1976. In this case, alas, the architect's inspiration failed him: the **Nueva Basílica** (New Basilica) is a gigantic, circular mass of wood, steel, and polyethylene that feels like a stadium rather than a church. The famous image of the Virgin is encased high up in its altar at the back and can be viewed from a moving sidewalk that passes below. The holiday itself is a great time to visit if you don't mind crowds; it's celebrated with various kinds of music and dancers.

It's possible to take the metro here—La Villa-Basílica station is just a couple of blocks south. But it's not the safest or most scenic part of town, and it's quicker and more secure to go by Uber. ✉ *Calz de Guadalupe, Greater Mexico City* ☎ *55/5118–0500* ⊕ *www.virgendegua-dalupe.org.mx.*

★ Museo del Juguete Antiguo México

A riotously colorful and curious collection of some 45,000 toys, some dating back to the 19th century, fill this playful museum and ode to pop culture in the Doctores neighborhood. There's little rhyme or reason to the manner in which everything is arranged, other than, perhaps, the whimsical eye and sly sense of humor of the museum's founder, architect Roberto Shimizu Kinoshita. You'll find cases of Barbie dolls, model cars and planes, stuffed animals, dioramas, and tons of Luche Libre and other elements of Mexican culture. The shop on the ground floor sells some very cool antique toys. The district is just a 15-minute walk east of Roma and although it is slowly becoming safer, it can be a bit dicey, especially at night or if you're walking alone. Consider taking an Uber. ✉ *Calle Dr. Olvera 15, Doctores* ☎ *55/5588–2100* ⊕ *www.museodeljuguete.mx* 🎟 *MX$75* Ⓜ *Obrera.*

Museo Nacional del Virreinato

No visit to the lovely Spanish colonial city of Tepotzotlán is complete without checking out the National Museum of Viceroyalty of New Spain, which contains an exceptional collection of art, furniture, and other items from primarily the 1500s through the mid-1800s. The museum is set inside the former College of San Francisco Javier, which was built by Jesuit priests in 1580. The ornate baroque architecture—in particular the gilded interiors—of the museum and its surrounding complex of colonial buildings is reason alone to visit. But the decorative arts inside, including stunning carved cedar retablos covered in 23-karat gold-leaf, as well as fascinating exhibits that detail the 300 years of Mexico's New Spain period, are also tremendously impressive. The museum sits right on Centro Tepotzotlán's main Plaza de la Cruz. ✉ *Plaza Hidalgo 99, Tepotzotlán* ☎ *55/5876-0332* ⊕ *virreinato.inah.gob.mx* ☾ *Closed Mon.*

Parque Bicentenario

It's perhaps not surprising that in a city where disused hydroelectric and garbage heaps have been reimagined as parks and brand-new neighborhoods, a badly polluting former oil refinery has been converted into a stunning green space with seven sections to replicate different climate-vegetation zones. The 136-acre preserve in the north of the city opened in 2010 on the bicentennial of the country's independence from Spain (hence the park's name). Key features include a lake, picnic areas, a playground, jogging tracks, sporting fields and courts, an orchid greenhouse, and a gorgeous botanical garden. Concerts, festivals, and other noteworthy events take place here throughout the year—check the online calendar for what's coming up next. The park is a 10-minute drive north of Polanco and easily accessed from the Estación Refinería metro stop. ✉ *Av. 5 de Mayo 290, Ángel Zimbrón, Greater Mexico City* ☎ *55/9154-2244* ⊕ *www.parquebicentenario.com.mx* ☾ *Closed Mon.*

★ Teotihuacán

Just 50 km (31 miles) from the center of Mexico City, Teotihuacán is one of the most significant and haunting archaeological sites in the world. Imagine yourself walking down a pathway called Calzada de los Muertos (Avenue of the Dead). Surrounding you are some of Earth's most mysterious ancient structures, among them the Palace of the Jaguars, the Pyramid of the Moon, and the Temple of the Plumed Serpent. From the top of the awe-inspiring Pyramid of the Sun—at about 210 feet, the third-tallest pyramid in the world—you begin to appreciate your 248-stair climb as you survey a city that long ago was the seat of a powerful empire. This is Teotihuacán, meaning "place

where men become gods." You can easily spend several hours here seeing all of the key sites.

At its zenith, around AD 600, Teotihuacán (teh-oh-tee-wa-can) was one of the world's largest cities and the center of an empire that inhabited much of central Mexico. Archaeologists believe that Teotihuacán was once home to some 100,000 people. The questions of just who built this city, at whose hands it fell, and even its original name, remain a mystery, eluding archaeologists and fueling imaginations the world over.

Excavations here first began as part of the dictator Porfirio Díaz's efforts to prepare for the centennial celebration of Mexican independence. Between 1905 and 1910, he sent his official archaeologist, Leopoldo Batres, to work principally on the Pyramid of the Sun. Later studies of these excavations have shown that several elements of this pyramid were destroyed in the excavation and others were falsely presented as being part of the original pyramid.

In 2010, archaeologists took part in another commemorative excavation, this time to celebrate 100 years of archaeological work at Teotihuacán. They discovered a tunnel, about 40 feet down, that passes below the Templo de Quetzalcóatl and is thought to have been intentionally closed off between AD 200 and AD 250. The tunnel leads to chambers into which thousands of objects were thrown, perhaps as a kind of offering. Archaeologists hypothesized that, after a couple of months of digging, they might find the remains of some of the city's earliest rulers. Although rulers were often deified at other sites, no tombs, or even depictions of rulers, have ever been found at Teotihuacán.

The **Ciudadela** is a massive citadel ringed by more than a dozen temples, with the **Templo de Quetzalcóatl** (Temple of the Plumed Serpent) as the centerpiece. Here you'll find incredibly detailed carvings of the benevolent deity Quetzalcóatl, a serpent with its head ringed by feathers, jutting out of the facade.

One of the most impressive sights in Teotihuacán is the 4-km-long (2½-mile-long) **Calzada de los Muertos** (Avenue of the Dead), which once held great ceremonial importance. The Aztecs gave it this name because they mistook the temples lining either side for tombs. It leads all the way to the 126-foot-high **Pirámide de la Luna** (Pyramid of the Moon), which dominates the northern end of the city. Atop this structure, you can scan the entire ancient city. Some of the most exciting recent discoveries, including a royal tomb, have been unearthed here. In late 2002 a discovery of jade objects gave important evidence of a link between the Teotihuacán rulers and the Maya.

On the west side of the spacious plaza facing the Pyramid of the Moon is the **Palacio del Quetzalpápalotl** (Palace of the Plumed Butterfly); its expertly reconstructed terrace has columns etched with images of various winged creatures. Nearby is the **Palacio de los Jaguares** (Palace of the Jaguars), a residence for priests. Spectacular bird and jaguar murals wind through its underground chambers.

The awe-inspiring **Pirámide del Sol** (Pyramid of the Sun), the first monumental structure constructed here, stands in the center of the city. With a base nearly as broad as that of the pyramid of Cheops in Egypt, it is one of the largest pyramids ever built. Its size takes your breath away, often quite literally, during the climb up 248 steps on its west face. Deep within the pyramid, archaeologists have discovered a natural clover-shape cave that they speculate may have been the basis for the city's religion and perhaps the reason the city was built in the first place.

The best artifacts uncovered at Teotihuacán are on display at the exceptional Museo Nacional de Antropología in Mexico City. Still, the **Museo de la Sitio,** adjacent to the Pirámide del Sol, contains a number of noteworthy pieces, such as the stone sculpture of the saucer-eyed Tlaloc, some black-and-green obsidian arrowheads, and the skeletons of human sacrifices arranged as they were when first discovered.

More than 4,000 one-story adobe and stone dwellings surround the Calzada de los Muertos; these were occupied by artisans, warriors, and tradesmen. The best example, a short walk east of the Pirámide del Sol, is called **Tepantitla.** Here you'll see murals depicting a watery realm ruled by the rain god Tláloc. Restored in 2002, its reds, greens, and yellows are nearly as vivid as when they were painted more than 1,500 years ago.

There are five entrances to Teotihuacán, each near one of the major attractions. Around these entrances there are food and craft vendors as well as several restaurants. Among these, the most famous and interesting is **La Gruta** (⊕ www.lagruta.mx), which is near Pirámide del Sol and just a short walk east of Museo de Sitio Teotihuacán. The restaurant, which dates to 1906 and is set within an immense cave with dramatic rock ceilings, serves traditional Mexican food.

There are several ways to approach a visit to Teotihuacán. A number of companies give guided tours that include transportation. As good English-language guidebooks are sold at the site, it's actually quite easy to explore and learn about Teotihuacán on your own—don't feel a guided tour is a necessity. Another good option is either renting a car for the day and making the one-hour drive yourself (there's ample, reasonably priced parking on-site) or taking an Uber here and back (which will cost something in the neighborhood of MX$800 to

MX$1,200 each way). There's also frequent bus service to Teotihuacán from Terminal del Norte bus station and from outside the Portrero (line 3) metro station; the trip takes about an hour and one-way fare is around MX$55. ✉ *Carretera Federal 132 (follow signs), San Juan Teotihuacán* ☎ *594/956-0276* ⊕ *www.inah.gob. mx/zonas/23-zona-arqueologica-de-teotihuacan* ⛟ *MX$70.*

Tepotzotlán

Not to be confused with the similar-sounding town of Tepoztlán, which lies just a little farther from Mexico City but in the opposite direction, Tepotzotlán lies 40 km (19 miles) due north and makes for a pleasing half-day getaway. One of Mexico's 120 or so designated Pueblos Mágicos (and the closest one to CDMX), Tepotzotlán traces its human history back to around 2500 BC and became a center of religious training and education when Spanish Jesuits established a foothold here in the mid-16th century. The most prestigious of the city's institutions, the College of San Francisco Javier, is now the splendid Museo Nacional del Virreinato, and a must for visitors. It adjoins the city's striking cathedral, Templo de San Francisco Javier, and is situated in the picturesque and pedestrian-friendly Centro Histórico, officially known as the San Martín neighborhood. From here, you can stroll around the plaza, admire views of the surrounding mountains, and visit the smattering of galleries, shops, and eateries nearby. There's no shortage of lively cafés and restaurants, and if you'd prefer to make a night of it, Puerta Al Virreinato Hotel Boutique offers comfortable, upscale accommodations. Depending on traffic, it's about a 45-minute to 1-hour drive to Tepotzotlán (an Uber ride costs around MX$500 to MX$800 each way), or you can catch one of the Primera Plus buses (MX$70-MX$110 each way) that depart regularly from Central Poniente bus station, on the west side of CDMX (not far from Condesa). ✉ *Plaza Virreinal, at Av. Insurgentes, Tepotzotlán* ⊕ *www.turismotepotzotlan.com.mx.*

 Shopping

★ **Maizajo, Molino y Tortilleria**
Started by Santiago Muñoz, a passionate former chef at the famous regional Mexican Nico's (which is just a short drive south), Maizajo is practically a devotional to all things corn, and the role it plays in Mexico's diet, culture, and soul. At this humble shop, Muñoz sources corn from small, high-quality producers around the country to produce about 4,000 tortillas daily, using the time-honored and time-consuming nixtamalization process that has been practiced for centuries. Open from just 10 am until 2 pm every day but Sunday, the shop sells these flavorful, coarse-yet-soft multicolor tortillas, masa, tostadas, flautas, and related corn products to the public as well as to some of the top restaurants in the city. The shop also gives workshops on

tortilla-making (check the calender on its website). ⊠ *Av. Soledad 556, Azcapotzalco, Greater Mexico City* ☎ *55/7959-8540* ⊕ *www.maizajo.com* Ⓜ *Ferrería/Arena Ciudad de México.*

Mercado Jamaica

As sensory experiences go, the city's most impressive floral market, located about a mile east of Roma and south of Centro Histórico, is quite impressive. The nearly 1,200 stalls proffering boldly colored, radiant arrangements and cut flowers along with a huge variety of potted plants fill the air with fragrant aromas. You'll find about 300 vendors selling other goods, including snacks, fruits, and fresh juices, plus a good variety of ornate piñatas. ⊠ *Guillermo Prieto 45, Jamaica, Greater Mexico City* ☎ *55/5741-0002* Ⓜ *Jamaica.*

☕ Coffee and Quick Bites

⭐ Tacos Los Güeros

$ | Mexican. If you watched the addictively tantalizing Netflix food show Taco Chronicles, you may have witnessed the scenes of al pastor deliciousness filmed in this humble but beloved taqueria on Calle Lorenzo Boturini, which is actually lined with great eats, including a few others featured on the program (such as Taquería la Autentica and El Buen Taco). In this no-frills spot that's open until at least 1 am nightly (it doesn't open, however, until around 4 pm), you'll of course want to sample the al pastor tacos, but you'll find dozens of other kinds, plus fantastic birria. **Known**

for: flavorful tacos and tortas; hearty birria stew; Jamaica and horchata beverages. *Average main: 50 MP* ⊠ *Calle Lorenzo Boturini 4354, Aeronáutica Militar, Greater Mexico City* Ⓜ *Fray Servando.*

🍴 Dining

⭐ Carmela y Sal

$$$ | International. Named the country's top chef by the Mexican Gastronomical Council in 2019, young chef Gabriela Ruíz helms this handsome space with a high "living" green ceiling in fashionable Lomas de Chapultepec. Offering inventive interpretations on recipes she grew up with in her native Tabasco, Ruíz wows diners with complexly flavored dishes like goose pâté with a guava compote, and cannelloni filled with cochinita pibíl and topped with a kicky habanero sauce. **Known for:** molcajete-ground salsas and moles; first-rate cocktail mixology program; flourless chocolate cake with Tabasco chiles. *Average main: 385 MP* ⊠ *Torre Virreyes, Calle Pedregal N.24, Lomas de Chapultepec, Greater Mexico City* ☎ *55/7600-1280* ⊕ *www.carmelaysal. mx* ⊗ *No dinner Sun.*

Ekilore

$$ | Basque. Spanish expats and other fans of contemporary Basque cuisine think nothing of making the 20-km (12-mile) trek north of the city center to feast on foie gras with calvados sauce, bacalao-stuffed piquillo peppers, fish throat and clams with creamy rice, salmon with tangerine sauce, and the many other culinary highlights served in this modern yet unassuming restaurant. Chef-owner Pablo San Román hails from San Sebastian, and from the knowledgeable service to the thoughtfully curated wine list, he's created a dining experience on par with any other Spanish restaurant in the city. **Known for:** Basque shellfish dishes; excellent Spanish wine list; cuajada (sweet fermented sheep's milk) for dessert. *Average main: 285 MP ⊠ Calz. de los Jinetes 102, Las Arboledas, Greater Mexico City ☎ 55/5920–6473 ⊘ Closed Mon. No dinner Sun., Tues., and Wed.*

Gorka Altamar

$$$$ | Spanish. The Spanish cuisine turned out here by celebrated chef Gorka Bátiz is gorgeously plated, richly seasoned, and created with the finest possible ingredients, but it's also still accessible and in some respects traditional, free of the foams and arty flourishes that typify high-end Iberian fare. The contemporary dining room with wood paneling and views of the glass-walled wine cellar is inviting, but even more lovely is the light and airy patio. **Known for:** refined, authentic regional Spanish fare; world-class list of mostly Spanish wines; deft if slightly formal service. *Average main: 520 MP ⊠ Calle Volcán 150, Greater Mexico City ☎ 55/1151–0115 ⊕ www.gorka.mx ⊘ No dinner Sun. and Mon. Ⓜ Polanco.*

★ Ko Ma

$$$$ | Modern Mexican. The team behind the world-renowned (but indefinitely shuttered) Biko as well as the buzzy Lur in Polanco have created this exclusive temple to haute contemporary Mexican cuisine amid the opulent homes of Lomas de Chapultepec. Ko Ma presents a nightly changing eight or nine-course menú degustación with optional wine or mocktail pairings, and both the visual and flavor approach reflects an appreciation for, if not a strict adherence to, molecular gastronomy. **Known for:** molecular gastronomy meets Mexican ingredients; minimalist modern dining room; adventurous wine pairings. *Average main: 1350 MP ⊠ Av. Paseo de las Palmas 781, Greater Mexico City ☎ 55/5925–7244 ⊕ www.komamx.com ⊘ Closed Sun.*

★ Los Tolucos

$ | Mexican. Hungry diners come from all over the city to savor bowls of green pozole—a Guerrero specialty—at this casual, old-fashioned Mexican restaurant situated in working-class Algarin (by the Lázaro Cárdenas metro, a short way east of Roma Sur). Piled high with shredded chicken, chicharrón, avocado, and other savory ingredients, this is some of the best pozole around, and there's also a good selection of tacos. **Known for:** pozole Guerrerense-style; big, affordable portions; agua de horchata and Jamaica. *Average main: 85 MP ⊠ Calle Juan E. Hernández y Davalos 40, Greater Mexico City ☎ 55/5440–3318 Ⓜ Lázaro Cárdenas.*

Los Virreyes

$$ | Mexican. The best seats at this sprawling, multilevel restaurant in the heart of Tepotzotlán's historic center are on the upstairs terrace and take in sweeping views of Templo de San Francisco Javier and the surrounding mountains—it's especially dramatic and romantic at sunset. The kitchen turns out reliably good, quite traditional Mexican and European fare from rib-eye steaks to mole poblano, but the big draw here is the view. **Known for:** terrace views of Tepotzlán's historic center; hearty steaks and seafood grills; escamoles (ant larvae) and gusanos de maguey (mezcal worms). *Average main: 210 MP* ⊠ *Plaza Virreinal 32, Tepotzlán* ☎ *55/4608–1399* ⊕ *www.restaurante-losvirreyes.com.*

★ Nico's

$$$ | Mexican. A must-visit for fans of traditional Mexican cuisine who think they've tasted it all, this barely adorned, simply elegant restaurant in a workaday neighborhood—a 20-minute Uber ride from Polanco—is the domain of chef Gerardo Vázquez Lugo (whose parents opened Nicos in 1957), a stickler for ingredients sourced from small producers and dishes that can seem *nuevo* but are all rooted in history. The *sopa seca de natas*—several crepes layered with cream, tomato, and poblano chiles—is a 19th-century recipe from a convent in Guadalajara, and the octopus stewed in its ink with pecans, almonds, and pine nuts is a generations-old recipe from Veracruz. **Known for:** ribeye on the bone with a bitter-orange sauce; extensive artisanal mezcal selection; chiles en nogada (available only in September). *Average*

main: 330 MP ⊠ *Av. Cuitlahuac 3102, Greater Mexico City* ☎ *55/5396–7090* ⊕ *www.nicosmexico.mx* ⊗ *Closed Sun. No dinner* Ⓜ *Cuitláhuac.*

🍸 Bars and Nightlife

★ Barba Azul

Since 1951, this unabashedly campy cabaret in the eastern reaches of Doctores has been luring even shy patrons onto the central dance stage for salsa, merengue, and cumbia music. The live orchestra is almost as much fun to watch as the completely diverse crowd that includes everyone from white-haired couples to gay teens. Upstairs by the restrooms, be sure to check out the kitschy, obscene artwork. Although not terribly far from Roma or El Centro, the area can get a bit dodgy at night—it's best to Uber here. ⊠ *Gutiérrez Nájera 291, Obrera, Greater Mexico City* ☎ *55/5588–6070* Ⓜ *Obrera.*

🎭 Performing Arts

Palacio de los Deportes

Constructed in 1968 for basketball and volleyball games during the Mexico City Olympics, this massive arena relatively near the airport still hosts occasional sporting events but is best known as a venue for major music concerts. In recent years, Ariana Grande, Adele, Tame Impala, Billie Eilish, Beyoncé, and Madonna have performed here. ⊠ *Granjas México, Iztacalco, Greater Mexico City* ☎ *55/4743–1100* ⊕ *www.ocesa.com. mx* Ⓜ *Velódromo.*

Greater Mexico City South

👁 Sights

Espacio Escultórico UNAM

At the northern edge of UNAM's cultural center and an easy stroll from MUAC (Museo Universitario Arte Contemporáneo) and the concert halls, this mesmerizing and tranquil complex of contemporary sculpture is more of a wilderness than a garden. It contains strikingly dramatic and in some cases massive sculpture installations by six renowned artists, the frequent Barragán collaborator Mathias Goeritz as well as Helen Escobedo, Federico Silva, Manuel Felguérez, Sebastian, and Hersúa. The property abuts a massive nature preserve; if you have time, take a stroll through the rugged, arid landscape of rusty-hued volcanic rock and the flora that thrives here. It's a peaceful spot, although with little protection from the sun. ⊠ *UNAM, Centro Cultural Universitario, Ciudad Universiteria, Greater Mexico City* ☎ *55/1534-7102* ⊕ *www.cultura.unam.mx* ⊗ *Closed weekends* Ⓜ *Universidad*.

Estadio Azteca

Fútbol is the sport that Mexicans are most passionate about, which is evident in the size of their soccer stadium, Estadio Azteca, which holds 87,523 spectators and is the second largest in all of Latin America. Located in the south of the city, about 8 km (5 miles) beyond historic Coyoacán, it's the home turf of Club América, one of Mexico's top fútbol teams, as well

as the Primera División's Cruz Azul, multiple winners of the CONCACAF Champions League. Additionally, Mexico's national team plays here often, and there's an American NFL football game held here once a year. You can buy tickets at the stadium ticket windows on the same day of any minor game. For more important games, try to buy tickets a week in advance—it's easiest to do so via Ticketmaster. The Pumas, a popular university-sponsored team, play relatively nearby at the also massive Estadio Olímpico, at Universidad Nacional Autónoma de México (UNAM), a little south of San Ángel. You can't get to Azteca by Metro, but there is a light rail stop (Estadio Azteca) outside the stadium and it's a short walk to catch the light rail from the Tasqueña metro stop. Hour-long tours are also offered daily for MX$120. ⊠ *Calz. de Tlalpan 3465, Sta. Úrsula Coapa, Greater Mexico City* ☎ *55/5487-3215 tours* ⊕ *www.estadioazteca.com.mx.*

Estadio Olímpico Universitario

This hulking 84,000-seat stadium is near the south end of San Ángel, but is part of Ciudad Universitaria, the main campus for UNAM (National Autonomous University of Mexico). The striking elliptical building was an icon of modern architecture when it opened in 1952 and it played host to the main events of the 1968 Olympics and 1986 FIFA World Cup. Today it hosts soccer games of UNAM's Pumas Doradas as well as a number of other events. Note the sprawling relief mural by Diego Rivera that hangs above the main entrance of the stadium, on the east side of the building. ✉ *Av. de los Insurgentes Sur s/n, Greater Mexico City* 🕾 *52/5622–0580* Ⓜ *Copilco.*

Museo Diego Rivera–Anahuacalli

A devoted collector of pre-Hispanic art, Diego Rivera built his own museum to house the more than 45,000 artifacts he collected over his lifetime—which, sadly, came to an end several years before this impressive volcanic-rock building with a design inspired by ancient Mexican pyramids was completed in 1964. The third-floor studio, with its massive wall of windows, displays sketches for some of Rivera's most celebrated murals. Be sure to make your way to the rooftop, which affords sweeping city and mountain views, especially if it's a clear day. During the weeks surrounding Día de Muertos, you can view a remarkable altar in honor of Rivera himself. Although located in the larger delegación of Coyoacán, the museum is in the neighborhood of San Pablo Tepetlapa, about a 15-minute Uber ride south of Coyoacán's historic center; it's also a short walk from the Nezahualpilli light rail station. ✉ *Calle del Museo 150, Greater Mexico City* 🕾 *55/5617–4310* ⊕ *www.museoanahuacalli.org.mx* ✉ *MX$90 (includes admission to Museo Frida Kahlo)* ☯ *Closed Mon.*

Museo del Tiempo Tlalpan

This offbeat gem of a museum located in a handsome 19th-century former home on the west side of historic Tlalpan's Plaza de la Constitución contains an unexpectedly fascinating collection of antique clocks as well as old gramophones, movie cameras, phones, typewriters, jukeboxes, and even relatively modern gadgets from the 2000s, like old flip phones and adding machines. ✉ *Plaza de la Constitución 7, Greater Mexico City* 🕾 *55/5513–3310* ⊕ *www.museodeltiempo.com.mx* ✉ *MX$60* ☯ *Closed Mon.–Wed.*

⭐ Museo Dolores Olmedo

In Xochimilco, on the outskirts of the city, is a superb collection of paintings by Frida Kahlo and the largest private collection of works by Diego Rivera. The museum was established by Dolores Olmedo, his lifelong model, patron, and onetime mistress. The lavish display of nearly 150 pieces from his cubist, post-cubist, and mural periods hangs in a magnificent 17th-century hacienda with lovely gardens. Kahlo's paintings are in a separate, adjacent hall; however, more often than not in recent years, the museum has lent them for traveling exhibitions around the world, so check ahead to ensure they're here if this is the main reason you're visiting. Concerts and entertainment for children are presented on weekends, while gaggles of geese and strutting peacocks amble about the grounds, adding to the clamor. There is a lovely small café in a glassed-in gazebo, and a variety of compelling rotating exhibits are held in other buildings around the property. During the month of October, the museum presents one of the better Día de Muertos displays in the city. You can reach the museum by taking the metro to Tasqueña station, and then catching the light-rail to La Noria (*not* Xochimilco), which is a five- to seven-minute walk away. By car, it's about a 40- to 50-minute drive from El Centro, but many visitors combine a stop here with boating on the canals in Xochimilco or strolling around historic Tlalpan. ⊠ *Av. México 5843, Xochimilco, Greater Mexico City* ☎ *55/5555-1221* ⊕ *www.museodolo-resolmedo.org.mx* ⊠ *MX$100; free Tues.* ⊙ *Closed Mon.*

★ Museo Universitario Arte Contemporáneo (MUAC)

Although this gleaming, expansive contemporary art museum on the campus of UNAM—in the same cluster of buildings that make up the university's cultural center—has no permanent installation, the several gallery spaces, some intimate and some enormous, are staged with exceptional changing shows throughout the year. Additionally, parts of the university's extensive collection are shown at different times. MUAC is on par with any of the city's contemporary art museums, partly thanks to the gorgeous, angular design of noted architect Teodoro González de Leon, who also designed Reforma 222, Torre Manacar, and—in collabora-tion—Museo Rufino Tamayo (which bears a resemblance to MUAC). The glass facade rises at a sharp angle over a long reflecting pool, facing a broad courtyard that leads to the cultural center's performance venues. A long curving window in the back of the building looks out over the volcanic landscape on which the museum and the university are built, and a grand, freestanding staircase leads to a lower-level museum restaurant (the food is fine, if not spectacular, but the space is beautiful) and some additional galleries as well as a lecture hall. There are usually five or six shows taking place at any given time, and these rotate two or three times per year. Past shows have been devoted to works by Ai Weiwei, Zaha Hadid, Anish Kapoor, and Pola Weiss. The museum shop is also superb and carries a number of reasonably priced household items. ⊠ *Cto. Centro Cultural, Ciudad Universiteria, Greater Mexico City* ☎ *55/5622-6972* ⊕ *muac.unam.mx* ⊠ *MX$40* ⊙ *Closed Mon. and Tues.* Ⓜ *Universidad.*

Parque Nacional Bosque del Pedregal

Although part of the country's national park system, this hilly, arid 622-acre expanse of oak scrubland south of the city—just 3 km (2 miles) west of Tlalpan Centro—feels a bit more like a city park, given that its completely surrounded by residen-tial neighborhoods. It's also a highly popular destination for running and walking, with its paved central pathways easily accessible from the bustling neighborhood at the park's main entrance, where you'll also

find the stately Casa de la Cultura Tlalpan cultural center as well as a good-size parking area and a playground. Once you venture deeper into the park, along the gravel and dirt paths, it starts to feel a bit more like you're actually in a wilderness (signs with park maps are placed strategically throughout the park, making it easy to navigate). Jagged lava outcroppings are evidence of the eruption some 2,000 years ago of nearby Xitle volcano, and the park contains more than 200 kinds of flora, from wild orchids to towering palms, and a number of birds, snakes, and mammals. If you make a complete circuit around the park and venture out to its northwestern border, you'll also spy some strange, curving towers in the mid-distance, at which point the gleeful screams of passengers will clue you in that you're viewing the back side of Six Flags México amusement park. ⊠ *Camino de Sta. Teresa 703, Tlalpan, Greater Mexico City* ☎ *55/5171–4558* ⊕ *www.bosquet-lalpan.org.mx.*

Parque Nacional Cumbres del Ajusco

Mexico City is flanked by huge mountains, including the cloud-scraping peaks of 5,230-meter (17,160-foot) Iztaccíhuatl and its neighbor Popocatépetl, an extremely active volcano that's also the country's second-highest peak, at 5,426 meters (17,802 feet). Visible on clear days from the city center, Popocatépetl is more than 3,300 feet taller than the highest peak in the Lower 48, California's

Mount Whitney. But Izzi and Popo, as these twins are affectionately known, aren't actually within city limits (they're about 56 to 72 km [35 to 45 miles] south of El Centro). The highest peak within city limits is Mount Ajusco, which is the centerpiece of Parque Nacional Cumbres del Ajusco, located in the southwestern corner of CDMX and a highly popular destination for hikers. Summiting its 3,930-meter (12,894-foot) peak is no easy feat, however. You'll want to allow at least seven hours to make it up and back, and as trails aren't always well-marked and crime isn't unheard of in this minimally patrolled wilderness, it's best to attempt a hike here with a guide or locals who've done the climb before. At the very least, go with a friend and research online for good trail maps and directions— under no circumstances should you go it alone. The elevation gain from any of the hike's starting points is around 2,500 to 3,000 feet, and it is a steep 10-km (6-mile) round-trip or loop hike (depending on the route), beginning in lush coniferous meadows and rising well above the tree line. You should also be in good shape to make it all the way. But it's a wonderfully rewarding adventure, and the views from the summit of neighboring mountains as well as the entirety of Mexico City to the north are spectacular. An excellent starting point is the trail that leads up from beside the casual Mexican restaurant, Cabaña Mireles La Polea, which is on the north side of the mountain, on the road that encircles it. Uber drivers shouldn't have trouble finding it, and if you drive yourself, you can park at the restaurant (or others near it) if you dine here before or after (the food is quite tasty)—just ask permission first. ⌧ *Greater Mexico City* ⊕ *Best trailhead: beside Cabaña Mireles La Polea restaurant, Carretera Picacho-Ajusco, Km 21.5* ☎ *55/5449–7000.*

★ Parque Nacional Desierto de los Leones

The air is rare in this stunning alpine preserve, which in 1917 was declared Mexico's first national park. The 4,600-acre oasis of mostly conifer forest (with significant stands of oak trees as well) ranges in elevation between 2,600 meters (8,530 feet) and 3,700 meters (12,140 feet), and when you're scampering along the trails and beside the babbling brooks that lace this verdant wonderland, it's hard to believe that you're still completely within Mexico City limits (albeit close to the border with Estado de México). If the name had you picturing a vast arid plain of savage wild cats, note that "Desierto" is a reference to the distance from civilization, and while "leones" reportedly does relate to the one-time prevalence of wild critters living in the area, there were never any true lions out here, of course. The area was settled in 1606 by the Spaniards, who constructed a Carmelite convent nestled amid the pines. Now the focal point of the park and a must for any visitor, the current **Ex-Convento del Desierto de los Leones**—with its curving domes, high walls, and cloistered courtyards—was constructed in 1814, long after its predecessor had deteriorated through gradual weathering and wear. After exploring the ex-convent and the huge forest sanctuary behind it, stroll around the immediate grounds, where you'll find a number of crafts and food vendors as well as a colorful little restaurant with table service, El Leon Dorado. The park lies 20 km (12 miles) southwest of the city center, and just 10 km (6 miles) beyond the modern commercial district of Santa Fe, at the junction of the 134 and 57 federal highways. ⌧ *Calz. Desierto de los Leones, Greater Mexico City* ⊕ *Off Carretera Toluca-México (Federal 15)* ☎ *55/5814–1171* ⌧ *MX$20* ⊙ *Closed Mon.*

Santa Fe

It rises like a postmodern Oz or perhaps (depending on your ideas about urbanization) a Bladerunner-esque dystopia, but regardless, the district of Santa Fe looks and feels entirely distinct from the rest of Mexico City. And if you're headed to this thicket of futuristic high-rises situated about 18 km (11 miles) from the city center, there's a high probability you're going for work-related reasons. Developed in the early 2000s atop a massive garbage landfill, Santa Fe was designed emphatically with cars in mind as more of an edge city than a proper neighborhood. It's home to some interesting examples of contemporary architecture, one of the most impressive shopping malls in Latin America (Centro Santa

Fe), a massive convention center (Expo Santa Fe), a slew of major corporate offices, glitzy, mostly upscale chain hotels (Westin, AC Marriott, Hilton, InterContinental, and Camino Real among them), and high-end restaurants. Many of the latter are also major chains or outposts of other restaurants located elsewhere around the city. If business brings you here, or you're simply curious to check out this thoroughly posh if rather antiseptic district, do make a point of visiting Parque La Mexicana, an beautifully designed 72-acre urban green space opened in 2017 and offering a playground, skate park, dog park, running and bicycling trails, and an outdoor terrace café. Santa Fe is also relatively close to Desierto de los Leones National Park, and it's a good stepping off point for venturing farther west to the city of Toluca. To get here, driving or taking an Uber is practically a requirement, as there's no metro service and getting here by bus is time-consuming and a bit complicated for tourists. Around 2022, the new Mexico City–Toluca commuter rail is expected to open, and this will provide easier and faster access, with a stop right in the center of Santa Fe. ⊠ *Vasco de Quiroga, Greater Mexico City* ✛ *Off the México 134D/México 15D freeways.*

Six Flags México

Amusement park giant Six Flags operates this enormous, well-designed park in the south of Mexico City, near Tlalpan and about 18 km (11 miles) from the city center. You'll find acres of both extreme and fairly mild rides, plus live entertainment and other diversions, including multiple restaurants and souvenir stands. Areas have colorful themes, such as DC Super Heroes, Bugs Bunny Boom Town, and Polynesian Village. It's possible to get here cheaply via the Insurgentes Sur Metrobus, but Uber is more efficient. The company also operates Six Flags Hurricane Harbor Oaxtepec, a similarly popular water park near Cuernavaca, about a 90-minute drive southeast of Mexico City. ⊠ *Carretera Picacho-Ajusco Km 1.5, Jardines del Ajusco, Greater Mexico City* ☎ *55/5339–3600* ⊕ *www. sixflags.com.mx* ⊠ *From MX\$679.*

★ Tlalpan Centro

Extremely popular with Mexican families, especially as a place to stroll and people-watch on weekends, this historic and enchanting historic center laid out in the 1600s is sometimes described as what Coyoacán felt and looked like 20 years or 30 years ago, before it became such a popular destination. Slowly but surely, Tlalpan's narrow lanes of colorful, historic houses and its charming tree-shaded hub, Plaza de la Constitución, are drawing more sizable crowds, but a visit here still feels manageable and relaxed, like you've stumbled upon a small colonial village far from the big city. Do visit the Capilla de las Capuchinas, a few blocks away, to admire the strikingly modernist interior, which Luis Barragán completely redesigned in the late 1950s. You can also walk through the courtyard and view the interior of the imposing Parroquia de San Agustín de las Cuevas, on the east side of the plaza. Next door are a couple of good quick stops for a refreshment: historic La Jalisciense cantina for Spanish food and tortas, and an atmospheric branch of the local ice cream chain, La Nueva Michoacana (which has been going strong since the early 1950s). If you can visit on a Sunday, you can enjoy watching locals, many of them seniors, dancing around the grand kiosco in the Plaza. Vendors sell crafts, souvenirs, and food while just a few steps south, Mercado de la Paz is a traditional market that also has plenty of food vendors. And although Tlalpan isn't flashy as a dining destination, there are a number of mostly traditional restaurants, cantinas, and food vendors on the blocks around the plaza, especially along pedestrianized Calle Guadalupe Victoria (which extends south from the plaza western's edge). Along here you'll also find the quirky but excellent Museo del Tiempo Tlalpan and the Museo de Historia de Tlalpa that, while not a must, offers free admission and gives a good overview of the neighborhood's history. Finally, on the north side of the Plaza, the performance venue Multiforo Cultural Ollin Kan often has concerts and other interesting shows—it's worth checking to see what's on. Tlalpan is in the south, easily visited in conjunction with Xochimilco, and most conveniently via Uber. But you could also save some pesos by taking the Metro to Universidad or the light rail to Huipulco, and taking much shorter Uber rides from either. Or you can take the Insurgentes Metrobus line south to the Fuentes Brotantes stop in Tlalpan Centro. ⊠ *Plaza de la Constitución 1, Greater Mexico City.*

Universidad Nacional Autónoma de México (UNAM)

Some of the country's most celebrated modern architects—including Mario Pani, Enrique del Moral, and Teodoro González de Leon—designed buildings on the massive campus of UNAM, which sprawls across its own city within a city, the 2,500-acre (10-square-km) Ciudad Universitaria. Located in the southern reaches of the city, a little south of Coyoacán and San Ángel, the current campus was constructed in the 1950s on a then completely desolate field of petrified lava produced by the roughly AD 300 eruption of Xitle Volcano (a now dormant 1,000-foot-tall ash cone volcano about 8 km [5 miles] to the south). The university itself was established in 1910 and is one of the largest and most prestigious educational institutions in the world, with about 215,000 undergraduate and 30,000 graduate students enrolled across its numerous campuses around the country (as well as in extension schools in the United States and Canada). UNAM accepts only about 8% of applicants, and the campus here at Ciudad Universiteria is by far the largest and includes a number of outstanding architectural works and cultural attractions. Murals by

Diego Rivera, David Alfaro Siqueiros, and Juan O'Gorman appear on some buildings, most notably the 1956 functionalist Central Library, which O'Gorman designed in collaboration with Gustavo Saavedra and Juan Martinez de Velasco (and on which his massive murals appear). Another highlight on campus is Jardín Botánico, which contains thousands of species of plant life, both on its outdoor grounds and in greenhouses. UNAM also operates some other important institutions around the city, including Palacio de Mineria and Colegio de San Ildefonso (with its famous murals) in Centro Histórico, Casa del Lago in Parque Chapultepec, and Museo Universitario del Chopo in Santa Maria la Ribera. ⊠ Cto. Interior, Ciudad Universiteria, Greater Mexico City ✛ Off Av. Insurgentes Sur at Cto. Escolar ⊕ www.cultura.unam.mx Ⓜ Universidad.

Universum

The Museo de las Ciencias de la UNAM (or UNAM Science Museum) lies at the southeastern edge of the university's cultural center and is packed with touch-friendly, interactive exhibits as well as a planetarium and a particularly good oceanography area. Especially popular with families, highlights include an actual, touchable piece of the moon, a butterfly exhibit, dinosaurs, and more. ⊠ UNAM, Cto. Centro Cultural, Ciudad Universiteria, Greater Mexico City ☎ 55/5622–7260 ⊕ www.universum. unam.mx 🎟 MX$90 ☻ Closed Mon. Ⓜ Universidad.

★ Xochimilco Canals

A former pre-Hispanic city 21 km (13 miles) south of current-day CDMX city center, the Xochimilco neighborhood is well worth a visit to explore its vast, ancient network of canals and *chinampas* (man-made islands), which have been declared a UNESCO World Heritage Site. When the first indigenous settlers arrived in the Valley of Mexico, they found an enormous lake. As the years passed and their population grew, the land could no longer satisfy their agricultural needs. They solved the problem by devising a system of chinampas, rectangular structures akin to barges, which they filled with reeds, branches, and mud. They planted the barges with willows, whose roots anchored the floating gardens to the lake bed, creating a labyrinth of small islands and canals on which vendors carried flowers and produce grown on the chinampas to market.

Today Xochimilco is the only place in Mexico where the gardens still exist. Go on a Saturday, when the *tianguis* (market stalls) are most active, or, though it's crowded, on a Sunday. On weekdays the distinctive community is usually much less crowded, so it loses some of its vibrancy but also its chaos. It's considered almost a

mandatory custom to hire a *trajinera* (a flower-painted boat that's roughly akin to a large gondola); a colorfully painted arch over each boat spells out its name. You can hire the trajineras at several different points in town—the launch point at Calle de Mercado 133 tends to be a little less crowded, as it's farther from the light-rail station, and a pretty pedestrian bridge crosses the canal, allowing for some great photos of these colorful boats. Expect to pay MX$500 per hour for a boat that can accommodate up to around 18 passengers. Optional extras include beer, micheladas, and soft drinks along with mariachi and marimba bands, Bluetooth audio speakers, tour guides, and decorative arches for your boat made of actual flowers. As you sail through the canals, you'll pass mariachis and women selling tacos from other trajineras, and you'll pass by the bizarre Isla de las Munecas (the Island of Dolls), which you'll know when you see it. While a Xochimilco boat tour has become one of Mexico City's top experiences, note that it's not an activity for everyone—these are basically party boats that ply some pretty murky, badly polluted waters, and while the tours can be a lot of fun for groups of friends (less so for just a couple of passengers), Xochilmilco is a long way to go for a touristy tour on a crowded canal. To get here, it's about a 45-minute to 1-hour drive, or you can take the metro to Tasqueña station, and then catch the light-rail commuter train to Xochimilco (a journey

Situated among the ancient canals of Xochimilco, one of the city's most intriguing—and creepiest—photo ops is Isla de las Muñecas (Island of the Dolls), which you'll get a good view of if you book a ride in one of the famous, floral-painted *trajineras* that ply these waters. The island's late caretaker, Don Julian Santana Barrera, allegedly found a drowned little girl near the island and soon after located a doll floating in the canal. Believing the doll to be hers, he hung it on a tree on this island, as a tribute or memorial of sorts, and over time, he hung more and more dolls in an effort to appease her apparently restless spirit. Barrera's death was also the result of drowning, and as the story goes, his body was found exactly where he discovered the little girl.

 Share your photo with us! @FodorsTravel #FodorsOnTheGo

of about two hours each way).
✉ *Embarcadero Nuevo Nativitas, Calle del Mercado 133, Xochimilco, Greater Mexico City.*

Zona Arqueológica Cuicuilco

The occupants of cars and buses speeding along the city's Anillo Periférico (southern beltway) are sometimes surprised to see an ancient, conical pyramid rising just off the side of the highway, standing out rather strangely among the modern buildings that dominate the surrounding landscape of the city's Pedregal area. From around 1400 to 200 BC, an Aztec settlement with as many as 20,000 residents thrived here along the southern shoreline of Lake Texcoco, the now drained body of water on which Mexico City now stands. They built this impressive pyramid likely around 800 BC, several centuries before the construction of the massive pyramids of Teotihuacán (a settlement that some believe was created by descendants of Cuicuilco inhabitants). It's thus considered the oldest of the major archaeological sites in metro CDMX. Today you can visit the site, which has been remarkably well preserved in part because it was covered in lava by the eruption of nearby Xitle around 100 BC. A small museum designed by noted Mexican architect Luis Macgregor Krieger houses excellent exhibits tracing the settlement's history as well as countless pots, figurines, tools, and other artifacts unearthed on the site. You can also walk the grassy, verdant grounds and stand atop the pyramid. Cuicuilco is a five-minute drive from Tlalpan Centro and about a 15-minute drive from UNAM and Ciudad Universitaria. You can Uber here, or take the Insurgentes Sur Metrobus to the Villa Olímpica stop, from which it's an easy five-minute walk. ⊠ *Espacio Ecológico Cuicuilco, Insurgentes Sur at Anillo Anillo Periférico, Greater Mexico City* ⊕ *www.inah.gob.mx/ zonas/119-zona-arqueologica-cuicuilco.*

 Shopping

Centro Santa Fe

Remarkable for its sheer enormity, the country's largest shopping mall is in the heart of the appropriately upscale (although a bit soulless) modern Santa Fe commercial district. Centro Santa Fe contains more than 500 shops and restaurants, a huge central ice-skating rink, a luxury cinemaplex, a kids theme park, and is in immediate proximity to a giant convention center and several hotels. Anchor stores include some noted Mexican brands, including Casa Palacio, Liverpool, and El Palacio de Hierro, and you'll find a number of luxury boutiques, most of which have branches in Polanco or other more central neighborhoods. However, for ardent shopping enthusiasts, it's worth the 18-km (11-mile) trip from downtown. Until the Toluca–Mexico City commuter rail opens around 2022, a car is the best way to get here. ⊠ *Av. Vasco de Quiroga 3800, Greater Mexico City* ⊕ *www.centrosantafe.com.mx.*

Paseo Arcos Bosques

In the affluent Bosques de las Lomas neighborhood near Santa Fe, in the rolling hills west of the city center, this exclusive shopping mall stands out as much for its chic boutiques as for its location inside the iconic Arcos Bosques towers. They were designed by Teodoro González de León in 1996 and comprise two angular 35-story towers joined at the top by a four-story lintel. The shopping center isn't huge, but it contains an upscale food court and restaurants along with such retailers as Crate & Barrel, Hugo Boss, Lululemon, and Swarovski. ⊠ *Paseo de Los Tamarindos 90, Bosques de las Lomas, Greater Mexico City* ☎ *55/2167-9607* ⊕ *www.paseoarcosbosques.mx.*

🍴 Dining

Antigua Hacienda de Tlalpan

$$$$ | **Mexican.** One of the most beautiful restaurant settings in the city, this gracious 1837 hacienda in Tlálpan Centro oozes history and personality, from the peacocks strutting about the sweeping lawns and gardens to the plates of sophisticated, haute Mexican and European cuisine served on hand-painted plates. Although open late most evenings, it's especially nice to relax here over midday comida, soaking up the garden views while supping on chile relleno stuffed with duck and topped with tamarind sauce, or Gulf snapper prepared Veracruz style, with tomatoes, onions, green olives, and pickled jalapeños. **Known for:** elegant, historic setting; outdoor seating overlooking the beautiful grounds;

rich traditional Mexican and European cuisine. *Average main: 460 MP* ⊠ *Calz. de Tlalpan 4619, Greater Mexico City* ☎ *55/5655-7888* ⊕ *www.facebook.com/antiguahaciendadetlalpan* ⊗ *No dinner Sun.*

Arroyo

$$$ | **Mexican.** Whether it's truly the largest restaurant in Mexico, as it boasts, this cavernous spectacle on the edge of Tlalpan Centro is undoubtedly enormous and renowned for big family-style platters of pit-cooked lamb barbacoa and other traditional Mexican fare (carnitas, cecina, chicken leg, etc). Opened in 1940, Arroyo is decorated with tiled walls, brick archways, murals, and overhead rows of colorful papales picados. **Known for:** big portions of lamb barbacoa; live entertainment on weekends; a kids' playground. *Average main: 310 MP* ⊠ *Av. Insurgentes Sur 4003, Greater Mexico City* ☎ *55/5573-4344* ⊕ *www.restaurantearroyo.com.mx.*

Azul y Oro

$$$ | **Modern Mexican.** Opened by Ricardo Muñoz Zurita, one of the country's foremost experts on regional, historic Mexican cuisine, this unobtrusively elegant restaurant lies in the heart of UNAM's cultural center, making it a favorite spot before catching a concert or a show. The menu is a showcase of time-honored recipes from every corner of the country, including tacos with slow-baked pork and habanero sauce from Quintana Roo and duck *manchamanteles* (with a fragrant pineapple-pear-apple-plaintain ancho-chile mole) from

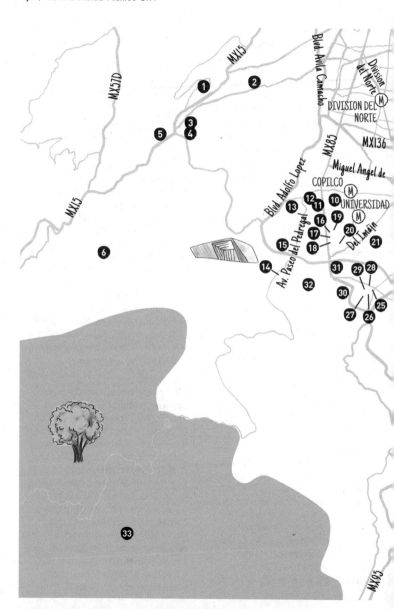

Ferrocarril Río Frío
Via Piedad

Calz de Tlalpan

Mexico
City

EJE
CENTRAL
Ⓜ Ⓜ ERMITA

MX136

Ⓜ 7 8

Ⓜ GENERAL ANAYA

Tasqueña Quevedo
Ⓜ

TASQUEÑA

9

Río Churubusco

22

23

24

Anillo Periférico

MX95D

Ⓐ

0 _____ 2 mi

0 _____ 2 km

SIGHTS

Espacio
Escultórico UNAM ...19

Estadio Azteca..........22

Estadio Olímpico
Universitario 11

Museo del
Tiempo Tlalpan 29

Museo Diego
Rivera–
Anahuacalli 9

Museo Dolores
Olmedo 23

Museo Universitario
Arte Contemporáneo
(MUAC).....................16

Parque Nacional
Bosque del
Pedregal 32

Parque
Nacional Cumbres
del Ajusco 33

Parque Nacional
Desierto de
los Leones 6

Santa Fe.....................2

Six Flags México 14

Tlalpan Centro 28

Universidad
Nacional Autónoma
de México (UNAM) ...10

Universum 20

Xochimilco Canals ...24

Zona Arqueológica
Cuicuilco...................31

SHOPPING

Centro Santa Fe 5

Paseo Arcos
Bosques.....................1

DINING

Antigua Hacienda
de Tlalpan................25

Arroyo 30

Azul y Oro 18

Market Kitchen 3

Michoacanissimo 21

Restaurante
Casa Club
de Académico...........12

Sud 777 15

Tetetlán 13

Toro............................4

BARS & NIGHTLIFE

Barra Alipus 27

Krox
International Beer 8

La Jalisciense 26

PERFORMING ARTS

Centro Nacional
de las Artes
(CENART)....................7

Centro Cultural
Universitario
de la UNAM 17

Puebla. **Known for:** authentic regional Mexican fare; impressive dessert list; lovely terrace. *Average main: 330 MP* ⊠ *Av. Insurgentes Sur 3000, Coyoacán* ☎ *55/5424–1426* ⊕ *www.azul.rest* ⏱ *No dinner Mon. and Tues.* Ⓜ *Universidad.*

Market Kitchen

$$$ | Modern American. Natural light pours into this airy, contemporary farm-to-table restaurant at the Westin Santa Fe, which also offers a spacious terrace with seating overlooking the surrounding greenery. An inviting option for a break from the hubbub of shopping at nearby Centro Santa Fe mall, Market offers moderately upscale fare like beef carpaccio with smoked mozzarella, black truffle–fontina pizzas, and seared red snapper with lentil-chorizo stew. **Known for:** American inspired farm-to-table cuisine; cheese and wine pairings; mix-and-match meat, seafood, and sauce options. *Average main: 330 MP* ⊠ *Park Plaza, Av. Javier Barros Sierra 540, Santa Fe, Greater Mexico City* ☎ *55/5089–8043* ⊕ *www.marketkitchendf.com.*

Michoacanissimo

$ | Mexican. Renowned for birria, this unfussy restaurant popular with families and locals serves a few kinds of the spicy stew popular in western Mexico states like Michoacán, including *surtida* (goat and a mix of other meaty bits like ribs, tongue, skin, and such) and the less adventurous but still robustly flavorful *maciza* (with pork). Expect a crowd—and maybe a wait—on weekends, when there's also some-

times mariachi music. **Known for:** Michoacán-style birria; micheladas; birria tacos and quesadillas. *Average main: 100 MP* ⊠ *Calle San Valentín 866, Pedregal de Sta Úrsula, Greater Mexico City* ☎ *55/5421–5576* ⊕ *www.michoacanisimo.com* ⏱ *No dinner* Ⓜ *Universidad.*

Restaurante Casa Club de Académico

$$ | International. It's worth making your way south to Cuidad Universitaria to dine at this distinctive and generally untouristy venue inside the UNAM faculty club, with a terrace that overlooks beautiful gardens and volcanic rocks. Open to the public and especially enjoyable for a late afternoon lunch, the restaurant serves a diverse menu of globally inspired dishes, such as shrimp pasta with a Thai red chile sauce, panela cheese enchiladas with mole verde, and roasted rosemary chicken with a Chardonnay reduction. **Known for:** live music, cultural programs, and kids' activities on weekend afternoons; diverse, international menu; suggested wine or beer pairings for each dish. *Average main: 180 MP* ⊠ *Av. Cd Universitaria 301, Greater Mexico City* ☎ *55/5616–1558* ⊕ *www. restaurantecasaclubdelacademico. com.mx* ⏱ *No dinner* Ⓜ *Copilco.*

★ Sud 777

$$$ | Modern Mexican. Young, celebrated chef Edgar Nunez has developed a thoroughly ambitious approach to contemporary cuisine that uses both Mexican and international ingredients—consider seared tuna with jocoque, fennel, smoked grapefruit, and citrus butter, or Veracruz-style beef tongue with quelites and onion. The gently modern space (a 10-minute drive south of San Ángel) merges indoors with outdoors and is one of the sexiest spots in town. **Known for:** stellar wine list; elaborate tasting menus with wine pairings; a separate sushi bar within the restaurant, Kokeshi. *Average main: 380 MP* ⊠ *Blvd. de la Luz 777, Greater Mexico City* ☎ *55/5568-4777* ⊕ *www.sud777. com.mx* ☾ *No dinner Sun.*

★ Tetetlán

$$$ | Modern Mexican. Adjacent to a gorgeous 1947 Luis Barragán–designed house (Casa Pedregal), this dramatic space with plexiglass floors that reveal a volcanic-rock landscape beneath is a favorite destination of both foodies and architecture aficionados. The kitchen turns out fancy, organic fare from early morning until late at night—consider a chia pudding or quinoa bowl in the morning, or sesame-crusted salmon with roasted cauliflower for dinner. **Known for:** stunning Luis Barragán–designed space; artfully presented organic food; first-rate on-site boutique and gourmet market. *Average main: 300 MP* ⊠ *Av. de Las Fuentes 180-B, Greater Mexico City* ☎ *55/5668-5335* ⊕ *www.tetetlan.com* Ⓜ *Copilco.*

★ Toro

$$$ | Modern Mexican. The swanky Santa Fe business district has plenty of good restaurants, but this buzzy spot operated by Mexican-born, Denver-based chef Richard Sandoval

is one of the few truly worth making a trip for. Decorated with Mexican pottery and eye-catching artwork, the contemporary space is a rarified environment for feasting on short rib or soft-shell crab tacos, several kinds of ceviche, wood-grilled rib-eye steaks, and other boldly flavored, creative fare. **Known for:** ceviche and other raw-bar dishes; wood-grilled steaks; inventive cocktails. *Average main: 410 MP* ⊠ *Park Plaza, Av. Javier Barros Sierra 540, Santa Fe, Greater Mexico City* ☎ *55/5292-4688* ⊕ *www.richardsandoval.com* ☾ *No dinner Sun.*

🍸 Bars and Nightlife

Barra Alipus

One of the most revered artisanal mezcal makers in the country, Oaxaca-based Alipus—which also runs the restaurants-bars Los Danzantes and Corazón de Maguey in Coyoacán—operates this unpretentious little bar in historic Tlalpan Centro. Stop by to sample the mezcal either straight up or in the extensive list of interesting cocktails, and note the well-prepared traditional Mexican food, including a number of Oaxacan specialties. ⊠ *Guadalupe Victoria 15, Tlalpan Centro, Greater Mexico City* ☎ *55/6363-4375* ⊕ *www.alipus.com.*

Krox International Beer

This small, lively craft-beer bar abuts the eastern edge of the CENART campus and is a great spot for drinks and a light bite to eat before or after seeing a performance, or perhaps a movie at the neighboring Cinemex multiplex. You'll find one of the city's largest selections of domestic and international beers, and most everything is also available to go. ⊠ *Av. Río Churubusco 85, El Prado, Greater Mexico City* ☎ *55/4444–2633* Ⓜ *General Anaya.*

★ La Jalisciense
Since 1875, this convivial cantina has been a favorite spot for hobnobbing, drinking, and dining on hearty Spanish fare in historic Tlalpan. This long, narrow space with an ornate wooden bar, vintage artwork, and brick archways is lively day or night. You can order delicious tortas and other items to go from a small take-out window up front and enjoy eating them on a picnic bench in nearby Plaza de la Constitución. ⊠ *Plaza de la Constitución 6, Mexico City* ☎ *55/5573–5586.*

 **Performing Arts**

★ Centro Cultural Universitario de la UNAM
A sprawling campus of exceptional museums, art spaces, and performance halls in the heart of Ciudad Universitaria, UNAM's cultural center is an excellent place to see concerts by the superb Orquesta Filarmónica de la UNAM (OFUNAM), which take place in the acoustically renowned Sala Nezahualcóyotl. Neighboring venues include the Centro Universitario de Teatro (CUT), Foro Sor Juana Ines de la Cruz, Teatro Juan Ruiz de Alarcón PUMA UNAM, Sala Carlos Chavez, and Filmoteca UNAM–Sala Miguel Covarrubias. Among these beautifully designed modern buildings, there's virtually always some sort of interesting performance (or several) taking place (except during occasional school breaks), including ballet, modern dance, choral, film, lecture, and theater. Tickets to performances are very reasonably priced. The excellent Azul y Oro restaurant sits within steps of these buildings. ⊠ *Cto. Centro Cultural, Ciudad Universiteria, Greater Mexico City* ⊕ *www.cultura.unam.mx* Ⓜ *Universidad.*

Centro Nacional de las Artes (CENART)
Situated a little east of Coyoacán and adjacent to Estudios Churubusco, CENART is the largest and most important film studio in Latin American. It was built in 1994 by a group of acclaimed Mexican architects led by Ricardo Legorreta, who clearly had Luis Barragán in mind with the design, which relies heavily on bright colors and geometric shapes. Created by the country's National Council for Culture and the Arts, the huge campus consists of performing arts schools and several venues, and there's virtually always something interesting going on, from dance and theater to music of all kinds. Also check out the terrific bookshop and hip little café on-site, and during the day, take a stroll through the surrounding gardens and walking paths. ⊠ *Av. Río Churubusco 79, Country Club Churubusco, Greater Mexico City* ☎ *55/4155–0000* ⊕ *www.cenart.gob.mx* Ⓜ *General Anaya.*

Photo Credits

Chapter 2: WitR/Shutterstock (48). **Chapter 3:** Inspired By Maps/Shutterstock (75).
Chapter 10: xeuphoriax/Shutterstock (230). **Chapter 12:** doleesi/Shutterstock (269).

NOTES

Fodor's INSIDE MEXICO CITY

Publisher: Stephen Horowitz, *General Manager*

Editorial: Douglas Stallings, *Editorial Director;* Jill Fergus, Jacinta O'Halloran, Amanda Sadlowski, *Senior Editors;* Kayla Becker, Alexis Kelly, Rachael Roth, *Editors*

Design: Tina Malaney, *Director of Design and Production;* Jessica Gonzalez, Graphic Designer; Mariana Tabares, *Design and Production Intern*

Production: Jennifer DePrima, *Editorial Production Manager;* Carrie Parker, *Senior Production Editor;* Elyse Rozelle, *Production Editor;* Jackson Pranica, *Editorial Production Assistant*

Maps: Rebecca Baer, Senior *Map Editor;* Mark Stroud (Moon Street Cartography), *Cartographer*

Photography: Viviane Teles, *Senior Photo Editor;* Namrata Aggarwal, Ashok Kumar, Carl Yu, *Photo Editors;* Rebecca Rimmer, *Photo Intern*

Business and Operations: Chuck Hoover, *Chief Marketing Officer;* Robert Ames, *Group General Manager;* Devin Duckworth, *Director of Print Publishing;* Victor Bernal, *Business Analyst*

Public Relations and Marketing: Joe Ewaskiw, *Senior Director Communications and Public Relations;* Esther Su, *Senior Marketing Manager*

Fodors.com: Jeremy Tarr, *Editorial Director;* Rachael Levitt, *Managing Editor;* Teddy Minford, *Editor*

Technology: Jon Atkinson, *Director of Technology;* Rudresh Teotia, *Lead Developer;* Jacob Ashpis, *Content Operations Manager*

Writers: Andrew Collins, Megan Frye, Molly McLaughlin, Michael Snyder

Editor: Amanda Sadlowski

Production Editor: Jennifer DePrima

Designers: Tina Malaney, Chie Ushio

1st Edition

ISBN 978-1-64097-268-1

ISSN 2688-9765

SPECIAL SALES
This book is available at special discounts for bulk purchases for sales promotions or premiums. For more information, e-mail SpecialMarkets@fodors.com.

PRINTED IN CANADA

10 9 8 7 6 5 4 3

MEXICO CITY METRO

RESOURCES

Mexico City's subway system is a wonder to behold. Its 12 color-coded lines ferry millions of visitors and commuters to most parts of the city quickly and efficiently, often much faster than traveling overland in the city's notorious traffic; rides cost MX$5. You can buy single-ride passes and transport cards at ticket windows at each station, but lines can be long. A better bet is to load up your card with credit at automated machines located at Metrobus stations. Metro stations are marked with graphical icons—a grasshopper, a fountain—as well as written names, in response to the city's relatively high illiteracy rate at the time of the system's construction. The metro has a reputation for being uncomfortably hot and sardine-packed during rush hour; women traveling solo may want to take advantage of the women-and-children-only cars, located at the front of each train. A recent government crackdown has reduced the number of mobile vendors that roam the cars hawking anything from socks and cigarette lighters to pirated CDs for MX$10, though you'll probably encounter a few. Keep a close eye on your belongings at all times while entering, exiting, and riding the metro.

Buses are also a cheap and convenient way to travel within Mexico City, particularly the city's modern bus rapid transit system, the Metrobus. The fleet's red buses travel along fixed routes in their own dedicated lanes and pick up passengers at designated stations, just like a metro. Transportation cards can be purchased with pesos at automated machines located at each station, then loaded up with credit that can also be used for the city's subway. Metrobus rides cost MX$6; the metro is MX$5. Like the metro, the Metrobus reserves the forward-most carriages for women and children—a good option for travelers seeking a bit more security on public transport, especially during peak travel times.

For short trips around central neighborhoods, the EcoBici bike share system is now available to tourists, though, inconveniently, it requires an in-person sign-up. With a passport and credit card, visitors can buy one-, three-, or seven-day memberships that allow access to public bikes for unlimited 45-minute trips. Memberships cost MX$104, MX$208, and MX$346, respectively, plus a hefty refundable deposit of MX$5,000. Bike lanes are scarce and Mexico City drivers are notoriously inconsiderate, but EcoBici is a welcome option for visitors comfortable with urban cycling.

ABOUT OUR WRITERS AND ILLUSTRATOR

Former Fodor's staff editor **Andrew Collins** lives in Coyoacán with his partner and three friendly cats. A lifelong nomad, he spends about half his time on the road, much of it in the Pacific Northwest and New England. He's contributed to more than 200 Fodor's guidebooks—most recently Inside Portland, Pacific Northwest, Santa Fe, New England, and National Parks of the West—and he's written for dozens of mainstream and LGBTQ publications, including *Travel + Leisure, New Mexico Magazine, AAA Living, The Advocate,* and *Canadian Traveller.* Additionally, Collins teaches travel writing and food writing for New York City's Gotham Writers Workshop. For *Inside Mexico City,* he wrote the Experience, Roma, Condesa, Coyoacán, San Ángel, and Greater Mexico City chapters. You can find more of his work at ⊕ *AndrewsTraveling.com.*

Megan Frye is an independent journalist, photographer, and translator specializing in stories about ethical travel, sustainability, history, culture, and food. Following a history in newsroom journalism and nonprofit management in Detroit, Michigan and escapades across the American West, she settled in Mexico City in 2015, where she appreciates a tranquil afternoon with good company at a mezcalería or hanging with her family (including two xoloitzcuintles and three cats) in her chosen neighborhood of Coyoacán. She wrote the Juárez and Anzures, San Rafael and Santa María la Ribera, and Benito Juárez chapters for this book.

Molly McLaughlin is an Australian travel and culture writer who moved to Mexico City in 2016. Her work has appeared in multiple publications including *Ozy, Lonely Planet, Refinery29,* and *TripSavvy,* as well as the *Fodor's Essential Australia* guidebook. She can often be found soaking up the sun at UNAM's botanic garden or searching for the city's best *elote.* For *Inside Mexico City,* she wrote the Polanco and Bosque de Chapultepec chapter.

Michael Snyder is a freelance journalist focused on food and architecture. He has lived in Mexico City's Centro Histórico since 2016 and, prior to that, spent over four years living in Mumbai, India. His work has appeared in a range of publications including *T Magazine, Lucky Peach, The Believer,* the *New York Times,* the *LA Times, Saveur, Food & Wine, Travel + Leisure,* and *The Nation,* among others. When he's not traveling, you can usually find him at one of his neighborhood's many historic cantinas. He wrote the Centro Histórico and Alameda Central chapters for this book.

Kathryn Holeman is a Philadelphia-based illustrator and graphic designer who shares her wanderlust for far-off places with her husband and two sons. With a treasured collection of Oaxacan pottery and Day of The Dead prints decorating the walls of her studio, Kathryn found inspiration in the vibrant colors and organic textures of Mexican art for her illustrations in this book. She was previously the illustrator for Fodor's *Inside Berlin.*